Lecture Notes in Computer Science 10776

Commenced Publication in 1973
Founding and Former Series Editors:
Gerhard Goos, Juris Hartmanis, and Jan van Leeuwen

More information about this series at http://www.springer.com/series/7407

Rio Yokota · Weigang Wu (Eds.)

Supercomputing Frontiers

4th Asian Conference, SCFA 2018
Singapore, March 26–29, 2018
Proceedings

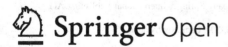

Editors
Rio Yokota
Tokyo Institute of Technology
Tokyo
Japan

Weigang Wu
Sun Yat-sen University
Guangzhou
China

ISSN 0302-9743   ISSN 1611-3349 (electronic)
Lecture Notes in Computer Science
ISBN 978-3-319-69952-3   ISBN 978-3-319-69953-0 (eBook)
https://doi.org/10.1007/978-3-319-69953-0

Library of Congress Control Number: 2018937379

LNCS Sublibrary: SL1 – Theoretical Computer Science and General Issues

This Springer imprint is published by the registered company Springer International Publishing AG
part of Springer Nature
The registered company address is: Gewerbestrasse 11, 6330 Cham, Switzerland

Preface

As the share of supercomputers in Asia continues to increase, the relevance of supercomputing in Asia has achieved a critical mass to merit the inauguration of a supercomputing conference for Asia. Supercomputing Asia (SCA) 2018 encompassed an umbrella of notable supercomputing events with the key objective of promoting a vibrant and relevant HPC ecosystem in Asian countries, and was held during March 26–29, 2018, at Resorts World Convention Centre, Singapore.

The technical program of SCA18 had its roots in Supercomputing Frontiers (SCF), which is Singapore's annual international HPC conference that provides a platform for leaders from both academia and industry to interact and discuss visionary ideas, important global trends, and substantial innovations in supercomputing. The conference was inaugurated in 2015 and helmed by A*STAR Computational Resource Centre (A*CRC). In March 2017, the National Supercomputing Centre (NSCC) Singapore took over hosting of Supercomputing Frontiers 2017 (SCF17). NSCC was established in 2015 and manages Singapore's first national petascale facility with available HPC resources to support science and engineering computing needs for academic, research, and industry communities. SCF17 was attended by over 450 delegates from over 12 different countries.

Riding on the success from the previous year, the SCA18 program highlights will included:

- HPC technology updates and case studies
- Scientific paper presentations
- Academic activities and workshop for students

The co-located HPC events include:

- Asia-Pacific Advanced Network Meeting (APAN45)
- Towards an Asia Research Platform (ARP)
- Conference on Next-Generation Arithmetic (CoNGA)
- Singapore–Japan Joint Sessions
- Supercomputing Frontiers Asia (SCFA)

SCFA represented the technical program for SCA18, consisting of four tracks:

- Application, Algorithms, and Libraries
- Programming and System Software
- Data, Storage, and Visualization
- Architecture, Network/Communications, and Management

We would like to express our gratitude to all our colleagues for submitting papers to the SCA18 scientific sessions, as well as to the members of the Program Committee for organizing this year's attractive program.

March 2018   Rio Yokota
                                                                             Weigang Wu

Organization

Technical Program Committee

Technical Papers Co-chairs

Rio Yokota	Tokyo Institute of Technology, Japan
Weigang Wu	Sun Yat-sen University, China

Application, Algorithms, and Libraries

Emmanuel Agullo	Inria, France
Ariful Azad	Lawrence Berkeley National Laboratory, USA
Costas Bekas	IBM, Switzerland
Aparna Chandramowlishwaran	University of California Irvine, USA
Kate Clark	NVIDIA, USA
Hal Finkel	Argonne National Laboratory, USA
Michael Heroux	Sandia National Laboratories, USA
Johannes Langguth	Simula, Norway
Piotr R. Luszczek	University of Tennessee at Knoxville, USA
Maciej Malawski	AGH University of Science and Technology, Poland
John Owens	UC Davis, USA
Vivek Pallipuram	University of the Pacific, USA
Antonio Pena	Barcelona Supercomputing Center, Spain
Min Si	Argonne National Laboratory, USA
Hari Sundar	University of Utah, USA
Nathan Tallent	Pacific Northwest National Laboratory, USA

Programming and System Software

Olivier Aumage	Inria, France
Sunita Chandrasekaran	University of Delaware, USA
Florina M. Ciorba	University of Basel, Switzerland
Bilel Hadri	King Abdullah University of Science and Technology, Saudi Arabia
Zbigniew Kalbarczyk	University of Illinois, USA
Hatem Ltaief	King Abdullah University of Science and Technology, Saudi Arabia
Arthur Maccabe	Oak Ridge National Laboratory, USA
Naoya Maruyama	Lawrence Livermore National Laboratory, USA
Ronald Minnich	Google Inc., USA
Raymond Namyst	University of Bordeaux, France
C. J. Newburn	NVIDIA, USA
Christian Perez	Inria, France

| Miquel Pericas | Chalmers University of Technology, Sweden |
| Mohamed Wahib | National Institute of Advanced Industrial Science and Technology, Japan |

Data, Storage, and Visualization

Janine Bennett	Sandia National Laboratories, USA
Mahdi Bohlouli	University of Koblenz, Germany
Steffen Frey	University of Stuttgart, Germany
Shadi Ibrahim	Inria, France
Hai Jin	Huazhong University of Science and Technology, China
Hideyuki Kawashima	University of Tsukuba, Japan
Quincey Koziol	Lawrence Berkeley National Laboratory, USA
Suzanne McIntosh	New York University, USA
Bogdan Nicolae	Huawei Technologies, China
David Pugmire	Oak Ridge National Laboratory, USA
Shinji Sumimoto	Fujitsu, Japan
Bronis R. de Supinski	Lawrence Livermore National Laboratory, USA
Daniela Ushizima	Lawrence Berkeley National Laboratory, USA
Jon Woodring	Los Alamos National Laboratory, USA
Amelie Chi Zhou	Inria, France

Architecture, Network/Communications, and Management

David Abramson	The University of Queensland, Australia
Eishi Arima	The University of Tokyo, Japan
Ali R. Butt	Virginia Tech, USA
Nikhil Jain	University of Illinois, USA
John Kim	Korea Advanced Institute of Science and Technology, Korea
John Shalf	Lawrence Berkeley National Laboratory, USA
Ryota Shioya	Nagoya University, Japan
Jeremiah J. Wilke	Sandia National Laboratories, USA
Weikuan Yu	Florida State University, USA

Contents

Big Data

HHVSF: A Framework to Accelerate Drug-Based High-Throughput Virtual Screening on High-Performance Computers

Pin Chen[1], Xin Yan[1], Jiahui Li[1], Yunfei Du[1,2(✉)], and Jun Xu[1(✉)]

[1] National Supercomputer Center in Guangzhou and Research Center for Drug Discovery, School of Data and Computer Science and School of Pharmaceutical Sciences, Sun Yat-Sen University, 132 East Circle at University City, Guangzhou 510006, China
yunfei.du@nscc-gz.cn, junxu@biochemomes.com
[2] School of Computer Science, National University of Defense Technology, Changsha 410073, China

Abstract. The High-performance High-throuhput Virtual Screening Framework (HHVSF) has been developed to accelerate High-Throughput Virtual Screening (HTVS) on high-performance computers. Task management and data management are two core components in HHVSF. Fine-grained computing resources are configured to support serial or threaded applications. Each task gets the input file from database through a preemptive algorithm and the failed tasks can be found and corrected. NoSQL database MongoDB is used as the data repository engine. Data is mobilized between the RAMDISK in computing node and the database. Data analysis is carried out after the computing process, and the results are stored in the database. Among the most popular molecular docking and molecular structure similarity packages, Autodock_vina (ADV) and WEGA were chosen to carry out experiments. Results show that when ADV was used for molecular docking, 10 million molecules were screened and analyzed in 22.31 h with 16000 cores, and the throughput reached up to 1324 molecules per second, averaging 145 molecules per second during the steady-running process. For WEGA, 958 million conformations were screened and analyzed in 34.12 min with 4000 cores, of which throughput reached up to 9448 molecules per second, 6430 molecules per second on average.

Keywords: High-Throughput Virtual Screening · Drug discovery
High-Performance Computing · Molecular docking
Molecular structure similarity

1 Introduction

Computational methodology has become a significant component in pharmaceutical industry for drug design and discovery [1–4]. Typically, molecular docking and molecular structure similarity are two frequently used computational approaches. High-Throughput Virtual Screening (HTVS) is known to computationally screen large compound libraries. These libraries contain a huge number of small-molecules varying

© The Author(s) 2018
R. Yokota and W. Wu (Eds.): SCFA 2018, LNCS 10776, pp. 3–17, 2018.
https://doi.org/10.1007/978-3-319-69953-0_1

from tens of thousands to millions, require a high volume of lots-of-small files scenario for a virtual screening campaign. With the development of high-performance computers, the virtual drug screening is accelerating. However, HTVS still faces challenges while a large scale virtual screening application is executed on High-Performance Computing (HPC) resources, such as distributing massive tasks, analyzing lots-of-small molecular structure files, and implementing fault tolerance.

Tools have been developed to accelerate the process of HTVS on HPC resources. Falkon [5] is a lightweight execution framework to enable loosely coupled program to run on peta-scale systems. The benchmark [6] shows that DOCK5 can scale up to 116,000 cores with high efficiency by Falkon. VinaMPI is a MPI version program based on ADV package, which uses a large number of cores to speed-up individual docking tasks. VinaMPI successfully ran on 84,672 cores on Kraken supercomputer and efficiently reduce the total time-to-completion. While all the above works focus on performance and efficiency of distributing tasks, ignoring the whole HTVS process, for instance, robustness, recoverability and result analysis. FireWorks (FWS) [7] is a workflow software for high-throughput calculation running on supercomputer, effectively solve the problem of concurrent task distribution and fault tolerance management, and provide an intuitive graphical interface. However, FWS pays more attention on versatility and usability. DVSDMS [8] is a distributed virtual screening data management system, only focusing on high-throughput docking process in the data management issues. Therefore, the architecture of high-performance computers, as well as the computational characteristics of the application, needs to be considered to design the framework for HTVS on high-performance computers.

In this work, we report a general framework - High-performance High-throughput Virtual Screening Framework (HHVSF) - to enable large-scale, multitasking and small-size input and output (IO) applications to efficiently execute on HPC resources. This framework contains task management and data management systems, which can handle thousands of tasks, manage a large volume of lots-of-small files, and reduce the long processing time for analyzing. The purpose of HHVSF is to provide high computational performance based on portability, availability, serviceability and stability (PASS).

2   Experimental and Computational Details

The framework of HHVSF is comprised of two parts: task management and distributed data management (see Fig. 1). In order to access and store data efficiently and flexibly, the executions of a program are coupled loosely by MongoDB C driver, while the application codes do not need to be modified. The following three subsections document the overall framework of HHVSF, the simulation parameters and the data sets of the experiments are introduced at the end of this section. ADV [9] and WEGA [10] are chosen as typical applications to carry out the experiments, and others can be integrated into the HHVSF in similar way.

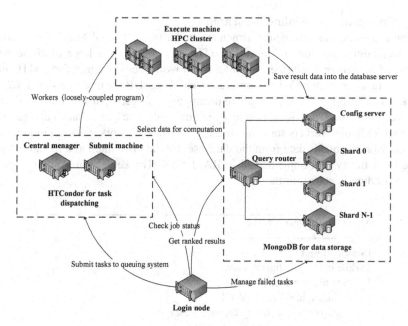

Fig. 1. The hardware and relevant operations in HHVSF.

2.1 Task Management

The followings are mainly considered in the task management system: two-level task scheduling, preemptive scheduling algorithm for worker and failed tasks recovery.

2.1.1 Task Scheduling

HTVS employs massive computing resources to support a large number of independent computing tasks. Because most molecular docking and molecular structure similarity tools, for instance, ADV, Gold [11], Glide [12], FlexX [13] and WEGA, are serial or threaded codes, these computing tasks are typical fine-grained Many-Task Computing (MTC) [6]. Such MTC tasks cannot take full advantage of the static scheduling solution with coarse scheduling granularity, while most traditional large-scale HPC resources are configured with coarse scheduling granularity under a control of batch queuing system such as Simple Linux Utility for Resource Management (SLURM) [14], Portable Batch System (PBS)/Torque [15], and Sun Grid Engine (SGE) [16].

Multi-level scheduling method can effectively solve the different application requirements for scheduling granularity, while maintaining the unified management of computing resources. The first level scheduler applies for a number of resources to the second level for task distribution. The second level scheduler can refine the computing resources and then distributes the tasks. HTCondor [17] is chosen to be the second level scheduler to dispatch tasks. HTCondor is full-featured batch workload management system for coordinating a large number of independent serial or parallel jobs in High-Throughput Computing (HTC) environment. We configure the HTCondor with one core per slot to provide more flexible task scheduling.

2.1.2 Preemptive Scheduling Algorithm

Molecular docking and molecular structure similarity are typical MTC applications, while maintaining millions of tasks by HTCondor to screen a large database with millions of ligands or conformers is still a touch work. Thus, we transform MTC into HTC by wrapping ADV or WEGA program with MongoDB C driver (version 1.4.2) as a worker. Each worker accesses database preemptively to get input files until all data is traversed. MongoDB provides atomic operation with "inc" to ensure data security when multitudinous workers start concurrently, so that each worker can get unique job. After the worker obtains data from the database, the data is written to a file and stored on the local file system implemented in RAMDISK. The kernel function's computational procedure is shown in the Fig. 2.

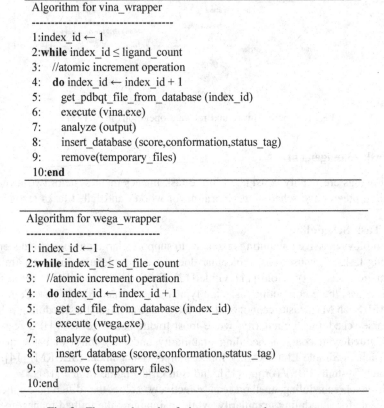

```
Algorithm for vina_wrapper
------------------------------------
1:index_id ← 1
2:while index_id ≤ ligand_count
3:   //atomic increment operation
4:   do index_id ← index_id + 1
5:     get_pdbqt_file_from_database (index_id)
6:     execute (vina.exe)
7:     analyze (output)
8:     insert_database (score,conformation,status_tag)
9:     remove(temporary_files)
10:end
```

```
Algorithm for wega_wrapper
----------------------------------
1: index_id ←1
2:while index_id ≤ sd_file_count
3:   //atomic increment operation
4:   do index_id ← index_id + 1
5:     get_sd_file_from_database (index_id)
6:     execute (wega.exe)
7:     analyze (output)
8:     insert_database (score,conformation,status_tag)
9:     remove (temporary_files)
10:end
```

Fig. 2. The pseudo code of vina_wrapper and wega_wrapper.

2.1.3 Fault Tolerance

Fault tolerance in this context can be simplified as the ability to automatically restart a task when the original run fails. When the HTVS scales to millions of tasks or run a long-time task, it is easy to get failures for bad input parameters, such as computing node fault, IO blocking, and network latency. There are two ways to consider fault tolerance in this case, one is monitoring the job status during the running by job management system, another is making a successful or failed tag on each task after the task is finished. HTCondor provides checkpoint mechanism in the standard universe by using condor_compile to relink the execution with the HTCondor libraries, while those coupled program vina_wrapper and wega_wrapper, containing system calls like system (), cannot provide check pointing services with HTCondor. As a result, we choose the second method. When a worker calls the execution of ADV or WEGA successfully, a tag that represents the task status will insert into the corresponding document in MongoDB database. After the job is finished, it needs to check the document's failed tag and then restart the failed jobs.

2.2 Data Management

Data storage, data relocation and data analysis are the bottlenecks when a virtual screening is scaled up to handle millions of tasks on thousands of cores. Such scattered lots-of-small files can overburden the shared file system with abundant IO operations if the plain files are accessed and stored directly. Database offers an attractive solution to both the storage and the data querying. In our framework, we avoid using shared file system by replacing it with the combination of MongoDB and local RAMDISK. The IO files are stored in MongoDB, while they are cached in the local RAMDISK during computation. The following three subsections describe the details on the data storage, data relocation and data analysis in HHVSF.

2.2.1 NoSQL Database for Storage

Chemical databases are the critical components of HTVS, which provide the basic information to build knowledge-based models for discovering and designing drug. Such as, PubChem [18], ZINC [19], ChEMBL [20], ChemDB [21], contain millions of compounds, provide shape data, physical properties, biological activities, and other information for pharmaceutical evaluations. Currently, many molecular docking programs and molecular structure similarity algorithms read the input and store the output in plain text files, which is not suitable for management when data grow up rapidly. Maintaining and analyzing such data are difficult.

MongoDB [22] is used as the data repository engine, which is a high performance, high availability, automatic scaling, open source NoSQL (Not Only SQL) database. This architecture is suitable for sparse and document-like data storage. By using MongoDB "index", molecules can be queried and ranked easily. In addition, MongoDB uses "sharding" (a method for distributing data across multiple machines) to support deployments with large data sets in high throughput manner, enhancing the computational performance by balancing query loading as the database growing. Finally, MongDB accepts big data up to 16 MB. MongDB is employed for WEGA to access the big conformation SDF input file.

2.2.2 Data Relocation

ADV and WEGA involve in processing large sized plain text files. Without modifying their source codes, the programs have to process huge number of small molecular structure files by moving on the shared file disks when screening a large-scale compound library. Hence, the RAMDISK in computing nodes are used to temporarily store the IO files needed by the applications (see Fig. 3). The RAMDISK provides high-speed, low-latency IO operations for handling lots-of-small files, while the high storage capacity of shared file disk is still fully occupied to store the resulting data. By relocating data between MongDB and RAMDISK, the IO pressure for shared file storage is effectively mitigated.

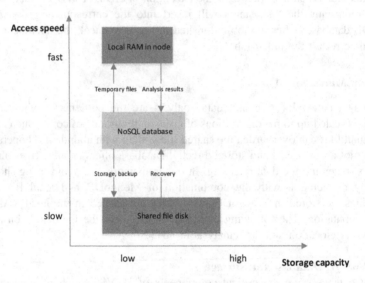

Fig. 3. The flowchart of the data relocation.

2.2.3 Data Analysis

For virtual screening using molecular docking and molecular structure similarity approaches, scores and molecular similarities have to be calculated before ranking the molecules in a large sized compound library. In consideration of high-performance computing systems with shared file storage, it is necessary to avoid IO overloading problems which are caused by a great number of small files. Thus, it is not wise to analyze the output files on the shared storage disk. When the computations are accomplished in the RAMDISK, the output files are analyzed and the compounds in the library are ranked based upon scores or similarities. This protocol minimizes the IO stress when the number of small files increases dramatically.

2.3 Simulation Parameters and Data Sets

2.3.1 ADV

About twenty million ligands with mol2 format file were obtained from ZINC database FTP server (http://zinc.docking.org/db/bysubset/6/). The pymongo (version 3.2.1) Python library was used for database operations. A python script was developed to insert mol2 files into MongoDB. MGLTools (version 1.5.6) was used to convert mol2 files into pdbqt file for docking. We prepared five different sized data sets (from zinc_ligand_1 ~ 5), as shown in Table 2. All data sets are sorted by heavy atom number arranged in ascending order. After finishing molecular docking, the result pdbqt file format was converted to mol file format by Open Babel package [23] (version 2.4.0).

The protein target is a crystal structure of the alpha subunit of glycyl tRNA synthetase (PDB codes: 5F5 W). The (x, y, z) coordinates (in Å) for the center of the docking site is (−94.666, 51.401, 8.991), and the side of the cubic box is (14, 18, 12). The argument of num_modes is set to 1.

2.3.2 WEGA

A SDF file containing about twenty million molecules was obtained from ZINC database FTP server. Approximately 958 million conformers were generated from the SDF file using the CAESAR algorithm [24] in discovery studio (version 3.5) [25] for shape-feature similarity calculation. In order to take advantage of the 16 MB storage space in MongoDB, the conformer files were split into smaller files which occupied 15 MB for each file, and then inserted into the database. Table 2 gives two data sets for WEGA (zinc_conformer_1 and zinc_conformer_2).

The query molecule is 4-amino-1-[4,5-dihydroxy-3-(2-hydroxyethyl)-1-cyclopent-2-enyl]-pyrimidin-2-one (ZINC ID: ZINC03834084). The method for molecular overlay is set to 2 (combing the shape similarity and pharmacophore similarity). Each SDF file corresponds up to 100 similar molecules. The Table 1 shows the detailed information of the data sets which are used throughout the article.

Table 1. Data sets for testing. The zinc_ligand_1 ~ 5 databases are prepared for Audock_vina, the zinc_ligand_2 ~ 5 databases were extracted from zinc_ligand_1 in accordance with a certain proportion. The zinc_conformer_1 ~ 2 databases are prepared for WEGA, and the zinc_conformer_2 are extracted from zinc_conformer_1 randomly.

Database name	Number	Description
zinc_ligand_1	20430347	ZINC purchasable subset
zinc_ligand_2	10^7	Enumerate one from every 2 molecules of ZINC purchasable subset
zinc_ligand_3	10^6	Enumerate one from every 20 molecules of ZINC purchasable subset
zinc_ligand_4	10^5	Enumerate one from every 200 molecules of ZINC purchasable subset
zinc_ligand_5	10^4	Enumerate one from every 2000 molecules of ZINC purchasable subset
zinc_conformer_1	$\sim 9.58 * 10^8$	Up to 50 conformers per molecule of ZINC purchasable subset
zinc_conformer_2	$\sim 10^6$	Up to 50 conformers per molecule of ZINC purchasable subset

All tests run on Tianhe-2 (MilkyWay-2) supercomputer, which consists of 16,000 computing nodes connected via the TH Express-2 interconnect. Each computing node is equipped with two Intel Xeon E5-2692 CPUs (12-core, 2.2 GHz), and configured with 64 GB memory. The storage subsystem contains 64 storage servers with a total capacity of 12.4 PB. The LUSTRE storage architecture is used as a site-wide global file system.

3   Results and Discussion

3.1   Load Balance

Time for screening a compound ranges from minutes to hours depending on the complexity of the molecular structure. Reports [9, 26] indicate that the compound complexity, for instance, number of active torsions or number of heavy atoms, dominates the computing time of molecular docking. In order to determine the relation between the number of heavy atoms computing time and the computing complexity, the zinc_lignad_5 data set was chosen to record the number of heavy atom in a ligand and computing time, as depicted in Fig. 4. The number of heavy atoms presents a linear relationship with time (logarithmic form), which indicates more heavy atoms in a small molecule requires longer computing time. For zinc_ligand_2 ~ 5 data sets are scaled down from zinc_ligand_1 by a certain percentage, the other data sets will also benefit from this approach. Based on this information, the zinc_ligand_4 data set was tested on 8,000 cores. Figure 5a and b demonstrate that the average computing time per worker is reduced by 8.83 s when load balancing protocol was used.

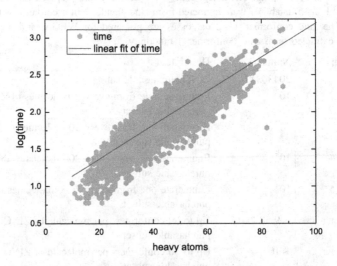

Fig. 4. The number of heavy atoms in a compound (x-axis), the computing time (logarithmic form) of a molecular docking (y-axis). The results are based upon zinc_ligand_5 data set.

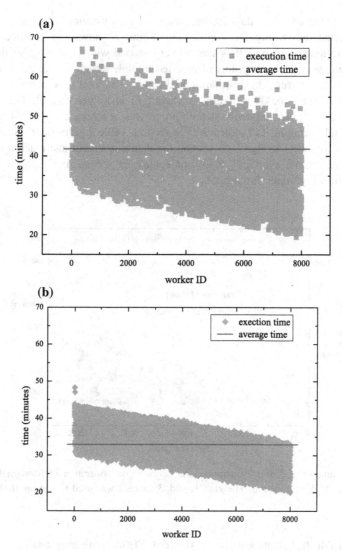

Fig. 5. (a) The computing time of each worker without load balancing. The red line is the average computing time per task. (b) The computing time per worker with load balance. The red line is the average computing time per task. (Color figure online)

3.2   Throughput with Data

The MongoDB monitors the status of a running instance. When a worker starts, a "connection" operation is activated by MongoDB's server. After the computing task is accomplished, the resulting data (score, structural conformation, and running status) will be inserted into MongoDB's collection. Figure 6 shows the "connection" and "insert" operations of MongoDB's server every second with vina_wrapper during the whole computing period, the points of inverted triangle clearly reveal the three stages of running tasks: startup, steady-running and finish. The total time during the startup was 1,396 s to start 16,000 workers, averaging 11 tasks per second. The points of rhombus become higher gradually as time progresses, reaching up to 1,324 molecules per second and averaging 145 molecules per second. Table 2 gives the results for other data sets. As for WEGA, Fig. 7 shows that the data throughput can reach up to 9,448 molecules per second, averaging 6,430 molecules per second, indicating a high performance and a high data throughput.

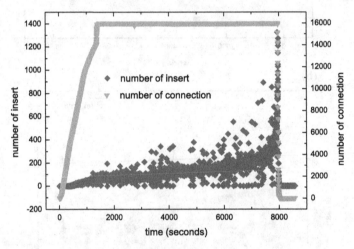

Fig. 6. The number of "insert" operation and "connection" operation in MongoDB's server when running ADV application. The zinc_ligand_3 data set was used to run on 16,000 cores.

Table 2. Data throughput for ADV and WEGA on different data sets.

Program	Test number	Cores	Startup time (second)	Maximum data throughput (molecules/second)	Average data throughput (molecules/second)
ADV	10^7	16000	1222	1957	130
ADV	10^6	16000	1396	1324	145
ADV	10^5	8000	564	473	76
WEGA	95712	4000	313	9448	6430

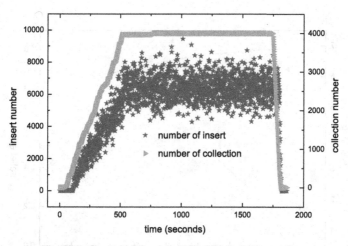

Fig. 7. The number of "insert" operation and "connection" operation in MongoDB's server when running WEGA application. The zinc_conformer_1 data set was used to run on 4,000 cores.

3.3 Scalability

To test scalability, we perform the experiments of speedup and parallel efficiency with zinc_ligand_4 data set and zinc_ligand_3 data set. Figure 8a shows zinc_ligand_4 data set can be scaled to 8,000 cores with parallel efficiency of 0.84, and the zinc_ligand_4 data set can be scaled to 16,000 cores with parallel efficiency of 0.83 (see Fig. 8b). It is shown that the parallel efficiency decreases sharply when computing resource is scaled up to more than 8,000 cores. This is because more cores represent more workers, and thus, more time will be cost by HTCondor to start those workers.

3.4 Fault Tolerance

Fault tolerance management can avoid task failures due to external environments, for instances, compute node fault, network blocking, IO latency, etc. Table 3 gives the information of failed tasks on different data sets. The zinc_ligand_2 data set has a high failure rate than others due to ten million ligands containing more ligands with high molecular weight which are not suitable for docking space of the protein (PDB code: 5W5F). In addition, longer calculations can lead to higher failures. The zinc_conformer_1 data set has fewer files (95712 SDF files in total) and less computing time, as a result, produces a low failure rate.

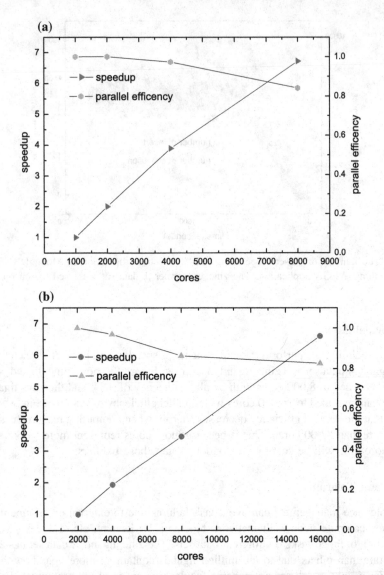

Fig. 8. (a) Speedup (right triangle) and parallel efficiency (read dot) of molecular docking experiment on zinc_ligand_4 data set. (b) Speedup (block dot) and parallel efficiency (upper triangle) of molecular docking experiment on zinc_ligand_3 data set.

Table 3. The failure rate and computing time for ADV and WEGA on different data sets.

Program	Data set	Cores	Failure rate	Last task time	Average time
ADV	zinc_ligand_2	16000	0.01171	22.31 h	20.14 h
ADV	zinc_ligand_3	16000	0.00390	3.34 h	2.43 h
ADV	zinc_ligand_4	8000	0.00001	48.10 min	31.31 min
WEGA	zinc_conformer_1	4000	0.00002	34.12 min	28.20 min

4 Conclusions

HHVSF includes task management and relocating data management, and supports the high-throughput applications of large-scale, multitasking and small sized IO files running on HPC resources. There are two types of virtual drug screening applications: (1) computation-intensive applications (such as molecular docking), and (2) data-intensive applications (such as molecular structure similarity based virtual screening campaigns). With HHVSF, two types of applications can run on Tianhe-2 supercomputer with high performance. Testing results show that when use ADV for molecular docking, the protein target (PDB code: 5W5F) was used to screen nearly half of compounds from the ZINC database within one day on 16,000 cores. For WEGA, 958 million conformations were screened by using about a half hour on 4,000 cores. The ranked ligands or conformers can be accessed in milliseconds by specifying the "sort" method from the database. Meanwhile, the IO pressure of shared file storage affected by lots-of-small files in HPC resources can be mitigated. Thus, HHVSF can significantly accelerate HTVS campaigns on HPC resources.

Acknowledgments. We would like to thank Prof. Xin Yan for permission to use WEGA program to test. Helpful discussions with Guixin Guo, Lin Li, Wen Wan and technical assistance by HTCondor Team (University of Wisconsin-Madison) are gratefully acknowledged. This work was performed by the auspices of the NSFC (U1611261), GD Frontier & Key Techn, Innovation Program (2015B010109004).

References

1. Manglik, A., Lin, H., Aryal, D.K., Mccorvy, J.D., Dengler, D., Corder, G., Levit, A., Kling, R.C., Bernat, V., Hübner, H.: Structure-based discovery of opioid analgesics with reduced side effects. Nature **537**(7619), 1 (2016)
2. Rodrigues, T., Reker, D., Schneider, P., Schneider, G.: Counting on natural products for drug design. Nat. Chem. **8**(6), 531–541 (2016)
3. Hao, G.F., Wang, F., Li, H., Zhu, X.L., Yang, W.C., Huang, L.S., Wu, J.W., Berry, E.A., Yang, G.F.: Computational discovery of picomolar Q(o) site inhibitors of cytochrome bc1 complex. J. Am. Chem. Soc. **134**(27), 11168–11176 (2012)
4. Forli, S., Huey, R., Pique, M.E., Sanner, M.F., Goodsell, D.S., Olson, A.J.: Computational protein-ligand docking and virtual drug screening with the AutoDock suite. Nat. Protoc. **11**(5), 905 (2016)
5. Raicu, I.: Falkon: a Fast and Light-weight tasK executiON framework, p. 43 (2007)
6. Raicu, I., Zhao, Z., Wilde, M., Foster, I., Beckman, P., Iskra, K., Clifford, B.: Toward loosely coupled programming on petascale systems, pp. 1–12 (2008)
7. Jain, A., Ong, S.P., Chen, W., Medasani, B., Qu, X., Kocher, M., Brafman, M., Petretto, G., Rignanese, G.M., Hautier, G.: FireWorks: a dynamic workflow system designed for high-throughput applications. Concurr. Comput. Pract. Exp. **27**(17), 5037–5059 (2015)
8. Zhou, T., Caflisch, A.: Data management system for distributed virtual screening. J. Chem. Inf. Model. **49**(1), 145–152 (2009)
9. Trott, O., Olson, A.J.: AutoDock Vina: improving the speed and accuracy of docking with a new scoring function, efficient optimization, and multithreading. J. Comput. Chem. **31**(2), 455–461 (2010)

10. Yan, X., Li, J., Liu, Z., Zheng, M., Ge, H., Xu, J.: Enhancing molecular shape comparison by weighted gaussian functions. J. Chem. Inf. Model. **53**(8), 1967–1978 (2013)
11. Jones, G., Willett, P., Glen, R.C., Leach, A.R., Taylor, R.: Development and validation of a genetic algorithm for flexible docking. J. Mol. Biol. **267**(3), 727–748 (1997)
12. Friesner, R.A., Banks, J.L., Murphy, R.B., Halgren, T.A., Klicic, J.J., Mainz, D.T., Repasky, M.P., Knoll, E.H., Shelley, M., Perry, J.K.: Glide: a new approach for rapid, accurate docking and scoring. 1. Method and assessment of docking accuracy. J. Med. Chem. **47**(7), 1739–1749 (2004)
13. Rarey, M., Kramer, B., Lengauer, T., Klebe, G.: A fast flexible docking method using an incremental construction algorithm. J. Mol. Biol. **261**(3), 470–489 (1996)
14. Yoo, A.B., Jette, M.A., Grondona, M.: SLURM: simple linux utility for resource management. In: Feitelson, D., Rudolph, L., Schwiegelshohn, U. (eds.) JSSPP 2003. LNCS, vol. 2862, pp. 44–60. Springer, Heidelberg (2003). https://doi.org/10.1007/10968987_3
15. Bode, B., Halstead, D.M., Kendall, R., Lei, Z., Jackson, D.: The Portable batch scheduler and the Maui Scheduler on Linux Clusters (2000)
16. Gentzsch, W.: Sun Grid Engine: Towards Creating a Compute Power Grid, pp. 35–36 (2001)
17. Thain, D., Tannenbaum, T., Livny, M.: Distributed computing in practice: the Condor experience: research articles. Concurr. Comput. Pract. Exp. **17**(2–4), 323–356 (2010)
18. Wang, Y., Xiao, J., Suzek, T.O., Jian, Z., Wang, J., Bryant, S.H.: PubChem: a public information system for analyzing bioactivities of small molecules. Nucleic Acids Res. **37** (Web Server issue), W623 (2009)
19. Irwin, J.J., Sterling, T., Mysinger, M.M., Bolstad, E.S., Coleman, R.G.: ZINC: a free tool to discover chemistry for biology. J. Chem. Inf. Model. **52**(7), 1757–1768 (2012)
20. Gaulton, A., Bellis, L.J., Bento, A.P., Chambers, J., Hersey, A., Light, Y., Mcglinchey, S., Michalovich, D., Allazikani, B.: ChEMBL: a large-scale bioactivity database for drug discovery. Nucleic Acids Res. **40**(Database issue), D1100 (2012)
21. Chen, J., Swamidass, S.J., Dou, Y., Bruand, J., Baldi, P.: ChemDB: a public database of small molecules and related chemoinformatics resources. Bioinformatics **21**(22), 4133–4139 (2005)
22. Banker, K.: MongoDB in Action. Manning Publications Co., Greenwich (2011)
23. O'Boyle, N.M., Banck, M., James, C.A., Morley, C., Vandermeersch, T., Hutchison, G.R.: Open babel: an open chemical toolbox. J. Cheminform. **3**(1), 1–14 (2011)
24. Li, J., Ehlers, T., Sutter, J., Varma-O'Brien, S., Kirchmair, J.: CAESAR: a new conformer generation algorithm based on recursive buildup and local rotational symmetry consideration. J. Chem. Inf. Model. **47**(5), 1923–1932 (2007)
25. Visualizer, D.S.: Release 3.5. Accelrys Inc., San Diego (2012)
26. Jaghoori, M.M., Bleijlevens, B., Olabarriaga, S.D.: 1001 ways to run AutoDock Vina for virtual screening. J. Comput. Aided Mol. Des. **30**(3), 1–13 (2016)

HBasechainDB – A Scalable Blockchain Framework on Hadoop Ecosystem

Manuj Subhankar Sahoo$^{(\boxtimes)}$ and Pallav Kumar Baruah

Sri Sathya Sai Institute of Higher Learning, Anantapur 515134,
Andhra Pradesh, India
subhankar.3eblue@gmail.com, pkbaruah@sssihl.edu.in

Abstract. After the introduction of Bitcoin, blockchain has made its way through numerous applications and been adopted by various communities. A number of implementations exist today providing a platform to carry on business with ease. However, it is observed the scalability of blockchain still remains an issue. Also, none of the framework can claim the ability to handle Big Data and support to perform analytics, which is an important and integral facet of current world of business. We propose HBasechainDB, a scalable blockchain-based tamper-proofed Big Data store for distributed computing. HBasechainDB adds the blockchain characteristics of immutability and decentralization to the HBase database in the Hadoop ecosystem. Linear scaling is achieved by pushing computation to the data nodes. HBasechainDB comes with inherent property of efficient big data processing as it is built on Hadoop ecosystem. HBasechainDB also makes adaptation of blockchain very easy for those organizations whose business logic are already existing on Hadoop ecosystem. HBasechainDB can be used as a tamper-proof, decentralized, distributed Big Data store.

Keywords: Blockchain · HBase · Big Data · Tamperproof
Immutability

1 Introduction

A Blockchain is a distributed ledger of blocks which records all the transactions that have taken place. It was first popularized by a person or a group under the pseudonym Satoshi Nakamoto, in 2008 by introducing Bitcoin [11]: A Peer-to-Peer Electronic Cash System. This technology revolutionized the decentralized paradigm by introducing and using a Consensus mechanism: Proof-of-Work (PoW). Proof-of-Work defines the requirement of an expensive calculation also called mining, to be performed so as to create a new trustless set of transactions, also called blocks on the blockchain. The major breakthrough for Bitcoin was the hash based blockchain which made the blocks of transactions tamper-proof, transparent and aversive to DoS attack.

Blockchains can support a variety of applications like decentralized financial services, Internet-of-Things [12], smart properties, etc. Several works have centered around the evaluation of potential use cases for the blockchain [3,9,13].

© The Author(s) 2018
R. Yokota and W. Wu (Eds.): SCFA 2018, LNCS 10776, pp. 18–29, 2018.
https://doi.org/10.1007/978-3-319-69953-0_2

Blockchains can also be seen as a tamper-proof, decentralized data store of a variety of data including government deeds, land ownership records, stock market transactions, etc. However, the PoW consensus protocol enforces major performance bottlenecks on the blockchain. Transaction latencies are as high as an hour and the theoretical peak transactions throughput is just 7 transactions per second. Further, the full nodes in the Bitcoin network which are capable of validating blocks and transactions are expected to maintain copies of the entire Bitcoin blockchain. This places heavy storage demands on the participating nodes. The Bitcoin blockchain is about 136 GB at the time of writing [1]. The communication model also places heavy demands on network bandwidth. The Bitcoin blockchain is also not scalable in that an increase in the number of nodes in the Bitcoin network does not help in increasing the network throughput, latency or capacity. As pointed out by Croman et al. [7], with the increasing adoption of blockchains, we need to address concerns about their scalability.

Apart from digital currency, blockchain technology has taken its own way through many types of industries which includes Finance and Accounting, Supply Chain and Logistics, Insurance etc. For example, financial institutions can settle securities in minutes instead of days. Manufacturers can reduce product recalls by sharing production logs with original equipment manufacturers (OEMs) and regulators. Businesses of all types can more closely manage the flow of goods and related payments with greater speed and less risk. For this reason various industries are trying to adopt blockchain for running their business process smoother and faster. Hyperledger Fabric and BigchainDB are the most widely used framework for blockchainifying business processes.

Today's business processes doesn't generate just data, they generates huge amount of data of wide variety with thrilling velocity. After putting these kinds of data on blockchain it is very important to process and analyze these data in an efficient way. Hadoop is a classic ecosystem which provides numerous functionalities with high efficiency for processing and analyzing these kind of data. A lot of business logic already exists in Hadoop ecosystem to process and analyze these data. Therefore it will be much more easier for the industries to adopt blockchain technology if there exists a scalable blockchain framework in Hadoop ecosystem. Towards this end, HBasechainDB is a first step towards providing a scalable blockchain framework in the Hadoop ecosystem. HBasechainDB is started by High performance Computing and Data (HPCD) Group, Department of Mathematics and Computer Science (DMACS), Sri Sathya Sai Institute of Higher Learning. This is achieved by imparting the blockchain characteristics of immutability and decentralization to the HBase database.

2   Background and Related Work

A lot of work has been underway for addressing the scalability of blockchains. Vukolic [14] has contrasted PoW-based blockchains to those based on BFT state machine replication for scalability. Eyal et al. [8] introduces Bitcoin-NG as a scalable blockchain protocol based on BFT consensus protocols. These approaches are focused upon improving the consensus protocol. McConaghy et al. [10] adopted a different approach to scalability. They started with a distributed database, MongoDB, and added the blockchain features of decentralized control, immutability while supporting the creation and movement of digital assets to provide a scalable, decentralized database BigchainDB. The major contribution of BigchainDB that enables this scalability is the concept of blockchain pipelining. In blockchain pipelining, blocks are added to the blockchain without waiting for the current block to be agreed upon by the other nodes. The consensus is taken care of by the underlying database. The validation of blocks is not done during block addition but eventually by a process of voting among nodes. This has huge performance gains and BigchainDB has points to transaction throughputs of over a million transactions per second and sub-second latencies.

In creating HBasechainDB, we have adopted an approach similar to that of BigchainDB. Instead of using MongoDB as the underlying database, we use the Hadoop database, Apache HBase. Apache HBase is a distributed, scalable Big Data store. It supports random, real-time read/write access to Big Data. Apache HBase is an open-source, distributed, versioned, non-relational, column-family oriented database modeled after Google's Bigtable [6]. HBase provides both linear and modular scaling, along with strongly consistent reads/writes. HBase tables are distributed on the cluster via regions. HBase supports automatic sharding by splitting and re-distributing regions automatically as data grows. HBasechainDB is a scalable, decentralized data store akin to BigchainDB.

3   Terminology

- **Blockchain:** A chain of blocks where every block has a hash link to the previous block i.e. every block stores the hash of the previous block. An advantage is, just by storing the hash of the last block we can easily detect if any change has been made to any of the block.
- **Double spending:** It is an attack where the asset is spent in more than one transaction. To prevent double spending, blockchain framework needs to check whether a particular asset is spent in any of the previous transactions. For instance: user U2 wants to spend/transfer an asset A1, in transaction T2, to another user U3. Say, the asset A1 was transferred to U2 by user U1 in some previous transaction T1. U2 specifies T1's Id in T2, which shows that T1 was the transaction which contained asset A1, and U2 got it from U1. Now, U2 wants to spend/transfer it to U3. So before validating transaction T2 with asset A1, a Blockchain framework checks all the transaction with asset A1 that has occurred/lies in between T1 and T2, in order. If A1 does not occur in any of the transactions then A1 is not double spent else it's double spent.
- **Blockchain Pipeline:** In Blockchain pipelining, blocks are written to the underlying database without waiting for a vote which confirms the block's validity. Voting for a block and forming a chain happens as a separate layer.

- **Changefeed:** It is a mechanism by which any update on the Blockchain is notified to the nodes. This automatic change notifications on the Blockchain brings another benefit: they improve tamper-detection (beyond what a blockchain offers). If a hacker somehow manages to delete or update a record in the data store, the hashes change (like any blockchain). In addition, a data-store with automatic change notifications would notify all the nodes, which can then immediately revert the changes and restore the hash integrity.
- **HBase region-server:** These are the basic elements of availability and distribution for tables, and are comprised of a store per Column Family.
- **HBase Master:** Responsible for coordinating Regions in the cluster and execute administrative operations.

4 Architecture

4.1 Data Model of Transaction

The Transaction Model of all Blockchain Platforms has three important fields: Transaction Id, List of Inputs, List of Outputs. Apart from these, there are fields which are platform dependent. HBasechainDB's transaction model consists of; Transaction Id, Asset, List of Inputs, List of Outputs and Metadata.

1. **ID:** The transaction Id uniquely identifies the transaction. It is a SHA3-256 hash of the asset, list of inputs, list of outputs and metadata.
2. **Asset:** A JSON format document associated with a transaction.
3. **List of Inputs:** Each input in the list of a transaction is spend-able/transferable if it has a link to the output of some previous transaction (in case of transfer transaction. Creation transaction doesn't have link to out of any previous transaction). This input is then spent/transferred by satisfying/fulfilling the crypto-conditions on that previous transaction output. A CREATE transaction should have exactly one input. A TRANSFER transaction should have at least one input (i.e. ≥ 1).
4. **List of outputs:** Each output in the list of a transactions indicates the crypto-conditions which must be satisfied by anyone who wishes to spend/transfer that output to some other transaction. It also indicates the number of shares of the asset tied to that output.
5. **Metadata:** User-provided transaction metadata. It can be any valid JSON document or NULL.

4.2 Design Details

HBasechainDB is a super peer-to-peer network operating using a federation of nodes. All the nodes in the federation have equal privileges which gives HBasechainDB its decentralization. Such a super peer-to-peer network was inspired by the Internet Domain Name System. Any client can submit or retrieve transactions or blocks, but only the federation nodes can modify the blockchain. The federation can grow or shrink during the course of operation of

HBasechainDB. Let us say there are n federation nodes N1, N2, ..., Nn. When a client submits a transaction t, it is assigned to one of the federation nodes, say Nk. The node Nk is now responsible for entering this transaction into the blockchain. Nk first checks for the validity of the transaction. Validity of a transaction includes having a correct transaction hash, correct signatures, existence of the inputs to the transaction, if any, and the inputs not having been already spent. Once Nk has validated a set of transactions, it bundles them together in a block, and adds it to the blockchain. Any block can only contain a specified maximum number of transactions. Let us say t was added in the block B.

When the block B is added to the blockchain its validity is undecided. Since the federation is allowed to grow or shrink during the operation of HBasechainDB, blocks also include a list of voters based on the current federation. All the nodes in the voter list for a block vote upon B for its validity. For voting upon a block, a node validates all the transactions in the block. A block is voted valid only if all the transactions are found to be valid, else it is voted invalid. If a block gathers a majority of valid or invalid votes, its validity changes from undecided to valid or invalid respectively. Only the transactions in a valid block are considered to have been recorded in the blockchain. The ones in the invalid blocks are ignored altogether. However, the chain retains both valid and invalid blocks. A block being invalid does not imply that all the transactions in the block are invalid. Therefore, the transactions from an invalid block are re-assigned to federation nodes to give the transactions further chance of inclusion in the blockchain. The reassignment is done randomly. This way, if a particular rogue node was trying to add an invalid transaction to the blockchain, this transaction will likely be assigned to a different node the second time and dropped from consideration. Thus, if block B acquires a majority of valid votes, then transaction t would have been irreversibly added to the blockchain. On the other hand, if B were invalid, then t would be reassigned to another node and so on until it is included in the chain or removed from the system.

As discussed in the previous section, the chain is not formed when blocks are created. When a block is entered into hbasechain table, the blocks are stored in HBase in the lexicographical order of their ids. The chain is actually formed during vote time. When a node votes on a block, it also specifies the previous block that it had voted upon. Thus, instead of waiting for all the federation nodes to validate the current block before proceeding to the creation of a new block, blocks are created independent of validation. This is the technique of blockchain pipelining described earlier. Over time, the blockchain accumulates a mix of valid and invalid blocks. The invalid blocks are not deleted from the chain to keep the chain immutable. What we also note here is that while it would seem that different nodes could have a different view of the chain depending upon the order in which they view the incoming blocks, it is not seen in practice in HBasechainDB due to the strong consistency of HBase and the fact that the blocks to be voted upon are ordered based on their timestamp. Thus, each node sees the same order of blocks, and we have the same chain view for different nodes.

To tamper with any block in the blockchain, an adversary will have to modify the block, leading to a change in its hash. This changed hash would not match the vote information for the block in the votes table, and also in subsequent votes that refer to this block as the previous block. Thus an adversary would have to modify the vote information all the way up to the present. However, we require that all the votes being appended by nodes are signed. Thus, unless an adversary can forge a node's signature, which is cryptographically hard, he cannot modify the node's votes. In fact, he has to forge multiple signatures to affect any change in the blockchain preventing any chances of tampering. This way HBasechainDB provides a tamper-proof blockchain over HBase.

4.3   Exploiting HBase

In this section we describe the distinction between MongoDB and HBase. We also justify the means to achieve greater performance with the proposed system design.

MongoDB is a document store database. A document is a big JSON block with no particular schema or format. This gives an edge to dynamic use cases and ever-changing applications. MongoDB does not provide triggers. Although MongoDB has its own advantages, the document store characteristic of MongoDB degrades its performance for following operations:

1. Working with individual columns.
2. Performing join operations.

HBase is a wide column store database. It is a distributed, scalable, reliable, and versioned storage system capable of providing random read/write access in real-time. It provides a fault-tolerant way of storing large quantities of sparse data. HBase features compression, in-memory operation and Bloom filters on a per-column basis.

We use the following characteristics of HBase extensively to derive performance:

1. HBase is partitioned to tables, and tables are further split into column families. Column families must be declared in the schema, and we can group certain set of columns together. One of the major operations in blockchain transaction is checking for Double-Spending. In order to make the check for double spending more efficient, we can keep the input column of all these transactions in a separate column family. This will allow us to perform the check for double spending faster because the region server will need to load only one column family which contains the input of the transaction. In case of database such as MongoDB the database server needs to load the whole document before filtering out the input column and performing Double Spent check.
2. HBase is optimized for reads, supported by single-write master, which results in a strict consistency model. And use of Ordered Partitioning supports row-scans. In Blockchain we need one write and many read operation because

the transactions are written only once but read many times for various purposes like checking double spending and performing checks on whether any tampering took place.

3. HBase provides us with various ways in which we can run our custom code on the region-server. HBase co-processor and custom filters are two such ways. HBase co-processor can act as database triggers. In our implementation we use these features in following ways:

   (a) The check for double spending is generally done by loading the transactions to the federation nodes(i.e. the client system). Loading this many transactions from region-server to the federations node system is a major bottleneck for the system throughput. In our approach, instead of pulling the data required for double spending check on to the client-system, we push the computation check to the region-server using HBase custom filter. This approach improves the performance in two ways:

      i. Data does not move towards the computation node rather computation moves towards the Data node. Since the code size is exponentially lesser than data size, we improve the system by decreasing the communication time.

      ii. Computation for double spending is done in parallel on multiple region-server compared to the traditional approach of checking on a single Client node.

   (b) Changefeed brings a great benefit to the Blockchain framework. We use HBase co-processor to implement changefeed which will notify immediately whenever a hacker tries to change or delete the content of the database.

5   Implementation Details

The Federation Nodes in HBasechainDB are initialized with a key-pair; Ed25519 [2,4] signing system. SHA3-256 [5] hashing scheme is used for hashing the transactions and blocks. The current implementation of HBasechainDB uses six HBase tables. A critical issue in the current design of HBase tables is that of designing the row key, since the region splits and the scans on HBase tables are done in the lexicographical order of the row key. The row key pattern depends upon the access pattern for the data in the Hbase table.

Following is the description of the HBase tables:

1. backLog: When a transaction is submitted to the Federation nodes, the transaction is randomly assigned to one of the nodes. All such assigned transactions are stored in the backlog table with each transaction stored in a single row. A node scanning the backlog table should only have to read the transactions assigned to itself. Thus, the first segment of the row key for backlog table is the public key of the node to whom the transaction was assigned, to ensure that a node can scan the backlog table with the row prefix being its own public key. The last segment of the row key contains the transaction reference id. So the row key looks like: <publicKey>_<transactionId>

2. block: This is the table that contains all the blocks in the blockchain. Each block is a logical block which contains only the id's of the transaction which are present in the block. The actual transaction details are stored in "hbasechaindb" table. Since the access pattern for this table is looking up blocks based on block id, the row key for this table is just the block id: <blockId>

3. hbasechaindb: This is the table where all the transaction details are stored after a transaction is put on the blockchain. In this table each row corresponds to a single transaction. Since the access pattern for this table is looking up transaction based on transaction link id, the row key of this table is <transaction link id>. The transaction link id consists of <block_id>_<transaction_id>. This transaction link id which is of previous output is used in inputs of current transaction while spending an asset

4. toVote: Every new block created has to be voted upon by the Federation nodes. For this, we need to inform the Federation nodes of their need to vote upon a newly created block. To this end, every block created is added to this table to signal the node for voting. It is removed from the table once the node has finished voting on it. The row key of this table is : <federation node's signing key>_<block id>

5. vote: This is the table in which all the votes are recorded. There has to be an entry for every federation node which votes for their respective blocks. The row key of the table is: <block_id>_<decision>_<Fed. Node public key>

6. reference: This is the table which stores the map between transaction link id and transaction id. This table acts as an index when the details of a transaction is queried. Since the access pattern of the table is transaction reference id, the row key of this table is just the transaction reference id: <transacation_link_Id>

When a transaction is submitted to HBasechainDB, it is first put in the *backLog* table. Federation nodes picks the transactions from *backLog* table in certain time interval, checks the validity of the transactions, bundles them into blocks and adds those blocks to the Blockchain. As show in Fig. 1, when a federation node forms a block, it updates 3 HBase tables. In *block* table, the transaction_Id of all the transactions are made as separate blocks and stored. In the *hbasechaindb* table, all the transaction details are stored. In the *toVote* table the information about newly created block is stored. The federation nodes refers this *toVote* table to vote for the block. All the Federation nodes, in certain time interval checks the *toVote* table and cast their vote after checking the validity of the block. All the votes are stored in the *vote* table. After the validity of a block, entries corresponding to all the transactions are made in the *reference* table.

The complete implementation of HBasechainDB is done using Java since the performance of HBase API for Java is best among the HBase API's present for different languages. HBase API for Java also gives advantage of writing custom filters and coprocessors.

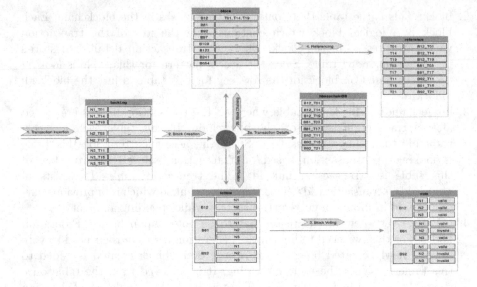

Fig. 1. Transaction flow of HBasechainDB

6 Performance

6.1 Experimental Setup

We have used three nodes for the initial performance testing of HBasechainDB with the following configurations:

- 3 nodes with Intel Core i5-4670 CPU @ 3.40 GHz*4 processor and 16 GB of memory, with Ubuntu 16.04 OS.
- Each of the 3 nodes runs HBase region-server. There is a HBase master running in one of the system.
- There is a Replication factor of 3 for the underlying HDFS.
- The HBase is backed by 3 quorum zookeeper.
- We consider only creation of transactions for our case.

6.2 Results

We have tested HBasechainDB for scalability over three nodes. There are two parameters that we describe the performance of HBasechainDB with:

- **Transaction Latency:** This is defined as the time elapsed since the submission of a transaction to HBasechainDB until the block in which it has been recorded is validated. The transaction latency is found for streaming transactions.
- **Throughput:** This is the number of transactions that are recorded in the blockchain per second. To find the peak throughput the blockchain is capable of, we store the transactions in the backlog beforehand and then run the nodes. The throughput observed then is the peak throughput.

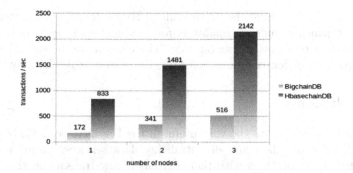

Fig. 2. Performance of BigchainDB and HBasechainDB

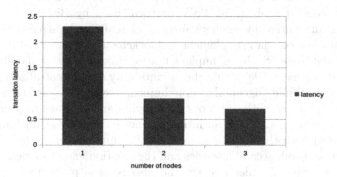

Fig. 3. Latency of HBasechainDB in sec.

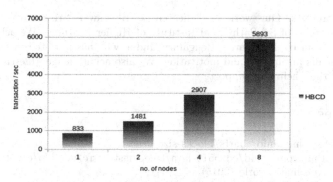

Fig. 4. Scalability of HBasechainDB upto 8 nodes

Figure 2 compares the transaction throughput of HBasechainDB and BigchainDB, using systems with 1, 2 and 3 nodes and Fig. 3 shows the latency of HBasechainDB. Figure 4 shows the scalability of HBasechainDB till 8 nodes. The result shows, as we add the nodes the transaction throughput of HBasechainDB scales linearly.

The main reason behind the linear scale of HBasechainDB is, almost all the computation which includes *computation for transaction's validity* and *check for double spending* is pushed to server side. Therefore if we increase the HBase nodes keeping the federation node constant, the system scales linearly.

7   Conclusion

Blockchain technologies can be very useful in the Big Data scenario by helping us immutably record data and decentralizing data services. However, current blockchain implementations with their extremely low transaction throughputs and high transaction latencies do not lend themselves to Big Data. Discussions on improving blockchain scalability have largely focused on using better consensus protocols as against the PoW protocol used by Bitcoin. BigchainDB provides an alternative idea where instead of scaling blockchains to provide scalable data stores, they implement a blockchain over an existing scalable distributed database. Such an implementation inherits the scalability of the underlying database, while adding the immutability and decentralization offered by blockchains. While BigchainDB was implemented upon the MongoDB and RethinkDB database, with our work we provide an alternate implementation over HBase. HBasechainDB is an hitherto unavailable blockchain implementation integrated with the Hadoop ecosystem. It supports very high transaction throughputs with sub-second latencies and the creation and movement of digital assets. HBasechainDB scales linearly and also is good platform for analyzing data that are present on blockchain.

Acknowledgments. Our work is dedicated to Bhagawan Sri Sathya Sai Baba, Founder Chancellor of Sri Sathya Sai Institute of Higher Learning. We acknowledge Adarsh Saraf from IBM Research, Bengaluru, India, who has initiated this work. We thank him for his inspiration and motivation. We also acknowledge Maestro Technology, USA for their help and support.

References

1. https://blockchain.info/charts/blocks-size
2. https://github.com/str4d/ed25519-java/tree/master/src/net/i2p/crypto/eddsa
3. Aron, J.: Automatic world (2015)
4. Bernstein, D.J., Duif, N., Lange, T., Schwabe, P., Yang, B.-Y.: High-speed high-security signatures. J. Cryptographic Eng. **2**(2), 1–13 (2012)
5. Bertoni, G., Daemen, J., Peeters, M., Van Assche, G.: Keccak specifications. Submission to NIST (Round 2) (2009)
6. Chang, F., Dean, J., Ghemawat, S., Hsieh, W.C., Wallach, D.A., Burrows, M., Chandra, T., Fikes, A., Gruber, R.E.: Bigtable: a distributed storage system for structured data. ACM Trans. Comput. Syst. (TOCS) **26**(2), 4 (2008)
7. Croman, K., et al.: On scaling decentralized blockchains. In: Clark, J., Meiklejohn, S., Ryan, P.Y.A., Wallach, D., Brenner, M., Rohloff, K. (eds.) FC 2016. LNCS, vol. 9604, pp. 106–125. Springer, Heidelberg (2016). https://doi.org/10.1007/978-3-662-53357-4_8

8. Eyal, I., Gencer, A.E., Sirer, E.G., Van Renesse, R.: Bitcoin-NG: a scalable blockchain protocol. In: NSDI, pp. 45–59 (2016)
9. Liebenau, J., Elaluf-Calderwood, S.M.:. Blockchain innovation beyond bitcoin and banking (2016)
10. McConaghy, T., Marques, R., Müller, A., De Jonghe, D., McConaghy, T., McMullen, G., Henderson, R., Bellemare, S., Granzotto, A.: BigchainDB: a scalable blockchain database. White paper, BigChainDB (2016)
11. Nakamoto, S.: Bitcoin: A Peer-to-Peer Electronic Cash System (2008)
12. Panikkar, S., Nair, S., Brody, P., Pureswaran, V.: Adept: an IoT practitioner perspective. IBM Institute for Business Value (2014)
13. Swan, M.: Blockchain: Blueprint for a New Economy. O'Reilly Media Inc., Sebastopol (2015)
14. Vukolić, M.: The quest for scalable blockchain fabric: proof-of-work vs. BFT replication. In: Camenisch, J., Kesdoğan, D. (eds.) iNetSec 2015. LNCS, vol. 9591, pp. 112–125. Springer, Cham (2016). https://doi.org/10.1007/978-3-319-39028-4_9

DETOUR: A Large-Scale Non-blocking Optical Data Center Fabric

Jinzhen Bao[1,2], Dezun Dong[2(✉)], and Baokang Zhao[2]

[1] PLA Academy of Military Science, Beijing, China
[2] National University of Defense Technology, Changsha, China
{baojinzhen,dong,bkzhao}@nudt.edu.cn

Abstract. Optical data center networks (DCNs) are attracting growing interest due to the technical strength compared to traditional electrical switching networks, which effectively eliminates the potential hotspot caused by over-subscription. However, the evolving traffics with high fan-out and various patterns pose new challenges to optical DCNs. Prior solutions are either hard to support high fan-out communications in large-scale or suffer from limited connections with low performance.

In this paper we propose DETOUR, a large-scale non-blocking optical switching data center fabric. DETOUR composes of optical circuit switches (OCSes) and connects them in a 2D-Torus topology. It supports up to 729 racks and 69K+ ports with each OCS having 96 wavelengths. DETOUR utilizes a broadcast-and-select mechanism and enables signals optically forwarded to any dimension. Moreover, it realizes non-blocking by recursively adjusting conflict links between the diagonal forwarding OCSes. Our extensive evaluation results show that DETOUR delivers comparable high performance to a non-blocking optical switching fabric. It outperforms up to 2.14× higher throughput, and reduces 34% flow completion times (FCT) and 21% energy consumption compared with the state-of-the-art works.

1 Introduction

Data centers as the infrastructure of cloud computing, are rapidly expanded to meet the increasing demand of cloud services, big data and high performance applications. Many novel network architectures have been proposed to efficiently connect tens of thousands servers inside data centers. Pure electrical switching architectures, such as Fat-Tree [4], BCube [13] and Jellyfish [20], provide static and uniform interconnections among servers, without considering the dynamic traffic patterns. Due to the mismatch between the static interconnections and the dynamic network traffic, pure electrical switching networks must pay extremely high cost and complex wiring to deliver high bisection bandwidth.

Owning on the traffic characteristics of frequently concentrated and bursty [14], optical switching technologies are introduced to DCNs due to their reconfigurability, higher bit-rates and lower power [8,9,12,17,21,25]. Optical DCNs

© The Author(s) 2018
R. Yokota and W. Wu (Eds.): SCFA 2018, LNCS 10776, pp. 30–50, 2018.
https://doi.org/10.1007/978-3-319-69953-0_3

support on-demand link connectivity and bandwidth allocation, which mitigating potential hotspots caused by the over-subscription. However, the increasing large-scale data-intensive applications have produced new traffic characteristics and pose challenges to existing optical DCNs:

(1) *High Fan-Out.* Traces from production clusters (e.g., Microsoft [16], Facebook [18], and Google [19]) show that source top-of-rack (ToR) electrical packet switches (EPSes) usually communicate with tens to hundreds of other EPSes simultaneously and have the stability across time periods from seconds to days. Constructing high fan-out EPSes connections in large-scale is significant to improve the network throughput and reduce flow completion times (FCT).

(2) *Various Communication Patterns.* The iterative computing frameworks (e.g., MapReduce, Spark, Hadoop) for large scale data analytics contain various communication patterns, such as unicast, multicast and broadcast (*-cast). Multicast and broadcast data dissemination are always the performance bottleneck for data analytics applications [11].

Along with the scale of DCN expanding, the ultimate goal is to provide non-blocking network services in large-scale with high flexibility. However, existing optical switching networks fail to meet all of the goals (as summarized in Table 1). Most designs are based on the techniques of Microelectromechanical system (MEMS) Optical Circuit Switch (OCS), Wavelength Division Multiplexing (WDM) and Wavelength Selective Switch (WSS).

(1) MEMS-based OCS is a $N \times N$ non-blocking switching matrix which mechanically rotates mirrors to direct any input signals to any one of the output ports. c-Through [21], Helios [12] and OSA [8] leverage a single MEMS-based OCS. However, the network scale is limited, since MEMS-based OCS is hard to scale and difficult to support high fan-out traffic patterns.

(2) WDM technology multiplexes multiple non-interfering wavelengths onto a single fiber, which supports up to 100 wavelengths by using Dense WDM (DWDM).

Table 1. Summary of prior optical DCNs and comparison to detour

Optical DCNs	Scalability(Ports)	Non-blocking	Flexibility
c-Through [21] Helios [12] OSA [8]	Low (~2000)	Yes	Yes
Wavecube [9]	High (Unlimited)	No	No
Mordia [17], MegaSwitch [10]	Low (~704) Low (~6000)	Yes	Yes
OvS [25]	High (100K+)	No	Yes
DETOUR	**High (69K+)**	**Yes**	**Yes**

(3) WSS is reconfigurable to switch the input multiplexed wavelengths to desired output. WDM and WSS are usually used together to construct a distributed optical switching fabric (e.g., Wavecube [9], Mordia [17], MegaSwitch [10] and OvS [25]). Although Wavecube is scalable, it is blocking due to the optical links are reconfigurable only between neighbor switches. Mordia, MegaSwitch and OvS construct a broadcast-and-select optical switching fabric. They naturally supports unicast, multicast and broadcast with high flexibility. However, Mordia and MegaSwitch have low scalability. OvS is scalable based on the 2D-Torus topology, but it blocked without supporting arbitrary connections.

In this paper, we propose DETOUR, a large-scale and non-blocking optical switching data center fabric. DETOUR utilizes the DWDM technique and connects OCSes in a 2D-Torus topology. It can easily extend up to 729 racks and 69K+ ports when each OCS supports 96 wavelengths. DETOUR utilizes broadcast-and-select optical switching mechanism. The multiplexed DWDM signals are broadcasted along the same horizontal and vertical dimensions with the source OCS, and can also be optically forwarded to other orthogonal dimensions by the crosspoint OCSes. DETOUR recursively adjusts the conflicting broadcasting paths between diagonal forwarding OCSes to realize a non-blocking optical switching fabric.

We summarize the contributions of this paper as follows:

- We propose a novel optical switching data center network architecture, which is non-blocking in large-scale, named DETOUR. DETOUR delivers high scalability with up to 729 racks and 69K+ ports. By utilizing the broadcast-and-select mechanism and enabling optically forwarding signals to other orthogonal dimensions, DETOUR delivers high flexibility with establishing directly connected and dynamic bandwidth links between arbitrary EPS pairs.
- We develop control algorithms to optimize the network performance, including demand estimation, topology generation, wavelength assignment, reconfiguration and so on. Especially, we realize a non-blocking wavelength assignment algorithm by recursively adjusting the conflicting wavelengths, which exploiting the topology properties of DETOUR. And we also prove the non-blocking property in theory.
- We realize an event-based flow level simulator and conduct extensive simulations. Our simulation results show that DETOUR delivers comparable high performance to a non-blocking optical switching fabric. It outperforms up to 2.14× higher throughput and reduces 34% FCT and 57% energy consumption compared with the state-of-the-art works.

The rest of this paper is organized as follows. Section 2 describes the architecture of DETOUR. Section 3 details the algorithms realized in the controller. In Sect. 4, we implement a flow level simulator and evaluate the performance of DETOUR. Section 5 summarizes the related work. Finally, Sect. 6 concludes the paper.

2   DETOUR Architecture Overview

In this section, we firstly give an overview of DETOUR and describe the architecture of OCS, which is the key device to construct DETOUR. Then we give an example to explain the specific broadcast-and-select workflow. Lastly, we analyze the scalability, feasibility and cost of DETOUR.

DETOUR is a distributed optical switching fabric, in which the OCSes are physically connected in 2D-Torus topology and configured by a centralized controller, as shown in Fig. 1. DETOUR overlays above ToR EPSes to construct a flattened and hybrid packet/circuit switched DCN. Each OCS in DETOUR has m ports directly connected with the below EPS, whose up-link ports are equipped with m DWDM transceivers. Thus, the EPSes are logically connected as a m-regular random graph [20] in the optical DCN.

DETOUR is based on the broadcast-and-select optical switching mechanism and uses multi-fibers for space division multiplexing different broadcast signals. For each sender OCS, the signals are statically broadcasted along the same horizontal (west-east) and vertical (south-north) dimensions. For OCSes in different dimensions, the desired signals are selected from the broadcasted signal sets by the crosspoint OCS, and optically forwarded from one dimension to the orthogonal dimension without being relayed by the crosspoint EPS. DETOUR constructs a non-blocking optical switching fabric that supports establishing directly connected optical links between arbitrary EPS pairs. Thus, it reduces the hop counts of EPS and improves network throughput.

Figure 2 illustrates the detailed architecture of OCS. Each OCS comprises of commercial optical components, such as $N \times 1$ Wavelength Selective Switch (WSS), Multiplexer (MUX), Demultiplexer (DEMUX), Optical Splitter, Coupler, Erbium Doped Fiber Amplifier (EDFA).

We firstly give a description about these optical elements. (1) $N \times 1$ WSS takes N fibers with k wavelengths each and outputs a non-interfering subset

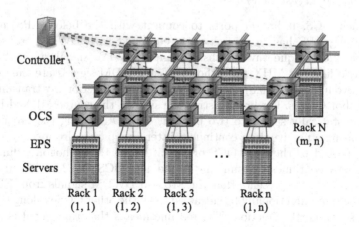

Fig. 1. The high-level architecture of DETOUR

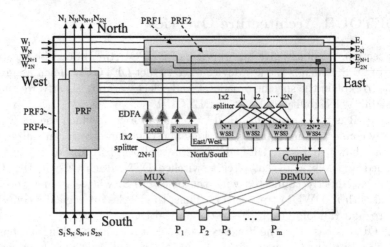

Fig. 2. The architecture of OCS

of the $k \times N$ wavelengths to an output fiber. The measured switching delay of $N \times 1$ WSS is less than $10\,\mathrm{ms}$ [25]. $2N \times 2$ WSS is composed of two $N \times 1$ WSSes and has N input ports for each horizontal and vertical dimension in the 2D-Torus topology. To construct a non-blocking optical switching fabric, there are at most $N + 1$ OCSes at each dimension. The option of N is the key factor to determine the number of other components. (2) MUX/DEMUX combines or separates optical signals at different wavelengths. (3) Splitter/Coupler are passive devices that combine or split optical power by a certain ratio. (4) EDFA is used to boost the signals and compensate losses.

In the following, we will detailedly explain the workflow of the specific broadcast-and-select optical switching mechanism.

– *From the Broadcasting View*

For each OCS, it has m ports to connect with the below EPS, and the corresponding EPS has m up-link ports equipped with DWDM transceivers, which have fixed unique wavelengths. The input DWDM signals are multiplexed into a single fiber by MUX. And the MUXed DWDM signals are then equally split into two fibers by a (5:5) optical splitter and unidirectionally transmitted to next neighbor OCSes. For broadcasting the signals, the source MUXed DWDM signals are statically split into two parts at each OCS along the broadcasting path. By using a passive drop-continue splitter, one part is dropped to the WSS for being passed to the local OCS or forwarded to the orthogonal dimension, the other part continues transmitting to the next OCS. As shown in Fig. 3, the multi-coloured line represents that the MUXed DWDM signals from EPS1 are statically and unidirectionally broadcasted to all the other OCSes along the west-east and south-north direction. The red line means that this signal is selected to be forwarded from west-east direction to south-north direction by WSS2. As optical splitter and connector insertion have signal losses, a single stage EDFA is

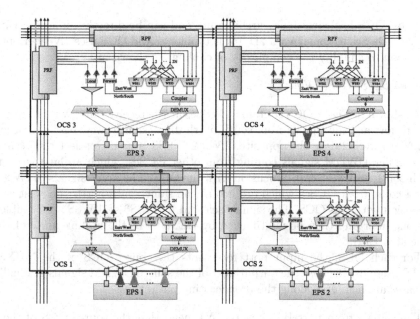

Fig. 3. An example of how DETOUR works (Color figure online)

used to boost the DWDM signals before being broadcasted out. This ensures all the dropped signals' intensity greater than the transceivers' receiver sensitivity, all signals can be recovered correctly.

To ensure the consistency of OCS architecture and simplify the connection between neighbor OCSes, OCS takes advantage of the uniform passive routing fabric (PRF) to reroute the multiple broadcasted signals. PRF also couples with passive drop-continue splitters to drop the broadcasted signals. The ratio of drop and continue is determined by the scale of DETOUR. As shown in Fig. 2, OCS contains 4 PRFs and each dimension has 2 PRFs. PRF1 and PRF3 are used for the signals that are broadcasted from the same dimension. PRF2 and PRF4 are used for the signals forwarded from other dimensions. Focusing on one dimension, for each OCS:

- The source DWDM signals are transmitted out from port E_1 and the source forwarded signals are transmitted out from port E_{N+1}.
- The signals from port W_i $(1 \leq i < N)$ are transmitted out from port E_{i+1} and dropped to the $(N+i)$-th (5:5) splitter.
- The signals from port W_i $(i = N)$ are only dropped to the $2N$-th (5:5) splitter.
- The signals from port W_i $(N + 1 \leq i < 2N)$ are transmitted out from port E_{i+1} and dropped to the i-th port of WSS4.
- The signals from port W_i $(i = 2N)$ are only dropped to the $2N$-th port of WSS4.

Thus, OCS has consistency architecture and can be directly connected with neighbor OCSes to construct a 2D-Torus topology. And OCS uses $2N$-fiber optical ribbon to simplify the complexity of cabling, as shown in Fig. 3.

– *From the Selecting View*

As shown in Fig. 2, OCS contains 4 WSSes at the receiver end. $N \times 1$ WSS1 is used to forward the signals from south-north dimension to west-east dimension and $N \times 1$ WSS2 does the opposite. $2N \times 2$ WSS3 is used to select the desired non-conflict DWDM signals coming from other OCSes, which are at the same north-south and west-east dimension with the OCS. The input signals of $2N \times 2$ WSS4 come from OCSes which are not at the same south-north and west-east dimension with this OCS. The signals selected by WSS3 and WSS4 are coupled into one fiber and then de-multiplexed by DEMUX to the up-link ports of the associated EPS.

For each OCS, the input port represents the source OCS of the MUXed DWDM signals. Because the output port of the source DWDM signals gradually increases at each OCS along the broadcasting path, thus:

– The signals from port W_i ($1 \leq i \leq N$) mean that the source OCS of these signals is the i-th OCS on the west of this OCS. The dropped signals are equally split by the $(N + i)$-th splitter, then transmitted to the i-th port of WSS2 and the $(N + i)$-th port of WSS3.
– The signals from port W_i ($N + 1 \leq i \leq 2N$) mean that they are forwarded by the $(i - N)$-th OCS on the west of this OCS, and the source OCS of these signals is on the south-north dimension passing the forwarding OCS. Then the dropped signals are transmitted to the i-th port of WSS4.
– The signal from port S_i ($1 \leq i \leq N$) means that the source OCS of these signals is the i-th OCS on the south of this OCS. The dropped signals are equally split by the i-th splitter, then transmitted to the i-th port of WSS1 and WSS3.
– The signals from port S_i ($N + 1 \leq i \leq 2N$) mean that they are forwarded by the $(i - N)$-th OCS on the south of this OCS, and the source OCS of these signals is on the west-east dimension passing the forwarding OCS. Then the dropped signals are transmitted to the $(i - N)$-th port of WSS4.

In DETOUR, the controller performs wavelength assignment algorithm, which will be introduced in the next section. Given the wavelength configuration demand, WSSes are configured to pass the desired wavelengths, and block the others. For each destination OCS:

– If the source OCS is in the same south-north or west-east dimension, WSS3 selects the demand wavelengths from the input port associated with the source OCS. As shown in Fig. 3, the optical channel from EPS1 to EPS2 is assigned a green wavelength, and from EPS1 to EPS3 is assigned a orange wavelength. So WSS3 of OCS2 passes the green wavelength from the $(N + 1)$-th port and WSS3 of OCS3 passes the orange wavelength from the 1-th port.

– If the source OCS are not in the same dimension, it needs jointly configure WSSes of the forwarding OCS and destination OCS. WSS1 or WSS2 of the forwarding OCS selects the demand wavelengths from the input port associated with the source OCS and broadcasts it to the orthogonal dimension. Then, WSS4 of the destination OCS passes the demand wavelengths from the input port associated with the forwarding OCS. As shown in Fig. 3, the optical channel from EPS1 to EPS4 is assigned a red wavelength and forwarded by OCS2. So WSS2 of OCS2 passes the red wavelength from the 1-th port and forwards it to the south-north dimension, then WSS4 of OCS4 passes the red wavelength from the 1-th port.

In the following, we will analyze the feasibility, scalability and cost of DETOUR.

We will give a detailed analysis on the feasibility through theory. The key to show the feasibility of DETOUR mainly focuses on two parts: (1) demonstrating the feasibility of the optical components shown in Fig. 2, (2) guaranteeing the receiving signals being correctly identified by DWDM transceivers.

The OCS in DETOUR uses existing commodity optical components, such as $N \times 1$ WSS, EDFA, Splitter, Coupler. And its architecture is similar to that of OvS [25] without introducing any novel optical devices. Zhu et al. have implemented a prototype of OvS and built a small testbed. The key difference between DETOUR and OvS is that DETOUR optically forwards signals to orthogonal dimensions by using the same WSS component. Therefore, the implementation of OvS, as a side effect, has also demonstrated the feasibility of the optical components in DETOUR.

Next, we will explore the Optical Signal Noise Ratio (OSNR) performance and how many times the optical signals can be split while guaranteeing correctness. To support a large scale, OCS adopts a bidirectional design, as shown in Fig. 4. The source signals are broadcasted along each direction and decrease when crossing one OCS. The signal specifications of optical components are listed in Table 2. Let l denote the transmittance $n/(m + n)$, which means the fraction of signal passing and reflecting. For each source OCS:

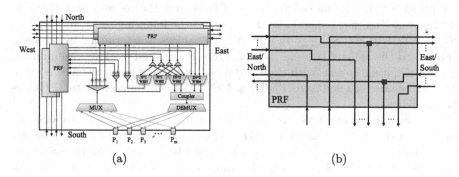

(a)   (b)

Fig. 4. Bidirectional design

Table 2. Optical component specifications

Contents		Specifications
Transceiver [1]	Output power	$-1 \sim 3\,$dBm
	Receiver sensitivity	$-7 \sim -23\,$dBm
EDFA [2]	Input power range	$-32 \sim -1\,$dBm
	Saturated output power	$17.3 \pm 0.3\,$dBm
1×2 splitter (m:n)	Dropped (m) loss	$-10log(m/(m+n))\,$dB
	Passed (n) loss	$-10log(n/(m+n))\,$dB
Connector loss		$1\,$dB
WSS loss		$4\,$dB
Coupler loss		$1\,$dB
DeMux loss		$2.5\,$dB
1×2 splitter/1×4 splitter		$3.5\,$dB/$7\,$dB

The signal loss S_{Loss}^{R} for the receiving side of i-th switch is calculated as follows:

$$S_{Loss}^{R} = -10log(l) * (i-1) - 10log(1-l) + i + 11$$

The signal loss S_{Loss}^{F} for the forwarding side of i-th switch is calculated as follows:

$$S_{Loss}^{F} = -10log(l) * (i-1) - 10log(1-l) + i + 11$$

And the forwarding signal loss S_{Loss}^{FR} for the receiving side of i-th switch is calculated as follows:

$$S_{Loss}^{FR} = -10log(l) * (i-1) - 10log(1-l) + i + 7.5$$

The source signals are firstly enhanced by EDFA up to 17.3 dBm. To be correctly recovered by transceivers or enhanced by EDFA, the attenuated signals should satisfy the input constraints of EDFA and the receiver sensitivity of transceivers. Hence the signal loss should under the following constraints: S_{Loss}^{R}, $S_{Loss}^{FR} \leq 40.3$ dB and $S_{Loss}^{F} \leq 49.3$ dB. The signal loss is determined by the OCS hops i and the splitter transmittance l. From the related work [6], the number of optical splits increases with transmittance l. When the transmittance is up to 0.9, the number of i equals to 13. Thus, DETOUR can support up to 27 OCSes in one dimension.

Through the above analysis, there are at most $min(27, N+1)$ OCSes at each dimension to construct a non-blocking optical fabric. With state-of-the-art technologies, the option N of a $N \times 1$ WSS can be as high as 32 at reasonable cost [25]. So DETOUR is scalable to connect 27×27 OCSes. A 27×27 2D-Torus network is then achievable to connect up to 729 OCSes. As described in the ITU-T G.692 standard, the C-band can be divided up to 96 wavelengths at

50 GHz channel spacing. By leveraging the standard 50 GHz wavelength spacing of DWDM technology, DETOUR supports up to 729 racks and 69K+ ports with each OCS supporting 96 wavelengths.

DETOUR has the advantage of high performance compared with OvS, but with the cost of modest optical components, e.g. $N \times 1$ WSS, Splitter, EDFA. $N \times 1$ WSS is the most expensive component compared with Splitter, EDFA and Coupler. While, the digital Liquid Crystal (LC) based optical switching technology used in the WSS has been proven to be a reliable and cost-effective technology [25]. In the future, silicon photonics (e.g., matrix switch by ring resonators) can further improve the integration level and reduce the cost.

3   The Control Loop

Inspired by most prior DCN designs [8,9,12,21,25], the hybrid DCN based on DETOUR employs a centralized controller to manage EPSes and OCSes. The controller maintains network information. And it performs demand estimation, wavelength assignment, reconfiguration and so on.

3.1   Traffic Demand Estimation

There exists many traffic demand estimation solutions. For example, the controller can periodically capture snapshots of the overall traffic demand. Hedera [5] and Helios [12] allocate bandwidth of elephant flows by guaranteeing max-min fairness in an ideal non-blocking network. c-Through [21] increases the socket buffer and uses large buffer occupancy to indicate the optical link demand. Moreover, researchers have started to forecast traffic demands of scientific and data-intensive parallel applications from diverse layers (e.g., application layer [22], compiler layer [7,14]). And for clusters that are orchestrated by centralized schedulers (e.g., MPICH2 Hydra, Hadoop YARN), the schedulers orchestrate jobs to compute, storage nodes, and make traffic demand visible.

As the reconfiguration delay of DETOUR is about 10 ms, DETOUR is suitable for the stable or predictable traffic demand which tolerates with the reconfiguration overhead, or DETOUR is preallocated to specific jobs. Overall, DETOUR is proposed to realize a fully reconfigurable interconnection with high scalability, performance and flexibility. And it works as topology-on-demand network resources to match with the upper demand.

3.2   Wavelength Assignment

Given a traffic demand matrix, the controller converts it into wavelength assignments and pushes them into OCSes. The converting algorithm can be accomplished by using weighted b-matching [8], in which b represents the number of ports connected with DETOUR at each ToR EPS. Through the weighted

b-matching algorithm, we get a wavelength demand matrix $G_w(V_w, E_w, \phi_w)$, in which $\phi_w(u, v)$ denotes the number of wavelengths assigned on directed edge (u, v). We need to assign non-conflicting wavelengths to satisfy ϕ_w. Non-conflicting refers that the same wavelengths can not coexist in the same fiber. Due to the specific architecture of OCS shown in Fig. 2, a feasible assignment is that no same wavelengths simultaneously exist in the sending fiber of one OCS, the same as receiving fiber, forwarding fiber from x to y and forwarding fiber from y to x. This problem is equivalent to edge-coloring problem on a multi-graph with extra constraints of the forwarding nodes. And non-conflicting edge coloring of multigraph G_b means that there are no same colors in each source node, destination node, forwarding node f_{xy} and f_{yx}.

Figure 5 illustrates an example of wavelength assignment process. As shown in Fig. 5(a), the OCSes are physically connected in a 3 * 3 2D-Torus topology, and each OCS has 4 unique wavelengths. Figure 5(b) denotes a specified wavelength demand matrix G_w. We transform it to a bipartite multigraph G_b, as shown in Fig. 5(c). The number of edges between OCSes u and v equals to the entry $\phi_w(u, v)$. We proceed to compute a wavelength assignment using existing edge-coloring algorithms of bipartite multigraph [9], as shown in Fig. 5(d), (e). The label f_{xy} on edge (u, v) means that the wavelength is forwarded from x dimension

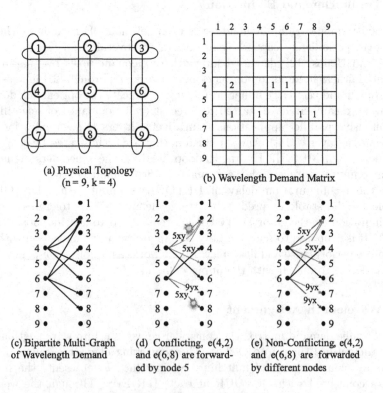

(a) Physical Topology
(n = 9, k = 4)

(b) Wavelength Demand Matrix

(c) Bipartite Multi-Graph of Wavelength Demand

(d) Conflicting, e(4,2) and e(6,8) are forwarded by node 5

(e) Non-Conflicting, e(4,2) and e(6,8) are forwarded by different nodes

Fig. 5. Wavelength assignment

to y dimension by OCS f, and f_{yx} does the opposite. Edge (4, 2) and edge (6, 8) are conflicting as they are assigned the same color and both forwarded from x dimension to y dimension by OCS 5. To avoid the conflict, we use OCS 9 to forward edge (6, 8), as shown in Fig. 5(e).

Considering the constraint of forwarding OCSes, we cast the wavelength assignment problem into a constrained edge-coloring solution on a bipartite multigraph. König's theorem [23] states that any bipartite graph G has an edge-coloring solution with $\Delta(G)$ (maximal degree) colors. The challenge in our situation is that whether the bipartite multigraph G_b converted from the wavelength demand matrix G_w is $\Delta(G_b)$-colorable. Since $\Delta(G_b) \leq k$, that ϕ_w can always be satisfied if G_b is $\Delta(G_b)$-colorable. We solve this problem by designing a conflict avoiding algorithm which utilizes the properties of DETOUR.

Theorem 1: *Given a wavelength demand matrix $G_w(V_w, E_w, \phi_w)$, we can always satisfy ϕ_w (non-conflicting) using $\Delta(G_b)$ wavelengths.*

The proof is motivated by Fig. 5. For bipartite multigraph G_b, we can always get an edge-coloring solution with $\Delta(G_b)$ matchings, without considering the forwarding constraints. Each source and destination port in matching M are assigned the same wavelength. For each matching M, if we could reassign the conflicting edges' forwarding nodes (Fig. 5(e)) and get a non-conflicting matching, we will finally get $\Delta(G_b)$ matchings and Theorem 1 will be proven.

We prove that a non-conflicting matching M always exists by recursively adjusting the forwarding nodes. The proof procedure is shown in Algorithm 1. $dict_{xy}$ and $dict_{yx}$ record the assigned forwarding nodes and the corresponding edge, and each forwarding node can only be used once for non-conflicting (line 2). The algorithm only considers the edges (u, v) whose source node u and destination node v are not in the same dimension (line 3–4). Edge (u, v) has two forwarding nodes f_x, f_y and only uses one forwarding node at the same time. Initially, the forwarding nodes are not assigned, and the previous edges of M can choose one of the remaining forwarding nodes (line 6–9). When both forwarding nodes of edge (u, v) are assigned, the algorithm recursively (line 11, 13, 25, 32) adjusts forwarding nodes with former conflicting edges until there is an unassigned forwarding node (line 20–23, 28–30). Since the initial edges only use one forwarding node, another forwarding node is unassigned. The algorithm will always recursively find an unassigned forwarding node except one situation. If the algorithm recursively runs to adjust edge (u_1, v_1) and (u_2, v_2). Edge (u_1, v_1) is assigned forwarding node f_x^{12} and another forwarding node is f_y^{12}. By contrast edge (u_2, v_2) is assigned forwarding node f_y^{12} and another forwarding node is f_x^{12}. This will cause a deadlock and can not find a solution. However, this situation will not happen because there are no two edges having the same forwarding nodes in the 2D-Torus topology. Thus, the algorithm can always find an unassigned forwarding node to all the conflicting edges in matching M. Proof of Theorem 1 is completed.

Algorithm 1. Conflict Avoiding Algorithm

Input: Matching M
Output: Forwarding Set $dict_{xy}$, $dict_{yx}$
1: **function** CONFLICT_FREE(M)
2: $\quad$ $dict_{xy} = \{\}$; $dict_{yx} = \{\}$ $\quad$ /*f: (u, v)*/
3: $\quad$ **for** (u, v) **in** M **do**
4: $\quad\quad$ **if** **not** $Is\_Same\_Dimension(u, v)$ **then**
5: $\quad\quad\quad$ $f_x, f_y = get\_forward(u, v)$
6: $\quad\quad\quad$ **if** f_x **not in** $dict_{xy}$ **then**
7: $\quad\quad\quad\quad$ $dict_{xy}[f_x] = (u, v)$
8: $\quad\quad\quad$ **else if** f_y **not in** $dict_{yx}$ **then**
9: $\quad\quad\quad\quad$ $dict_{yx}[f_y] = (u, v)$
10: $\quad\quad\quad$ **else** /*conflicting*/
11: $\quad\quad\quad\quad$ $Adjust(dict_{xy}, dict_{yx}, u, v, f_x, \text{`}xy\text{'})$
12: $\quad\quad\quad\quad$ **or**
13: $\quad\quad\quad\quad$ $Adjust(dict_{xy}, dict_{yx}, u, v, f_y, \text{`}yx\text{'})$
$\quad\quad$ **return** $dict_{xy}, dict_{yx}$
14: **function** ADJUST($dict_{xy}, dict_{yx}, u, v, f, flag$)
15: $\quad$ **if** $flag == \text{`}xy\text{'}$ **then**
16: $\quad\quad$ $(u_1, v_1) = dict_{xy}[f]$
17: $\quad$ **else** $flag == \text{`}yx\text{'}$
18: $\quad\quad$ $(u_1, v_1) = dict_{yx}[f]$
19: $\quad$ $f_x, f_y = get\_forward(u_1, v_1)$
20: $\quad$ **if** $flag == \text{`}xy\text{'}$ **then**
21: $\quad\quad$ **if** f_y **not in** $dict_{yx}$ **then**
22: $\quad\quad\quad$ $dict_{yx}[f_y] = (u_1, v_1)$; $dict_{xy}[f] = (u, v)$
23: $\quad\quad\quad$ ***Return***
24: $\quad\quad$ **else**
25: $\quad\quad\quad$ ***Adjust***($dict_{xy}, dict_{yx}, u_1, v_1, f_y, \text{`}yx\text{'}$)
26: $\quad\quad\quad$ $dict_{yx}[f_y] = (u_1, v_1)$; $dict_{xy}[f] = (u, v)$
27: $\quad$ **else**
28: $\quad\quad$ **if** f_x **not in** $dict_{xy}$ **then**
29: $\quad\quad\quad$ $dict_{xy}[f_x] = (u_1, v_1)$; $dict_{yx}[f] = (u, v)$
30: $\quad\quad\quad$ ***Return***
31: $\quad\quad$ **else**
32: $\quad\quad\quad$ ***Adjust***($dict_{xy}, dict_{yx}, u_1, v_1, f_x, \text{`}xy\text{'}$)
33: $\quad\quad\quad$ $dict_{xy}[f_x] = (u_1, v_1)$; $dict_{yx}[f] = (u, v)$

3.3 Reconfiguration

To instantiate the new topology, the controller needs to configure OCSes of DETOUR and update the flow tables of EPSes. It may lead to network instable during the reconfiguration. We adopt two strategies to minimize the influence on network performance during reconfiguration.

Minimizing Wavelength Shifting. During the process of calculating new wavelength matchings, we utilize current wavelengths distribution and the G_b matchings to calculate new k-perfect matchings. Then we assign colors to the

k-perfect matchings based on Hungarian algorithm, which minimizes the overlap of wavelength shifting to previous assignments. And for each colored matching, we use Algorithm 1 to get the non-conflicting forwarding sets.

Seamless Reconfiguration. From the above minimizing wavelength shifting algorithm, we will get a subset of wavelengths which does not need to adjust. And each EPS also reserves m-k static wavelengths to ensure the network connectivity. So there exists a stable subnetwork during the reconfiguration. To seamlessly reconfigure the network, each EPS maintains two flow tables: $table_{com}$, $table_{mid}$. $table_{com}$ is used for the complete network and $table_{mid}$ is used for the intermediate subnetwork. The controller maintains topology informations and active flow rules for each network.

Before adjusting the optical links, the controller updates flow rules of $table_{mid}$ based on the difference of new and old subnetwork. This way avoids forwarding packets to a dynamical link, which will cause packet loss. During reconfiguration, the controller enables $table_{mid}$ and calculates new flow rules based on the intermediate network. And it also deletes the flow rules affected by the adjusted links. When the configuration of OCSes finished, the controller enables $table_{com}$ and calculates flow rules based on the new network.

4   Evaluation

In this section, we evaluate the performance of DETOUR via flow-level simulation. We first introduce the simulation methodology and then analyze the performance of DETOUR by conducting extensive simulations.

4.1   Simulation Setting

(1) *Simulator:* Because existing packet-level simulators (e.g., NS2, NS3) are time consuming to simulate hundreds to thousands servers, and we are more interested in network throughput rather than packet-level behaviors. Therefore, we implemented a event-based flow-level simulator to perform simulations at large scale. The simulator takes flows with start time, size, source server and destination server as input. When the network status changes (e.g., flow arrival, flow departure, EPS and OCS reconfiguration), it updates the rate and remaining size of all active flows. The rate of each active flow is calculated by the progressive filling algorithm [3], which allocates bandwidth satisfying max-min fairness without considering the detailed transport layer protocol behaviors. A flow transmission is finished when the receiver receives all the data. In this simulator, we also realized a centralized controller, which maintains a global view of the network and manages all the EPSes and OCSes. It periodically (0.1 s in our simulation) predicts the traffic demand between ToRs and assigns optical wavelengths to meet the demand. The OCS reconfiguration and controller communication overhead is setted to 10 ms.

(2) **Topology:** We compare the performance of DETOUR against Jellyfish [20], OvS [25] and non-blocking optical switching network. Jellyfish is a pure electrical switching network and randomly connects ToR EPSes into a k-regular topology. It has higher bisection bandwidth and lower mean path length over other static network topologies. The typical optical solutions such as MegaSwitch [10], Mordia [17] and OSA [8] all construct non-blocking optical switching networks and support multiple wavelengths, but has limited scalability. We will compare the performance gap between DETOUR and these non-blocking solutions. OvS is a 2D-Torus optical switching fabric similar with DETOUR but it is blocked with limited connections. In this experiment, we simulate a 8 * 8 2D-Torus topology, each EPS has 18 ports with 10 ports connected with servers and the other 8 ports connected to the optical switching networks. We reserve 2 ports static in each EPS and connect the EPSes as base mesh, which ensures the network connectivity.

(3) **Traffic Patterns:** We synthetic the following traffic patterns used in [10]:
   - *Server-Level Stride.* We index the servers from 1 to 640. In each round, we randomly select the stride k and each servers i talks with $(i + k)$ mod 640.
   - *ToR-Level Stride.* We index the ToR from 1 to 64. In each round, we randomly select the stride k, all the servers in ToR i talk to all the servers in ToR $i + k$ mod 64.
   - *Random.* In each round, each server in ToR i talks to servers in up to 4 randomly selected ToRs. Each server randomly communicates with other severs. In this pattern, many flows may select the same path, creating sparse bottleneck links.
   - *MapReduce-Demand.* We use the Hive/MapReduce trace collected from a 3000-server, 150-rack cluster, which contains many shuffle processes. And we duplicate the traffic demands onto DETOUR using spatial replication.

(4) **Metrics:** We evaluate DETOUR from the following aspects. Firstly, we measure the network throughput under the above typical static traffic patterns. Second, we quantify the effect on reducing FCT and energy consumption under dynamic MapReduce traffic patterns. Third, we analyze the network performance on reconfiguration.

4.2   Network Practical Throughput

Figure 6 illustrates the average (max/min) network throughput under server-stride, ToR-stride and random workloads when running 10 instances. From the figure, we find that DETOUR achieves the same performance as non-blocking optical switching networks under all traffic patterns. And it increases the average throughput by 1.34–2.14× and 2.28–5.7× compared to OvS and Jellyfish respectively under all traffic patterns. The reason is that DETOUR can dynamically allocate directly connected links to perfectly match the traffic demand. While OvS needs multiple hops if the demand pair acrosses different dimensions. Forwarding high bandwidth traffic through multiple hops will consume bandwidth per link and incur load on each EPS it traverses.

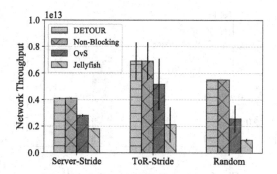

Fig. 6. Network practical throughput

4.3 Overall FCT and Energy Consumption

In this experiment, we evaluate the FCT and energy consumption performance under the dynamic MapReduce traffic pattern. Figure 7(a) and (b) shows the cumulative distribution function (CDF) of FCTs and the overall average FCT, respectively. From Fig. 7, we find that DETOUR achieves the same FCT performance as non-blocking switching networks. The FCTs for all the flows under DETOUR are less than the FCTs under OvS and Jellyfish. And DETOUR reduces the overall average FCT by ~34% and ~57% compared with OvS and Jellyfish, respectively. The reason is that the large flows in DETOUR are allocated directly connected links with demanded bandwidth, which reduces the FCT of large flows. Meanwhile, it also reduces the bandwitch preemption between small and large flows, which in trun reduces the FCT of small flows.

Compared with EPS, OCS delivers considerably less energy consumption and avoids unnecessary optical-electrical-optical conversions. The typical per port power values of commercially SFP+ transceivers, EPS switching and OCS switching are 1 W, 8.75 W and 0.14 W, respectively. The energy consumption of each flow is calculated based on per port power and transmission time. Figure 8 illustrates the average energy consumptions under the MapReduce workload.

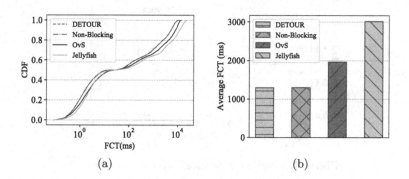

(a)   (b)

Fig. 7. (a) CDF distribution of FCT and (b) overall average FCT

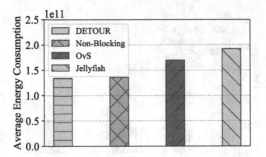

Fig. 8. Average energy consumption

From the figure, we find that DETOUR reduces the overall average energy consumption by ∼21% and ∼30% compared with OvS and Jellyfish, respectively. The reason is that flows in DETOUR traverse through less EPSes and OCSes compared with OvS and Jellyfish.

4.4　Network Performance on Reconfiguration

Figure 9 illustrates the 10 ms reconfiguration impact on network throughput. From the figure, we find that the throughput increases along time with the flows' injection. The throughput of DETOUR and non-blocking optical switching network increase to a relative higher value after each reconfiguration, which are greater than OvS. The reason is that the controller calculates new wavelength assignments to better match with traffic demands in each reconfiguration. During each reconfiguration, the being adjusted optical links are unable to use, and the network bisection bandwidth will temporarily degrades. So we adopt seamless reconfiguration strategies, which ensures the minimal network bisection bandwidth and minimize the reconfiguration impact on small flows.

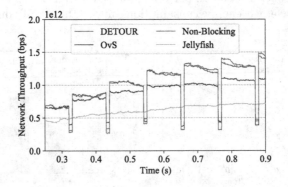

Fig. 9. Network performance on reconfiguration

4.5   Overhead of the Central Controller

The centralized controller maintains network status, estimates traffic demand and allocates wavelengths. In this experiment, we realized the simulator in python language, and we used the existed maximum weight matching and maximum matching algorithms in the networkx package. The time complexity of maximum weight matching and maximum matching are $O(n^3)$ and $O(n)$ respectively, in which n represents the number of racks. We run this simulator on Intel(R) Core(TM) i5-5257U CPU @ 2.70 GHz. We measure the time cost under 10 random seleted traffic patterns. The total time is about 46 ms under 64 switches and 8 wavelengths, in which demand estimation and max-weight matching algorithm consume the dominant. And when the network scales up to ~700 switches, the runtime increases up to hundreds to thousands microseconds. In order to reduce the impact of the controller overhead to support large scale DCNs, the controller on the one hand can use traffic predicting mechanism, on the other hand can increase the demand estimation period. Moreover, our demand estimation and wavelength reconfiguration algorithms are adopted from Hedera [5] and Wave-Cube [9] respectively, which has been optimized to consume less than 100 ms for large data centers via parallelization. This means that there is a large room to speed up controller algorithms with advanced technologies to support large scale DCNs.

5   Related Work

Our work is mostly inspired by prior solutions on reconfigurable DCN. We summarize the existing reconfigurable techniques by three categories: Optical Circuit Switching (OCS), 60 GHz Wireless and Free-Space Optics (FSO).

Most solutions (e.g., c-Through [21], Helios [12], and OSA [8]) rely on MEMS-based optical switches, which has high reconfiguration latency and low port counts. They leverage a single MEMS-based optical switch to establish optical links between ToR EPSes. The DCN scalability is limited by the low port density of MEMS. Wavecube [9] removes the core MEMS and connects WSSes in mesh topology. Although Wavecube is scalable to support unlimited racks, the network diameter increases with the scalability as links are only reconfigured between neighbors. Mordia [17], MegaSwitch [10] and OvS [25] are based on the broadcast-and-select mechanism. Mordia takes microseconds switching technologies and establishes optical links with time-sharing. This is not efficient for high-out and stable traffic patterns. OvS uses multi-fiber multiplexing and connects OCSes into 2D-Torus topology. But it only supports establishing directly optical circuits between OCSes in the same dimension.

Flyway [14] was firstly proposed to augment the traditional data center with 60 GHz wireless devices, which relieves hotspot traffic. In Mirror [24], beams were bounded off the data center ceiling to eliminate the line-of-sight constraint. Unlike optical technology, 60 GHz wireless suffers from limited throughput and low distance, which is hard to use in large scale data centers.

Firefly [15] equips ToR EPSes with free-space optics and uses Galvo or switchable mirrors to dynamically establish optical links. ProjecToR [16] combines digital micromirror device (DMD) and mirror assembly to construct a high-fanout free-space topology. However, the beam of FSO is narrow and susceptible to interferences.

6   Conclusion

We presented DETOUR, a large-scale non-blocking optical data center fabric, which supports up to 700+ racks and 69K+ servers. We designed a recursive wavelength assignment algorithm based on the architecture of DETOUR. And We also implemented a flow-level simulator and realized the control algorithms. Extensive evaluation results show that DETOUR delivers high performance comparable to a non-blocking switching fabric. It outperforms up to 2.14× higher throughput, reduce 34% FCT and 21% energy consumption compared with the state-of-the-art works.

Acknowledgments. The work is supported by the project of National Key Research and Development Program of China under Grant No. 2016YFB0200400, and FANEDD under Grant No. 201450.

References

1. Cisco DWDM SFP+ module. http://www.cisco.com/c/en/us/products/collateral/interfaces-modules/dwdm-transceiver-modules/data_sheet_c78-711186.html
2. Cisco ONS15501 erbium doped fiber amplifier. http://www.cisco.com/en/US/products/hw/optical/ps2011/products_data_sheet09186a008008870d.html
3. Progressive filling algorithm. https://en.wikipedia.org/wiki/Max-min_fairness
4. Al-Fares, M., Loukissas, A., Vahdat, A.: A scalable, commodity data center network architecture. In: ACM SIGCOMM (2008)
5. Al-Fares, M., Radhakrishnan, S., Raghavan, B., Huang, N., Vahdat, A.: Hedera: dynamic flow scheduling for data center networks. In: NSDI (2010)
6. Bao, J., Dong, D., Zhao, B., Luo, Z., Wu, C., Gong, Z.: FlyCast: free-space optics accelerating multicast communications in physical layer. In: ACM SIGCOMM (2015)
7. Barker, K.J., Benner, A., Hoare, R., Hoisie, A., Jones, A.K., Kerbyson, D.K., Li, D., Melhem, R., Rajamony, R., Schenfeld, E., et al.: On the feasibility of optical circuit switching for high performance computing systems. In: IEEE SC (2005)
8. Chen, K., Singla, A., Singh, A., Ramachandran, K., Xu, L., Zhang, Y., Wen, X., Chen, Y.: OSA: an optical switching architecture for data center networks with unprecedented flexibility. In: NSDI (2012)
9. Chen, K., Wen, X., Ma, X., Chen, Y., Xia, Y., Hu, C., Dong, Q.: WaveCube: a scalable, fault-tolerant, high-performance optical data center architecture. In: IEEE INFOCOM (2015)
10. Chen, L., Chen, K., Zhu, Z., Yu, M., Porter, G., Qiao, C., Zhong, S.: Enabling wide-spread communications on optical fabric with megaswitch. In: NSDI 2017, Boston, MA, pp. 577–593 (2017)

11. Chowdhury, M., Stoica, I.: Coflow: a networking abstraction for cluster applications. In: ACM HotNets (2012)
12. Farrington, N., Porter, G., Radhakrishnan, S., Bazzaz, H.H., Subramanya, V., Fainman, Y., Papen, G., Vahdat, A.: Helios: a hybrid electrical/optical switch architecture for modular data centers. In: ACM SIGCOMM (2010)
13. Guo, C., Lu, G., Li, D., Wu, H., Zhang, X., Shi, Y., Tian, C., Zhang, Y., Lu, S.: BCube: a high performance, server-centric network architecture for modular data centers. In: ACM SIGCOMM (2009)
14. Halperin, D., Kandula, S., Padhye, J., Bahl, P., Wetherall, D.: Augmenting data center networks with multi-gigabit wireless links. In: ACM SIGCOMM (2011)
15. Hamedazimi, N., Qazi, Z., Gupta, H., Sekar, V., Das, S.R., Longtin, J.P., Shah, H., Tanwer, A.: Firefly: a reconfigurable wireless data center fabric using free-space optics. In: ACM SIGCOMM (2015)
16. Monia (Manya), G., Ratul, M., Amar, P., Nikhil, R., Gireeja, R., Jana, K.: Projector: agile reconfigurable data center interconnect. In: ACM SIGCOMM (2016)
17. Porter, G., Strong, R., Farrington, N., Forencich, A., Chen-Sun, P., Rosing, T., Fainman, Y., Papen, G., Vahdat, A.: Integrating microsecond circuit switching into the data center. In: ACM SIGCOMM (2013)
18. Roy, A., Zeng, H., Bagga, J., Porter, G., Snoeren, A.C.: Inside the social network's (datacenter) network. In: ACM SIGCOMM (2015)
19. Singh, A., Ong, J., Agarwal, A., Anderson, G., Armistead, A., Bannon, R., Boving, S., Desai, G., Felderman, B., Germano, P., et al.: Jupiter rising: a decade of clos topologies and centralized control in Google's datacenter network. In: ACM SIGCOMM (2015)
20. Singla, A., Hong, C.Y., Popa, L., Godfrey, P.B.: Jellyfish: networking data centers randomly. In: NSDI (2012)
21. Wang, G., Andersen, D.G., Kaminsky, M., Papagiannaki, K., Ng, T., Kozuch, M., Ryan, M.: c-Through: part-time optics in data centers. In: ACM SIGCOMM (2010)
22. Wang, H., Chen, L., Chen, K., Li, Z., Zhang, Y., Guan, H., Qi, Z., Li, D., Geng, Y.: Flowprophet: generic and accurate traffic prediction for data-parallel cluster computing. In: IEEE ICDCS (2015)
23. Wikipedia: König's theorem (graph theory) – wikipedia, the free encyclopedia (2015)
24. Zhou, X., Zhang, Z., Zhu, Y., Li, Y., Kumar, S., Vahdat, A., Zhao, B.Y., Zheng, H.: Mirror mirror on the ceiling: flexible wireless links for data centers. In: ACM SIGCOMM (2012)
25. Zhu, Z., Zhong, S., Chen, L., Chen, K.: Fully programmable and scalable optical switching fabric for petabyte data center. Opt. express **23**(3), 3563–3580 (2015)

Querying Large Scientific Data Sets with Adaptable IO System ADIOS

Junmin Gu[1], Scott Klasky[2], Norbert Podhorszki[2], Ji Qiang[1],
and Kesheng Wu[1(✉)]

[1] Lawrence Berkeley National Laboratory (LBNL), Berkeley, USA
kwu@lbl.gov
[2] Oak Ridge National Laboratory (ORNL), Oak Ridge, USA

Abstract. When working with a large dataset, a relatively small fraction of data records are of interest in each analysis operation. For example, while examining a billion-particle dataset from an accelerator model, the scientists might focus on a few thousand fastest particles, or on the particle farthest from the beam center. In general, this type of selective data access is challenging because the selected data records could be anywhere in the dataset and require a significant amount of time to locate and retrieve. In this paper, we report our experience of addressing this data access challenge with the Adaptable IO System ADIOS. More specifically, we design a query interface for ADIOS to allow arbitrary combinations of range conditions on known variables, implement a number of different mechanisms for resolving these selection conditions, and devise strategies to reduce the time needed to retrieve the scattered data records. In many cases, the query mechanism can retrieve the selected data records orders of magnitude faster than the brute-force approach.

Our work relies heavily on the *in situ* data processing feature of ADIOS to allow user functions to be executed in the data transport pipeline. This feature allows us to build indexes for efficient query processing, and to perform other intricate analyses while the data is in memory.

1 Introduction

Modern scientific experiments such as large accelerators rely heavily on high-performance simulations for design, calibration and data analysis [13,24]. These simulation programs typically need to read and write a vast amount of data, for example to read the definition of the complex geometry of an accelerator design, to checkpoint the state of the simulation, and to produce analysis output [23]. The output from these simulations is used to understand the experimental observations and to guide the next experiment. Often, the critical information is only a small fraction of a large data collection. Reading and writing the necessary data records efficiently is the challenge we address in this work.

R. Yokota and W. Wu (Eds.): SCFA 2018, LNCS 10776, pp. 51–69, 2018.
https://doi.org/10.1007/978-3-319-69953-0_4

Current high-performance computing systems are typically massively parallel platforms consisting of millions of CPU cores and thousands of secondary storage devices. A significant amount of programming effort is needed to make effective uses of such a system. Programmers have to make difficult choices among available options. Take the checkpointing task as an example, an efficient solution to write a large amount data is to have each process of the simulation program write its own file. However, this option can create millions of files when millions of processes are used. On some file systems, an attempt to list these files will slow the metadata servers to a crawl, even crash the whole file system. Usually, the checkpoint files are also used for data analyses. During a typical analysis operation, only a fraction of the data records are needed for a specific analysis operation. Locating these data records from a petabyte data collection is a challenging task requiring auxiliary information such as indexes. It may be necessary to restart the simulation program with a different number of processes, for example, to reduce the computation time or to increase the fidelity of the simulation. When there is one checkpoint file per process, these checkpoint files may have to be combined in complex ways in order to restart the simulation properly. For these reasons, many researchers have explored options to simplify the IO operations for large simulation programs.

The process of locating and retrieving these selected records is typically through a query interface. The best known querying tools do not support scientific data, which is typically stored in large data files as numbers. For example, internet search engines are widely used by primarily designed to process text documents; and database systems could work on both numerical values and text string, but require the data to be under its full control. Scientific projects usually does not have the budget to pay for the extra storage and software license fee for database systems. The alternative we pursue is to add query interface to high-level IO libraries.

A number of high-level IO libraries are in wide use, the most commonly used are ADIOS [16], HDF5 [10], and netCDF [22]. Among these three popular libraries, netCDF is primarily used by the climate community and it is in the process of switching to use HDF5 as the backend storage layer. For this work, we primarily consider choosing between HDF5 and ADIOS. Both ADIOS and HDF5 are used in a variety of large scientific applications, and the authors have first-hand experience with both [5,7,16,26]. In this particular case, we plan to use ADIOS because it offers a distinctive feature that is not available in any other IO libraries. That is, ADIOS supports *in situ* processing, which allows us to build the indexes while generating the data files. This has a distinct advantage of as soon as the data files are available, the associated indexes are also available. This should make it much more efficient to select a relatively small number of critical data records from a large data collection. In addition, the *in situ* processing capability would also enable dynamic analysis capability to improve the usefulness of a simulation program. Thus, the core of this work is to develop a query interface for ADIOS.

The key contributions of this work are as follows:

- Design and develop a query interface for ADIOS.
- Evaluate strategies to minimize the time needed to retrieve scatter data records from a ADIOS file.
- Exercise the query interface with a large application dataset.
- Introduce *in situ* processing feature to an application that does not yet have this feature, and demonstrate the usefulness of this feature.
- Measure the performance of ADIOS in completing the checkpoint operations.

2   Related Work

In commercial applications, large datasets are typically managed by a data management system [15,18,25]. These systems take control of the user data and provide high-level languages for analysis tasks. In contrast, most scientific projects store their data as files and use the file systems as the primary tools for data management [24]. This file-based approach allows users full control of their data and their analysis tasks; however, it also requires the users to spend much more time to manage their data than using a data management system. In this work, we combine a number of techniques to reduce the data management time, more specifically the time to select a relatively small fraction of the data records. In this section, we briefly review the key technologies involved.

2.1   High-Level IO Libraries

Scientific datasets are frequently organized as multidimensional arrays and the commonly used IO libraries are designed to store and organize these arrays. Earlier we mentioned three: HDF5 [10], netCDF [22] and ADIOS [16]. Next, we provide a brief description for each of them.

HDF5 is a short-hand for Hierarchical Data Format version 5[1] [10,11]. It is highly flexible, efficient, portable and extensible. Many application domains have developed their own data organization standards based on HDF5 [10]. The recent releases of HDF5 software exposes the Virtual Object Layer (VOL) to make it even easier to extend the functionality of the software library, such as to provide query services [8] and to work with Burst Buffers [9].

NetCDF is a short-hand for network common data format[2] [22]. It is widely in the climate modeling community, with many petabytes of data stored in this format. Some of the largest collections are used to compile the assessment reports commissioned by the Intergovernmental Panel on Climate Change[3].

ADIOS is a short-hand for Adaptable IO System[4] [16,17]. First released in 2008 [17], it is a new library among the commonly used scientific formats. However, it has attracted much attention because its simplicity and efficiency [16].

---

[1] HDF5 software is available at https://support.hdfgroup.org/HDF5/.
[2] NetCDF software is available at https://www.unidata.ucar.edu/software/netcdf/.
[3] The most recent IPCC report AR5 is available at https://www.ipcc.ch/report/ar5/.
[4] Software available at https://www.olcf.ornl.gov/center-projects/adios/.

For example, it accepts an XML configuration file for users to describe the variables, their types, and the path to take from memory to disk. This capability allows the users to change how they process the data without changing the simulation program. This approach gives a level of adaptability that no other IO system could match. A special feature created by this flexibility is the *in situ* processing capability to be described next. To effectively support the querying capability over ADIOS files, we also utilize this *in situ* capability to create indexes, which reduces the effort required to generate indexes and ensures the indexes are available as soon as the data is available.

2.2   In Situ Processing

Writing to disk is generally much slower than writing the same data to memory, therefore, it is highly desirable to perform as many analysis operations as possible while the data is still in memory. This type of *in situ* processing also makes it possible to produce analysis results without storing the original data. On a HPC system, the IO operations typically need to pass data among the compute nodes, IO nodes, and disk systems. While the data is being transferred among these subsystems, it is possible to perform a considerable amount of analysis operations. ADIOS supports these options by separating API for data producers from that for data consumers.

A data producer outputs the data following a set of API styled after the familiar POSIX write interface. The content generated by the producer is sent to the downstream processing code by the ADIOS transport system based on the instructions provided by the user. The consumers of the data could be located on the same CPU as the producer, or elsewhere on the network. The ADIOS transport system will schedule the data movement in a reliable manner [17].

The benefits of *in situ* processing is widely recognized for large scientific simulations and a number of efforts are under way to develop alternatives to ADIOS. Bauer et al. have produced an excellent review of the state of art in 2016 [1]. As of this writing, ADIOS is the most mature system for *in situ* processing and has extensive IO capability, therefore, we have selected to use ADIOS for this work.

2.3   Querying and Indexing

A data management system such as a DBMS typically provides a query interface for accessing the data under its management. In contrast, the data access functions for a file generally need to follow the structure of the file, such as, move file pointer to a location and read the next 40 bytes. This structure-based access functions require the user to know more details about the file organization than most application users are familiar with, and therefore, not as user-friendly as the query-based data access methods. A query on a scientific dataset might be "finding all data records from collection A where temperature and pressure are in the specified ranges." In this example, the user only needs to know the name of the variables and quantities of interest, thus a query interface is much easier to use for an application scientist.

To effectively support the queries, the system needs to create indexes [12], such as, B-Tree [6], bitmap index [26], and hashing [28]. Because the scientific data collections are typically analyzed without modification (or with infrequently modifications), we plan to concentrate on indexing techniques that are designed for query-intensive workloads. The queries on scientific data typically returns a number of data records instead of a single record. Additionally, the users often explore a large variety of combinations of query conditions. From research literature, we see that bitmap indexes satisfy these requirements. To support newly designed ADIOS query interface, we choose to use an open source bitmap index library named FastBit[5] [26]. At the same time, we are also exploring additional indexing techniques that might be better suited for ADIOS [27].

2.4 Application Use Cases

In this work, we use a couple of large scientific applications to illustrate the functionality we are developing. Next, we give a brief description of IMPACT and S3D. They are selected as examples of large scientific simulation programs. These large simulations produce a large amount of data and require complex data analyses, where ADIOS indexing and querying capability could play important roles.

IMPACT[6] is a parallel particle-in-cell code designed to model the dynamics of multiple charged particle beams in accelerators. This program uses longitudinal position (z) as an independent variable and includes the effects of externally applied fields from magnets and accelerating cavities as well as the effect of self-fields (as space charge fields). It is written in Fortran 90 with MPI for interprocess communication. It has been applied to studies of halo formation and coupling resonance in high intensity beams, microbunching instability in high brightness electron linac, beam dynamics in SNS linac, JARPC linac, RIA driver linac, CERN superconducting linac, LEDA halo experiment, Proton Synchrotron at CERN, and so on [19–21]. In this work, we primarily use IMPACT to exercise the *in situ* processing capability because it is a capability not available in IMPACT yet.

S3D is a high-performance direct numerical simulation (DNS) of combustion with detailed chemistry [4,14]. It is designed to study the interaction between turbulence and combustion chemistry. It is extensively used to understand the flame characteristics of lean mixture flame in the next generation of diesel and alternative fuel engines, as well as the flame stability features in large industrial burners such as those for gas-fired power plants. A large run of this code typically divides its simulation domain into billions of cells and then follow the evolution of the combustion process for many thousands of time steps. The checkpoint files and the *in situ* analysis output could easily be many terabytes per run [4]. Since extensive work on *in situ* processing has been performed before with S3D, in this work we primarily use a set of S3D data to test the query processing capability to be developed.

---

[5] FastBit software is available at http://sdm.lbl.gov/fastbit/.

[6] IMPACT Software available at http://amac.lbl.gov/~jiqiang/IMPACT/.

3   ADIOS Overview

In the next three sections, we describe our work on ADIOS to address various IO challenges. We start with the basic bulk IO operation of checkpointing, then move on to *in situ* processing and querying in the next two sections.

ADIOS is known for its simple API and high performance. The core insight guiding the ADIOS design is to separate the description of IO operations from the IO strategies employed for the actual lower level operations. This allows the application programming interface (API) to only describe what variables to read or write, while leaving the responsibility of selecting the actual transport operations to the ADIOS system. In particular, ADIOS has implemented a variety of transport mechanisms [16]. Its ability to seamlessly select the best transport mechanism is also at the root of its support for *in situ* operations. Other important factors contributing the high-performance include log-based file format, buffered writing, subfiling, asynchronous transport operations, and so on [16].

ADIOS was designed in 2005 to reduce the IO time for a number of mission critical applications [17]. Since then, ADIOS has been the leading software system for *in situ* data processing on many of largest high-performance computers. Some of the early success stories include improving the IO rate of S3D checkpoint operation by more than a factor of 10 from 3 GB/s to over 30 GB/s [16]. The developers of ADIOS have published a number of studies showing the dramatic improvement of IO performance for various applications. Next, we add our experience with the IMPACT code.

IMPACT employs the particle-in-cell paradigm to model the dynamics of particles. Each particle has immutable properties such as rest mass and charge, and dynamic properties such as position and momentum, recorded as x, y, z, p_x, p_y, and p_z. IMPACT produces two types of output for analyses: checkpoint files and particle statistics. We describe our work on checkpointing in this section and the work on utilizing *in situ* processing to accelerate the production of particle statistics in the next section.

Because the particles on each processor are independent from other particles, IMPACT produces its checkpoint files by writing one file per processor. This option has the advantage of minimizing the coordinate needed among the processors and could significantly reduce the time spent on IO operations.

ADIOS offers a variety of IO options and the parallel file system (Lustre) additionally offers a number of file system parameters; all of these parameters could affect IO performance. Instead of providing an exhaustive exploration of these parameters, in Fig. 1, we provide one set of performance measurements to show that ADIOS is able to support very efficient IO operations. This particular set of measurements was collected on Edison at NERSC. The measurements are conducted on Lustre file system with 24 OST and a peak IO rate of 168 GB/s. To avoid contention with other active jobs, we only used 16 OST for each ADIOS file, which have a nominal peak IO rate of about 112 GB/s.

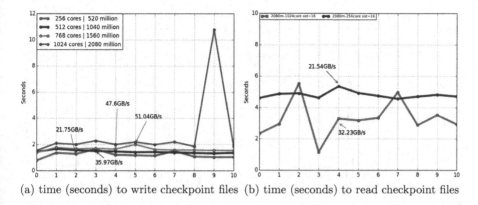

(a) time (seconds) to write checkpoint files (b) time (seconds) to read checkpoint files

Fig. 1. Time to read and write checkpoint files with ADIOS.

The write tests were performed with a fixed number of particles on each MPI process. The reported IO rates in Fig. 1 are computed using the median observed IO time. The write operations reported in Fig. 1(a) all uses 16 OST and uses about 2 million particles per MPI process. Up to 1024 processes, the average write speeds rises to over 50 GB/s.

In Fig. 1(b), we reported the observed performance of reading the different checkpoint files. Clearly, the number of OST used to store the files has a strong influence on the observed read performance. One important feature we want to demonstrate is the reading of the same checkpoint files with a different number of processes. In this particular case, reading the same file with different number of processes took about the same amount of time and producing about the same aggregate IO speed.

4   *In Situ* Indexing

The checkpoint files capture the position and momentum of each particle periodically, but infrequently. To capture more dynamic behavior of the particles, IMPACT also compute high-level statistics about the particles at a much higher frequency. However, these statistics are programmed by the developers of IMPACT code and is difficult for the end users to modify to suit their own needs. The *in situ* processing capability of ADIOS is a flexible mechanism to introduce these custom statistics. It can also be used to provide asynchronous computation including index building, without blocking the main simulation computation. Next we describe a simple test to compute histograms at every simulation step to demonstrate the capability of ADIOS.

Using the ADIOS framework, IMPACT sends the positions and momentums to the *libsim* system, and a histogram function from *VTK* is attached to produce 1-D and 2-D histograms for each of the six variables. The histogram functions are instructed to divide the data records into 100 equal-width bins between the minimum and maximum values.

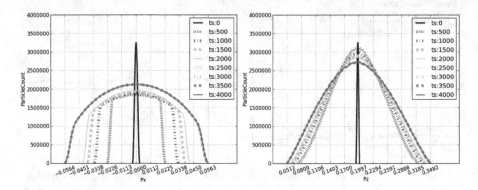

Fig. 2. Histogram of p_x and p_z at time steps 0, 500, 1000, 1500 and 2000 of an IMPACT run. Histogram of p_y is similar to that of p_x.

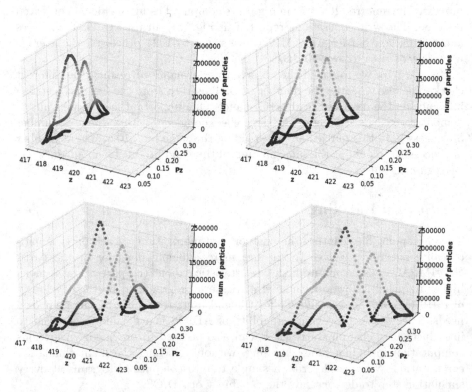

Fig. 3. Histogram of z and p_z at time steps 500, 1000, 1500, and 2000 of an IMPACT run (time progresses from left to right, top to bottom). The two tall peaks appear to move to the right indicating the bulk of the particles are moving along the z direction with increased momentum p_z.

Figure 2 shows a sample output from the histogram computation. In this simulation, the particles travel in the z direction. From the histograms of p_x, we see very sharp drop as momentums along x (and y) directions increase in magnitude reflecting the fact that the accelerators are designed to limit the motions perpendicular to z direction. In contrast, we see the histograms of p_z have a more gradual drop off as the momentum deviates from the center.

Figure 3 shows a series of 2D histograms of z and p_z. In this case, as time progresses (from left to right, top to bottom), we see that the peak of the curves move to the right indicating the bulk of the particles are moving along z direction as designed. There appears to be two groups of particles following different trajectories over time.

The above figures demonstrate two analysis options among many possible particle statistics could be computed with *in situ* analysis capability. We note two important ADIOS features in this use case. First, ADIOS *in situ* framework can effectively support analysis tasks with zero-copy data transfers. This is an important feature since the analysis task may require a large amount of data and copying the data would require extra memory and computer time. Second, we demonstrate that the ADIOS framework can easily work with a Fortran program. This is a useful feature since a large number of popular science codes are in Fortran.

Additionally, we have tested the options of the *in situ* processing capability of ADIOS to compute all the built-in statistics on a small set of separate compute nodes. Since the computation of the statistics involve a large number of global reductions, reducing the number of processors involved also reduce the overall cost of completing the simulation and the computation of the statistics. Using the common measure of CPU-core-hour (number of CPU cores used multiply the number of hours elapsed), the *in situ* processing option could reduce the overall CPU-core-hour by as much as 20% by overlapping the main simulation with the computation of the statistics.

Figure 4 shows a careful measurement of fraction of total execution time devoted to I/O operations with the standard I/O option (of writing data to files stored on a large parallel file system) and with the ADIOS *in situ* mechanism

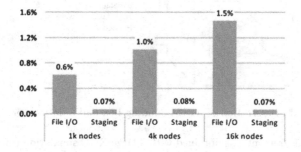

Fig. 4. The fraction of total execution time spent on I/O operations: using File I/O vs using ADIOS *in situ* capability to staging the output data before committing to disk.

to stage the data away from the compute nodes before committing the data to disk[7]. We note that the fraction of time spent on I/O operations is dramatically reduced. More importantly, it is possible to attach an index generation function and the above mentioned statistics computation to the *in situ* workflow without delaying the main simulation computation.

5   Query API

A common query interface is web search box on a web browser, where user enters a set of keywords to locate relevant pages on the web. A similar interface for finding interesting data records in large scientific data collection would also be very useful, however, this functionality is not widely available. An important reason for this lack of querying function is that most scientific datasets are stored as files. Because the POSIX file systems treat a file as a container of bytes, there is no general way of extracting meaningful data records for querying. The first step in breaking this limitation is to have a model to describe the data records. In this work, we are using the ADIOS library and will follow the array data model. In the remaining of this section, we will describe this data model and the query use cases. The latest version of ADIOS release contains the query interface and detailed description of how to use the functions is available in the user's manual[8].

5.1   Array Data Model

In ADIOS, the bulk of data is expressed as multi-dimensional arrays. In Fig. 5, we provide a simple illustration of a 3D array. Often such an array is produced from a simulation program, and each element of the array corresponds to a point or a cell from the 3D space being simulated. In such a case, there might be a number of different variables associated with each point or cell in space, e.g.,

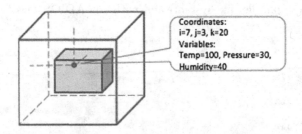

Fig. 5. Illustration of a 3D bounding box and a data record.

---

[7] This time measurement was obtained with a large XGC simulation running on titan at ORNL.

[8] ADIOS source code and documentation could be found at https://www.olcf.ornl.gov/center-projects/adios/.

temperature, pressure and humidity as shown in Fig. 5. We view all variables at a single point as a data record, which allows us to ask for the temperature values at points where pressure is between 20 and 40, and humidity is greater than 35.

On a parallel computer, a large multidimensional array is commonly divided onto different processors in blocks that could be expressed as bounding boxes. The existing ADIOS interface supports selective accesses to these bounding boxes. For example, to divide the above 3D array onto 1000 processors, each processor might have 1/1000th of the 3D array. A bounding box in ADIOS is expressed as an offset and extent. Say the 3D array has 1000 element along each of the three directions, then the bounding box for the entire array can be expressed as offset $= [0, 0, 0]$ and size $= [1000, 1000, 1000]$. One way to divide this array into 1000 pieces might be to have each of the subarrays with the size of $[100, 100, 100]$. In a simple case, we can view the $1000 \times 1000 \times 1000$ array to be defined on a $1000 \times 1000 \times 1000$ mesh. To simplify the following discussion, we assume this is the case. However, the elements of an array may have a much more complex relationship with the underlying physical domain of the simulation. For example, irregular mesh points are often packed into 1D arrays with additional arrays used to describe the physical location of the mesh points and how the mesh points are connected.

5.2   Query Use Cases

Case 1: Regular mesh data, all variables are named explicitly. Given a dataset defined on m dimensions: $D_1, D_2, \ldots, D_m$, the n physical properties such as temperature, pressure and humidity, could be defined as separate m-dimensional arrays: $A_1, A_2, \ldots, A_n$. Each of these variables can be thought of as a column of a relational table and each point of the mesh as a row of the same table. Given this simple mapping between multidimensional data model and the relational data model, we can transplant all SQL queries to queries on mesh data. For example, "select humidity from mesh_data where temperature > 280 and pressure > 100000" is meant to select all mesh points where temperature and pressure values satisfy the specified conditions and then output the values of humidity on those mesh points.

Case 2: using bounding boxes to partition arrays of the same shape and size. Given a dataset defined on a 3-D mesh of size $10 \times 20 \times 30$, we might divide this mesh for 8 processors as a $2 \times 2 \times 2$ blocks. To accommodate this use case, we will define a set of 8 non-overlapping bounding boxes, one for each of the 8 processors. This would allow each processor to answer queries on 1/8th of the data, corresponding to mesh size $5 \times 10 \times 15$.

A query over this structure consists of 3 parts:

1. The selection box to limit the points considered,
2. The query conditions - in a form of query predicates connected with AND/OR operators,
3. The query output - the values of variables for the points that qualify.

An example of a query could be:

1. Selection box: starts = [5, 0, 15], sizes = [5, 10, 15]
2. Query conditions: temperature > 5 AND pressure < 40
3. Query output: humidity

Case 3: Composite array structures. Users sometimes combine multiple variables into a single array. Continuing with the example involving temperature, pressure, and humidity, assume the mesh size to be 10 × 20 × 30. The 3 dimensions could be linearized into a single dimension with 6000 elements. The three variables could then be put into a 6000 × 3 2D array illustrated in Fig. 6.

In such a case the individual variables could be specified with bounding boxes. Assuming the overall array is named A, the same query from the previous example could be expressed as follows, where temperature ≡ $A[0 : 6000, 0 : 1]$, pressure ≡ $A[0 : 6000, 1 : 2]$, and humidity ≡ $A[0 : 6000, 2 : 3]$; and the query specified in the previous use case could be expressed as,

SELECT A[0 : 6000, 2 : 3] WHERE A[0 : 6000, 0 : 1] > 5 AND A[0 : 6000, 1 : 2] < 40.

Note that the bounding boxes are associated with each variable in the query expression separately, and the sizes of the bounding boxes must be the same; but the offsets (the starting positions) could be different.

Case 4: A general array structure. It is possible that some of the variables are packed together while others are not. More generally, the arrays may have more

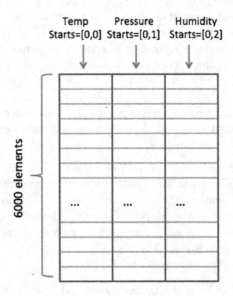

Fig. 6. Illustration of a use case with different variables packed as another dimension of the data array.

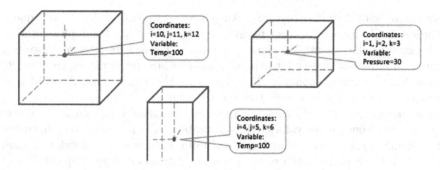

Fig. 7. Illustration of a user query involving multiple arrays of different shapes and sizes.

complex relationship than described above. For example, the values for temperature, pressure, and humidity, could be produced from different measuring instruments and recorded as different time resolutions in space and time, as illustrated in Fig. 7.

Now if we want to compare values at a particular city, we will need to use different bounding boxes on these arrays. This use case is similar to the previous one, the key difference is that the array names would be different. Again, the bounding boxes are required to be of the same size, i.e., having the same number of data points.

5.3 Additional Design Considerations

Reading Multiple Variables. To start with, the current design of the ADIOS query interface retrieves values from on variable at a time. If a use case requires multiple output variables, the caller needs to repeat the invocation of the read function. Introducing a mechanism to specify multiple output variables at once will increase the likelihood of additional optimization in the implementation. However, we choose to keep the interface relatively simple so that we can explore the implementation challenges associated with the basic tasks of integrating with indexing techniques. This and other performance optimization issues will be considered in the future.

Expressing Query Conditions. To avoid the need to introducing a query parser, we have opted to introduce a set of functions for users to compose query expressions instead of allowing the user to specify the query conditions in the string form, even though the string form is a more common form of query interface. This choice also has the benefit of not imposing any restrictions on the variable names. A typical database management system supports query in the SQL language, which imposes a number of restrictions on the variable names, such as, not allowing punctuations, which would introduce extra challenge is expressing the bounding boxes.

Integration with Indexing Software. An effective implementation of the query interface would need to connect to an indexing capability. Our implementation is designed to allow multiple indexing systems to be used. In later tests, we will explore two different ones: a bitmap indexing software library named FastBit [26] and a *MinMax* index capability built into the ADIOS software. A set of user specified conditions may select data records that are scattered randomly in a multidimensional array. Since reading randomly scattered values are much slower than reading consecutive values, some optimization is necessary to reduce the time needed to read the selected values. In our work, we have developed a set of heuristics to combine small random read operations into large sequential read operations.

6   Query Performance

The naive way of resolving a query would be to read through all data records to find those satisfying the user specified conditions. This option is generally known as *scanning*. In this work, we plan to use two different indexing techniques, Fast-Bit index and block MinMax index, to accelerate the query answering process.

FastBit implements a number of different bitmap indexes that have been shown to work well for a number of scientific use case [26]. The block MinMax index is a structure that keeps the minimum and maximum for each variable in a data block. It is a mechanism developed to take advantage of the metadata already captured in the ADIOS BP file format. When processing a user query, this mechanism first examine each data block's header information to determine whether there are any possible entries satisfying the specified conditions using the minimum and maximum values. It only examines the data values in a block if there are possible hits. The mechanism allows us to avoid some blocks. For the data blocks with hits, since the minimum unit of an IO operation is a block, this query answering mechanism is reading the minimum number of blocks and performing the minimum amount of IO operations.

Figure 8 shows the time needed to resolve the queries with three different mechanisms: scanning the raw data, using FastBit indexes, and using the Min-Max mechanism. We see that using the two indexing schemes could dramatically reduce the query processing time compared to scanning the raw data. Compared these two indexing mechanisms, we see that the FastBit indexing is typically faster, however, the FastBit indexes take up a lot more storage space than the MinMax mechanism, which can be regarding as not using any extra space in ADIOS BP format.

Another important observation from Fig. 8 is that the time needed to read the selected values (i.e., the difference between "FastBit + read" and "FastBit") is significantly longer than resolving the query using one of the indexing techniques. This is because the query results are typically randomly scattered in the data file. Extracting these randomly scattered values takes a long time. Often, reading a relatively small number of bounding boxes to encompass the randomly scattered points and then extract the selected values could reduce the overall time need to extract these values.

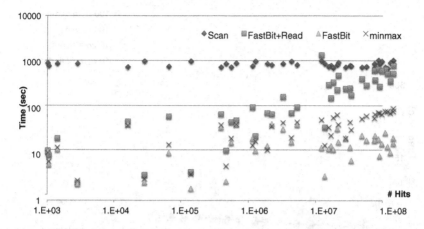

Fig. 8. Query processing time with a set of S3D data (total number of records is 1.67×10^9, organized into a 3D array of $1100 \times 1080 \times 1408$).

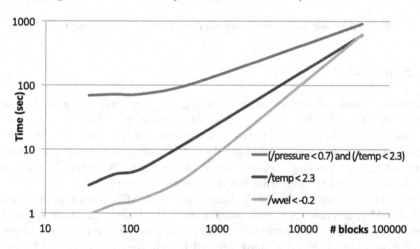

Fig. 9. Query processing time changes dramatically with the number of blocks.

When working with a large dataset, we typically employ multiple CPUs and process each data blocks independently on each CPU core. However, the query processing time could be dramatically affected by the number of blocks used to generated the indexes. Figure 9 shows the query processing time of a small number of queries when the FastBit indexes are generated on different number of blocks. Clearly, the more blocks are used the longer it takes to resolve a query. This is largely because the extra work needed to process each index block. On the other hand, using more processors can significantly reduce the query response time, as shown in Fig. 10. Additional studies are needed to further optimize these and other parameters affecting the performance of indexing and query processing techniques [27].

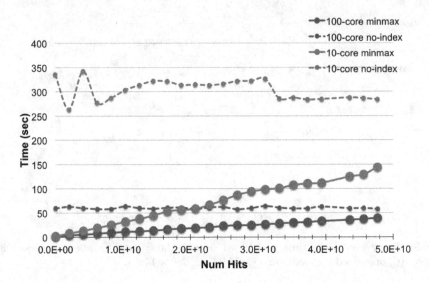

Fig. 10. Using more processors reduces the query processing time.

7   Summary

This work reports our experience in designing and implementing a query interface for ADIOS. We explored a number of different indexing data structures for supporting such a query interface. We observe that for queries that select a relatively small fraction of total number of records in a dataset, answering a query with these indexing methods could be dramatically faster than reading the whole data and then filtering the data records in memory.

In addition to using external indexing libraries, ADIOS also implements a block MinMax mechanism to take advantage of the built-in blocking structure. Tests show that it has the potential to significantly accelerate the query answering process. One challenge we have noticed is that the number of blocks has a strong impact on the overall system performance. We have started exploring possible options to select this and other parameters affecting the query processing time [27].

This work also demonstrates two useful capability of ADIOS in improving the IO pipeline of a simulation program called IMPACT: checkpointing and customizing analysis. In reading and writing of checkpoint files, ADIOS allows the user to manage the IO operations more efficiently. We rely on the *in situ* processing capability of ADIOS to enable IMPACT users to customize the particle statistics during the simulation process.

The *in situ* mechanism is also used to generate the indexes needed to accelerate the query processing algorithms, without increasing the elapsed time used by the simulation programs. It allows the indexes to be generated when the data file is generated, which means the indexes are available when the data is ready. This is very convenient for the users.

In the future, we plan to more fully explore the two capabilities described above. In addition, we plan to compare the query capability with well-known systems such as RasdaMan [2] and SciDB [3].

Acknowledgment. This work was supported by the Office of Advanced Scientific Computing Research, Office of Science, of the U.S. Department of Energy under Contract No. DE-AC02-05CH11231 (for LBNL) and DE-AC05-00OR22725 Mod 877 (for ORNL). This research also used resources of the National Energy Research Scientific Computing Center supported by the same funding agency.

References

1. Bauer, A.C., Abbasi, H., Ahrens, J., Childs, H., Geveci, B., Klasky, S., Moreland, K., O'Leary, P., Vishwanath, V., Whitlock, B., Bethel, E.W.: In situ methods, infrastructures, and applications on high performance computing platforms. Comput. Graph. Forum **35**(3), 577–597 (2016)
2. Baumann, P.: rasdaman - raster data manager, January 2018. rasdaman.org
3. Brown, P.G.: Overview of sciDB: large scale array storage, processing and analysis. In: Proceedings of the 2010 ACM SIGMOD International Conference on Management of Data, SIGMOD 2010, pp. 963–968. ACM, New York (2010)
4. Chen, J.H., Choudhary, A., De Supinski, B., DeVries, M., Hawkes, E.R., Klasky, S., Liao, W.-K., Ma, K.-L., Mellor-Crummey, J., Podhorszki, N., et al.: Terascale direct numerical simulations of turbulent combustion using S3D. Comput. Sci. Discov. **2**(1), 015001 (2009)
5. Chou, J., Wu, K., Rübel, O., Howison, M., Qiang, J., Prabhat, Austin, B., Bethel, E.W., Ryne, R.D., Shoshani, A.: Parallel index and query for large scale data analysis. In: SC11 (2011)
6. Comer, D.: The ubiquitous B-tree. Comput. Surv. **11**(2), 121–137 (1979)
7. Dong, B., Byna, S., Wu, K.: Expediting scientific data analysis with reorganization of data. In: 2013 IEEE International Conference on Cluster Computing (CLUSTER), pp. 1–8, September 2013. http://ieeexplore.ieee.org/xpls/abs_all.jsp?arnumber=6702675
8. Dong, B., Byna, S., Wu, K.: SDS: a framework for scientific data services. In: Proceedings of the 8th Parallel Data Storage Workshop (2013). http://www.pdsw.org/pdsw13/papers/p27-pdsw13-dong.pdf
9. Dong, B., Byna, S., Wu, K., Prabhat, Johansen, H., Johnson, J.N., Keen, N.: Data elevator: low-contention data movement in hierarchical storage system. In: 2016 IEEE 23rd International Conference on High Performance Computing (HiPC), pp. 152–161, December 2016
10. Folk, M., Heber, G., Koziol, Q., Pourmal, E., Robinson, D.: An overview of the HDF5 technology suite and its applications. In: Proceedings of the EDBT/ICDT 2011 Workshop on Array Databases, pp. 36–47. ACM (2011). http://www.hdfgroup.org/HDF5/
11. Gosink, L., Shalf, J., Stockinger, K., Wu, K., Bethel, W.: HDF5-FastQuery: accelerating complex queries on HDF datasets using fast bitmap indices. In: SSDBM 2006, Vienna, Austria, July 2006, pp. 149–158. IEEE Computer Society Press (2006)
12. Graefe, G.: Query evaluation techniques for large databases. ACM Comput. Surv. (CSUR) **25**(2), 73–169 (1993)

13. Hey, T., Tansley, S., Tolle, K. (eds.): The Fourth Paradigm: Data-Intensive Scientific Discovery. Microsoft, Redmond (2009)
14. Im, H.G., Chen, J.H., Law, C.K.: Ignition of hydrogen/air mixing layer in turbulent flows. In: Twenty-Seventh Symposium (International) on Combustion, The Combustion Institute, pp. 1047–1056 (1998)
15. Lee, K.-H., Lee, Y.-J., Choi, H., Chung, Y.D., Moon, B.: Parallel data processing with mapreduce: a survey. ACM SIGMOD Record 40(4), 11–20 (2012)
16. Liu, Q., Logan, J., Tian, Y., Abbasi, H., Podhorszki, N., Choi, J.Y., Klasky, S., Tchoua, R., Lofstead, J., Oldfield, R., Parashar, M., Samatova, N., Schwan, K., Shoshani, A., Wolf, M., Wu, K., Yu, W.: Hello ADIOS: the challenges and lessons of developing leadership class I/O frameworks. Concurr. Comput. Pract. Exp. 26, 1453–1473 (2014). https://www.olcf.ornl.gov/center-projects/adios/
17. Lofstead, J.F., Klasky, S., Schwan, K., Podhorszki, N., Jin, C.: Flexible IO and integration for scientific codes through the adaptable IO system (ADIOS). In: CLADE 2008, pp. 15–24. ACM, New York (2008)
18. Ozsu, M.T.: Principles of Distributed Database Systems, 3rd edn. Prentice Hall Press, Upper Saddle River (2007)
19. Qiang, J., Lidia, S., Ryne, R.D., Limborg-Deprey, C.: Three-dimensional quasistatic model for high brightness beam dynamics simulation. Phys. Rev. Spec. Topics-Accel. Beams 9(4), 044204 (2006)
20. Qiang, J., Ryne, R.D., Habib, S., Decyk, V.: An object-oriented parallel particle-in-cell code for beam dynamics simulation in linear accelerators. J. Comput. Phys. 163(2), 434–451 (2000)
21. Qiang, J., Ryne, R.D., Venturini, M., Zholents, A.A., Pogorelov, I.V.: High resolution simulation of beam dynamics in electron linacs for X-ray free electron lasers. Phys. Rev. ST Accel. Beams 12, 100702 (2009)
22. Rew, R., Davis, G.: NetCDF: an interface for scientific data access. IEEE Comput. Graphics Appl. 10(4), 76–82 (1990). http://www.unidata.ucar.edu/software/netcdf/
23. Roman, E.: A survey of checkpoint/restart implementations. Technical report, Lawrence Berkeley National Laboratory (2002)
24. Shoshani, A., Rotem, D. (eds.): Scientific Data Management: Challenges, Technology, and Deployment. Chapman & Hall/CRC Press, Boca Raton (2010)
25. White, T.: Hadoop - The Definitive Guide: MapReduce for the Cloud. O'Reilly, Sebastopol (2009)
26. Wu, K., Ahern, S., Bethel, E.W., Chen, J., Childs, H., Cormier-Michel, E., Geddes, C., Gu, J., Hagen, H., Hamann, B., Koegler, W., Lauret, J., Meredith, J., Messmer, P., Otoo, E., Perevoztchikov, V., Poskanzer, A., Prabhat, Rübel, O., Shoshani, A., Sim, A., Stockinger, K., Weber, G., Zhang, W.-M.: FastBit: interactively searching massive data. In: SciDAC 2009. LBNL-2164E (2009)
27. Wu, T., Chou, J., Podhorszki, N., Gu, J., Tian, Y., Klasky, S., Wu, K.: Apply block index technique to scientific data analysis and I/O systems. In: Proceedings of the 17th IEEE/ACM International Symposium on Cluster, Cloud and Grid Computing, CCGrid 2017, pp. 865–871. IEEE Press, Piscataway, May 2017
28. Zhang, H., Wen, Y., Xie, H., Yu, N.: Distributed Hash Table: Theory, Platforms and Applications. Springer, New York (2013). https://doi.org/10.1007/978-1-4614-9008-1

On the Performance of Spark on HPC Systems: Towards a Complete Picture

Orcun Yildiz[1] and Shadi Ibrahim[2(✉)]

[1] Inria, Univ Rennes, CNRS, IRISA, Rennes, France
[2] Inria, IMT Atlantique, LS2N, Nantes, France
shadi.ibrahim@inria.fr

Abstract. Big Data analytics frameworks (e.g., Apache Hadoop and Apache Spark) have been increasingly used by many companies and research labs to facilitate large-scale data analysis. However, with the growing needs of users and size of data, commodity-based infrastructure will strain under the heavy weight of Big Data. On the other hand, HPC systems offer a rich set of opportunities for Big Data processing. As first steps toward Big Data processing on HPC systems, several research efforts have been devoted to understanding the performance of Big Data applications on these systems. Yet the HPC specific performance considerations have not been fully investigated. In this work, we conduct an experimental campaign to provide a clearer understanding of the performance of Spark, the *de facto* in-memory data processing framework, on HPC systems. We ran Spark using representative Big Data workloads on Grid'5000 testbed to evaluate how the latency, contention and file system's configuration can influence the application performance. We discuss the implications of our findings and draw attention to new ways (e.g., burst buffers) to improve the performance of Spark on HPC systems.

Keywords: HPC · MapReduce · Spark · Parallel file systems
Contention

1 Introduction

Data is a driving power in almost every aspect of our lives and thus large amounts of data generated everyday. For instance, International Data Research report [6] estimates that the global data volume subject to data analysis will grow by a factor of 50 to reach 5.2 zettabytes in 2025. This huge growth in the data volumes, the deluge of Big Data, results in a big challenge in managing, processing and analyzing these gigantic data volumes.

To benefit from this huge amount of data, different data processing models have emerged [13,20]. Among these models, MapReduce [13,23] has stood out as the most powerful Big Data processing model, in particular for batch processing. MapReduce, and its open-source implementation Hadoop [3], is adopted in both industry and academia due to its simplicity, transparent fault tolerance and scalability. For instance, Yahoo! claimed to have the world's largest Hadoop cluster [7] with more than 100000 CPUs in over 40000 machines running MapReduce jobs.

R. Yokota and W. Wu (Eds.): SCFA 2018, LNCS 10776, pp. 70–89, 2018.
https://doi.org/10.1007/978-3-319-69953-0_5

With the wide adoption of MapReduce in different domains, diverse Big Data applications (e.g., stream data processing, graph processing, analysis of large scale simulation data) have emerged where obtaining timely and accurate responses is a must. This, on the one hand, motivates the introduction of new Big Data analytic frameworks which extend the MapReduce programming model [4,10,11,36]. Such frameworks keep data processing in memory and therefore try to efficiently exploit its high speed. Among these frameworks, Spark [36] has become the de facto framework for in-memory Big Data analytics. Spark is recently used to run diverse set of applications including machine learning, stream processing and etc. For example, Netflix has a Spark cluster of over 8000 machines processing multiple petabytes of data in order to improve the customer experience by providing better recommendations for their streaming services [5]. On the other hand, high performance computing (HPC) systems recently gained a huge interest as a promising platform for performing fast Big Data processing given their high performance nature [1,17]. HPC systems are equipped with low-latency networks and thousands of nodes with many cores and therefore have the potential to perform fast Big Data processing. For instance, PayPal recently shipped its fraud detection software to HPC systems to be able to detect frauds among millions of transactions in a timely manner [26].

However, when introducing Big Data processing to HPC systems, one should be aware of the different architectural designs in current Big Data processing and HPC systems. Big Data processing systems have shared nothing architecture and nodes are equipped with individual disks, thus they can co-locate the data and compute resources on the same machine (i.e., data-centric paradigm). On the other hand, HPC systems employ a shared architecture (e.g., parallel file systems) [19] which results in separation of data resources from the compute nodes (i.e., compute-centric paradigm). Figure 1 illustrates these differences in the design of these two systems. These differences in the design of these two systems introduce two major challenges: Big Data applications will face *high latencies* when performing I/O due to the necessary data transfers between the parallel file system and computation nodes. Moreover, *I/O contention* (i.e., performance degradation observed by any single application/task running in contention with other applications/tasks on the same platform [15,33]) is a well-known problem in HPC systems which often detracts the performance of a single-application

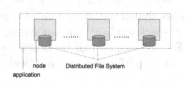

(a) Data-centric paradigm.

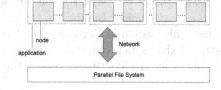

(b) Compute-centric paradigm.

Fig. 1. The different designs in Big Data and HPC systems.

from the high performance offered by these systems due to their large sizes and shared architecture [16,18,25,33].

In response, several efforts have been conducted to leverage Spark for fast Big Data processing on HPC systems. These works have mainly tried to alleviate the high latency problem by focusing on the *intermediate data* storage (i.e., map output for batch jobs and temporary output produced between stages for iterative jobs) [12,21,28,32,34]. For example, Islam et al. [21] utilized NVRAM as an intermediate storage layer (i.e., burst buffer) between compute nodes and Lustre file system [14]. This brought 24% improvement to the application performance by reducing the latency when reading/writing the intermediate data. However, Big Data applications mostly run in batches and there is a continuous interaction with the parallel file system for reading the input data and writing the output data, thus it is important to study the impact of latency on the performance of Big Data applications by considering the different phases of Big Data applications as input, intermediate and output data. Moreover, none of these efforts considered the contention problem which can contribute to a significant performance degradation by up to 2.5x [33]. Hence, *as we argue in this paper, current efforts and solutions to adopt Spark on HPC systems may fail in practice to achieve the desired performance and this may hinder such adoption.*

Our Contributions. In an effort to complement existing efforts on understanding the performance of Big Data applications on HPC systems, in this paper, we perform an experimental study characterizing the performance of Spark [36] on HPC systems. We use representative Big Data workloads on the Grid'5000 [22] testbed to evaluate how the *latency, contention,* and *file system's configuration* impact the application performance. We make the following contributions:

- *A quantitative analysis of the impact of latency on the application performance.* We find that resulting latency during the data movement between compute nodes and parallel file system can degrade the application performance seriously. Specifically, we show evidence that the high latency of reading the input data and writing the output data to the parallel virtual file system (PVFS) [27] have higher impact on performance degradation compared to the intermediate data.
- *The role of contention on the application performance.* Our results show that contention can result in severe performance penalties for Big Data applications on HPC systems due to employing a shared storage system.
- *An analysis of the impact of the file system specific properties on the application performance.* Similar to [12] which shows that metadata operations in Lustre file system [14] create a bottleneck for Spark applications, we demonstrated that synchronization feature of PVFS [27], which can be necessary for providing resilience, can reduce the application performance dramatically by 14x.
- *Towards an efficient adoption of Spark on HPC systems.* We discuss the implications of our findings and draw attention to new ways (e.g., burst buffers) to improve the performance of Spark on HPC systems.

The rest of the paper is organized as follows. Section 2 describes an overview of our methodology and Sect. 3 presents different sets of experiments highlighting the possible performance bottlenecks for Big Data applications on HPC systems. We discuss the implications of our findings to the new ways (i.e., burst buffers) to improve the performance of Big Data applications on HPC systems in Sect. 4. In Sect. 5 we present related work. Finally, we conclude the paper and propose our future work in Sect. 6.

2 Methodology

We conducted a series of experiments in order to assess the impact of the potential issues regarding HPC systems (i.e., latency, contention, file system's configuration) on the performance of Big Data applications. We further describe the experimental environment: the platform, deployment setup, and Big Data workloads.

2.1 Platform Description

The experiments were carried out on the Grid'5000 testbed. We used the Rennes site; more specifically we employed nodes belonging to the *parasilo* and *paravance* clusters. The nodes in these clusters are outfitted with two 8-core Intel Xeon 2.4 GHz CPUs and 128 GB of RAM. We leveraged the 10 Gbps Ethernet network that connects all nodes of these two clusters. Grid'5000 allows us to create an isolated environment in order to have full control over the experiments and obtained results.

2.2 Spark Deployment

We used Spark version 1.6.1 working with Hadoop distributed file systems (HDFS) version 1.2. We configured and deployed a Spark cluster using 51 nodes on the *paravance* cluster. One node consists of the Spark master and the HDFS NameNode, leaving 50 nodes to serve as both slaves of Spark and DataNodes. We used the default value (number of available cores on the node) for the number of cores to use per each node. Therefore, the Spark cluster can allocate up to 800 tasks. We allocated 24 GB per node for the Spark instance and set Spark's default parallelism parameter (spark.default.parallelism) to 800 which refers to the number of RDD partitions (i.e., number of reducers for batch jobs). At the level of HDFS, we used a chunk size of 32 MB and set a replication factor of 2 for the input and output data.

The OrangeFS file system (a branch of PVFS2 [27]) version 2.8.3 was deployed on 12 nodes of the *parasilo* cluster. We set the stripe size which defines the data distribution policy in PVFS (i.e., analogous to block size in HDFS) to 32 MB in order to have a fair comparison with HDFS. Unless otherwise specified, we disabled the synchronization for PVFS (Sync OFF) which indicates that the incoming data can stay in kernel-provided buffers. We opted for Sync OFF configuration since Spark is also using the memory as a first storage level with HDFS.

2.3   Workloads

We selected three representative Big Data workloads including Sort, Wordcount and PageRank which are part of HiBench [2], Big Data benchmarking suite.

Wordcount is a map-heavy workload which counts the number of occurrences of each word in a data set. The map function splits the input data set into words and produces the intermediate data for the reduce function as a key, value pair with word being the key and 1 as the value to indicate the occurrence of the word. The reduce function sums up these intermediate results and outputs the final word counts. Wordcount has a light reduce phase due to the small amount of the intermediate data.

Sort is a reduce-heavy workload with a large amount of intermediate data. This workload sorts the data set and both map and reduce functions are simple functions which take the input and produce its sorted version based on the key. This workload has a heavy shuffling in the reduce phase due to the large amount of intermediate data it produces.

PageRank is a graph algorithm which ranks elements according to the number of links. This workload updates these rank values in multiple iterations until they converge and therefore it represents the iterative set of applications.

For Sort and Wordcount workloads, we used 200 GB input data set generated with RandomTextWriter in HiBench suite. For the PageRank workload, we also used HiBench suite which uses the data generated from Web data with 25 million edges as an input data set.

3   Experimental Results

In this section, we provide a detailed analysis of the experimental results we obtained which highlights the implications of the potential performance bottlenecks for Big Data applications on HPC systems.

3.1   How Does Latency Affect the Application Performance?

First, we try to understand the impact of the data location on the application performance. While storage resources are co-located with Spark tasks under the data-centric paradigm (i.e., when using Spark with HDFS), Spark tasks need to communicate with the parallel file system either to fetch the input data or to write the output data under the compute-centric paradigm (i.e., when Spark is using PVFS as the storage space). This remote data access results in a higher latency compared to the data-centric paradigm which leverages data locality (i.e., executing tasks on the machines where the input data resides). Figure 2 shows how latency can affect the application performance. Note that, intermediate data is stored locally on the aforementioned settings for Spark in order to focus on the latency resulting from reading the input data in map phase. We explore the intermediate data storage separately in the next subsection.

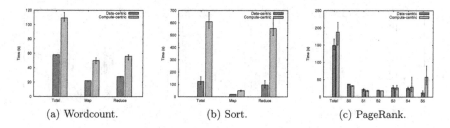

(a) Wordcount.   (b) Sort.   (c) PageRank.

Fig. 2. Performance of Big Data workloads on Spark under data-centric and compute-centric paradigms.

Figure 2(a) displays the execution time of the Wordcount workload for both paradigms with a performance in map and reduce phases. Overall, Wordcount performs 1.9x worse under the compute-centric paradigm compared to the data-centric one. When we look at the performance in each phase, we observe that the performance degradation contributed by the map phase (2.3x) is higher compared to the reduce phase. This stems from the fact that Wordcount has a light reduce phase and generates only a small amount of output data.

Similarly, in Fig. 2(b) we observe that the data-centric configuration outperforms the compute-centric one by 4.9x for the Sort workload. In contrast to Wordcount, the reduce phase is the major contributor to the performance degradation. For the Sort workload, the amount of the output data is equal to the input data thus it suffers from a higher latency in the reduce phase as data is written to the parallel file system. As a result, having a higher latency on both input and output phases led to higher performance degradation for the compute-centric paradigm.

Lastly, we ran the PageRank workload in both settings for Spark and Fig. 2(c) shows the results. Here, performance degradation with the compute-centric paradigm is only 26%. The reason behind this is that I/O phases of the PageRank workload (i.e., Stage 0 and Stage 5 (denoted as S0 and S5)) accounts for a small fraction of PageRank execution time and Spark computes the iterations (i.e., Stage 1, 2, 3 and 4) locally.

The Impact of the Input Data Sizes. We also investigated the impact of the input data size on the application performance. To do so, we ran the Wordcount workload with different input sizes as 2 GB, 20 GB and 200 GB. Figure 3 displays the performance of the Wordcount workload in each phase for data and compute-centric paradigms. Overall, we observe that the impact of I/O latency is only visible in the map phase for the compute-centric paradigm with increasing input sizes: there is a performance degradation for the map phase by 1.2x, 1.8x and 2.3x with 2 GB, 20 GB and 200 GB input sizes, respectively. This is mainly due to the fact that Wordcount is a map-heavy workload which generates a small amount of output data and therefore reduce phase results do not vary significantly with respect to different data sizes. To further investigate

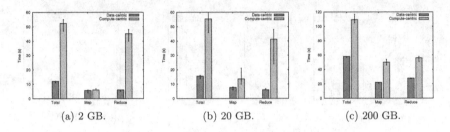

(a) 2 GB.   (b) 20 GB.   (c) 200 GB.

Fig. 3. Performance of the Wordcount workload with different input sizes.

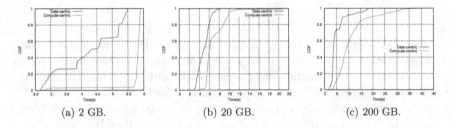

(a) 2 GB.   (b) 20 GB.   (c) 200 GB.

Fig. 4. CDFs of running times of map tasks in the Wordcount workload.

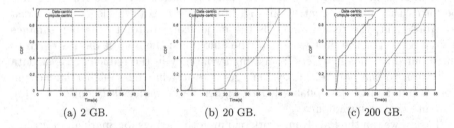

(a) 2 GB.   (b) 20 GB.   (c) 200 GB.

Fig. 5. CDFs of running times of reduce tasks in the Wordcount workload.

these different behaviors in map and reduce phases, we display the CDF of map and reduce task durations in Figs. 4 and 5.

Interestingly, Fig. 4(a) shows that some map task durations are smaller for the compute-centric paradigm compared to the data-centric one. This is due to the fact that Spark employs delay scheduling [35] to increase the chances of a map task to be launched locally for the data-centric paradigm. This delay while launching the map tasks, which results in a performance degradation for the jobs with small input data sizes, is due to the default Spark configuration for the maximum waiting time (i.e., 3 s) in scheduling the map tasks. This is only valid for the data-centric paradigm since there is no data locality objective when scheduling the tasks in the compute-centric paradigm where all the machines have an equivalent distance to the parallel file system. On the other hand, we observe an increase in the map task durations with larger input sizes for the compute-centric paradigm. This results from the higher latency while fetching the input data from parallel file system with larger input sizes.

Another interesting trend we observe is that the maximum map task duration also increases with the increasing data sizes, especially with 200 GB input data size in Fig. 4(c). We believe that this behavior is due to the higher contention with the increased number of concurrent map tasks. It is important to note that there are 33, 594 and 800 concurrent map tasks with 2 GB, 20 GB and 200 GB input sizes. Moreover, we see that this increase is much higher with the compute-centric paradigm which can highlight the severity of the contention problem for this paradigm. We will further explain the impact of the contention on the application performance in Sect. 3.2.

In Fig. 5, we observe a similar trend for the reduce task durations for the compute-centric paradigm. With larger data sizes, we observe an increase in those durations too. This again stems from an increased amount of the remote data transfer while writing the reducer outputs to the parallel file system. Moreover, we discover that there is a high performance variability in the reduce phase and the maximum task duration is quite high even with 2 GB data size. This is due to the static Spark configuration which employs 800 reducers regardless of the input data size. These high number of reducers overload the parallel file system and results in this performance variability. Hence, we do not see the impact of latency in Fig. 3 for the reduce phase. However, when the output data size is large enough as shown for the Sort workload in the previous experiment (Fig. 2(b)), the impact of the I/O latency is quite clear as it results in a significant performance degradation.

For the data-centric paradigm, this time we see that reduce task durations are inlined with the data sizes, different from the map phase. While for the map phase there is an increase in the maximum task duration due to the increased number of concurrent map tasks, for the reduce phase the number of reduce tasks is fixed and the increase in the reduce task durations is mainly due to the increased amount of reducer output with larger input sizes.

Intermediate Data Storage. In Big Data processing systems, intermediate data are typically stored locally. However, nodes in some of the HPC systems may not have individual disks attached to themselves. This gives rise to the question of how to store the intermediate data when running Big Data applications on HPC systems. As a naive solution, we employed PVFS also for storing the intermediate data as well as storage space for input and output data like in the experiments so far. We ran the Sort workload with PVFS since it generates an intermediate data equal to the input data size and thus it is a good fit for evaluating the intermediate data storage for HPC systems. Figure 6 compares the performance of Sort depending on the intermediate data location: local storage (on disk) or remote storage (on PVFS). We see that using PVFS also for storing the intermediate data results in 9% performance degradation.

When we analyze the performance of the Sort workload in each phase, we see that this performance degradation is 16% for the map phase which stems from writing the intermediate data to the parallel file system. For the reduce

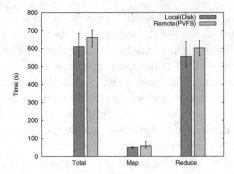

Fig. 6. Impact of the location of intermediate data on the performance of the Sort workload.

phase, we observe that there is a 8% increase in the completion time due to the additional I/O latency when fetching the intermediate data from PVFS.

Findings. In all of the workloads, we observe that the remote data access to the parallel file system leads to a significant performance degradation, especially for the input and output data. We also confirm that the degree of this performance degradation depends on the characteristics of the workloads and on the input data size.

3.2   The Role of Contention

Given the shared architecture of HPC systems, contention is likely to occur when running Big Data applications on a HPC system. To assess the impact of contention on the performance of Big Data applications, we designed the following experiments:

Measuring the contention when running concurrent Big Data applications. Since the storage system is shared by all the nodes, this can create a serious contention problem on the storage path including network, server and storage devices. Here, we ran two Wordcount workloads concurrently under compute and data-centric paradigms by employing the Fair scheduler in Spark. The Fair scheduler allows these workloads to have equal share of the resources in the Spark cluster (i.e., each workload employ 400 tasks which is equal to the half of the cluster capacity). Figure 7 displays the execution times of the Wordcount workload when it runs alone and together with the other identical Wordcount workload for data and compute-centric paradigms. As shown in Fig. 7(a), the performance degradation when running in contention with the other Wordcount workload is negligible with the data-centric paradigm. In contrast, we observe that there is a 41% performance degradation with the compute-centric paradigm when two work-loads are running concurrently. This stems from sharing the same parallel file system with compute-centric paradigm while these two workloads perform their I/O operations on their individual storage devices in the data-centric paradigm.

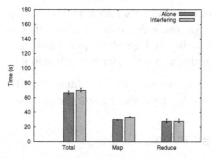 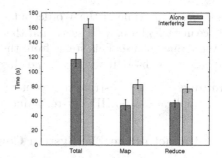

(a) Performance of concurrent Wordcount workloads under a data-centric paradigm.

(b) Performance of concurrent Wordcount workloads under a compute-centric paradigm.

Fig. 7. Performance of concurrent Wordcount workloads under different paradigms.

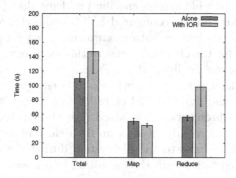

Fig. 8. Performance of the Wordcount workload when running alone and together with IOR workload.

In particular, Fig. 7(b) highlights that this performance degradation is mainly due to the map phase. This is because Wordcount is a map-heavy workload and therefore the number of I/O operations is quite large in the map phase compared to the reduce phase.

Measuring the contention when co-locating HPC and Big Data applications. This contention problem can even become more significant when we consider the ultimate objective of the HPC and Big Data convergence which is co-locating scientific and Big Data applications on a same platform. To emulate this objective, we ran the Wordcount workload alone and together with the IOR workload. IOR [29] is a popular I/O benchmark that allows users to specify different I/O configurations and thus measures the I/O performance of HPC systems. For IOR workload, we employed 224 processes (on a different set of nodes separated from the ones running the Wordcount workload) where each process issues a 512 MB write request in 32 MBs of chunks. Figure 8 shows the execution times of the Wordcount workload for both cases. Due to resource sharing (file system and network) with the IOR workload, there is a 1.4x performance degradation in the total execution time of the Wordcount workload. When we look at the performance in each phase, we observe that this performance degradation is mainly due to the reduce phase. This stems from the fact that reduce phase performs write operations as the IOR workload and this results in a write/write contention.

Findings. We demonstrate that contention appears as a limiting factor for Big Data applications on HPC systems due to employing a shared storage system.

3.3 Impact of the File System Configuration

Besides the generic problems of HPC systems as latency and contention, we can also encounter performance issues with the file system specific problems when running Big Data applications on HPC systems. For example, [12] reported that metadata operations on Lustre create a bottleneck for Spark applications. Thus, we wanted to investigate file system specific problems that Spark applications can encounter. To this end, we configured PVFS with synchronization enabled (Sync ON). This synchronization feature can be necessary for providing a better reliability guarantee for the clients. To ensure this, each request is immediately flushed to the disk before finalizing the request.

We ran the Wordcount workload with two different synchronization options for PVFS: Sync ON and Sync OFF. Figure 9 shows that Wordcount performs 1.5x worse when synchronization is enabled. We observe that this significant performance degradation mainly stems from the reduce phase. This is expected since the output data is sent to the file system during the reduce phase and each request is flushed to the disk thus resulting in a major bottleneck for the application performance.

We also ran the Sort workload with two different configurations of PVFS and Table 1 shows that Sort performs 4.5x worse when synchronization is enabled. In contrast to Wordcount, we observe a much higher performance degradation with the Sort workload. This is because while Sort is generating a large amount of output data (200 GB as the input data size), Wordcount has a light reduce phase and generates only a small amount of output data.

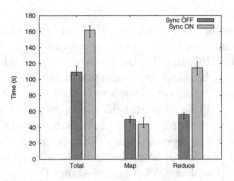

Fig. 9. Performance of the Wordcount workload under different configurations of PVFS.

Table 1. Execution time of the Sort workload and its phases under different configurations of PVFS.

Configuration	Execution time	Map	Reduce
Sync ON	2708.5 s	42.7 s	2665.8 s
Sync OFF	597.6 s	42.6 s	555.0 s

Findings. Parallel file systems are equipped with several features which are important for HPC applications (i.e., synchronization feature in PVFS to provide resiliency, distributed locking mechanism in Lustre to ensure file consistency). However, as we demonstrated in our experiments and also reported earlier in [12,32], these features may bring a significant performance degradation for Big Data applications.

3.4 Burst Buffers: Impact of Their Capacities and Location

We believe that there is a significant potential for improving the performance of Big Data applications using burst buffers. Although burst buffers promise a large potential, leveraging them efficiently for Big Data processing is not trivial. For example, there is a trade-off between the capacity and the throughput of the storage devices that are used in the burst buffers. Although, storage devices such as SSDs or NVRAMs can provide high throughput, they are limited in the *storage capacity*. Moreover, we demonstrated in our experiments that we should tackle all the I/O phases (i.e., input, intermediate and output data) while addressing the latency problem. Therefore, the problem of having limited capacity will be amplified when we try to use the burst buffer for all the I/O phases. By analyzing the traces collected from a research cluster (i.e., M45) [8], we observed that the amount of processed data was almost 900 TBs during 9 months. Hence, data management strategies for the burst buffers will play a crucial role on their efficiency. Similarly, it is important to decide when and which data to evict when running multiple concurrent applications.

Another challenge would be choosing the optimal *deployment location* for the burst buffers. Some of the possible deployment locations are within the compute nodes [32] or using a dedicated set of nodes [12] as burst buffers. While co-locating burst buffers and compute nodes can prevent the aforementioned capacity constraints since compute nodes are greater in size compared to dedicated nodes, this may result in a computational jitter due to sharing of the resources as also reported in [9].

To find out the impact of the aforementioned factors on the application performance when using burst buffers, we emulated a naive adoption of burst buffers by using the *ramdisk* (e.g., /dev/shm/) as a storage space and performed the following experiments:

Measuring the impact of the storage capacity on the application performance. Here, we ran the Wordcount workload with two different storage capacities for

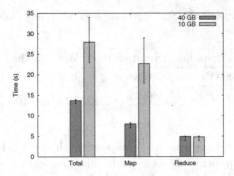

Fig. 10. Impact of the memory capacity of the burst buffer on the performance of the Wordcount workload.

the burst buffer as 40 GB and 10 GB memory. Note that, we used a smaller input data size than previous experiments which has a data size of 20 GB. The burst buffer is employing 5 dedicated nodes. Figure 10 shows the execution time of the Wordcount workload for different burst buffer configurations. We observe a 2.1x performance degradation when the burst buffer has 10 GB storage capacity. When we look at the performance of the workload in each phase, we see that this performance degradation is attributed to the map phase. This results from not having enough space for storing the input data on the burst buffer. Hence, compute nodes have to fetch the input data from the parallel file system thus resulting in a high I/O latency in the map phase. On the contrary, all I/O operations performed between burst buffer nodes and compute nodes when there is enough storage capacity. For the reduce phase, we do not observe any performance degradation since the output data to be written is small enough to fit into the burst buffer storage space, for this workload.

Measuring the impact of the deployment location of the burst buffer. We ran the Wordcount workload with the same configuration as in the previous experiment and deployed the burst buffer in two scenarios: in the first one, the burst buffer is deployed as a disjoint set of nodes and in the second one it is located as a subset of the compute cluster. Figure 11 displays that Wordcount performs better when burst buffer is deployed as a separate set of nodes. We hypothesize the following explanation. When the burst buffer is using the subset of the nodes of the compute cluster, I/O and compute tasks on those nodes conflict with each other thus resulting in a significant performance degradation (38% slowdown). This is in line with the observations reported in [9].

Findings. Our experiments show that the storage capacity and the location of burst buffers can have a significant impact on the performance of Big Data applications. With limited storage capacity, we demonstrate that burst buffers can not mitigate the latency problem fully since compute nodes still need to fetch most of the data from the parallel file system. For the deployment location, we

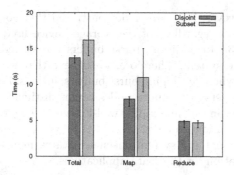

Fig. 11. Impact of the location of the burst buffer on the performance of the Wordcount workload.

observe that co-locating the burst buffer and compute resources on the same node can not be appropriate due to the possible interference among them.

4 Discussion and Implications

Here, we summarize our findings and discuss their implications to the design of burst buffer solutions. Our experiments reveal that Big Data applications encounter serious performance issues when running on HPC systems. First, we show that latency has a significant impact on the application performance and this impact depends on the characteristics of the Big Data applications.

Implications (1). Prior studies [12, 21, 32] have focused on mitigating the latency resulting from writing and reading intermediate data by introducing an intermediate storage layer (i.e., burst buffer); which is a blind adoption of burst buffers for HPC applications—burst buffers are used to store temporary data (i.e., checkpoints). We observe that using burst buffers for intermediate data can bring an improvement of at most 16%—when intermediate data have the same size as input data. As a result, the latency introduced by intermediate data is not really the bottleneck for a major fraction of Big Data applications: by analyzing traces collected from three different research clusters we observe that the amount of the intermediate data is less than 20% of the input data size for 85% of the applications [8]. On the other hand, we find that the latencies resulting from reading input data and writing output data significantly impact the performance. Thus, it is very important to mitigate the high latency resulting from accessing those data when developing burst buffer solutions. Moreover, prefetching techniques and mechanisms to overlap I/O and computation time could be adopted to further hide the high latency of remote data accesses between compute nodes and the parallel file system.

Second, we demonstrate that contention can severely degrade the performance of Big Data applications on HPC systems.

Implications (2). One could argue that using burst buffers would mitigate the contention problem as well since they are equipped with high throughput storage devices. However, it is earlier demonstrated that contention is present in the HPC I/O stack regardless of the storage device used (e.g., SSDs, local memory or disk) [33]. In addition, burst buffers are shared by all the nodes as in the parallel file system. Therefore, we believe that we must address the contention problem when developing burst buffer solutions. For instance, we can try to make distinct sets of compute nodes target distinct sets of burst buffer nodes. Moreover, we can further employ well-known I/O aggregation techniques to minimize the contention problem.

We also observe that file system specific features may bring a significant performance degradation for Big Data applications.

Implications (3). Even burst buffers can improve the performance of Big Data applications, they still rely on a parallel file system. Thus, we should tackle the file system specific issues as well for efficient Big Data processing on HPC systems.

Lastly, we confirm that an effective exploitation of burst buffers for Big data applications in HPC systems strongly depends on the size and location settings of burst buffers.

Implications (4). To tackle the limited storage capacity problem, we can develop smarter data fetching techniques for the burst buffer. For instance, instead of trying to fit all the input data set into the burst buffer storage space, we can fetch a subset of the data set (i.e., one wave) as compute cluster computes one wave at a time. For instance, cluster consists of 800 tasks in our experiments and therefore they can only compute 25 GB data at one iteration. In this way, compute tasks can fetch all the data from the burst buffer nodes and therefore the latency problem can be mitigated.

5   Related Work

Several research efforts have been conducted to evaluate the performance of Big Data analytics frameworks on HPC systems. Wang et al. [32] performed an experimental study where they investigated the characteristics of Spark on a HPC system with a special focus on the impact of the storage architecture and locality-oriented task scheduling. Tous et al. [31] evaluated the Spark performance on a MareNostrum supercomputer. In particular, they studied the impact of different Spark configurations on the performance of Sort and K-means applications. In [30], the authors compared the performance of MapReduce applications on PVFS and HDFS file systems by using Hadoop framework and give insights into how to emulate HDFS behavior by using PVFS. Li and Shen [24] compared the performance of MapReduce applications on scale-up and scale-out clusters and proposed a hybrid scale-up/out Hadoop architecture based on their findings.

Aforementioned studies provide useful findings towards leveraging HPC systems for Big Data processing. However, they do not illustrate a complete analysis of the potential performance issues (e.g., latency and contention). For the latency problem, most of the studies focus on the intermediate data storage and ignore the latencies which can occur in other I/O phases. We provide a detailed analysis of the impact of latency on the application performance by giving a breakdown of the latency problem into its different phases (i.e., input, intermediate and output data). Although these studies mention contention as a problem, none of them investigate its impact on the application performance. Hence, we aim to complement those studies by providing a detailed analysis of the impact of latency and contention on the performance of Spark applications. Furthermore, we show potential performance issues specific to different PVFS configurations.

Some works proposed adoption of burst buffers for efficient Big Data processing on HPC systems. Chaimov et al. [12] employed a dedicated set of nodes with NVRAM as the storage space for the intermediate data of Big Data applications. This in turn improved the scalability of the Spark framework compared to the scenario when using Lustre file system as the storage space. Islam et al. [21] proposed a novel design for HDFS which uses NVRAM-based burst buffer nodes on top of a parallel file system for improving the performance of Spark applications. Yildiz et al. [34] present Eley, a burst buffer solution that helps to accelerate the performance of Big Data applications while guaranteeing the performance of HPC applications. Eley employs a prefetching technique that fetches the input data of these applications to be stored close to computing nodes thus reducing the latency of reading data inputs. Moreover, Eley is equipped with a full delay operator to guarantee the performance of HPC applications. Similarly, our findings illustrate that there is a need for burst buffer solutions to alleviate

Table 2. Our major findings on the characteristics of Big Data applications on HPC systems.

The impact of I/O latency
We confirm that I/O latency resulting from the remote data access to the parallel file system leads to a significant performance degradation for all the Big Data workloads. However, in contrary to existing studies [12,21], we demonstrate that intermediate data storage is not the major contributor to this latency problem. We also observe that the impact of this latency problem depends on the characteristics of the Big Data applications (e.g., map-heavy, iterative applications) and on the input data size
The role of contention
We demonstrate that contention appears as a limiting factor for Big Data applications on HPC systems due to employing a shared storage system
The impact of the file system configuration
Parallel file systems are equipped with several features which are important for HPC applications (i.e., synchronization feature in PVFS to provide resiliency, distributed locking mechanism in Lustre to ensure file consistency). However, as we demonstrated in our experiments and also reported earlier in [12,32], these features may bring a significant performance degradation for Big Data applications

the latency problem. In addition, we give insights into designing efficient burst buffer solutions. Specifically, we claim that future burst buffer implementations should be aware of the contention problem and also try to eliminate the latency problem for the input phase and output phase.

6   Conclusion and Future Work

We have recently witnessed an increasing trend toward leveraging HPC systems for Big Data processing. In this paper, we undertook an effort to provide a detailed analysis of performance characteristics of Big Data applications on HPC systems, as first steps towards efficient Big Data processing on HPC systems. Our findings demonstrate that one should carefully deal with HPC-specific issues (e.g., latency, contention and file system configuration) when running Big Data applications on these systems. An important outcome of our study is that negative impact of latency on the application performance is present for all I/O phases. We further show that contention is a limiting factor for the application performance and thus Big Data solutions should be equipped with contention-aware strategies. Lastly, we reveal that enabling synchronization for PVFS in order to provide resilience can create a serious performance bottleneck for Big Data applications.

We summarize our findings in Table 2. We believe that these findings can help to motivate further research leveraging HPC systems for Big Data analytics by providing a clearer understanding of the Big Data application characteristics on these systems.

Acknowledgment. This work is supported by the ANR KerStream project (ANR-16-CE25-0014-01). The experiments presented in this paper were carried out using the Grid'5000/ALADDIN-G5K experimental testbed, an initiative from the French Ministry of Research through the ACI GRID incentive action, INRIA, CNRS and RENATER and other contributing partners (see http://www.grid5000.fr/ for details).

References

1. Big Data and Extreme-scale Computing (BDEC) Workshop. http://www.exascale.org/bdec/
2. HiBench Big Data microbenchmark suite. https://github.com/intel-hadoop/HiBench
3. The Apache Hadoop Project. http://www.hadoop.org
4. Apache Storm (2012). https://storm.apache.org/
5. Apache Spark primer (2017). http://go.databricks.com/hubfs/pdfs/Apache_Spark_Primer_170303.pdf
6. IDC's Data Age 2025 study (2017). http://www.seagate.com/www-content/our-story/trends/files/Seagate-WP-DataAge2025-March-2017.pdf
7. Powered by Hadoop (2017). http://wiki.apache.org/hadoop/PoweredBy/
8. Hadoop Workload Analysis. http://www.pdl.cmu.edu/HLA/index.shtml. Accessed Jan 2017

9. Bent, J., Faibish, S., Ahrens, J., Grider, G., Patchett, J., Tzelnic, P., Woodring, J.: Jitter-free co-processing on a prototype exascale storage stack. In: 2012 IEEE 28th Symposium on Mass Storage Systems and Technologies (MSST), pp. 1–5. IEEE (2012)

10. Bu, Y., Howe, B., Balazinska, M., Ernst, M.D.: Haloop: efficient iterative data processing on large clusters. Int. J. Very Large Databases **3**(1–2), 285–296 (2010)

11. Carbone, P., Katsifodimos, A., Ewen, S., Markl, V., Haridi, S., Tzoumas, K.: Apache flink: stream and batch processing in a single engine. Bull. IEEE Comput. Soc. Tech. Comm. Data Eng. **36**(4), 28–38 (2015)

12. Chaimov, N., Malony, A., Canon, S., Iancu, C., Ibrahim, K.Z., Srinivasan, J.: Scaling Spark on HPC systems. In: Proceedings of the 25th ACM International Symposium on High-Performance Parallel and Distributed Computing, pp. 97–110. ACM (2016)

13. Dean, J., Ghemawat, S.: MapReduce: simplified data processing on large clusters. Commun. ACM **51**(1), 107–113 (2008)

14. Donovan, S., Huizenga, G., Hutton, A.J., Ross, C.C., Petersen, M.K., Schwan, P.: Lustre: building a file system for 1000-node clusters (2003)

15. Dorier, M., Antoniu, G., Cappello, F., Snir, M., Sisneros, R., Yildiz, O., Ibrahim, S., Peterka, T., Orf, L.: Damaris: addressing performance variability in data management for post-petascale simulations. ACM Trans. Parallel Comput. (TOPC) **3**(3), 15 (2016)

16. Dorier, M., Antoniu, G., Ross, R., Kimpe, D., Ibrahim, S.: CALCioM: mitigating I/O interference in HPC systems through cross-application coordination. In: Proceedings of the IEEE International Parallel and Distributed Processing Symposium (IPDPS 2014), Phoenix, AZ, USA, May 2014. http://hal.inria.fr/hal-00916091

17. Fox, G., Qiu, J., Jha, S., Ekanayake, S., Kamburugamuve, S.: Big data, simulations and HPC convergence. In: Rabl, T., Nambiar, R., Baru, C., Bhandarkar, M., Poess, M., Pyne, S. (eds.) WBDB -2015. LNCS, vol. 10044, pp. 3–17. Springer, Cham (2016). https://doi.org/10.1007/978-3-319-49748-8_1

18. Gainaru, A., Aupy, G., Benoit, A., Cappello, F., Robert, Y., Snir, M.: Scheduling the I/O of HPC applications under congestion. In: International Parallel and Distributed Processing Symposium, pp. 1013–1022. IEEE (2015)

19. Guo, Y., Bland, W., Balaji, P., Zhou, X.: Fault tolerant MapReduce-MPI for HPC clusters. In: Proceedings of the International Conference for High Performance Computing, Networking, Storage and Analysis, p. 34. ACM (2015)

20. Isard, M., Budiu, M., Yu, Y., Birrell, A., Fetterly, D.: Dryad: distributed data-parallel programs from sequential building blocks. In: Special Interest Group on Operating Systems Review, vol. 41, pp. 59–72. ACM (2007)

21. Islam, N.S., Wasi-ur Rahman, M., Lu, X., Panda, D.K.: High performance design for HDFS with byte-addressability of NVM and RDMA. In: Proceedings of the 2016 International Conference on Supercomputing, p. 8. ACM (2016)

22. Jégou, Y., Lantéri, S., Leduc, J., Melab, N., Mornet, G., Namyst, R., Primet, P., Quetier, B., Richard, O., Talbi, E.G., Iréa, T.: Grid'5000: a large scale and highly reconfigurable experimental grid testbed. Int. J. High Perform. Comput. Appl. **20**(4), 481–494 (2006)

23. Jin, H., Ibrahim, S., Qi, L., Cao, H., Wu, S., Shi, X.: The MapReduce programming model and implementations. In: Buyya, R., Broberg, J., Goscinski, A. (eds.) Cloud Computing: Principles and Paradigms, pp. 373–390. Wiley, New York (2011)

24. Li, Z., Shen, H.: Designing a hybrid scale-up/out hadoop architecture based on performance measurements for high application performance. In: 2015 44th International Conference on Parallel Processing (ICPP), pp. 21–30. IEEE (2015)

25. Lofstead, J., Zheng, F., Liu, Q., Klasky, S., Oldfield, R., Kordenbrock, T., Schwan, K., Wolf, M.: Managing variability in the I/O performance of petascale storage systems. In: International Conference for High Performance Computing, Networking, Storage and Analysis, pp. 1–12. IEEE (2010)

26. Lopez, I.: IDC talks convergence in high performance data analysis (2013). https://www.datanami.com/2013/06/19/idc_talks_convergence_in_high_performance_data_analysis/

27. Ross, R.B., Thakur, R., et al.: PVFS: a parallel file system for Linux clusters. In: Annual Linux Showcase and Conference, pp. 391–430 (2000)

28. Sato, K., Mohror, K., Moody, A., Gamblin, T., de Supinski, B.R., Maruyama, N., Matsuoka, S.: A user-level infiniband-based file system and checkpoint strategy for burst buffers. In: 2014 14th IEEE/ACM International Symposium on Cluster, Cloud and Grid Computing (CCGrid), pp. 21–30. IEEE (2014)

29. Shan, H., Shalf, J.: Using IOR to analyze the I/O performance for HPC platforms. In: Cray User Group Conference 2007, Seattle, WA, USA (2007)

30. Tantisiriroj, W., Patil, S., Gibson, G.: Data-intensive file systems for internet services: a rose by any other name. Parallel Data Laboratory, Technical report UCB/EECS-2008-99 (2008)

31. Tous, R., Gounaris, A., Tripiana, C., Torres, J., Girona, S., Ayguadé, E., Labarta, J., Becerra, Y., Carrera, D., Valero, M.: Spark deployment and performance evaluation on the MareNostrum supercomputer. In: 2015 IEEE International Conference on Big Data (Big Data), pp. 299–306. IEEE (2015)

32. Wang, Y., Goldstone, R., Yu, W., Wang, T.: Characterization and optimization of memory-resident MapReduce on HPC systems. In: 2014 IEEE 28th International Parallel and Distributed Processing Symposium, pp. 799–808. IEEE (2014)

33. Yildiz, O., Dorier, M., Ibrahim, S., Ross, R., Antoniu, G.: On the root causes of cross-application I/O interference in HPC storage systems. In: IPDPS-International Parallel and Distributed Processing Symposium (2016)

34. Yildiz, O., Zhou, A.C., Ibrahim, S.: Eley: on the effectiveness of burst buffers for big data processing in HPC systems. In: 2017 IEEE International Conference on Cluster Computing (CLUSTER), pp. 87–91, September 2017

35. Zaharia, M., Borthakur, D., Sen Sarma, J., Elmeleegy, K., Shenker, S., Stoica, I.: Delay scheduling: a simple technique for achieving locality and fairness in cluster scheduling. In: Proceedings of the 5th European Conference on Computer Systems, pp. 265–278. ACM (2010)

36. Zaharia, M., Chowdhury, M., Franklin, M.J., Shenker, S., Stoica, I.: Spark: cluster computing with working sets. In: HotCloud 2010, p. 10 (2010)

Experiences of Converging Big Data Analytics Frameworks with High Performance Computing Systems

Peng Cheng[1,2]([✉]), Yutong Lu[3], Yunfei Du[3], and Zhiguang Chen[1,2]

[1] College of Computer, National University of Defense Technology,
Changsha, China
peng_cheng_13@163.com
[2] State Key Laboratory of High Performance Computing, Changsha, China
[3] National Supercomputer Center in Guangzhou (NSCC-GZ),
Guangzhou, China

Abstract. With the rapid development of big data analytics frameworks, many existing high performance computing (HPC) facilities are evolving new capabilities to support big data analytics workloads. However, due to the different workload characteristics and optimization objectives of system architectures, migrating data-intensive applications to HPC systems that are geared for traditional compute-intensive applications presents a new challenge. In this paper, we address a critical question on how to accelerate complex application that contains both data-intensive and compute-intensive workloads on the Tianhe-2 system by deploying an in-memory file system as data access middleware; we characterize the impact of storage architecture on data-intensive MapReduce workloads when using Lustre as the underlying file system. Based on our characterization and findings of the performance behaviors, we propose shared map output shuffle strategy and file metadata cache layer to alleviate the impact of metadata bottleneck. The evaluation of these optimization techniques shows up to 17% performance benefit for data-intensive workloads.

Keywords: High performance computing · Big data · Convergence
File system · Hadoop

1 Introduction

The strong need for increased computational performance has led to the rapid development of high-performance computing (HPC) systems, including Sunway TaihuLight [1], Tianhe-2 [2], Titan [3], etc. These HPC systems provide an indispensable computing infrastructure for scientific and engineering modeling and simulations [4–6]. While HPC systems mostly focus on large computational workloads, the emerging big data analytics frameworks target applications that need to handle very large and complex data sets on commodity machines. Hadoop MapReduce [7] and Spark [8] are the most commonly used frameworks for distributed large-scale data processing and gained wide success in many fields over the past few years.

© The Author(s) 2018
R. Yokota and W. Wu (Eds.): SCFA 2018, LNCS 10776, pp. 90–106, 2018.
https://doi.org/10.1007/978-3-319-69953-0_6

Recently, many researchers have predicted the trend of converging HPC and big data analytics frameworks to address the requirements of complex applications that contains both compute-intensive and data-intensive workloads [9, 10]. The motivation behind this converging trend is twofold. Firstly, traditional data analytics applications need to process more data in given time, but the dynamics of the network environment and cloud services result in a performance bottleneck. Compared with normal machines, HPC systems that equipped with better hardware and high performance network can provide much higher capacity. Secondly, scientific applications are more complex to fully utilize the computing capacity of the HPC systems and the high resolution data from advanced sensors. For example, in the NASA Center for Climate Simulation (NCCS), climate and weather simulations can create a few terabytes of simulation data [11]. To visualize the data of interesting events such as hurricane center and thunderstorms, part of these data need to be processed by a visualization tool under Hadoop environment. These complex applications contain both compute-intensive and data-intensive jobs and need to be processed in HPC environment.

However, the converging trend presents a new challenge when data-intensive applications migrate to HPC systems that are geared for traditional compute-intensive applications, mainly due to the different workload characteristics and optimization objectives.

System architectures are designed to best support the typical workloads running on the clusters. Traditional HPC systems are invented to solve compute-intensive work-loads, such as scientific simulation, with the optimization goal of providing maximum computational density and local bandwidth for given power/cost constraint. In contrast, big data analytics systems aim to solve data-intensive workloads with the optimization goal of providing maximum data capacity and global bandwidth for given power/cost constraint. Consequently, big data analytics systems are different to HPC systems, as shown in Fig. 1.

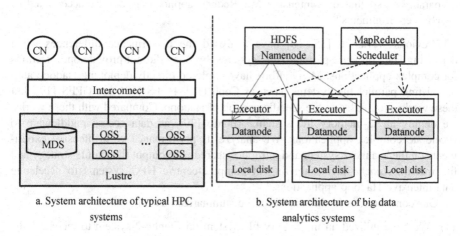

a. System architecture of typical HPC systems

b. System architecture of big data analytics systems

Fig. 1. System architecture comparison

Typical HPC systems consist of a large collection of compute nodes (CN), which are connected through high-speed, low-latency interconnects (such as InfiniBand [12]). Parallel file system (e.g. Lustre [13]) on top of disk array are used for persistent data storage. In most HPC systems, the compute node is diskless and performs well for compute-intensive workloads with high ratios of compute to data access. Parallel file systems simplify data sharing between compute nodes, but its performance is bottlenecked by metadata operations and fails to provide spatial data locality for computation tasks.

Big data processing frameworks like Hadoop and Spark utilize low-cost commodity machines to solve data-intensive problems, where each machine co-locate processing unit and local disks together. Hadoop distributed file system (HDFS [14]) is built on top of these local disks to provide the ability of persistent storage. Computation tasks are launched on physical machines where the data locality of required data can be leveraged maximally.

On the one hand, these distinctions between HPC and big data analytics systems have significant performance implications for different types of application workloads. On the other hand, the converging trend of HPC and big data is imperative and provides a lot of chance for researchers to make their attempt.

In this paper, we try to figure out three problems:

1. How to accelerate the complex application that contains both simulation and analytics jobs? The output data of HPC workloads are stored in parallel file systems, while traditional big data analytics frameworks rely on HDFS to read or write data. Hence, it is highly desirable to utilize a middleware that allows applications to access data stored in different data source without redundant data movement.
2. What is the impact of using Lustre parallel file system as the underlying file system of big data analytics frameworks since compute nodes in most HPC systems are diskless?
3. How to reconcile and converge the architectural differences between the two paradigms so that data-intensive MapReduce applications can be accelerated in HPC environments?

Previous works in [15, 16] have analyzed the performance differences when deploying Hadoop and Spark on HPC systems, but they did not provide optimizations for complex applications. Many efforts have explored directly deploying Hadoop atop of existing parallel file systems, such as Ceph [17], PVFS [18] and GPFS [19], but these works are limited to the specific version of Hadoop. Compared with these works, we deploy an in-memory file system, Alluxio [20], as data access middleware to accelerate complex applications. We analyze its performance with intensive experiments on the Tianhe-2 system and introduce shared map output file shuffle strategy and file metadata cache layer targeting at compute-centric HPC systems to accelerate data-intensive Hadoop applications.

Our contributions in this paper can be summarized as follows.

(1) We have utilized an in-memory file system on Tianhe-2 system to reconcile the architectural differences and accelerate complex applications.
(2) We have evaluated the feasibility and performance impacts of in-memory file system through different workloads.

(3) We proposed advanced acceleration techniques, including shared map output file shuffle strategy and file metadata cache layer, to accelerate data-intensive MapReduce applications on HPC systems.

Section 2 gives a brief background of this paper. Section 3 explore the feasibility of data access middleware and analyze the performance impact. We propose our design of shared map output file shuffle strategy and file metadata cache layer in Sect. 4. Section 5 provides some related studies currently existing in the literature. We conclude the paper and talk about the future work in Sect. 6.

2 Background

In this section, we give a direct comparison between HDFS and Lustre file system and review the design of Alluxio.

2.1 HDFS vs Lustre

HDFS and Lustre file system is the representative underlying file system for big data analytics frameworks and HPC applications, respectively. Table 1 summarizes their key differences.

Table 1. Comparison between HDFS and Lustre

	POSIX compliant	Access model	Data locality information
HDFS	No	Write once read many	Yes
Lustre	Yes	Many write many read	No

HDFS is a distributed file system designed to run on commodity hardware. HDFS has a master/slave architecture, the namenode is the master that manages the file system namespace and regulates access to files by clients, datanodes are the slaves that stores data blocks and are responsible for serving read and write requests from the file system's clients. HDFS is highly fault tolerant since every data block is replicated three times by default to minimize the impact of a data center catastrophe. All the data block info are stored in the master node, which allow the computation tasks to launch on physical machines where the data locality of required data can be leveraged maximally. Because of the nature of big data analytics workloads that most data won't be modified once it is generated, HDFS relaxes consistency and provide a write once read many access model to improve file access concurrency.

Lustre is a POSIX-compliant, open-source distributed parallel file system, and is deployed in most modern HPC clusters due to the extremely scalable architecture. Lustre is composed of three components: metadata servers (MDSs) manage file metadata, such as file names, directory structures, and access permissions. Object storage servers (OSSs) expose block devices and serves data. The clients issue the I/O requests. To access a file, a client must send a request to MDS first to get the file metadata, including file attributes, file permissions, and the layout of file objects in the form of extended attributes (EA). With the EA, the client can communicate with corresponding OSSs to get the file data.

2.2 Alluxio

Due to the growing I/O bandwidth gap between main memory and disk, the storage layer became the bottleneck that limits the application scalability. To alleviate the storage pressure, a variety of in-memory file systems that act as a fast, distributed cache are developed to enhance I/O performance [21–23].

Alluxio is an open source memory speed virtual distributed storage system that sits between the underlying storage systems and processing framework layers. It has the same architecture as HDFS where a master is primarily responsible for managing the global metadata of the system. Alluxio workers store data as blocks in local resources. These resources could be local memory, SSD, or hard disk and are user configurable. Alluxio provides Hadoop API, Java API and POSIX interface for user applications and computation frameworks while it can connect with different underlying storage systems such as Amazon S3, Apache HDFS through encapsulated adapters. Because of the memory-centric design and the outstanding compatibility with different computation frameworks and storage systems, Alluxio plays an important role in the big data ecosystem.

We choose Alluxio as data access middleware to converge big data analytics frameworks with HPC systems because of the compatibility to different kinds of underlying file system and the POSIX-compliant interface it provides.

3 Experiment and Analysis

To explore an efficient way of accelerating complex applications on HPC systems and analyze the performance impact of different architecture between big data analytics and HPC, we use three benchmarks to cover the performance space: (1) IOZone benchmark [24] and Mdtest benchmark [25] tests the basic file system performance of HDFS and Lustre; (2) HiBench benchmark [26] evaluates the efficiency of big data analytics frameworks through micro workloads, machine learning workloads, etc. (3) Simulation of complex applications where RandomWriter simulates HPC workload and generates 10 GB data per node, Sorter simulates data analytic workload that analyzes the output data of RandomWriter in Hadoop environment.

3.1 Experiment Setup

We used 64 nodes to conduct our experiments on the data analytics cluster of the Tianhe-2 system at national supercomputer center in Guangzhou (NSCC-GZ), where each node is equipped with two 2.20 GHz Intel Xeon E5-2692 processors (24 cores per node) and 64 GB of RAM. We allocate 32 GB RAM for MapReduce jobs and reserve 32 GB for ramdisk. Besides, there is one HDD of 1 TB storage space mounted on each node as the local disk. All nodes run Linux 3.10.0 kernels and are connected via Tianhe high performance interconnects.

We used 32 nodes to simulate the typical data analytics environment where HDFS is set on top of the local disk. Spark-2.1.0, Hadoop-2.7.3 and Oracle Java 1.8.0 are used. The HDFS block size is set to 128 MB.

Another 32 nodes are used to simulate the typical HPC environment. We did not utilize the local disk as underlying storage but mounted Lustre file system on these nodes. In our test environments, the mounted Lustre file system contains 48 OSTs. To enable Hadoop and Spark to read/write data from/to Lustre, we deployed Alluxio-1.4.0 on these nodes.

As mentioned, we evaluate IOZone, Mdtest, HiBench benchmark and a simulated complex application on HPC and data analytics environment, where the underlying file system is Lustre and HDFS respectively. Each benchmark has been executed at least three times and we report the mean performance.

3.2   Data Access Middleware

As discussed in the introduction, the converging trend of big data analytics and HPC is imperative, it's important to give a feasible solution that can allow Hadoop or Spark to access data stored in Lustre. A straightforward way to use Hadoop or Spark in HPC environment is to copy data from Lustre to HDFS. However, this will result in tremendous data movement cost and is a waste of storage space.

After considering these issues, we deploy Alluxio in HPC systems and compare its performance against Hadoop adapter for Lustre (HAL) [27]. HAL, which is developed by the Intel high performance data division, is used to make Hadoop work on Lustre, instead of HDFS, without any Lustre changes. HAL modifies Hadoop's built-in LocalFileSystem class to add the Lustre file system support by extending and over-riding default file system behavior. Moreover, HAL optimizes the shuffle strategy by avoiding repetitive data movements. In the default implementation of Hadoop shuffle strategy, reduce tasks send the data fetch requests to remote servers which in turn retrieve the data from their local directories and send them back across the network. Because of Lustre can provide a shared file system view for reduce tasks, default shuffle strategy will result in repetitive data movements, HAL reimplements the shuffle phase so that each reduce task can accesses Lustre to retrieve the data written by remote nodes directly.

HAL is packaged as a single Java library, Hadoop and Spark applications can access Lustre without modifying their code after HAL library is added to the Hadoop classpath and the configuration files are updated. What's important for users to know is that HAL-Lustre is not compatible with HDFS, which means the applications can access only Lustre file system after changing the configuration files. Besides, HAL cannot provide data locality information for map/reduce tasks.

We allocate 20 GB ramdisk for Alluxio worker to store data blocks on each node. Alluxio acts as an in-memory HDFS while communicating with different underlying storage systems like S3 or Lustre simultaneously. Compared with HAL, Alluxio provides data locality information if data were stored in Alluxio worker. Moreover, it allows the applications to access HDFS or Lustre file system by mounting them to Alluxio namespace without modifying configuration files.

We compare the performance of HAL and Alluxio via HiBench benchmark. All input data are stored in Lustre and we run each workload in data analytics environment where each node can write the intermediate data to local disk. We did not use the shuffle strategy implemented in HAL because of the existence of local disk. Figure 2 shows the performance comparison of different data access strategy where hdfs-put means copy data from Lustre to HDFS before running the workload, hadoop-hdfs represents Hadoop workload read input data from HDFS and hadoop-alluxio represents Hadoop workload read input data from Lustre directly via Alluxio by such analogy. All the intermediate data are stored in the local disk. Obviously, both Alluxio and HAL provide an efficient way for Hadoop and Spark workloads to read data stored in Lustre without redundant data movement.

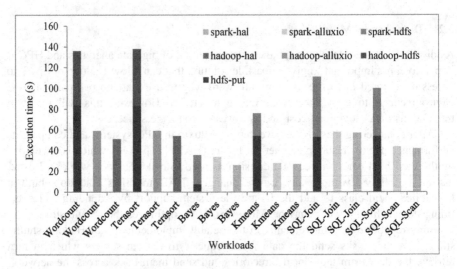

Fig. 2. HiBench benchmark performance

It is worth mentioning that Hadoop/Sprak over HAL run faster than over Alluxio. The reason behind this phenomenon is that Alluxio provides HDFS view for user application which in turn makes a more complicated data access process than HAL. In Fig. 3, to access a file that stored in underlying file system, a client requests the Alluxio master to get file metadata. After receiving the metadata request, the master will create an inode object and generate file metadata in HDFS metadata format according to the information from underlying file system and sent back to the client. According to the metadata, the client will construct the underlying file system info and sent to Alluxio worker if the file is not stored in Alluxio and the block locations info is null. After receiving the data requests from the client, Alluxio worker will create a packet reader and act as a client of underlying file system to read file data and sent them back. Data access in HAL is much simpler because each client sent data access request to underlying Lustre file system directly without providing HDFS function for user application.

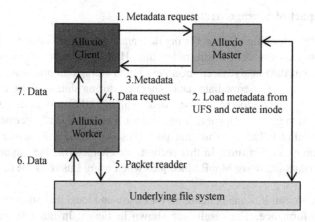

Fig. 3. Reading a file stored in underlying file system in Alluxio

Although the data access performance of HAL is better, Alluxio can provide a memory-centric distributed storage space and is compatible with different underlying file system simultaneously. We believe that Alluxio is a better choice for complicated applications. To validate our assumption, we define a complex application that consists of RandomWriter and Sorter. RandomWriter simulates HPC workload, which is executed in HPC environment and generates 10 GB data per node. Sorter simulates data analytic workload that analyzes the output data of RandomWriter in Hadoop environment. The results are shown in Fig. 4. We scale the number of nodes from 1 to 32, RandomWriter-HAL indicates that RandomWriter writes data into Lustre and Sort-HAL read data from Lustre via HAL. RandomWriter-Alluxio represents the output data of RandomWriter are stored in Alluxio and Sort-Alluxio can read data from Alluxio directly. Obviously, Sort-Alluxio spent less time than Sort-HAL since the output data are stored in memory and can be accessed directly while Sort-HAL needs to read data from underlying Lustre file system.

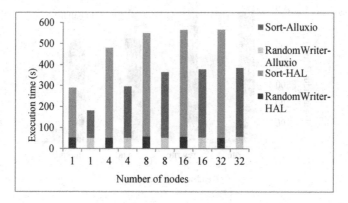

Fig. 4. Simulation of complex application

3.3   The Impact of Storage Architecture

Alluxio provides a feasible solution for big data analytics frameworks like Hadoop and Spark to access data stored in Lustre rather than HDFS. However, the key distinction between HPC and data analytics environment is the storage architecture. In data analytics environment, the intermediate data generated during shuffle phase can be stored in the local file system on top of the local disk, while in HPC environments, these data need to be stored in underlying parallel file system. The location of intermediate data is a critical factor that influences shuffling performance, which will further dominate a MapReduce job execution time. In this section, we characterize the impact of storage architecture on data-intensive MapReduce jobs when using Lustre as the underlying file system.

First of all, we run IOZone benchmark on Lustre and local disk to analyze the basic file system performance. The results are shown in Fig. 5: In our test environments, Lustre provides a much higher read or write bandwidth than local disk because files stored in Lustre are broken into stripes, which are typically stored on multiple object storage targets (OSTs), allowing parallel read and write access to different parts of the file. In contrast, the bandwidth of local disk is limited and may become the bottleneck of HDFS that build on it.

Secondly, to investigate the influence of metadata latency, we run Mdtest benchmark, a MPI-coordinated metadata benchmark that performs open/stat/close operations on files and directories and then reports the performance. Figure 6 shows the result of Mdtest, local file system performs much better than Lustre as expected. Local file system can perform 32397 file create operations and 240534 file read operations per second while Lustre can perform only 880 file create operations and 1578 file read operations per second. Lustre file system uses a limited number of MDSs to manage the file metadata, the centralized metadata management is a potential bottleneck and will result in serious performance loss when gigantic metadata requests need to be processed during shuffle phase.

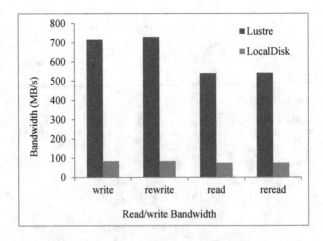

Fig. 5. IOZone benchmark performance

To validate the speculation, we run the terasort workload of HiBench benchmark in both HPC and data analytics environment where the intermediate data are stored in Lustre file system and local disk respectively. During the evaluation, terasort workload reads the input data from Lustre via HAL or Alluxio and writes the output back to Lustre, the generated intermediate data size is equal to the input size. Figure 7 illustrates the performance of terasort when intermediate data resides in different storage architectures. HAL-Local disk means that terasort workload read data from Lustre via HAL and stored intermediate data in local disk, while HAL-Lustre means intermediate data are stored in Lustre. In general, as data size grows, Lustre-based intermediate data storage results in serious performance loss and HAL-Lustre performs even worse than Alluxio-Lustre. The reason of performance differences can be ascribed to the characteristic of shuffle phase and the metadata operation bottleneck of Lustre.

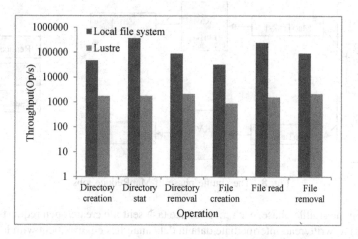

Fig. 6. Metadata operation throughput of Lustre and local file system

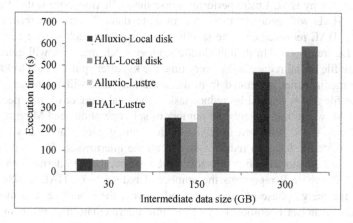

Fig. 7. Impact of intermediate data location

The shuffle phase of MapReduce jobs is shown in Fig. 8: (1) each map task is assigned a portion of the input file and applies the user-defined map function on each key-value pair. The processed key-value data are stored in a memory buffer named kvbuffer first and will be spill to the intermediate data directory every time the available space of kvbuffer is less than 20%. These spill files will be sorted and merged into one output file before each map task finished. (2) Reduce tasks starts fetching these intermediate data that stored in local disk form each node after all map tasks finished. These data from different map output files are sorted and merged again to generate one final input data for each reduce task. Overall, the shuffle phase contains gigantic file create and read/write operations and is sensitive to network latency and disk bandwidth.

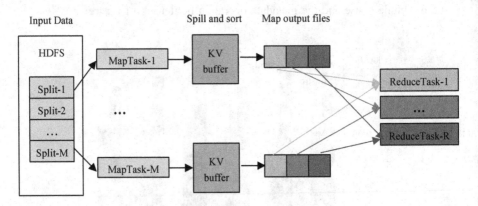

Fig. 8. The shuffle phase of MapReduce jobs

During the shuffle phase, each map/reduce task sent file create/open requests to local file system to write/read intermediate data in data analytics environment with local disk, and its performance is subject to network latency and disk latency. In HPC environment, however, these requests will be sent to the underlying parallel file system, and its performance is subject to metadata latency along with network latency and disk latency.

The reason why HAL-Lustre performs worse than Alluxio-Lustre is that the shuffle strategy in HAL will generate more intermediate data. To prevent repetitive data movements, HAL reimplements the shuffle phase to allow each reduce task retrieve data from Lustre directly. In default shuffle strategy, each map task will generate one intermediate file for all reduce tasks every time the kvbuffer spill the data to local disk. These intermediate files generated from the same map task will be merged into one final output file and is fetched by reduce tasks. The total number of intermediate files will be n * M, where n represents the number of spill operations and M represents the number of map tasks. However, in HAL shuffle strategy, each map task will generate one intermediate file for each reduce task and all the intermediate files that belong to one reduce task are stored in one directory. The total number of intermediate files will be n * M * R, where R represents the number of reduce tasks. HAL shuffle strategy can avoid the merge phase of map tasks and prevent the repetitive data movements cost, but the metadata operation cost to gigantic intermediate files result in the performance loss.

In summary, when using Lustre as the underlying file system of big data analytics frameworks, Lustre can provide higher aggregate bandwidth than traditional HDFS that build on top of the local disk, but the costly metadata operation may result in serious performance loss if massive intermediate data were stored in Lustre.

4 Optimization and Evaluation

To support data analytics frameworks on compute-centric HPC systems effectively, there are two performance issues that need to be addressed based on the characterization of Sect. 3.3. Firstly, the total number of intermediate files that generated in shuffle phase need to be reduced. Secondly, the costly metadata operations need to be accelerated. Accordingly, we propose two optimizations: shared map output shuffle strategy and file metadata cache layer.

4.1 Shared Map Output Shuffle Strategy

Shared map output shuffle strategy is intended to reduce the total number of intermediate files while utilizing the shared file system view provided by Lustre. The design of this shuffle strategy is shown in Fig. 9.

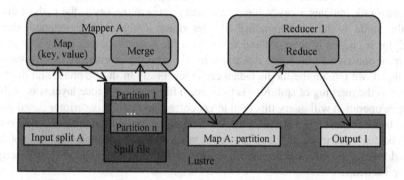

Fig. 9. Shared map output shuffle strategy

Firstly, each map task generates one intermediate file every time the kvbuffer spill the data to underlying Lustre file system. Each spill file contains multiple partitions and every partition stores the data that corresponding to one reduce task. Secondly, all the spill files generated by each map task are retrieved and sorted. Due to the effect of large memory space in a compute node, it is likely that those spill files still reside in local memory and can be retrieved quickly. Finally, the sorted map output data are stored in multiple intermediate files where each intermediate file contains the data that belongs to one reduce task. In other words, each map task generates R intermediate files no matter how many spill operations it went through, where R is the number of reduce tasks. The intermediate files that will be processed by the same reduce task are stored in the same directory.

The proposed shuffle strategy has several advantages: (1) It can utilize the effect of large memory space in a compute node and reduce the time of retrieving spill files. (2) Compared with the shuffle strategy of HAL described in Sect. 3.3, the proposed shuffle strategy can reduce the total number of intermediate files form n * M * R to M * R, where n represents the number of spill operations, M represents the number of map tasks and R represents the number of reduce tasks. Therefore, the number of costly metadata operations can be reduced. (3) Compared with default shuffle strategy, each reduce task can fetch the map output files from the corresponding directory via Lustre directly without repetitive data movements cost.

4.2 File Metadata Cache Layer

We introduce file metadata cache layer to facilitate metadata operations. During the shuffle phase, each map task creates multiple segments to fetch data partition by partition, where a segment represents a partition of a spill file. The spill file will be opened every time a segment is created and closed after each segment is closed. As a result, each spill file will be opened and read multiple times. In data analytics environments, file open and read requests can be processed quickly, while in HPC systems that deployed a parallel file system, these requests would take more time because of the centralized metadata bottleneck.

To alleviate the stress of metadata server, we implement a file metadata cache layer. Each map task initiates a key-value data structure, where the key is the path of the file and the value is the corresponding file descriptor. Once a file is opened, the file descriptor is cached in the pool and subsequent file open requests can retrieve the file descriptor and create a new file input stream. To keep the original file read operations unchanged, we initiate the file metadata cache layer only in shuffle phase and disable it as soon as the merging of spill files is finished. If file metadata cache layer was enabled, file open operation will query this pool to get corresponding file descriptor based on file name. If the response is not null, a new file input stream will be created based on the retrieved file descriptor. If the response is null, which means this file has not been opened before, this file will be opened via Java FileInputStream and the file descriptor will be cached.

In the current implementation, the capacity of the key-value data structure is set to 20 based on experiments. Besides, we use the first in first out (FIFO) eviction policies to solve capacity conflicts.

4.3 Evaluation

To validate the effectiveness of our proposed optimizations, we run the terasort workload of HiBench benchmark in the HPC environment, and the results are shown in Fig. 10. Default strategy represents the default shuffle strategy of Hadoop. HAL represents the original HAL shuffle strategy without optimizations. Shared shuffle represents the proposed shared map output shuffle strategy and file metadata cache represents using file metadata cache layer with shared map output shuffle strategy together. We vary the data size from 300 GB to 1500 GB and all the intermediate data are stored in Lustre file system.

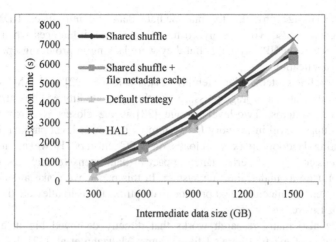

Fig. 10. Performance of HiBench-Terasort

When intermediate data size is less than 1200 GB, the default shuffle strategy performs the best since the data server that serves the requests of reduce tasks can fetch the intermediate data from local memory due to the effect of large buffer cache in a compute node. As intermediate data size grows, the memory space of compute node is insufficient to store all the intermediate data, data servers need to fetch data from Lustre and sent them back to reduce tasks. The repetitive data movement cost in default shuffle strategy results in the performance loss.

In contrast, our proposed optimizations allow reduce tasks to fetch data from underlying Lustre file system directly without repetitive data movement cost. Moreover, it reduces the total number of intermediate files and shows obvious performance benefit compared to original HAL shuffle strategy. For 1500 GB data size, shared map output shuffle strategy has a performance benefit of 11% compared to HAL and it can provide 17% benefit when file metadata cache layer is used together.

5 Related Work

In recent years, big data analytics has gained great success in different fields. Previous work [9, 28–30] has identified and analyzed the characteristic of bid data and discussed the big data challenges, including data storage and transfer, data security, scalability of data analytics systems etc.

Many efforts have been conducted to integrate big data analytics frameworks with HPC infrastructure. Chaimov et al. [15] ported Spark on Cray XC systems and evaluate a configuration with SSDs attached closer to compute nodes for I/O acceleration. Wang et al. [16] characterizes the performance impact of key differences between compute-centric and data-centric paradigms and then provides optimizations to enable a dual-purpose HPC system that can efficiently support conventional HPC applications and new data analytics applications. Wasi-ur-Rahman et al. [31] proposed a high-performance design for running YARN MapReduce on HPC clusters by utilizing

Lustre as the storage provider for intermediate data and introduced RDMA-based shuffle approach. These works analyzed the performance differences when deployed Hadoop and Spark on HPC systems, but they were lacking in providing optimizations for complex applications.

In-memory file systems like MemFS [21], FusionFS [22] and AMFS [23] are developed to alleviate the storage pressure, but they provide limited compatibility with underlying file systems. Two-level storage [32] is the closest research work that integrates an upper-level in-memory file system with a lower-level parallel file system for accelerating Hadoop/Spark workloads on HPC clusters. However, it lacks an in-depth discussion on the performance impact of data-intensive analytics workloads when using Lustre as underlying file system. In this paper, we make a detailed comparison of system architectures and provide two optimizations to alleviate the metadata bottleneck of Lustre.

There are also many research works that directly deployed big data analytics frameworks atop of existing parallel file systems. Maltzahn et al. [17] describe Ceph and its elements and provide instructions for installing a demonstration system that can be used with Hadoop. Yang et al. [18] propose PortHadoop, an enhanced Hadoop architecture that enables MapReduce applications reading data directly from HPC parallel file systems. Xuan et al. [32] present a two-level storage system that integrates an upper-level in-memory file system with a lower-level parallel file system. Comparing with previous works, this paper presents our experiences of converging big data analytics frameworks with the Tianhe-2 system. We aim at the growing need of complex applications and provide a feasible solution to accelerate it by utilizing an in-memory file system.

6 Conclusion

In this paper, we deployed an in-memory file system as data access middleware to reconcile the differences of system architectures between HPC systems and big data analytics systems. We characterized the impact of storage architecture on big data analytics frameworks when using Lustre as underlying file system. The result of experiments shows that the centralized metadata management of Lustre is a potential bottleneck and can result in serious performance loss when gigantic intermediate data are stored in Lustre. To alleviate the impact of metadata bottleneck and accelerate data-intensive MapReduce applications in HPC environments, we proposed shared map output shuffle strategy and file metadata cache layer. Our results ensure up to 17% performance benefit for data-intensive workloads.

Overall, it's critical to find a solution that can accelerate complex applications under the converging trend of HPC and big data analytics. Our work provides useful experience and gives a feasible solution. In the future, we plan to investigate the performance impact of big data analytics frameworks when high-capacity NVM is equipped in compute nodes and provide better data management strategy based on the results.

Acknowledgment. This work was supported by National Nature Science Foundation of China under Grant No. U1611261 and No. 61433019, the National Key R&D Program of China 2017YFB0202201, and the Program for Guangdong Introducing Innovative and Entrepreneurial Teams under Grant No. 2016ZT06D211.

References

1. Fu, H.H., Liao, J.F., Yang, J.Z., Wang, L.N., Song, Z.Y., Huang, X.M., et al.: The Sunway TaihuLight supercomputer: system and applications. Sci. China Inf. Sci. **59**(7), 1–16 (2016)
2. Liao, X.K., Xiao, L.Q., Yang, C.Q., Lu, Y.T.: Milkyway-2 supercomputer: system and application. Front. Comput. Sci. **8**(3), 345–356 (2014)
3. Titan - Cray XK7 (2017). https://www.olcf.ornl.gov/titan/
4. Wang, F., Yang, C.Q., Du, Y.F., Chen, J., Yi, H.Z., Xu, W.X.: Optimizing Linpack benchmark on GPU-accelerated petascale supercomputer. J. Comput. Sci. Technol. **26**(5), 854–865 (2011)
5. Yang, C., Wu, Q., Tang, T., Wang, F., Xue, J.: Programming for scientific computing on peta-scale heterogeneous parallel systems. J. Cent. South Univ. **20**(5), 1189–1203 (2013)
6. French, S., Zheng, Y., Romanowicz, B., Yelick, K.: Parallel Hessian assembly for seismic waveform inversion using global updates. In: IEEE International Parallel and Distributed Processing Symposium (IPDPS), pp. 753–762. IEEE (2015)
7. Bhandarkar, M.: MapReduce programming with apache Hadoop. In: IEEE International Symposium on Parallel and Distributed Processing (IPDPS), p. 1 (2010)
8. Zaharia, M., Chowdhury, M., Das, T., Dave, A., Ma, J., Mccauley, M.: Resilient distributed datasets: a fault-tolerant abstraction for in-memory cluster computing. In: USENIX Conference on Networked Systems Design and Implementation, p. 2 (2012)
9. Kambatla, K., Kollias, G., Kumar, V., Grama, A.: Trends in big data analytics. J. Parallel Distrib. Comput. **74**(7), 2561–2573 (2014)
10. Reed, D.A., Dongarra, J.: Exascale computing and big data. Commun. ACM **58**(7), 56–68 (2015)
11. NASA Center for Climate Simulation (2017). http://www.nasa.gov/topics/earth/features/climate-sim-center.html
12. InfiniBand Homepage (2017). http://www.infinibandta.org/
13. Donovan, S., Kleen, A., Wilcox, M., Huizenga, G., Hutton, A.J.: Lustre: building a file system for 1,000-node clusters. In: Proceedings of the Linux Symposium, p. 9 (2003)
14. Shvachko, K., Kuang, H., Radia, S., Chansler, R.: The Hadoop distributed file system. In: MASS Storage Systems and Technologies, pp. 1–10 (2010)
15. Chaimov, N., Malony, A., Canon, S., Iancu, C., Ibrahim, K.Z., Srinivasan, J.: Scaling Spark on HPC systems. In: Proceedings of the 25th ACM International Symposium on High-Performance Parallel and Distributed Computing (HPDC), pp. 97–110 (2016)
16. Wang, Y., Goldstone, R., Yu, W., Wang, T.: Characterization and optimization of memory-resident MapReduce on HPC systems. In: IEEE International Symposium on Parallel and Distributed Processing (IPDPS), pp. 799–808 (2014)
17. Maltzahn, C., Molinaestolano, E., Khurana, A., Nelson, A.J., Brandt, S.A., Weil, S.: Ceph as a scalable alternative to the Hadoop distributed file system. The Magazine of USENIX and SAGE, pp. 38–49 (2010)
18. Yang, X., Liu, N., Feng, B., Sun, X.H., Zhou, S.: PortHadoop: support direct HPC data processing in Hadoop. In: IEEE International Conference on Big Data, pp. 223–232 (2015)

19. Fadika, Z., Dede, E., Govindaraju, M., Ramakrishnan, L.: MARIANE: MApReduce implementation adapted for HPC environments. In: International Conference on Grid Computing, pp. 82–89 (2011)
20. Li, H., Ghodsi, A., Zaharia, M., Shenker, S., Stoica, I.: Tachyon: reliable, memory speed storage for cluster computing frameworks. In: Proceedings of the ACM Symposium on Cloud Computing, pp. 1–15. (2014)
21. Uta, A., Sandu, A., Costache, S., Kielmann, T.: Scalable in-memory computing. In: International Symposium on Cluster, Cloud and Grid Computing, pp. 805–810 (2015)
22. Zhao, D., Zhang, Z., Zhou, X., Li, T.: FusionFS: toward supporting data-intensive scientific applications on extreme-scale high-performance computing systems. In: IEEE International Conference on Big Data, pp. 61–70 (2014)
23. Zhang, Z., Katz, D.S., Wozniak, J.M., Espinosa, A.: Design and analysis of data management in scalable parallel scripting. In: International Conference on High PERFORMANCE Computing, Networking, Storage and Analysis, pp. 1–11 (2012)
24. IOzone Filesystem Benchmark (2017). http://www.iozone.org/
25. MDTest Metadata Benchmark (2017). https://github.com/MDTEST-LANL/mdtest
26. Huang, S., Huang, J., Dai, J., Xie, T., Huang, B.: The HiBench benchmark suite: characterization of the MapReduce-based data analysis. In: International Conference on Data Engineering Workshops, pp. 41–51 (2010)
27. Hadoop Adapter for Lustre (HAL) (2017). https://github.com/intel-hpdd/lustre-connector-for-hadoop
28. Hu, H., Wen, Y., Chua, T.S., Li, X.: Toward scalable systems for big data analytics: a technology tutorial. IEEE Access 2(1), 652–687 (2017)
29. Brohi, S.N., Bamiah, M.A., Brohi, M.N.: Identifying and analyzing the transient and permanent barriers for big data. J. Eng. Sci. Technol. 11(12), 1793–1807 (2016)
30. Tolle, K.M., Tansley, D.S.W., Hey, A.J.G.: The fourth paradigm: data-intensive scientific discovery [point of view]. Proc. IEEE 99(8), 1334–1337 (2011)
31. Wasi-ur-Rahman, M., Lu, X., Islam, N.S., Rajachandrasekar, R., Panda, D.K.: High-performance design of YARN MapReduce on modern HPC clusters with Lustre and RDMA. In: IEEE International Symposium on Parallel and Distributed Processing (IPDPS), pp. 291–300 (2015)
32. Xuan, P., Ligon, W.B., Srimani, P.K., Ge, R., Luo, F.: Accelerating big data analytics on HPC clusters using two-level storage. Parallel Comput. 61, 18–34 (2016)

GPU/FPGA

MACC: An OpenACC Transpiler
for Automatic Multi-GPU Use

Kazuaki Matsumura[1,2]([✉]), Mitsuhisa Sato[3,4], Taisuke Boku[4], Artur Podobas[1],
and Satoshi Matsuoka[1,2]

[1] Tokyo Institute of Technology, Tokyo, Japan
{matsumura.k.ak,podobas.a.aa,matsu}@m.titech.ac.jp
[2] AIST-Tokyo Tech Real World Big-Data Computation
Open Innovation Laboratory, Tokyo, Japan
[3] RIKEN Advanced Institute for Computational Science, Kobe, Japan
msato@riken.jp
[4] University of Tsukuba, Tsukuba, Japan
taisuke@cs.tsukuba.ac.jp

Abstract. Graphics Processing Units (GPUs) perform the majority of
computations in state-of-the-art supercomputers. Programming these
GPUs is often assisted using a programming model such as (amongst
others) the directive-driven OpenACC. Unfortunately, OpenACC (and
other similar models) are incapable of automatically targeting and distributing work across several GPUs, which decreases productivity and
forces needless manual labor upon programmers. We propose a method
that enables OpenACC applications to target multi-GPU. Workload distribution, data transfer and inter-GPU communication (including modern GPU-to-GPU links) are automatically and transparently handled by
our compiler with no user intervention and no changes to the program
code. Our method leverages existing OpenMP and OpenACC backends,
ensuring easy integration into existing HPC infrastructure. Empirically
we quantify performance gains and losses in our data coherence method
compared to similar approaches, and also show that our approach can
compete with the performance of hand-written MPI code.

Keywords: Programming language · Compiler · Multi-GPU

1 Introduction

Graphics Processors Units (GPUs) are the workhorse of modern, state-of-the-
art, supercomputers. Each node in a supercomputer node often consists of several GPUs, each carrying its own distributed memory and each being capable
of executing asynchronously to one another. Due to GPU's high performance
and compute-to-power ratio (FLOPs/Watt), modern supercomputers such as
TSUBAME3.0 [1], DGX SATURNV [2] and the upcoming SUMMIT [3] include
multiple GPUs per supercomputing node.

Programming GPUs has historically been done through low-level programming languages (often derivatives or dialects of C) such as CUDA [4] and

© The Author(s) 2018
R. Yokota and W. Wu (Eds.): SCFA 2018, LNCS 10776, pp. 109–127, 2018.
https://doi.org/10.1007/978-3-319-69953-0_7

OpenCL [5]. Here the programmer is responsible for both creating the program code, and — in cases where multiple GPUs are involved — orchestrating the concurrent execution of multiple GPUs; an often non-trivial task.

A better (and arguably more portable) way is to use compiler directives to indicate sources of potential parallelism in the application. A compiler can then use these directives to abstract the complex architectural details away from the programmer and instead automatically generated device-specific program code. One example of such directive-driven approach is OpenACC [6] and OpenMP [7].

While models such as OpenACC increase productivity through raised programming abstraction, they are currently limited in targeting only a single GPU device. The user is still responsible for manually orchestrating the multi-GPU execution.

We propose a method to enable OpenACC-annotated applications to exploit multiple GPUs. We implemented a source-to-source compiler (*transpiler*) that analyzes and optimizes OpenACC applications. Our transpiler is *transparent* to the user— kernel scheduling, data-movement and inter-GPU communication (including the recent GPU-to-GPU links) are automatically done.

Our contributions in short:

(1) A transpiler that extends the OpenACC programming model to allow applications to seamlessly use multiple GPUs.
(2) A novel communication algorithm that preserves data coherency across GPUs by extracting source-code information.
(3) An empirical evaluation of above contributions using well-known HPC benchmark, positioning the performance against hand-written MPI code and the recent Unified Memory abstraction layer.

The remaining of this paper is organized as follows. Section 2 discusses related work. Section 3 provides an overview of OpenACC. Section 4 describes our proposed method. Section 5 describes our experimental methodology. In Sect. 6, we evaluate our transpiler. Finally, Sect. 7 concludes this paper.

2   Related Work

NVIDIA provides Unified Memory [8], which allows multiple NVIDIA GPUs to share the global address space between each other. Unified Memory recently supports coherence through the NVLink interconnect [9], and allows GPUs to effortlessly communicate between each other. Unlike Unified Memory, which is very architecture dependent, our approach is more general and oblivious of which accelerator is being targeted as long as compilers' OpenACC backend supports it. Moreover, our method is able to accelerate GPU-to-GPU communications using GPU interconnects. We also see performance benefits using our method as compared to Unified Memory in Sect. 6.

Komada et al. [10] used a compiler to distribute OpenACC fairly across GPUs and execute them in parallel. Their approach is to divide loop iterations into chunks of equal size and also keep these chunks coherent across different GPUs.

Their coherence mechanism is similar to that of Unified Memory, except that the chunk size can be changed manually by the user and the chunks are prepared for each array. Unlike Komada et al., we focus on identifying where communication needs to happen between GPUs through data-flow analysis inside the transpiler.

Rameshekar et al. [11] propose to execute parts of application (written in C) on multiple GPUs by analyzing loops using the polyhedral model. The polyhedral compilation precisely detects necessary communication between GPUs using superpositions of fine regions and a buffer management. However, their approach is only applicable to loops with affine iteration and array accesses. We (unlike Rameshekar et al.) build and extend upon OpenACC, which allows us to have more information regarding the sources of parallelism, increasing generality as long as the application uses OpenACC. However, we complement their study and show how the polyhedral compilation can enhance our method in certain cases.

HYDRA [12] is a compiler system for distributed environments that use a single GPU per node. We both share a similar system of determining communication patterns between GPUs. Unlike HYDRA, which takes as input simple directives and generates a distributed application, our method leverages OpenACC and OpenMP and hence focuses parallelism within a single "shared" node. The output of our transpiler uses both OpenACC and OpenMP, and thus can further use existing OpenACC and OpenMP profiling tools to further improve performance. In evaluation, we compare hand-written MPI code with our transpiled code.

Scogland et al. [13] combine a well-designed task-based runtime with directive-driven model to facilitate efficient work-sharing in heterogeneous systems. They provide new directives that help to identify data dependency. We consider extending our work to leverage existing task-based runtime systems to perform the load-balancing.

Xu et al. [14] present new directives to extend OpenACC to support multiple accelerators. The proposal is based on an evaluation using the hybrid model of OpenACC and OpenMP.

Accelerate [15] is a purely-functional domain-specific language for array processing. Accelerate has a potential to utilize multi-GPU [16].

Also, programming models targeting accelerator clusters are proposed [17,18]. These models provide explicit functions to distribute computations over multiple accelerators.

3 Overview of OpenACC

Introduced in 2011, OpenACC aims to bridge accelerator programmability gaps by leveraging compiler directives. Rather than programming with vendor-specific languages, the programmers instead focus on exposing available parallelism in his/her source-code. A compiler uses these directives to automatically generate device-specific application code.

3.1 Execution Model

Programmers are responsible for specifying which regions of the OpenACC application are offloaded onto accelerators. A programmer, when using OpenACC to parallelize the application, must enclose regions to-be accelerated on the device using the `parallel` and `kernels` construct. Each construct is specified by its directive.

A region enclosed by the `parallel` construct is called a *parallel region* and will be executed on an accelerator. Controlling the granularity of loops found within the parallel region is done using the `loop` construct. The `loop` construct allows various controls of computation, including collective operations (by `reduction` clause), loop-carried dependency (by `independent` or `seq` clause), coarse-grained parallelism (called `gang`), fine-grained parallelism (called `worker`), and SIMD-level parallelism (called `vector`). These granularities represent the naturally forms of parallelism found in modern accelerators.

A nested loop executed parallely on an accelerator is called *kernel*. A region enclosed by the `kernels` construct will treat each of the subsequent loops in the region as accelerator kernels.

3.2 Memory Model

Prior to execution, accelerators with local memory (often called *device memory*) must receive the data they operate on from the host. Similarly, when accelerators finish computing using some data as the result, that data must be transferred back to the host.

OpenACC allows data on the device to be explicitly controlled using the `data` construct. Any region enclosed by the `data` construct will place specified data on-to the accelerator and insert proper transfers between host and accelerator according to specified clauses. Although OpenACC can automatically deduce where to place data, using the `data` clause is often encouraged for the prevention of incomplete or inefficient data transfers. A `present` clause of the `data` construct indicates that the data already is defined in the region, to prevent duplicated data transfers.

OpenACC defines the `update` directive that allows programmers to change data shared between host and accelerator. In the case of `update`, the OpenACC runtime system can reflect the recent changes to the variable on both the accelerator and the host.

3.3 A Motivational Example

We show an example which utilizes multi-GPU. In OpenACC, several efforts are required even to distribute a simple kernel over multiple GPUs.

OpenACC Single-GPU Example. We illustrate the needless and error-prone (manual) effort of re-purposing an OpenACC application into targeting multi-GPUs using a simple vector-multiplication example, seen in Fig. 1(a). For clarity

(a) Single-GPU Use

(b) Multi-GPU Use

```
#pragma acc data\
  copyout(x[0:N]) present(y)
#pragma acc kernels
for (int i = 0; i < N; i++)
  x[i] = y[i] * y[i];
```

```
numgpus = acc_get_num_devices(DEVICE_TYPE);
#pragma omp parallel num_threads(numgpus)
{
  int tnum = omp_get_thread_num();
  int sz = N / numgpus;
  int lb = sz * tnum; int ub = lb + sz;
  acc_set_device_num(tnum, DEVICE_TYPE);
#pragma acc data copyout(x[lb:sz]) present(y)
#pragma acc kernels
  for (int i = lb; i < ub; i++)
    x[i] = y[i] * y[i];
}
```

Fig. 1. Two examples illustrating the difference in OpenACC code that targets (a) single-GPU use, and (b) multi-GPU use through mixed OpenMP/OpenACC

purposes, we leave out non-trivial optimizations such as deducing (and minimizing) inter-GPU communication and coherence; such optimizations further complicate the manual re-targeting process (which is automatically handled by our proposed transpiler).

Figure 1(a) shows OpenACC directives in for a simple vector-multiplication. The programmer — knowing that the loop is inherently parallel — annotates the region with a kernels construct and also informs the compiler that he expects the host's memory to be updated after the loop has finished (copyout). The compiler will use these directives to offload the parallelized loop onto a single device.

OpenACC Multi-GPU Example. OpenACC only provides functionality for exposing parallelism onto a single accelerator. To use multiple GPUs, the programmer must manually orchestrate the execution, distribution and data transfers between the GPUs. This includes ensuring that data are coherent between the GPUs that work on similar sets of data.

Figure 1(b) shows the earlier vector multiplication example but with manual augmentation for multi-GPU execution. Here we use OpenMP (a related directive-driven model) to launch a team of threads and have each thread computation which subset of the loop's iteration-space it should execute. Finally, each thread encounters the OpenACC directives, which each launch the kernel onto the earlier (acc_set_device_num()) specified accelerator.

We can see that there is significant effort of code rewriting between Fig. 1(a) and (b), which further motivates the need for our work. Furthermore, in case of real applications, data dependencies between multiple OpenACC kernels must be considered.

4 MACC: A OpenACC Transpiler for Multi-GPU Use

We present MACC — a transpiler that eliminates the effort of using OpenACC in multi-GPU environments. Our transpiler allows OpenACC (which traditionally targets a single GPU) to run on multiple GPUs without changing the source code. Our approach is to source-to-source transform the OpenACC application into post source-code that exploits both OpenACC and OpenMP.

The operations performed by MACC can be condensed down to three steps:

(1) The source code is parsed and OpenACC directive understood and abbreviated notation (e.g. "parallel loop", "kernels copy(..)") flattened. Tightly-nested (which has just one loop inside except for the innermost) or loop-directive-specified loops within a kernels construct are transformed to use an OpenACC parallel construct (and loop directives with the reduction clause if any collective operation is found and the independent clause if our basic checker statically finds no loop-carried dependency between iterations).
(2) Array reference expressions are extracted using our data-flow analysis (described in Subsect. 4.3) and code to dynamically find data dependencies at runtime are constructed.
(3) MACC outputs post source-code, which effectively is hybrid OpenMP and OpenACC version of the original code but capable of multi-GPU execution (described in Subsect. 4.4).

The final output can then be compiled with any compiler supporting OpenACC and OpenMP. Our compiler pass is generic and thus untied to any specific compiler backend. Host-to/from-GPU and GPU-to-GPU communication in the post source-code are automatically generated based on our communication algorithm to resolve data dependencies, leveraging shared host memory and GPU interconnects (described in Subsect. 4.2).

We have deliberately chosen to have the transpiled source-code use a hybrid OpenACC and OpenMP approach. There are no formal requirements behind using OpenMP and our methodology can be extended to use less abstract models such as POSIX Threads. However, by leveraging OpenMP we can more easily use existing infrastructure (such as) to debug or analyze the performance. Furthermore, future work of ours includes code multi-versioning to enable hybrid execution of single-/multi-GPU and general purpose processor accelerators; it is here we expect our design decision to bear fruit as OpenMP traditionally (prior to the 4.0 accelerator directives) target general purpose processors.

4.1 Execution on Multi-GPU Environments

Since OpenACC primarily target loop-level parallelism of the outermost loop, we need to make sure to avoid data dependencies on the memory accesses happening between processors executing the parallelized loop.

In MACC, we divide and distribute the outermost loop of OpenACC kernels equally for each GPU. We only enable multiple GPUs when all writes in the kernel are affine with respect to the loop counters and the write-section does not intersect with the write-section of other GPUs; we fall back on single GPU execution if the state condition does not hold. Switching between single- and multi-GPU execution occurs at runtime. Also, the number of GPUs used can dynamically be decided and changed, leaving room for autotuners.

4.2 Generating Host-to/from-GPU and GPU-to-GPU Communcation Patterns

Understanding what data-regions a GPU will work on is crucial when parallelizing loop constructs to execute over multiple GPUs. A too optimistic approach can fail to fully include all data, leading to incorrect execution; a too pessimistic approach will on the other hand lead to unnecessary transfer and maintenance overheads.

Algorithm 1. Generate copyin

1: Create DIRTY
2: **for** each gpu $i \in$ GPUs **do**
3:     Communicate specified array from Host to GPU i
4:     DIRTY[i].valid $\leftarrow$ false
5: **end for**

Identifying the data-regions needed for the GPUs is difficult because the order of kernel executions is dynamically decided. Therefore, we replicate Host-to-GPU communications according to `data` constructs (`copyin`) for all GPUs (Algorithm 1).

When multiple GPUs are used, it is important to resolve the data dependencies between the GPUs because each GPU is (often) a discrete device with its own distributed memory. We have adopted Kwon et al. [19] 's method (from distributed-memory programming) to identify the necessary communication across GPUs. Our implementation calculates the section of the read (called USE) and the write (called DEF) for each combination of parallel regions, GPUs and data (arrays). We apply data-flow analysis (described in Subsect. 4.3) to derive necessary information.

Before each execution of parallel regions, we compute the necessary communication among GPUs based on the superpositions of the calculated sections; after that, we update the section (called DIRTY) for each combination of GPUs and data/arrays. Here, we call the section whose master is a GPU, as DIRTY. Algorithm 2 describes this process.

All sections contain an upper- and a lower-bound. Communication between GPUs is performed either through host memory (CPU-to-GPU) or — if supported — using the interconnected (GPU-to-GPU or *P2P*). MACC also removes any duplicated transfers in order to reduce the amount of communication needed.

Algorithm 2. Generate communications before an execution of a parallel region

---
1: **for** each gpu $i \in$ GPUs **do**
2:     **if** DIRTY$[i] \cap$ DEF$[i] = \emptyset$ or $\exists$ d $\in$ (DEF $\setminus$ DEF$[i]$); DIRTY$[i] \cap$ d $\neq \emptyset$ **then**
3:         Communiate DIRTY$[i]$ from GPU i to Host and all other GPUs
4:         DIRTY$[i] \leftarrow \emptyset$
5:     **else if** P2P IS ENABLED **then**
6:         **for** each gpu $j \in$ GPUs; $j \neq i$ **do**
7:             COMM$[j] \leftarrow$ DIRTY$[i] \cap$ USE$[j]$
8:             Communicate COMM$[j]$ from GPU i to GPU j
9:         **end for**
10:    **else**
11:        **for** each gpu $j \in$ GPUs; $j \neq i$ **do**
12:            COMM$[j] \leftarrow$ DIRTY$[i] \cap$ USE$[j]$
13:        **end for**
14:        GHs $\leftarrow$ BIND(COMM) /* Optimize GPU-to-Host communication */
15:        Communicate GHs from GPU i to Host
16:        **if** $\exists$ gh $\in$ GHs; DIRTY$[i] \subset$ gh **then**
17:            DIRTY$[i]$.valid $\leftarrow$ false
18:        **end if**
19:        **for** each gpu $j \in$ GPUs; $j \neq i$ **do**
20:            Communiate COMM$[j]$ from Host to GPU j
21:        **end for**
22:    **end if**
23:    DIRTY$[i] \leftarrow$ DIRTY$[i] \cup$ DEF$[i]$
24: **end for**

Algorithm 3. Generate copyout

1: **for** each gpu $i \in$ GPUs **do**
2:     Communicate DIRTY$[i]$ from GPU i to Host
3: **end for**
4: Delete DIRTY

Algorithm 4. Generate update of GPU-to-Host

1: US $\leftarrow$ the update section
2: **for** each gpu $i \in$ GPUs **do**
3:     Communicate DIRTY$[i] \cap$ US from GPU i to Host
4: **end for**

When encountering GPU-to-Host communication of the data constructs (copyout), only the data constructs that fail meeting coherence are transferred. Hence, each GPU will execute a copyout transfer of its own DIRTY section (Algorithm 3).

When encountering a update directive for Host-to-GPU communication, the host will update all GPUs with the new data. If update directive for a GPU-to-Host communication is encountered, only the sections overlapping the DIRTY-section (Algorithm 4) will be transferred.

4.3 Data-Flow Analysis

MACC uses data-flow analysis to identify USE and DEF sections of parallel regions. Data-flow analysis is invoked on every parallel region to extract array references/indices for read and write accesses. Array references are composed of constants and loop iterator variables, as well as variables defined outside the parallel region. Note that MACC only synthesize the code for automatically analyzing the USE and DEF sections; the actual analysis is performed at runtime during execution before every parallel region.

During data-flow analysis, we collect array references/indices as well as extracting variables that are defined or overwritten in the parallel region. We iteratively analyze the parallel region to account for all paths of the control-flow graph as long as the collected array references/indices change (so-called Iterative Data-Flow Analysis [20]).

In MACC, we do these through the following two steps:

(1) We transform source-code into static single assignment form (SSA [20]).
(2) Array indices are collected and all variables (except the loop counter) are extracted.

A variable represented by an expression using the variable itself and other values, is considered to have indefinite value. A section that is calculated using a non-affine index, when regarding variables other than loop counters as constants, or indefinite value will force the section to pessimistically contain the whole target array. For indices that are affine we can compute the sections by substituting upper- and lower-limits of the affected loop counters into them owing to convexity.

In the final generated post source-code we execute the parallel region on multi-GPU when:

(1) all write accesses for each array are affine and definite,
(2) the outermost loop of the kernel in the parallel region is dividable (which statically-or-dynamically has an affine range and statically has no loop-carried dependency), and
(3) the write-sections are not duplicated among GPUs.

Single-GPU execution is invoked if above conditions do not hold.

4.4 Output Formats

In MACC, each OpenACC directive will be transformed to use a combination of OpenMP and OpenACC. To realize the communication generation (described in Subsect. 4.2), we wrap the existing OpenACC communication routines around our own. These wrapper maintains the DIRTY section for each the {GPU:Array} combinations and also generates the communications. We use and link-against vendor-supplied libraries (in this case NVIDIA CUDA libraries) only when P2P (GPU-to-GPU) communication is available.

The data construct and update directive are converted into corresponding concurrent versions using OpenMP's parallel construct, seen in Fig. 2(a) and (b) respectively. When transforming data-constructs, MACC will always append appropriate present clause to parallel sections within data construct in order to specify that the data are already on the GPUs.

Figure 2(c) shows how we transpile OpenACC's parallel constructs. We start by identifying the loop ranges by calculating USE and DEF sections. Once we know the loop ranges, we spawn one OpenMP thread for each GPU device. Each thread then continues to generate the needed communication based on the algorithm described in Subsect. 4.2; a barrier is inserted to synchronize all threads before entering the compute part. Finally, the parallel region is executed by all the threads and the GPU they orchestrate.

If the parallel region satisfies the conditions described in Subsect. 4.3, the outermost loop is divided and the execution is distributed to each GPU. An actual example of the transpilating is shown in Fig. 3. At section calculations,

(a) data construct

```
#pragma acc data copy(x[0:N])
{ /* ... */ }
```

```
#pragma omp parallel num_threads(NUMGPUS)
{
    copyin_routine(omp_get_thread_num(),x,0,N);
}
{ /* ... */ }
#pragma omp parallel num_threads(NUMGPUS)
{
    copyout_routine(omp_get_thread_num(),x);
}
```

(b) update directive

```
#pragma acc update host(x[a:b])
```

```
#pragma omp parallel num_threads(NUMGPUS)
{
    int tid = omp_get_thread_num();
    update_host_routine(tid, x, a, b);
}
```

(c) parallel construct

```
#pragma acc parallel
{ /* PARALLEL REGION */ }
```

```
if (/* sections are changed */)
{ /* recalculate sections */ }
#pragma omp parallel num_threads(NUMGPUS)
{
    int tnum = omp_get_thread_num();
    set_gpu_num(tnum);
    set_data_section(/* ... */);
#pragma omp barrier
#pragma acc parallel
    { /* PARALLEL REGION */ }
}
```

Fig. 2. This mapping illustrating how MACC transpiles each directive including construct (left) into combined OpenMP/OpenACC code (right)

(a) Original Code

```
#pragma acc parallel loop gang reduction (+ : sum) present(a)
for (i = X; i < Y; i++) {
  sum += a[i + p];
}                                               PARALLEL REGION
```

(b) Transpiled Code

```
{
    static int sections_are_changed = 1;
    sections_are_changed =
      (sections_are_changed || last_p != p || last_X != X || last_Y != Y);

    if (sections_are_changed) {
      section_are_changed = 0; last_p = p; last_X = X; last_Y = Y;

      calc_loop_sections(loop_sections, X, Y,
                         1 /* increment */,
                         0 /* whether to execute when X==Y */);

      init_uses(a_uses, 1 /* affine */); init_defs(a_defs, 0 /* none */);
      for (i = 0; i < NUMGPUS; i++) {
        update_section(a_uses[i], loop_sections[i].lb + p);
        update_section(a_uses[i], loop_sections[i].ub + p);
      }

      if (is_overlapping(a_defs)) {
        /* reconstruct for single GPU execution */
      }
    }
}                                               SECTION CALCULATION
```

```
#pragma omp parallel num_threads(NUMGPUS) reduction (+ : sum) private (i)
{
    int tnum = omp_get_thread_num();
    set_gpu_num(tnum);
```

```
    set_data_section(tnum, a, a_uses, a_defs);
#pragma omp barrier                             COMMUNICATION
```

```
#pragma acc parallel present(a)
#pragma acc loop gang reduction (+ : sum)
    for(i = loop_sections[tnum].lb; i <= loop_sections[tnum].ub; i++) {
      sum += a[i + p];
    }                                           PARALLEL REGION
}
```

Fig. 3. This actual example showing how OpenACC kernel is transpiled and where MACC inserts section calculation, communication and parallel region

the last result is used as long as all component values are not changed from the last calculation. Since variables defined outside the parallel region are shared among threads, our multi-GPU execution can overwrite them. As an exception, variables used as loop counters are duplicated on every thread by `private` clauses of OpenMP. Reductions are firstly calculated for each GPU by OpenACC, then the overall results are computed among threads by OpenMP's reduction clause.

4.5   Polyhedral Extension

It is important for transpilers (such as the one we present) to easily be integrated into existing tool-chains, frameworks and compilations techniques.

To show this, we show that MACC can be complemented with other techniques to further the performance benefits. One such extension we support is the *polyhedral compilation*, here materialized using PLUTO [21].

By using PLUTO prior to MACC invocation, we can automatically split OpenACC kernels through loop fission, and thus extract the parallelism that MACC can exploit over multiple GPUs by just appending the directive of the `kernels` construct.

5   Experimental Methodology

5.1   Implementation

MACC was implemented as a prototype coupled with the Omni [22] compiler's C frontend/backend using XcodeML [23]. Currently, MACC only support OpenACC applications written using the C language (and not, for example, FORTRAN). This is a minor limitation (and resolving it is more of an engineering effort), since the methods and techniques introduced in this paper is general enough to not be tied to any specific programming language.

MACC also requires that arrays copied to GPU devices are contiguous, as multidimensional arrays are converted into singledimensional arrays. The size of coarse-grain parallelism `gang` specified in input is divided for each GPU equally, and other parallelisms (`worker`, `vector`) are kept.

We evaluated the three versions of MACC: baseline which conducts GPU-to-GPU communications through shared host memory, MACC with NVIDIA Unified Memory (UM) which entrusts data coherency to UM, and MACC with P2P. We also leveraged PLUTO together with MACC where applicable (for one of the benchmarks). We compared transpiled code against the original version of the benchmark, and also against MPI + ACC versions that we prepared by appending OpenACC directives to the official MPI code.

Each benchmark was executed 10 times and we used the average to represent the performance. We report performance with respect to computational performance or execution time (OP/s, FLOP/s or seconds depending on benchmark) as well as speedup over the original version ($speedup = t_{\text{original}}/t_{\text{multi-GPU}}$).

5.2 Topology Options

MACC allows the user to specify a topology mapping, which dictates what OpenMP thread handles what GPU device. Such information can be crucial in system with non-homogeneous links between the GPU devices.

While not the primary focus of the present study, we found that by reassigning the thread-to-GPU mapping on P2P-enabled GPUs (NVIDIA's to be precise), we can get a performance increase. The topology mapping is conveyed to MACC through an environmental variable.

5.3 Environment

We evaluated the performance using a single node on the new TSUBAME3.0 supercomputer at the Global Scientific Information and Computing Center (GSIC), Tokyo Institute of Technology. A node in the TSUBAME3.0 supercomputer contains 4 NVIDIA P100 GPUs [24]. The GPUs are interconnected in an all-to-all fashion using NVLink technology; note, however, that the links are heterogeneous and different: two of the links ($GPU_0 \leftrightarrow GPU_2$, $GPU_1 \leftrightarrow GPU_3$) have 80 GB/s bidirectional bandwidth and the remaining links have 40 GB/s bidirectional bandwidth. Each TSUBAME 3 node also contain two CPUs (Intel Xeon E5-2680v4) with a total of 28 general-purpose x86-64 cores. Table 1 provides more detailed system information.

For all experiments, we used PGI Compiler version 17.10 and NVIDIA CUDA version 9.0. Inside MACC we have OpenMP threads each orchestrate individual GPU; more specifically, the mapping is as follows: {$thread_0$, GPU_0}, {$thread_1$, GPU_2}, {$thread_2$, GPU_1}, {$thread_3$, GPU_3}. Our mapping follows the heterogeneous links of the GPU interconnect.

PGI Compiler supports UM only for dynamically allocated memory. We implemented an extension in MACC to force static allocations to be dynamically allocated.

Table 1. Specifications of TSUBAME3.0

CPU	Intel Xeon E5-2680 V4 (Broadwell-EP, 14 core, 2.4GHz) × 2
CPU memory	256 GiB
GPU	NVIDIA Tesla P100 for NVLink-Optimized Servers × 4
GPU memory	16 GB HBM2@732 GB/s / GPU
OS	SUSE Linux Enterprise Server 12 SP1
Compiler	PGI Compiler 17.10
Compiler option	-O4 -fastsse -ta=tesla,cuda9.0 -acc -mp -Munsafe_par_align -Mmovnt -mcmodel=medium
CUDA	CUDA 9.0

5.4 Benchmarks

We selected four benchmarks to evaluate our transpiler.

Himeno Benchmark [25] is a benchmark which solves a 3-D Poisson's equation by Jacobi method. We created an OpenACC version of this benchmark by adding directives to the official code. In the baseline OpenACC version of code, the calculation part and the substitution part are executed on an accelerator, and they are repeated for certain time-steps. Each part consists of three loops, and they are tightly nested and have no loop-carried dependency between the iteration. The baseline code collapses three-nested loops into single loops. The loop has SIMD parallelism vector (the size is 256), and coarse-grain parallelism gang and fine-grain parallelism worker are not specified (their size is decided by compiler's runtime). In multi-GPU execution by MACC, halo communications between GPUs are inserted for each execution of the calculation part. As the problem size, we chose Large $(i \times j \times k) = (256 \times 256 \times 512)$.

NAS Parallel Benchmarks CG (NPB-CG) [26] is a benchmark which calculates the minimum eigenvalue of a sparse symmetric positive matrix. We used an OpenACC version of this benchmark, created by Xu et al. [27]. In the baseline program, sparse matrix multiplications (SpMV) and eigenvalue calculations are offloaded to an accelerator and they are repeated for certain times. The SpMV execution applies gang to the iteration over each row, and applies both worker and vector to the inner loop over each non-zero element of the row. The gang size is equal to the row size of the matrix, worker size 4, and vector size 32. In multi-GPU execution by MACC, a communication of the row size from each GPU to all other GPUs are generated for each execution of SpVM. We chose the problem Class C (rowsize = 150,000) for the evaluation.

For comparison, we prepared hand-coded MPI code (MPI+ACC) of Himeno Benchmark and NPB-CG by adding OpenACC directives to the official MPI code in same parallelization style as above. Regarding only NPB-CG, the official code is written by Fortran and the number of process is limited to N^2.

The Scalable Heterogeneous Computing Benchmark Suite MD (SHOC-MD) [28] is a benchmark which performs an N-body computation (the Lennard-Jones potential from molecular dynamics) using a neighbor-list algorithm. In evaluation, the N-body computation against 73,728 atoms is performed 512 times in double precision. There is no data dependency between the 512 computations. We obtained SHOC-MD's OpenACC source-code from the official repository. The source-code has one OpenACC kernel which is just enclosed by the kernels construct to execute one-time N-body computation.

PolyBench/ACC [29] is a polyhedral benchmark suite targeting accelerators. We chose the covariance code (COVAR) from PolyBench/ACC to test MACC's polyhedral extension. We used the OpenACC source-code of the official repository. In evaluation, a large covariance matrix $(16,384 \times 16,384)$ is calculated. The one compute-bound kernel is originally not parallelizable by MACC due to a symmetric-matrix creation while calculating covariances.

6   Results

The performance with respect to the number of GPUs is seen in Fig. 4. Overall, we see that our transpiler do provide the means to increase the performance of the application by multi-GPU. However, depending on the application characteristics, different behaviors are observed.

Using MACC, we measured the performance of two data coherence implementations: our own described in Sect. 4 (with and without P2P support), and using NVIDIA Unified Memory (UM). Despite the fact that UM internally use P2P, we find that our implementation without P2P outperforms it in all but one case; enabling P2P in our implementation always executes faster than UM.

We also find that for applications whose data patterns require plenty inter-GPU communication (e.g. NPB-CG and in-parts the Himeno benchmark), enabling the P2P acceleration inside MACC can have significant performance increases. For applications that MACC's transform is inadequate, we show that we can leverage other optimization techniques (the polyhedral compilation in case of this evaluation) to overcome bottlenecks otherwise hard to deal with. Finally, we also find that MACC can automatically generate multi-GPU code that is performance comparable to handwritten MPI+OpenACC code.

The remaining section continues to in-detail provide the analysis on a per-benchmark basis.

Himeno Benchmark. The speedup for the Himeno benchmark is shown in Fig. 4 (a). Using only the MACC compiler yields an average speedup of $2.55\times$ with four GPUs activated without P2P; further performance can be reached by allowing MACC to exploit the P2P communication between GPUs, which can yield an up-to 32.1% performance increase ($3.36\times$ speedup) on average. Using UM yields performance similar to MACC without the P2P addition. One MPI version ($N \times 1 \times 1$) which divides the i, j and k dimension by N, 1 and 1 respectively as with baseline MACC, and another MPI version ($2 \times 2 \times 1$) which is minimizing communications between processes yield slightly lower performance (-12.6% and -1.6% respectively) compared to baseline MACC.

NPB-CG. Performance results for the NPB-CG is shown in Fig. 4(b). We see that MACC (with and without P2P) scales with the given GPUs, yielding a $2.16\times$ and $1.54\times$ performance speedup respectively. MACC with P2P enabled scales stably better (19.9%, 34.9% and 40.9% when using $2 \sim 4$ GPUs respectively). Direct data transfer between MPI processes incurs a large 72.9% overhead when using 4 GPUs, which limits scalability; the average increase in performance experienced by the MPI version is $1.09\times$. Note that our version that use UM experience a *loss* of application performance (negative scaling) when increasing the number of GPUs. We found that UM thashes the memory (by thrashes we mean that it frequent causes page faults and page migrations), which leads to large performance losses.

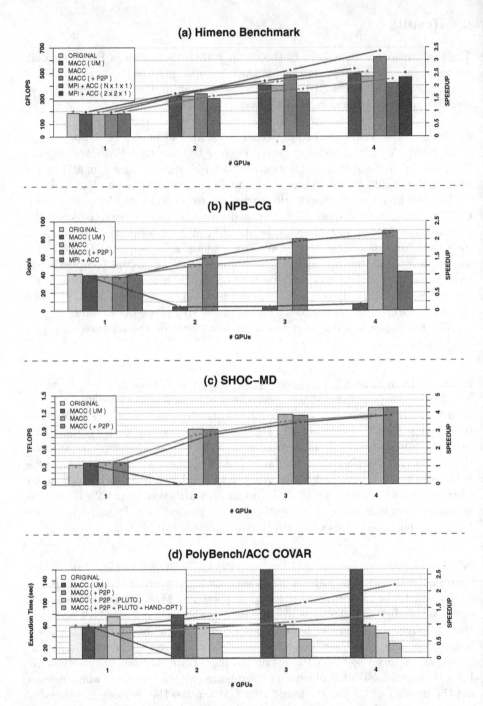

Fig. 4. This result with respect to number of GPUs displaying computational performance or execution time as well as speedup against original version

SHOC-MD. Performance results for the SHOC-MD benchmark is shown in Fig. 4(c). Unlike the other benchmarks, SHOC-MD do not benefit from P2P communication, since the application is inherently parallel. The cause for the observed superlinearity when moving from one to two GPUs ($2.78\times$ speedup on average) is not known (and it is kept even if we manually set the parallelism sizes prior to transpiling). The UM version again thrashes memory, which significantly reduced application scalability.

PolyBench/ACC COVAR. The result for the COVER benchmark is shown in Fig. 4(d). By our proposed method, the benchmark does not scale at all due to the most computation is done by a single GPU. On the other hand, by combining MACC with PLUTO, the symmetric-matrix creation (SC) and the covariance calculation (CC) are separated. This allows the application to exploit multiple GPUs on the CC. However, the SC becomes executed sequentially due to both MACC's and PGI Compiler's inability to resolve the loop-carried dependency, which drastically reduces the performance. We overcome this problem by manually adding a single directive of `loop` construct to make sure the SC loop parallelizable (HAND-OPT in Fig. 4(d)). This manual optimization can be automated by a direct operation of the polyhedral model (we consider this future work). The HAND-OPT code (SC is still performed on single-GPU though) reaches a performance of $2.20\times$ speedup on average. Using UM drastically reduces performance— again due to memory thrashing.

7   Conclusion

In this paper, we proposed MACC — an OpenACC transpiler to automatically use multiple GPUs. We described and revealed how our transpiler performs the transformations, how data are kept coherent and how multiple GPUs are used. We showed that our proposed framework can transparently use or easily be integrated into existing infrastructure by leveraging architecture-specific P2P support (NVLink), external polyhedral compiler passes (PLUTO), and Unified Memory— an alternative to our custom data coherence protocol.

We evaluated our implementation with respect to four, well-know and important benchmarks. We quantified the performance of our transpiler. We found that our custom data coherence protocol outperforms that of Unified Memory and that using P2P communication can drastically improve scalability. We also illustrated a case where our transpiler can use external compilation strategies to overcome bottlenecks otherwise impossible to overcome. Finally, we also showed that for some applications we can compete with handwritten MPI code.

In the future, we plan to continue developing the transpiler to include more optimizations and evaluate more benchmarks. Moreover, we do plan to support a more variety of accelerators, such as FPGAs or many-core accelerators (Xeon Phis).

Acknowledgements. This work was supported by JST-CREST under Grant Number JPMJCR1303 and JPMJCR1687, and JSPS KAKENHI under Grant Number JP16F16764.

References

1. Global Scientific Information and Computing Center, Tokyo Institute of Technology. TSUBAME. http://www.gsic.titech.ac.jp/en/tsubame
2. NVIDIA: DGX SATURNV Supercomputer for AI and Deep Learning. https://www.cscs.ch/computers/piz-daint/
3. Oak Ridge Leadership Computing Facility. Summit. https://www.olcf.ornl.gov/summit/
4. NVIDIA: About CUDA. https://developer.nvidia.com/about-cuda
5. The Khronos Group Inc.: OpenCL Overview. https://jp.khronos.org/opencl/
6. OpenACC-standard.org. OpenACC. https://www.openacc.org/
7. The OpenMP ARB: The OpenMP API specification for parallel programming. http://www.openmp.org
8. Unified Memory in CUDA 6: NVIDIA. https://devblogs.nvidia.com/parallelforall/unified-memory-in-cuda-6/
9. NVIDIA NVLink High-Speed Interconnect. NVIDIA. http://www.nvidia.com/object/nvlink.html
10. Komoda, T., Miwa, S., Nakamura, H., Maruyama, N.: Integrating multi-GPU execution in an OpenACC compiler. In: The 42nd International Conference on Parallel Processing (ICPP) (2013)
11. Ramashekar, T., Bondhugula, U.: Automatic data allocation and buffer management for multi-GPU machines. ACM Trans. Architect. Code Optim. (TACO) **10**(4) (2013)
12. Sakdhnagool, P., Sabne, A., Eigenmann, R.: HYDRA: extending shared address programming for accelerator clusters. In: Shen, X., Mueller, F., Tuck, J. (eds.) LCPC 2015. LNCS, vol. 9519, pp. 140–155. Springer, Cham (2016). https://doi.org/10.1007/978-3-319-29778-1_9
13. Scogland, T.R.W., Feng, W.-C., Rountree, B., de Supinski, B.R.: CoreTSAR: core task-size adapting runtime. IEEE Trans. Parallel Distrib. Syst. (TPDS) **26**(11), 2970–2983 (2015)
14. Xu, R., Tian, X., Chandrasekaran, S., Chapman, B.: Multi-GPU support on single node using directive-based programming model. In: Scientific Programming (2015)
15. Chakravarty, M.M.T., Keller, G., Lee, S., McDonel, T.L., Grover, V.: Accelerating haskell array codes with multicore GPUs. In: The Sixth Workshop on Declarative Aspects of Multicore Programming (DAMP) (2011)
16. Svensson, B.J., Vollmer, M., Holk, E., McDonell, T.L., Newton, R.R.: Converting data-parallelism to task-parallelism by rewrites. In: 4th ACM SIGPLAN Workshop on Functional High-Performance Computing (FHPC) (2015)
17. Nakao, M., Murai, H., Shimosaka, T., Tabuchi, A., Hanawa, T., Kodama, Y., Boku, T., Sato, M.: XcalableACC: extension of XcalableMP PGAS language using OpenACC for accelerator clusters. In: 2014 First Workshop on Accelerator Programming using Directives (WACCPD) (2014)
18. Kim, J., Lee, S., Vetter, J.S.: An OpenACC-based unified programming model for multi-accelerator systems. In: The 20th ACM symposium on Principles and Practice of Parallel Programming (PPoPP) (2015)

19. Kwon, O., Jubair, F., Min, S.-J., Bae, H., Eigenmann, R., Midkiff, S.P.: Automatic scaling of OpenMP beyond shared memory. In: Rajopadhye, S., Mills Strout, M. (eds.) LCPC 2011. LNCS, vol. 7146, pp. 1–15. Springer, Heidelberg (2013). https://doi.org/10.1007/978-3-642-36036-7_1
20. Aho, A.V., Lam, M.S., Sethi, R., Ullman, J.D.: Compilers: Principles, Techniques, and Tools, 2nd edn. Addison-Wesley, Reading (2006)
21. Bondhugula, U., Hartono, A., Ramanujam, J., Sadayappan, P.: A practical automatic polyhedral parallelizer and locality optimizer. In: ACM SIGPLAN Programming Languages Design and Implementation (PLDI) (2008). http://pluto-compiler.sourceforge.net
22. Omni Compiler Project: Omni Compiler. http://omni-compiler.org
23. Omni Compiler Project: XcodeML. http://omni-compiler.org/xcodeml.html
24. NVIDIA: Tesla P100 Most Advanced Data Center Accelerator. http://www.nvidia.com/object/tesla-p100.html
25. ACCC: RIKEN. Himeno benchmark. http://accc.riken.jp/en/supercom/himenobmt/
26. NASA Advanced Supercomputing Division. NAS Parallel Benchmarks. https://www.nas.nasa.gov/publications/npb.html
27. Xu, R., Tian, X., Chandrasekaran, S., Yan, Y., Chapman, B.: NAS parallel benchmarks for GPGPUs using a directive-based programming model. In: Brodman, J., Tu, P. (eds.) LCPC 2014. LNCS, vol. 8967, pp. 67–81. Springer, Cham (2015). https://doi.org/10.1007/978-3-319-17473-0_5. https://github.com/uhhpctools/openacc-npb
28. Danalis, A., Marin, G., McCurdy, C., Meredith, J.S., Roth, P.C., Spafford, K., Tipparaju, V., Vetter, J.S.: The scalable heterogeneous computing (SHOC) benchmark suite. In: Third Workshop on General-Purpose Computation on Graphics Processing Units (GPGPU-3) (2010). https://github.com/vetter/shoc/tree/openacc
29. Grauer-Gray, S., Xu, L., Searles, R., Ayalasomayajula, S., Cavazos, J.: Auto-tuning a high-level language targeted to GPU codes. In: Proceedings of Innovative Parallel Computing (InPar) (2012). https://cavazos-lab.github.io/PolyBench-ACC/

Acceleration of Wind Simulation Using Locally Mesh-Refined Lattice Boltzmann Method on GPU-Rich Supercomputers

Naoyuki Onodera[✉] and Yasuhiro Idomura

Japan Atomic Energy Agency, Chiba, Japan
onodera.naoyuki@jaea.go.jp

Abstract. A real-time simulation of the environmental dynamics of radioactive substances is very important from the viewpoint of nuclear security. Since airflows in large cities are turbulent with Reynolds numbers of several million, large-scale CFD simulations are needed. We developed a CFD code based on the adaptive mesh-refined Lattice Boltzmann Method (AMR-LBM). AMR method arranges fine grids in a necessary region, so that we can realize a high-resolution analysis including a global simulation area. The code is developed on the GPU-rich supercomputer TSUBAME3.0 at the Tokyo Tech, and the GPU kernel functions are tuned to achieve high performance on the Pascal GPU architecture. The code is validated against a wind tunnel experiment which was released from the National Institute of Advanced Industrial Science and Technology in Japan Thanks to the AMR method, the total number of grid points is reduced to less than 10% compared to the fine uniform grid system. The performances of weak scaling from 1 nodes to 36 nodes are examined. The GPUs (NVIDIA TESLA P100) achieved more than 10 times higher node performance than that of CPUs (Broadwell).

Keywords: High performance computing · GPU · Lattice boltzmann method
Adaptive mesh refinement · Real-time wind simulation

1 Introduction

A real-time simulation of the environmental dynamics of radioactive substances is very important from the viewpoint of nuclear security. In particular, high resolution analysis is required for resident areas or urban cities, where the concentration of buildings makes the air flow turbulent. In order to understand the details of the air flow there, it is necessary to carry out large-scale Computational Fluid Dynamics (CFD) simulations. Since air flows behave as almost incompressible fluids, CFD simulations based on an incompressible Navier-Stokes equation are widely developed. The LOcal-scale High-resolution atmospheric DIspersion Model using Large-Eddy Simulation (LOHDIM-LES [1]) has been developed in Japan atomic energy agency (JAEA). The LOHDIM-LES can solve turbulent wind simulation with Reynolds numbers of several million. However, an incompressible formulation sets the speed of sound to infinity, and thus, the pressure Poisson equation has to be solved iteratively with sparse matrix solvers. In such large-scale problems, it is rather difficult for sparse matrix solvers to

© The Author(s) 2018
R. Yokota and W. Wu (Eds.): SCFA 2018, LNCS 10776, pp. 128–145, 2018.
https://doi.org/10.1007/978-3-319-69953-0_8

converge efficiently because the problem becomes ill-conditioned with increasing the problem size and the overhead of node-to-node inter-communication increases with the number of nodes.

The Lattice Boltzmann Method (LBM) [2–5] is a class of CFD method that solves the discrete-velocity Boltzmann equation. Since the LBM is based on a weak compressible formulation, the time integration is explicit and we do not need to solve the pressure Poisson equation. This makes the LBM scalable, and thus, suitable for large-scale computation. As an example, researches performing large-scale calculation using the LBM were nominated for the Gordon Bell prize in SC10 [6] and SC15 [7]. However, it is difficult to calculate multi-scale analysis with a uniform grid from the viewpoint of computational resources and calculation time. In this work, we address this issue based on two approaches, one is the development of an adaptive mesh refinement (AMR) method for the LBM, and the other is optimization of the AMR-LBM on the latest Pascal GPU architecture.

The AMR method was proposed to overcome this kind of problem [8, 9]. Since the AMR method arranges fine grids only in a necessary region, we can realize a high-resolution multi-scale analysis covering global simulation areas. AMR algorithms for the LBM have been proposed, and they have achieved successful results [10, 11].

Recently, GPU based simulations have been emerging as an effective technique to accelerate many important classes of scientific applications including CFD applications [12–14]. Studies on LBM have also been reported on implementation of GPU [15, 16]. Since there are not many examples of AMR-based applications on the latest GPU architectures, there is a room for research and development of such advanced applications. In this work, we implement an AMR-based LBM code to solve multi-scale air flows. The code is developed on the GPU-rich supercomputer TSUBAME3.0 at the Tokyo Institute of Technology, and the GPU kernel functions are tuned to realize a real-time simulation of the environmental dynamics of radioactive substances.

This paper reports implementation strategies of the AMR-LBM on the latest Pascal GPU architectures and its performance results. The code is written in CUDA 8.0 and CUDA-aware MPI. The Host/Device memory is managed by using Unified memory, and the GPU/CPU buffers are directly passed to a MPI function. We demonstrate the performance of both CPU and GPU on the TSUBAME3.0. A single GPU process (a single NVIDIA TESLA P100 processor) achieves 383.3 mega-lattice update per second (MLUPS) when leaf size equals to 4^3 in single precision. The performance is about 16 times higher than that of a single CPU process (two Broadwell-EP processors, 14×2 cores, 2.4 GHz). Regarding the weak scalability results, the AMR-LBM code achieves 22535 MLUPS using 36 GPU nodes, which is 85% efficiency compared with the performance on a single GPU node.

2 Lattice Boltzmann Method

The LBM solves the discrete Boltzmann equation to simulate the flow of a weakly compressible fluid. The flow field is expressed by a limited number of pseudo particles, which evolve through streaming and collision processes. The configuration space is discretized by uniform grids. Since pseudo particles move onto the neighbor lattice points after one time step in the streaming process, this process is completed without any error. The macroscopic diffusion and the pressure gradient are expressed by the local collisional process. The time evolution of the discretized velocity function is

$$f_i(x + c_i \Delta t, t + \Delta t) = f_i(x, t) + \Omega_i(x, t). \tag{1}$$

Here, Δt is the time interval, c_i is the lattice vectors of pseudo particles, and Ω_i is the collision operator.

It is important to choose a proper lattice velocity (vector) model by taking account of the tradeoff between efficiency and accuracy. Since their low computational cost and high efficiency, the D3Q15 and D3Q19 models are popular. Recently, it was pointed out that these velocity models do not have enough accuracy at high Reynolds number with complex geometries [17]. On the other hand, the D3Q27 model is suitable model for a weakly compressible flow at high Reynolds number.

Figure 1 shows schematic figures of the above velocity vector models. Since airflows in urban cities are turbulent with high Reynolds number, we adapt the D3Q27 model. The components of the velocity vector are defined as

$$c_i = \begin{cases} (0,0,0) & i = 0 \\ (\pm c, 0, 0), (0, \pm c, 0), (0, 0, \pm c) & i = 1 - 6 \\ (\pm c, \pm c, 0), (0, \pm c, \pm c), (\pm c, 0, \pm c) & i = 7 - 18 \\ (\pm c, \pm c, \pm c) & i = 19 - 26 \end{cases} \tag{2}$$

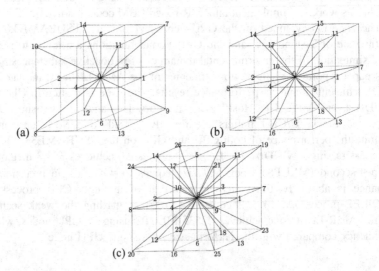

Fig. 1. Components of the velocity vector of (a) D3Q15, (b) D3Q19, and (c) D3Q27 models.

Here, c is sound speed, and is normalized as $c = 1$. Each velocity refers the predetermined upwind quantity. Since memory accesses are simple and continuous, the streaming process is suitable for high performance computing.

2.1 Single Relaxation Time Model

The macroscopic diffusion and the pressure gradient are expressed by the collisional process. The lattice BGK model [18] is widely used in most of the previous studies because of its simplicity. A collision operator of a single relaxation time (SRT) model are defined as

$$\Omega_{i(x,t)} = -\frac{1}{\tau}(f_i(x,t) - f_i^{eq}(x,t)), \tag{3}$$

where τ is relaxation time, and f_i^{eq} is a local equilibrium distribution function. The relaxation time in the collisional process is determined using the dynamic viscosity and the sound speed

$$\tau = \frac{1}{2} + \frac{3v}{c^2 \Delta t}. \tag{4}$$

In this wind simulation, since the Mach number is less than 0.3, the flow can be regarded as incompressible. The equilibrium distribution function f_i^{eq} of incompressible model is given as

$$f_i^{eq}(x,t) = \omega_i \left(1 + \frac{3c_i \cdot \vec{u}}{c^2} + \frac{9(c_i \cdot \vec{u})^2}{2c^4} - \frac{3\vec{u}^2}{2c^2} \right). \tag{5}$$

Here, ρ is the density and $\vec{u}$ is the macroscopic velocity vector. The collision operator is equivalent to the viscous term in the Navier-Stokes equation. The corresponding weighting factors of the D3Q27 model are given by

$$\omega_i = \begin{cases} 64/216 & i = 0 \\ 16/216 & i = 1 - 6 \\ 4/216 & i = 7 - 18 \\ 1/216 & i = 19 - 26 \end{cases}. \tag{6}$$

Since the SRT model is unstable at high Reynolds number, a Large-Eddy Simulation (LES) model has to be used to solve the LBM equation. The dynamic Smagorinsky model [19, 20] is often used, but it requires an averaging process over a wide area to determine the model constant. This is a huge overhead for large-scale computations, and it will negate the simplicity of the SRT model.

2.2 Cumulant Relaxation Time Model

The cumulant relaxation time model [21, 22] is a promising approach to solve the above problems. This model realizes turbulent simulation without LES model, and we can determine the equilibrium distribution function locally. Unlike the SRT model, the collisional process is not determined in the momentum space. We redefine physical quantities in the following. We take the two-sided Laplace transform of distribution function as

$$F\left(\vec{\Xi}\right) = \mathcal{L}\left\{f\left(\vec{\xi}\right)\right\} = \int_{-\infty}^{\infty} f\left(\vec{\xi}\right) e^{-\vec{\Xi}\cdot\vec{\xi}} d\vec{\xi}. \tag{7}$$

Here, $\vec{\Xi}$ is the velocity frequency variable. $\vec{\xi} = (\xi, \upsilon, \zeta)$ are the microscopic velocities. The coefficients of the series as countable cumulants $c_{\alpha\beta\gamma}$ are written as

$$c_{\alpha\beta\gamma} = c^{-\alpha-\beta-\gamma} \frac{\partial^{\alpha}\partial^{\beta}\partial^{\gamma}}{\partial^{\alpha}\Xi\partial^{\beta}\Upsilon\partial^{\gamma}Z} \ln(F(\Xi,\Upsilon,Z)). \tag{8}$$

Here, the subscripts α, β, and γ are indices of the cumulant. All decay processes are computed by

$$c^{*}_{\alpha\beta\gamma} = c^{eq}_{\alpha\beta\gamma} + (1 - \omega_{\alpha\beta\gamma})c_{\alpha\beta\gamma}. \tag{9}$$

The asterisk $*$ is the post collision cumulant, and $\omega_{\alpha\beta\gamma}$ is the relaxation frequency. The Maxwellian equilibrium is expressed as a finite Taylor expansion.

$$\ln(F^{eq}(\Xi,\Upsilon,Z)) = \ln\left(\frac{\rho}{\rho_0}\right) - \Xi u - \Upsilon v - Zw + \frac{c^2\theta}{2}\left(\Xi^2 + \Upsilon^2 + Z^2\right)). \tag{10}$$

The velocities u, v, and w are the components of macroscopic velocity vector $\vec{u}$, and θ is a parameter. Cumulants are calculated by using local quantities as discretized velocity function f_i and macroscopic velocities $\vec{u}$. Since this model is a computationally intensive algorithm with local memory access, it should be well suited to achieve high efficiency for GPU computing.

2.3 Boundary Treatment

The LBM is suitable for modeling boundary conditions with complex shapes. The bounce-back (BB) scheme and the interpolated bounce-back (IBB) scheme make it easy to implement the no-slip velocity condition. Immersed boundary methods (IBM) [23, 24] are also able to handle complex boundary conditions by adding external forces in the LBM.

In this work, we applied the IBB scheme [25, 26] because of their flexibility and compute efficiency. Figure 2 shows schematic figures of the IBB scheme. The IBB scheme directly applies the following conditions to the velocity distribution function depending on a distance function Δ

$$f^{*}_{i,(-1)}(x,t) = \begin{cases} 2\Delta f_{i,(+1)}(x,t) + (1 - 2\Delta)f_{i,(+1)}(x - c_i\Delta t, t) + F_{i,(-1)} & \Delta < \frac{1}{2} \\ \frac{1}{2\Delta}f_{i,(+1)}(x,t) + \frac{(2\Delta-1)}{2\Delta}f_{i,(-1)}(x,t) + \frac{1}{2\Delta}F_{i,(-1)} & \Delta \geq \frac{1}{2} \end{cases}, \tag{11}$$

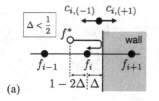 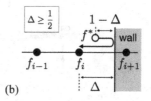

Fig. 2. Interpolated bounce-back boundary conditions of (a) $\Delta < \frac{1}{2}$ and (b) $\Delta \geq \frac{1}{2}$. The velocity distribution function f^* is computed by a linear interpolation in the upwind cell.

where subscript (± 1) is the direction of each velocity component, and F_i is force on the solid boundary given as

$$F_{i,(-1)} = -3\omega_i \rho \frac{c_i \cdot \vec{u_b}}{c^2}. \tag{12}$$

Here $\vec{u_b}$ is a velocity vector of the boundary. Since each velocity function refers the predetermined neighbor upwind and downwind quantities, it is more suitable for high performance computing than the IBM [23, 24].

3 Adaptive Mesh Refinement (AMR) Method

3.1 Block-Structured AMR Method

Since a lot of buildings and complex structures make the air flow turbulent in large urban areas, it is necessary to carry out multi-scale CFD simulations. However, it is difficult to perform such a multi-scale analysis with uniform grids from the viewpoint of computational resources and calculation time. The AMR method [8, 27] is a grid generation method, which can arrange high-resolution grids only in a necessary region. In the AMR methods based on a forest-of-octrees approach [16, 28], one domain named a leaf is subdivided into four leaves in two dimensions (quadtree) and eight leaves in three dimensions (octree). Since the leaf is recursively subdivided into half, it is easy to implement the algorithm for parallel computing, and the same number of leaves are assigned to each process.

The block-structured AMR method [29, 30] is an efficient method suitable for multithread computation. Since a leaf contains N^3 grid points and these memory accesses are continuous, it is suitable for GPU computation. Figure 3(a) shows a schematic figure of computational leaves at the interface of leaves at different levels, where each level needs the halo region across the interface. In such halo leaves, data is constructed from data on another level. Figure 3(b) shows an example of the leaf arrangement in 2D case, where the calculation region at each level is surrounded by the halo region, which is constructed from the data on leaves at the next level. Therefore, only one level difference is allowed at the interface of leaves at different levels.

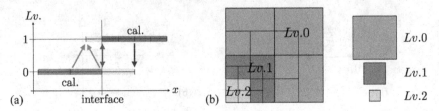

Fig. 3. Schematic figures of computational leaves: (a) Interpolating operations of (red) linear interpolation, (green) exchange values between coarse and fine grids, (blue) copy values from fine to coarse grid in 1D case. (b) An example of leaf arrangement in 2D case. Calculation region is surrounded by the halo (boundary) region of the same refined level. (Color figure online)

The AMR method is applied to resolve the boundary layer near the buildings. The octree is initialized at the beginning of the simulation and does not dynamically change the mesh during the time step.

3.2   LBM with AMR

The LBM is a dimensionless method in time and space. It is necessary to arrange these parameters according to the resolution of AMR grids [5]. The kinematic viscosity, defined in the LBM, depends on the time step size with

$$v = \frac{1}{3}\left(\tau - \frac{1}{2}\right)c^2 \Delta t \tag{13}$$

To keep a constant viscosity on coarse and fine grids, the relaxation time τ satisfies the following expression

$$\left(\tau_f - \frac{1}{2}\right) = m\left(\tau_c - \frac{1}{2}\right). \tag{14}$$

Here the super- and sub-scripts c and f denote the value of the coarse and fine grids, respectively. The coefficient m is the refinement factor. The time step is also redefined for each resolution as $\Delta t_f = (\Delta t_c)/m$. To take account of the continuity of hydrodynamic variables and their derivatives on the interface between two resolutions, the distribution functions satisfy the following equations

$$f_i^c = f_i^{eqf} + m\frac{\tau_c - 1}{\tau_f - 1}\left(f_i^f - f_i^{eqf}\right), \tag{15}$$

$$f_i^f = f_i^{eq,c} + \frac{1}{m}\frac{\tau_f - 1}{\tau_c - 1}\left(f_i^c - f_i^{eq,c}\right). \tag{16}$$

The refinement factor m is set to 2 for stability and simplicity reasons.

Figure 4 illustrates the flowchart of the computational procedure on coarse grid and fine grid. At first, streaming and collision terms are calculated on each grid. Before the fine grid calculation starts at time $t + \Delta t/2$, boundary values around the fine grid are interpolated from the coarse grid. MPI communications are executed after the computational procedures ① and ③. Temporal and spatial interpolations in halo region are executed at ② and ④.

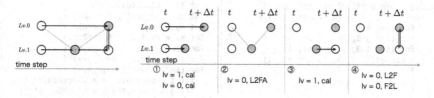

Fig. 4. Flowchart of the computational procedure on coarse grid ($Lv.0$) and fine grid: ($Lv.1$) ① Streaming and collision on each grid, ② time and space interpolation, ③ streaming and collision on fine grid, and ④ space interpolation on each level. Processes ② and ④ are executed in halo region.

4   Implementation and Optimization

4.1   CPU and GPU Implementation

In this section, we describe implementation of wind simulation code. The code is written in CUDA 8.0. We adopted the Array of Structures (AoS) memory layout to optimize multi-threaded performance. Each array is allocated by using the CUDA runtime API "cudaMallocManaged" which defines CPU and GPU memory space in the same address space. The CUDA system software automatically migrates data between CPU and GPU, so that it keeps the portability.

Figure 5 shows pseudocodes for stencil computation on CPU and GPU. The calculation code consists of a calling function (Fig. 5 top), loop functions (Fig. 5 middle), and a kernel function (Fig. 5 bottom). The calling function and the kernel function are shared by CPU and GPU. The loop functions generate indices for multi-threaded computation. CUDA threads are assigned to grid points in the leaf, and thread blocks are assigned to leaves.

The code is parallelized by the MPI library. OpenMPI 2.1.1 is CUDA-aware MPI that enables to send and receive CUDA device memory directly. OpenMPI 2.1.1 also supports Unified Memory, and the GPU/CPU buffers can be directly passed to a MPI function. MPI communications are executed in each leaf unit, and the leaf unit is transferred by one-sided communication of "MPI_Put" function implemented by MPI-2.

```
void launch_func() {
#ifdef CPU_CAL_
  func_cpu(num_leaves, nx_leaf, arguments);
#elif  GPU_CAL_
  dim3 grid(thread_x_max, thread_y_max, thread_z_max);/*less than nx_leaf*/
  dim3 block(num_leaves, 1, 1);

  func_gpu <<<grid, block>>> (num_leaves, nx_leaf, arguments);
  cudaDeviceSynchronize();
#endif
}
```

```
void func_cpu(num_leaves, nx_leaf, argu-          __global__     void     func_gpu(num_leaves,
ments) {                                          nx_leaf, arguments) {
#pragma omp parallel for collapse(4)                int l  = blockIdx.x;
  for (int l=0; l<num_leaves; l++) {                int mx = nx_leaf / blockDim.x;
    for (int k=0; k<nx_leaf; k++) {                 int my = nx_leaf / blockDim.y;
      for (int j=0; j<nx_leaf; j++) {               int mz = nx_leaf / blockDim.z;
        for (int i=0; i<nx_leaf; i++) {             for (int _k=0; _k<mz; _k++) {
          kernel(i, j, k, l, arguments);             for (int _j=0; _j<my; _j++) {
        }                                              for (int _i=0; _i<mx; _i++) {
      }                                                  int i = threadIdx.x + blockDim.x*_i;
    }                                                    int j = threadIdx.y + blockDim.y*_j;
  }                                                      int k = threadIdx.z + blockDim.z*_k;
}
                                                         kernel(i, j, k, l, arguments);
                                                       }
                                                     }
                                                   }
                                                 }
```

```
inline __host__ __device__ void kernel(i, j, k, l, arguments) {
  /* do something on CPU or GPU */
}
```

Fig. 5. Pseudocodes for stencil computation as (top) function to call CPU or GPU instruction, (middle left) function executed on the CPU, (middle right) function executed on the GPU, and (bottom) common function of both CPU and GPU.

4.2 Optimization for GPU Computation

In our GPU implementation, the streaming and collision processes are fused to reduce global memory accesses. In order to achieve high performance, it is also necessary to use thousands of cores in GPUs. The upper limit of the number of threads is limited by the usage of registers per streaming multiprocessor (SM), and it is determined at compile time. For example, according to the GP100 Pa whitepaper of NVIDIA [32], the Pascal GP100 provides 65536 32-bit registers on each SM. If one thread requires 128 registers, only 512 threads are executed on SM simultaneously. On the other hand, if one thread requires 32 registers, 2048 threads are executed and that is the upper limit of the Pascal GP100. Since the D3Q27 model and its cumulant collision operator need a lot of register memories on GPUs, the number of threads executed is limited by the lack of registers.

As a simple solution to reduce the amount of registers, it is effective to create a kernel function for each conditional branch. The main conditional branch of the streaming and collision function is the boundary condition on the object. The IBB scheme (Eq. (13)) requires a level-set function and velocity vector of boundary, and this branch requests more memory read/write and registers. In this research, since the boundary objects are fixed, optimal kernel functions are created at the beginning of calculation. We show the PTX information generated by NVIDIA CUDA Compiler 8.0.61 in single precision.

• Func1: stream_collision_without_boundary_condtion
0 bytes stack frame, 0 bytes spill stores, 0 bytes spill loads
ptxas info: Used 88 registers, 108 bytes smem, 364 bytes cmem[0],
260 bytes cmem[2]
• Func2: stream_collision_with_boundary_condition
328 bytes stack frame, 0 bytes spill stores, 0 bytes spill loads
ptxas info: Used 93 registers, 108 bytes smem, 396 bytes cmem[0],
264 bytes cmem[2]

As described above, the function without boundary conditions (Func1) can reduce the number of registers compared to the original function (Func2). By executing two functions asynchronously, it is possible to use more threads than the original calculation. Details of computational performance are discussed in Sect. 6.1 below.

5 Numerical Verification and Validation

5.1 Lid-Driven Cavity Flow

The validity of the adopted local grid refinement was verified by simulating the classical problem of lid-driven cavity flow in two-dimensions [33]. The computational domain is surrounded by walls, and its top boundary wall moves in the horizontal direction (left to right). Table 1 shows the discretization parameters. The whole computational domain is divided into 8 × 8 sub-domains. The coarse-resolution leaves are located in 6 × 6 sub-domains of the center part, and the middle-resolution leaves are located around coarse-resolution leaves, and the fine-resolution leaves are located near the walls. Each leaf contains 8 × 8 grid points. The total number of grid points in 2D-surface is 20992. It is equivalent to 32% grid points compared to the finest uniform grids in the whole domain.

Table 1. Discretization parameters for 2D lid-driven cavity flow.

AMR lv.	Δleaf	Δx	# of leaves	# of grid points
0	L/8	L/64	$36 = 6^2$	2304
1	L/16	L/128	$52 = 14^2 - 12^2$	3328
2	L/32	L/256	$240 = 32^2 - 28^2$	15360
Total	–	–	328	20992

Figure 6 shows velocity profiles of velocities along a vertical line and a horizontal line passing through the center of the cavity at (a) Re = 1000, (b) Re = 3200, (c) Re = 5000, and (d) Re = 10000. Calculation results are in good agreement with the reference results. If we used the SRT model, calculation was diverged at a high Reynolds number such as 3200. We conclude that our simulation is robust against high Reynolds number, and physical phenomena can be reproduced with few grid points.

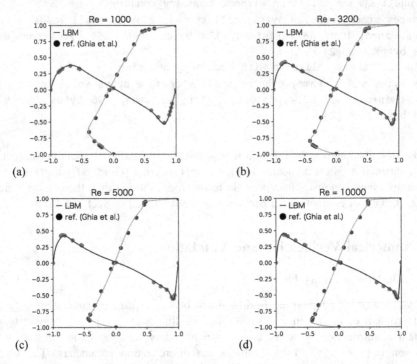

Fig. 6. Velocity profiles of u along a vertical line (green solid line) and v along a horizontal line (orange solid line) passing through the center of the cavity at (a) Re = 1000, (b) Re = 3200, (c) Re = 5000, and (d) Re = 10000. Each axis is normalized by the half-length of computational domain and the velocity of the moving wall. (Color figure online)

5.2   Wind Tunnel Test

The code is validated against a wind tunnel test, which was released from the National Institute of Advanced Industrial Science and Technology (AIST) in Japan [34]. Figure 7 shows schematic figures of a wind tunnel test. A cube is placed on the center of the floor. Inflow and outflow boundary conditions are applied in the streamwise direction. Periodic boundary conditions are assumed in the spanwise direction. A non-slip condition is imposed on the ground, and a moving boundary condition is given on the top in the vertical direction. The inlet velocity is set to be

$$u(z) = u_s \left(\frac{z}{z_s}\right)^{\frac{1}{7}}, \tag{17}$$

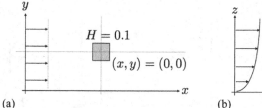
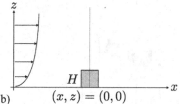

Fig. 7. Schematic figures of the wind tunnel test: (a) top view and (b) side view. A cube is placed on the center of the floor.

where the ground roughness is $z_s = 0.5$ m and wind velocity coefficient is $u_s = 2.14$ m/s. The Reynolds number, which is evaluated from the inlet velocity and physical properties of the air, is about 14000 at the top of the cube ($z = 0.1$ m).

Table 2 shows the discretization parameters for wind tunnel test. The computational domain size is from $(-19.2, -1.2, -0.2)$ to $(19.2, 1.2, 2.2)$ corresponding to the streamwise, spanwize and vertical direction, respectively. The bottom boundary condition is given at z = 0.0, and the top boundary condition is given at z = 2.0.

Table 2. Discretization parameters for wind tunnel test.

AMR lv.	$\Delta x (H = 0.1 m)$	Domain size $(X_{min,max}/Y_{min,max}/Z_{min,max})$	# of leaves	# of grid points $(\times 10^6)$
0	$H/4$	-1.5, 1.5/-0.5, 0.5/-0.2, 0.75	24048	12.31
1	$H/8$	-4.0, 4.0/-1.0, 1.0/-0.2, 1.5	25800	13.21
2	$H/16$	-19.2, 19.2/-1.2, 1.2/-0.2, 2.2	24000	12.29
Total	–	–	73848	37.81

We compute a simulation with three refinement levels. Fine-resolution leaves are located near the cube, and middle-resolution leaves are surrounding the fine-resolution leaves, and coarse-resolution leaves are used in the outer region. The total number of grid points is 3.78×10^7, which corresponds to 4.2% compared to the finest uniform grids in the whole domain.

Figure 8 shows mean velocity profiles in the stream wise direction. Red solid lines show calculation results and blue dots show experimental data. Figure 8(a) shows mean velocity profiles horizontal plane at the center of the cube ($z = H/2$). Calculation results are smooth around a cube and in good agreement with the reference results. Figure 8(b) shows mean velocity profiles in vertical plane at the center of the cube ($y = 0$). The flow behind the cube is captured well, and calculation results are also in good agreement with the reference results. We conclude that our simulation can reproduce the wind tunnel experiment with an optimal number of grid points.

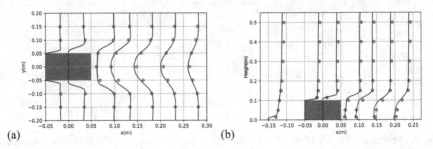

Fig. 8. Mean velocity profiles (m/s) in stream wise direction: (a) in horizontal plane at the center of the cube (z = 1/2H), and (b) in vertical plane at the center of the cube (y = 0). Red solid lines show calculation results and blue dots show experiment data as $u_{plot} = 0.02u_{mean} + x_{line}$. Simulation and experiment data have been measured along the lines: $x_{line} = (-50, 0, 65, 100, 150, 200, 250mm)$. (Color figure online)

6 Performance on the TSUBAME 3 Supercomputer

The TSUBAME 3.0 supercomputer at the Tokyo Institute of Technology is equipped with more than 2,000 GPUs (NVIDIA TESLA P100). The peak performance is 12.15/24.3 PFLOPS in double/single precision, respectively, and has achieved 8.125 PFLOPS on the Linpack benchmark. Table 3 shows the specification of TSUBAME 3.0. A compute node consists of two Intel Xeon E5-2680 V4 Processor (Broadwell-EP, 14 cores, 2.4 GHz) and four NVIDIA TESLA P100 processors. We measured the performance of our LBM code on TSUBAME 3.0.

Table 3. TSUBAME 3.0 specification of a node.

	Architecture	Bandwidth/node (GB/s)
CPU	Intel Xeon E5-2680 V4 (14 cores) × 2	153.6 (76.8 × 2)
GPU	NVIDIA TESLA P100 (16 GB, SXM2) × 4	2928 (732 × 4)
Network	Intel Omni-Path HFI 100 Gbps × 4	50 (12.5 × 4)
Memory	DDR4-2400 DIMM 256 GB	–
PCI Express	PCI Express Gen3 × 16	–

6.1 Performance on a Single Process

We show the performance results of the application on a single process by comparing three versions as follows. A CPU version is the original code parallelized by using OpenMP library, and executed on a single node (two CPU sockets). A GPU version is written in CUDA, and executed on a single GPU. An Optimal GPU version is optimized by using a boundary separate technique described Sect. 4.2 above. CPU and GPU codes are compiled with the NVIDIA CUDA Compiler 8.0.61 (-O3 -use_-fast_math -restrict -Xcompiler fopenmp –gpu-architecture = sm_60 -std = C++ 11). As for OpenMP parallelization, we use 28 threads on two Intel Xeon E5-2680 V4 Processor, while for GPU computation, the number of threads is set to $min(N_{Leaf}, 256)$.

Table 4 shows the benchmark parameters and the single process performance on TSUBAME 3.0. Here, the single process performance is estimated by subtracting the communication cost from the total cost. We scan the number of grid points in a leaf (Nleaf), while the total number of grid point are set to be equal. The performances in mega-lattice update per second (MLUPS) are measured in single precision. Table 4 shows the performances of the GPU version are about 10 times higher than those of the CPU version under various leaf size. It is unclear why the GPU performance is much higher than the ratio of GPU and CPU memory bandwidth. We estimate that the main kernel is compute intensive, and the NVIDIA CUDA compiler may not generate the SIMD-optimized CPU code. There is a possibility that the Intel compiler can generate faster CPU code.

Table 4. Performance on a single process in a single node of TSUBAME 3.0.

Nleaf	# of leaves in each level (Lv. = 0/1/2)	CPU (2 sockets) MLUPS	GPU MLUPS	Optimal GPU MLUPS
4^3	19008 /73728 /294912	23.3	231.6	383.5
8^3	2448 /9216 /36864	17.4	237.4	369.7
16^3	324 /1152 /4608	18.0	229.0	342.7
32^3	45 /144 /576	13.2	184.4	243.5

The performances of the Optimal GPU version are about 1.5 times higher than those of the GPU version under the conditions of $N_{Leaf} = (4^3, 8^3, 16^3)$. Since the benchmark is executed including the whole AMR leaves, the boundary separate technique works well under the condition with a small leaf size.

6.2   Performance on Multiple Processes in a Single Node

We show the performance results of the application on multiple processes in a single node. A communication cost of GPU based applications becomes a large overhead compared with that of CPU based ones. Table 3 shows that the memory bandwidth of GPUs is 19 times higher than that of CPUs in a single node. In other words, an impact of the communications cost on GPUs are 19 times larger than that on CPUs.

Table 5 shows the performance the Optimal GPU version with 4 MPI processes in a single node. The total number of leaves is 4 times larger than the condition used in Table 4. Although the performances in a single node is higher than those in a single GPU, the communication time occupies most of the total calculation time particularly when leaf size equals to 4^3. Since MPI communications are executed in each leaf unit, it is difficult to obtain high network bandwidth with a small message size. Unfortunately, MPI communications using Unified memory in OpenMPI 2.1.2 are slower than using Device or Host memory. This may be resolved by using GPUDirect RDMA or NVLink. We will address this issue in future work.

Table 5. Performance of GPU computation in a single node.

Nleaf	# of leaves in each process (Lv. = 0/1/2)	MLUPS (4 GPUs)	MPI cost %
4^3	19008/73728/294912	261.0	88.2
8^3	2448/9216/36864	729.5	65.4
16^3	324/1152/4608	840.6	48.8

(Note: OpenMPI 2.1.2 supports GPUDirect RDMA, which enables a direct P2P (Peer-to-Peer) data transfer between GPUs. However, we do not succeed in MPI communications using the GPUDirect RDMA in TSUBAME 3.0.)

6.3 Performance on Multiple Nodes

We show the performance results of the application in multiple nodes. The leaf size is set to 8^3 considering the performance and applicability to real problems. The number of leaves in a node is the same as that in Sect. 6.2 above.

Figure 9 presents weak scalabilities of CPU and GPU performances on TSUBAME 3.0. In these figures, the horizontal axis indicates the number of nodes, and the vertical axis indicates the MLUPS per step respectively.

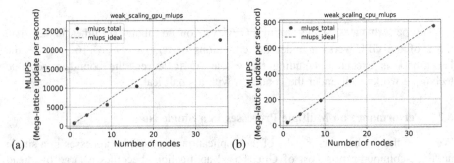

Fig. 9. Weak scaling results of the LBM simulation on (a) GPUs and (b) CPUs. 4 MPI processes are executed in each node.

In the weak scaling tests, the parallel efficiencies from 1 node to 36 nodes of CPUs and GPUs are 98% and 85%, respectively. Although CPUs show better scalability, the performance on a single GPU node (733MLUPS) is comparable to that on 36 CPU nodes (767MLUPS).

6.4 Estimation of Performance in Wind Simulation

Our final goal is to develop a real-time simulation of the environmental dynamics of radioactive substances. We estimate the minimum mesh resolution $\Delta x_{real\,time}$, at which a wind simulation can be executed in real time. The mesh resolution can be easily estimated from the Courant–Friedrichs–Lewy (CFL) condition as

$$\Delta x_{realtime} = \frac{U_{target}}{CFL_{target}} \times \Delta t_{cal}. \tag{18}$$

Here U_{target} is a wind velocity, and CFL_{target} is the CFL number at U_{target}, and Δt_{cal} is the elapse time per step.

We estimate the mesh resolution under the condition of $(U_{target}, CFL_{target})$ $= (5.0 m/s, 0.2)$. The computational condition is based on a single GPU node case in the previous Subsect. 6.3. The fine leaves are placed near the ground surface, and the resolution changes in the height direction. The leaves are arranged with $24 \times 24 \times 17$ at Lv. 0, $48 \times 48 \times 16$ at Lv. 1, and $96 \times 96 \times 16$ at Lv. 2. The computational performance is achieved 733MLUPS using a single GPU node. The minimum mesh resolution becomes $\Delta x_{realtime} = m$ that corresponds to the whole computation domain size of $(L_x, L_y, L_z) = (2.8\,km, 2.8\,km, 3.3\,km)$. The above estimation shows that a detailed real-time wind simulation is realized by GPU computing.

7 Summary and Conclusions

This paper presented the GPU implementation of air flow simulations on the environmental dynamics of radioactive substances. We have successfully implemented the AMR-based LBM with a state-of-the-art cumulant collision operator. Our code is written in CUDA 8.0, and executed both on CPUs and GPUs by using the CUDA runtime API "cudaMallocManaged". Since the LBM kernel needs a lot of register memories on GPUs, the number of threads executed is limited by the lack of registers. We propose the effective optimization to create a kernel function for each conditional branch. This technique can reduce the number of registers compared to the original function, and the single GPU performance is accelerated by ~ 1.5 times. The performance of a single GPU process (NVIDIA TESLA P100) achieved 383.3 mega-lattice update per second (MLUPS) with the leaf size of 4^3 in single precision. The performance is about 16 times higher than that of a single CPU process (two Broadwell-EP 14 cores 2.4 GHz).

We have also discussed the weak scalability results. Regarding the weak scalability results, 36 GPU nodes achieved 22535 MLUPS with the parallel efficiency of 85% compared with a single GPU node. The present scaling studies revealed a severe performance bottleneck due to MPI communication, which will be addressed via GPUDirect RDMA or NVLink in the future work.

Finally, we estimate the minimum mesh resolution $\Delta x_{realtime}$ at which air flow simulations can be executed in real time. The above estimation shows that a detailed real-time wind simulation is realized by GPU computing. We conclude that the present scheme is one of efficient approaches to realize a real-time simulation of the environmental dynamics of radioactive substances.

Acknowledgements. This research was supported in part by the Japan Society for the Promotion of Science (KAKENHI), a Grant-in-Aid for Scientific Research (C) 17K06570 and a

Grant-in-Aid for Scientific Research (B) 17H03493 from the Ministry of Education, and "Joint Usage/Research Center for Interdisciplinary Large-scale Information Infrastructures" in Japan (Project ID: jh170031-NAH). Computations were performed on the TSUBAME 3.0 at the Tokyo Institute of Technology, and the ICEX at the Japan Atomic Energy Agency.

References

1. Nakayama, H., Takemi, T., Nagai, H.: Adv. Sci. Res. **12**, 127–133
2. Rothman, D.H., Zaleski, S.: J. Fluid Mech. **382**(01), 374–378 (1997)
3. Inamuro, T.: Fluid Dyn. Res. **44**, 024001 (2012). 21 pp.
4. Inagaki, A., Kanda, M., et al.: Boundary-Layer Meteorology, pp. 1–21 (2017)
5. Kuwata, Y., Suga, K.: J. Comp. Phys. **311** (2016)
6. Rahimian, A., Lashuk, I., et al.: In: Proceedings of the 2010 ACM/IEEE International Conference on High Performance Computing, Networking, Storage and Analysis, pp. 1–11. IEEE Computer Society (2010)
7. Rossinelli, D., Tang, Y.H., et al.: In: Proceedings of the 2015 ACM/IEEE International Conference on High Performance Computing, Networking, Storage and Analysis, vol. 2. IEEE Computer Society (2015)
8. Berger, M.J., Oliger, J.: J. Comp. Phys. **53**(3), 484–512 (1984)
9. Zhao, Y., Liang-Shih, F.: J. Comp. Phys. **228**(17), 6456–6478 (2009)
10. Zhao, Y., Qiu, F., et al.: Proceedings of 2007 Symposium on Interactive 3D Graphics, pp. 181–188 (2007)
11. Yu, Z., Fan, L.S.: J. Comput. Phys. **228**(17), 6456–6478 (2009)
12. Wang, X., Aoki, T.: Parallel Comput. **37**(9), 521–535 (2011)
13. Shimokawabe, T., Aoki, T., et al.: In: Proceedings of the 2010 ACM/IEEE International Conference on High Performance Computing, Networking, Storage and Analysis, pp. 1–11. IEEE Computer Society (2010)
14. Shimokawabe, T., Aoki, T., et al.: In: Proceedings of the 2011 ACM/IEEE International Conference on High Performance Computing, Networking, Storage and Analysis, vol. 3. IEEE Computer Society (2011)
15. Feichtinger, C., Habich, J., et al.: Parallel Computing **37**(9), 536–549 (2011)
16. Zabelock, S., et al.: J. Comput. Phy. **303**(15), 455–469 (2015)
17. Kang, S.K., Hassan, Y.A.: J. Comput. Phys. **232**(1), 100–117 (2013)
18. Zou, Q., He, X., et al.: Phys. Fluid **9**(6), 1591–1598 (1996)
19. Germano, M., Piomelli, U., Moin, P., Cabot, W.H.: Physics of Fluids A: Fluid Dynamics 3 (7), pp.1760–1765 (1991)
20. Lilly, D.K.: Phys. Fluids A **4**(3), 633–635 (1992)
21. Geier, M., Schonherr, M., et al.: Comput. Math. Appl. **70**(4), 507–547 (2015)
22. Geier, M., Psquali, A., et al.: J. Comput. Phys. **348**, 889–898 (2017)
23. Kim, J., Kim, D., Choi, H.: J. Comput. Phys. **171**(20), 132–150 (2001)
24. Peng, Y., Shu, C., et al.: J. Comput. Phys. **218**(2), 460–478 (2006)
25. Chun, B., Ladd, A.J.C.: Phys. Rev. E **75**(6), 066705 (2007)
26. Yin, X., Zhang, J.: J. Comput. Phys. **231**(11), 4296–4303 (2012)
27. Guzik, S.M., Weisgraber, T.H., et al.: J. Comput. Phys. **259**(15), 461–487 (2014)
28. Laurmaa, V., Picasso, M., Steiner, G.: Comput. Fluids **131**(5), 190–204 (2016)
29. Zuzio, D., Estivalezes, J.L.: Comput. Fluids **44**(1), 339–357 (2011)
30. Usui, H., Nagara, A., et al.: Proc. Comput. Sci. **29**, 2351–2359 (2014)

31. Open MPI: Running CUDA-aware Open MPI. https://www.open-mpi.org/faq/?category=runcuda
32. NVIDIA: Whitepaper, NVIDIA Tesla P100. https://images.nvidia.com/content/pdf/tesla/whitepaper/pascal-architecture-whitepaper.pdf
33. Ghia, U., Ghia, K.N., Shin, C.T.: J. Comput. Phys. **48**, 387–411 (1982)
34. National Institute of Advanced Industrial Science and Technology, Database, (in Japanese). https://unit.aist.go.jp/emri/ja/results/db/01/db_01.html

Architecture of an FPGA-Based Heterogeneous System for Code-Search Problems

Yuki Hiradate, Hasitha Muthumala Waidyasooriya$^{(\boxtimes)}$ (iD), Masanori Hariyama, and Masaaki Harada

Graduate School of Information Sciences, Tohoku University, 6-3-09, Aramaki-Aza-Aoba, Aoba, Sendai, Miyagi 980-8579, Japan
hiradate.yuki.p5@dc.tohoku.ac.jp, {hasitha,hariyama}@tohoku.ac.jp, mharada@m.tohoku.ac.jp

Abstract. Code search problems refer to searching a particular bit pattern that satisfies given constraints. Obtaining such codes is very important in fields such as data encoding, error correcting, cryptography, etc. Unfortunately, the search time increases exponentially with the number of bits in the code, and typically requires many months of computation to find large codes. On the other hand, the search method mostly consists of 1-bit computations, so that reconfigurable hardware such as FPGAs (field programmable gate arrays) can be used to successfully obtain a massive degree of parallelism. In this paper, we propose a heterogeneous system with a CPU and an FPGA to speed-up code search problems. According to the evaluation, we obtain over 86 times speed-up compared to typical CPU-based implementation for extremal doubly even self-dual code search problem of length 128.

1 Introduction

Fields such as cryptography, data encoding, error correcting, etc. often requires bit patterns that satisfy particular conditions. However, finding such bit patterns is a very time consuming problem. For example, in order to find 64-bit code that satisfies particular conditions, we have to search 2^{64} bit patterns. Even if we can search one bit pattern in one clock cycle using a 4 GHz CPU, it requires over 146 years to search all combinations. For a 128-bit code search problem, the required processing time exceeds the age of the universe. Therefore, how we can solve such code search problems. Mathematicians propose many algorithms to generate a particular code that satisfies the conditions, instead of search for all possible bit patterns. For example, to find all 64-bit numbers that are divisible by four, we can fix the least significant two bits to zero and generate all combinations of bit patterns of the other 62 bits. This increases the processing speed by four times. For more complex problems, many different methods are available to reduce the amount of searches. Most of those methods use bit operations or fixed-point computations. On the other hand, CPUs and GPUs are specialized for floating-point computations, and using those for such simple bit operations is not an efficient method.

© The Author(s) 2018
R. Yokota and W. Wu (Eds.): SCFA 2018, LNCS 10776, pp. 146–155, 2018.
https://doi.org/10.1007/978-3-319-69953-0_9

In this paper, we use re-configurable hardware call FPGA (field programmable gate array) [1] to efficiently compute bit operations. FPGAs contain over millions of multi-input logic gates and registers [2]. Since all these logic gates and their interconnections are configurable, we can design custom processing elements and datapaths to efficiently execute the required operation with a massive degree of parallelism. Recently, OpenCL-based FPGA design [3] has been introduced to design accelerators using C-like high-level programming. This design method allows us to exploit the full potential of an FPGA while reducing the design time [4]. OpenCL is not only can be used to design FPGA accelerator, but also can be used to design a whole heterogeneous system including the computations of a CPU and also the data transfers between a CPU and an FPGA.

In this paper, we propose an FPGA-based heterogeneous accelerator to speed-up the "extremal doubly even self-dual code" search problem [5–7]. To solve this problem, the work in [8] proposes a method that contains many bit-operations that can be done in parallel. The proposed FPGA accelerator contains thousands of processing elements to perform bit-operations in parallel while the CPU computes complex but sequential operations in a higher clock frequency compared to the FPGA. The FPGA accelerator design and the heterogeneous system implementation are done using OpenCL. According to the evaluation, we obtain over 86 times speed-up compared to a typical CPU-based implementation for extremal doubly even self-dual code search problem of length 128.

2 Code-Search Problems

In this paper, we consider the acceleration of extremal doubly even self-dual code search [8], as an example to show the efficiency of the FPGA-based heterogeneous system for such problems. Self-dual codes are an important class of linear codes with both theoretical importance and practical applications [7]. It is important in the fields such as cryptography, error correcting, etc. In this section, we briefly explain the extremal doubly even self-dual code search algorithm. Note that, we restrict the details of the mathematical background since it is not in the scope of this paper. Readers can refer [8] for the details. We focus on the types of computations required in such code search problems, and how to accelerate those computations using FPGA-based heterogeneous system.

2.1 Extremal Doubly Even Self-dual Code Search

In the work in [8], the extremal doubly even self-dual code is described as follows. "A binary self-dual code C of length n is a code over $\mathbb{F}_2$ satisfying $C = C^\perp$ where the dual code $C^\perp$ of C is defined as $C^\perp = \{x \in \mathbb{F}_2^n | x \cdot y = 0 \text{ for all } y \in C\}$ under the standard inner product $x \cdot y$. A self-dual code C is *doubly even* if all codewords of C have hamming weight divisible by four, and *singly even* if there is at least one codeword of hamming weight $\equiv 2 \pmod 4$. Note that a doubly even self-dual code of length n exists if and only if n is divisible by eight. It was shown in [9] that the minimum hamming weight d of a doubly even self-dual code of length n is bounded by $d \leq 4[n/24] + 4$. A doubly even self-dual code meeting this upper bound is called *extremal.*"

For example, an extremal doubly even self-dual code C of length 128 satisfies the following three conditions.

1. Hamming weight $\equiv 0 \pmod 4$
2. $C = C^{\perp}$
3. $d(C) = 24$

To find such a code, work in [8] proposes the following algorithm that contains four steps.

Step 1: $x \in \mathbb{F}_2^{64}$ and $wt(x) \equiv 3 \pmod 4$

Step 2: If $AA^{\mathrm{T}} + BB^{\mathrm{T}} \neq I_{32}$ go to step 1. A and B are circulant matrices given by Eq. (1).

$$A = \begin{pmatrix} x_1 & x_2 & \cdots & x_{32} \\ x_{32} & x_1 & \cdots & x_{31} \\ \vdots & \vdots & & \vdots \\ x_2 & x_3 & \cdots & x_1 \end{pmatrix}, \quad B = \begin{pmatrix} x_{33} & x_{34} & \cdots & x_{64} \\ x_{64} & x_{33} & \cdots & x_{63} \\ \vdots & \vdots & & \vdots \\ x_{34} & x_{35} & \cdots & x_{33} \end{pmatrix} \tag{1}$$

Step 3: The matrices G and H in Eq. (2) are the generator matrices of C and $C^{\perp}$ respectively. If the hamming weight of the sum until the 10th row of G is less than 20, go to step 1. If the hamming weight of the sum until the 10th row of H is less than 20, go to step 1.

$$M = \begin{pmatrix} A & B \\ B^{\mathrm{T}} & A^{\mathrm{T}} \end{pmatrix}, \quad G = (I_{64}, M), \quad H = \left(M^{T}, I_{64}\right) \tag{2}$$

Step 4: A code is found and exit.

In order to satisfy the step 3 of the code search algorithm, the hamming weight of $\{x_1 \cdots x_{64}\}$ must be equal or larger than 19. That is, at least 19 bits of the 64 bits in the code must be ones. Therefore, we have to search k-out-of-64 codes where $19 \leq k \leq 64$. Searching for such a code is a very time consuming problem.

3   FPGA-Based Heterogeneous Architecture

3.1   Exploiting the Parallelism

Since FPGA is a reconfigurable device, we can implement both space parallelism and time parallelism. Space parallelism is similar to SIMD (single instruction multiple data) operations in GPUs where the same operation is performed on multiple data simultaneously. Time parallelism is implemented using pipelines, where multiple operations are performed on different data. In order to design

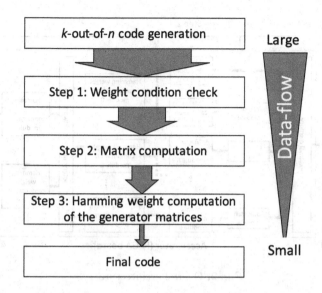

Fig. 1. The amount of data transferred among each step of the code search method.

an efficient architecture, we have to exploit the parallelism of the code search problem. Figure 1 shows the amount of data transferred among each step of the code search method. As explained in Sect. 2, if the conditions are not met in each step, further computations are terminated and go back the step 1. Therefore, the amount of data transferred to the latter steps become smaller and smaller in each step. To utilize this efficiently, we use a large amount of parallel computations in the initial steps but a small amount of parallel computations in the latter steps. In addition, multiple steps are computed in parallel for different data using a pipelined architecture.

3.2 Overall Architecture of the FPGA-Based Heterogeneous System

Figure 2 shows the overall architecture of the FPGA-based heterogeneous system. It consists of a CPU and an FPGA accelerator. The CPU and the FPGA works together to generate k-out-of-n codes that satisfies the step 1 of the algorithm explained in Sect. 2.1. For each k-out-of-n code, matrix calculations in step 2 is performed in parallel. After the matrix computation is done, hamming weight is calculated as explained in step 3.

Amount of parallel computations are decreases from step 1 to step 3. As shown in Fig. 2, we have used a CPU and 64 bit-shift modules in step 1. There are 64 matrix calculation modules in step 2. However, there are only 10 modules in step 3. Since the amount of data transferred to each stage is getting smaller and smaller, we decrease the amount of parallel computations. This way, we can efficiently use the FPGA resources by spending more resources on bottleneck stages that process a large amount of data.

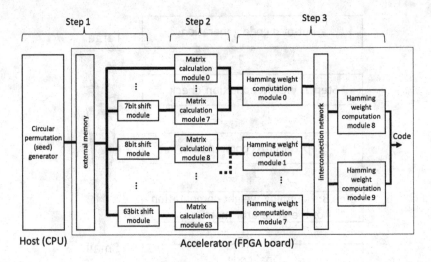

Fig. 2. Overall architecture.

3.3 *k*-out-of-*n* Code Generation

There are a few methods such as [10, 11] for *k*-out-of-*n* code generation. However, these methods have a data dependency among code searches. That is, the search of a new bit pattern must be started only after the search of the previous bit pattern is finished. As a result, it is extremely difficult to accelerate such methods using parallel processing. Therefore, we use the "circular permutation generation algorithm" proposed in [12] to accelerate *k*-out-of-*n* code generation. A *p*-ary circular permutation of length *n* is an *n*-character string of an alphabet of size *p*, where all rotations of the string are considered as equivalent. Therefore, we can regard a circular permutation code as a seed and generate the other bit patterns by rotating the bits. Figure 3 shows two seeds and the generated bit patterns of 2-out-of-4 codes. The rotation of bits can be done in parallel using bit-shift operations. Therefore, even if we generate the seeds in serial, we can still have a large amount of parallel operations.

The algorithm to generate circular permutation [12] is a serial one. Therefore, the only way to increase the processing speed of the circular permutation generation is to increase the clock frequency. Unfortunately, the clock frequency of an FPGA is usually less than 300 MHz. Therefore, we use a CPU for the permutation generation which has more than 10 times larger clock frequency compared to that of an FPGA. Once the permutations are generated, those are transferred to the external memory (DRAM) of the FPGA board. The FPGA accelerator access those data and performs 63 shift operations in parallel and select the codes that satisfies the step 1 of the algorithm explained in Sect. 2.1. The permutation generation and bit-shift can be done in parallel as shown in Fig. 4. The time required for a circular permutation generation and parallel bit-shift operations are nearly equal. This way, the CPU and the FPGA are used in parallel manner.

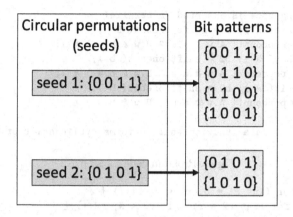

Fig. 3. 2-out-of-4 bit pattern generation using seeds.

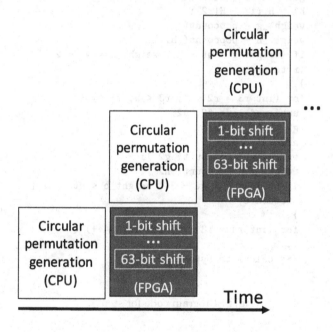

Fig. 4. Parallel processing of k-out-of-n code generation using a CPU and FPGA.

3.4   Matrix Calculation and Hamming Weight

In step 2, we do the matrix calculation of $AA^{\mathrm{T}} + BB^{\mathrm{T}} \neq I_{32}$ is a simple bit operation. Since there are 64 codes generated in parallel in step 1, we use 64 modules in parallel in step 2 for matrix calculation. Only a small percentage of codes satisfy this condition, so that the amount of data proceeds to the next step is small. As a result, we use one "hamming weight computation" modules in step 3 for every 8 matrix calculation results. As a result, the number of modules in

```
//The following code is executed in parallel
a = shift_onebit( A ); b = shift_onebit( B );
out.BIT.b30 = popcount( A.w & a.w ^ B.w & b.w ) & 1;
a = shift_onebit( a ); b2 = shift_onebit( b );
out.BIT.b29 = popcount( A.w & a.w ^ B.w & b.w ) & 1;
a = shift_onebit( a ); b2 = shift_onebit( b );
out.BIT.b28 = popcount( A.w & a.w ^ B.w & b.w ) & 1;
...
/** shift_onebit is a function that performs cyclic shift of 32 bits **/
```

Fig. 5. Program code for step 2.

```
for (int r1 = 0; r1 < N; r1++) {
 for (int r2 = r1 + 1; r2 < N; r2++) {
  unsigned long g1, h1;
  g1 = G[r1] ^ G[r2];
  h1 = H[r1] ^ H[r2];
  weight_g = popcount( g1 );
  weight_h = popcount( h1 );
  if (weight_g < wt - 2 | weight_h < wt - 2) {
   return 0;
  }
  for (int r3 = r2 + 1; r3 < N; r3++) {
   unsigned long t2, s2;
   g2 = t1 ^ G[r3];
   h2 = s1 ^ H[r3];
   weight_g = popcount( g2 );
   weight_h = popcount( h2 );
   if (weight_g < wt - 3 | weight_h < wt - 3) {
    return 0;
   }
   for (int r4 = r3 + 1; r4 < N; r4++) {
    ...
    /** calculate upto r10. **/
}
```

Fig. 6. Program code for step 3.

step 2 is reduced without affecting the total processing time. A part of matrix calculation program code is shown in Fig. 5.

In step 3, hamming weight until the 10th row is calculated. However, most codes can be rejected by computing the hamming weight until the first few rows. Therefore, we divide the step 3 into two stages. In the first stage, the hamming weight until the first 5 rows are computed. The codes satisfy this condition go to the second stage. We use only 2 modules in the second stage since a smaller degree of parallelism is required. A part of step 3 program code is shown in Fig. 6.

4   Evaluation

We used two systems for the evaluation, where one contains only one CPU and the other contains one CPU and one FPGA. In the CPU only system, the CPU is Intel Xeon E5-1650 v3 (3.50 GHz). In the heterogeneous system, the CPU is Intel Xeon E5-2643, and the FPGA is Terasic DE5a-net FPGA board [13] with Intel Arria 10 FPGA. FPGA is configured using Quartus prime pro 16.1 and Intel FPGA SDK for OpenCL [14]. CPU codes are compiled using Intel compiler 17.0 with OpenMP directives for parallel computation.

Table 1 shows the comparison of the processing time of k-out-of-n code generation using different methods. In this evaluation, n is 64 and k is 8. The fastest CPU implementation is a nested-loop implementation that search all bit patterns to find the desired code. Some part of the loop can be processed in parallel so that the processing time is reduced. Compared to that, proposed heterogeneous implementation produced over 2.4 times speed-up compared to the nested-loop implementation.

Table 2 shows the comparison of the total processing time of extremal doubly even self-dual code search. Note that the clock frequency of the FPGA is reduced to 207 MHz from 309 MHz in Table 1 due to increased computation. Even with such low clock frequency, the speed-up of the proposed implementation is 86.9 times compared to the CPU-only implementation. This shows that FPGAs are very efficient for bit operations. Moreover, nearly 64 codes can be checked per clock cycle in FPGA due to its massively parallel computations.

Table 3 shows the resource usage of the FPGA. Since only 37% of the logic resources are used, there is a potential to increase the processing speed further by doing more parallel computations. If we increase the degree of parallelism, the bottleneck would be the circular permutation generation in the CPU. Therefore,

Table 1. Comparison of the processing time of k-out-of-n code generation

	[10]	[11]	Nested loops	Proposed
Device	CPU	CPU	CPU	CPU & FPGA
Clock frequency (MHz)	3500	3500	3500	CPU:3300, FPGA:309
Processing time (s)	35	9.04	0.6	0.25

Table 2. Results

	Conventional	Proposed
Device	CPU only	CPU & FPGA
Clock frequency (MHz)	3500	207
Processing time (s)	29.13	0.33
Number of clock cycles (10^9)	10.21	0.07
Codes checked per clock cycle	0.04	63.5

Table 3. FPGA resource utilization

Resource type	Utilization (Percentage %)
Logic	143,186 (34)
Memory bits	3,899,280 (7)
RAM blocks	425 (16)

decreasing the processing time of circular permutation generation is critical for future improvements.

The evaluation is done for only k-out-of-64 codes where k equals 8. We also found similar results for 19-out-of-64 codes. Neither of those search results have given a solution for extremal doubly even self-dual code of length 128. Therefore, it is still an unsolved problem. In order to find a solution for this problem, we have to search other k values and that is one of our future works. Also note that, the data transferred to the FPGA for the CPU are only the circular permutation data generated in CPU. Therefore, the DRAM access by the FPGA is minimal. Although the FPGA board has a small memory bandwidth of 25.6 GB/s bandwidth, it is not a bottleneck for the code search problems.

5   Conclusion

In this paper, we propose an FPGA-based heterogeneous system for extremal doubly even self-dual code search. Although we are yet to solve the problem, there is a great potential to find a solution in near future due to over 86 times of speed-up of the proposed system compared to a conventional one with only a CPU. Moreover, we used only 34% of the FPGA resources, so that further increase of speed is possible. It is very important to exploit the possibility of accelerating other code search problems using FPGAs in future.

References

1. Marchal, P.: Field-programmable gate arrays. Commun. ACM **42**(4), 57–59 (1999)
2. https://www.altera.com/content/dam/altera-www/global/en_US/pdfs/literature/hb/arria-10/arria_10_aib.pdf
3. Czajkowski, T.S., Neto, D., Kinsner, M., Aydonat, U., Wong, J., Denisenko, D., Yiannacouras, P., Freeman, J., Singh, D.P., Brown, S.D.: OpenCL for FPGAs: prototyping a compiler. In: Proceedings of the International Conference on Engineering of Reconfigurable Systems and Algorithms (ERSA), p. 1 (2012)
4. Waidyasooriya, H.M., Hariyama, M., Uchiyama, K.: Design of FPGA-Based Computing Systems with OpenCL (2017)
5. MacWilliams, F.J., Sloane, N.J.A.: The Theory of Error-Correcting Codes. North-Holland, Amsterdam (1977)
6. Pasquier, G.: A binary extremal doubly even self-dual code (64, 32, 12) obtained from an extended Reed-Solomon code over F16. IEEE Trans. Inform. Theory **27**, 807–808 (1981)

7. Rains, E., Sloane, N.J.A.: Self-dual codes. In: Pless, V.S., Huffman, W.C. (eds.) Handbook of Coding Theory, pp. 177–294. Elsevier, Amsterdam (1998)
8. Harada, M.: An extremal doubly even self-dual code of length 112. Electron. J. Comb. **15**, 1–5 (2008)
9. Mallows, C.L., Sloane, N.J.A.: An upper bound for self-dual codes. Inform. Control **22**, 188–200 (1973)
10. Harbison, S.P., Steele Jr., G.L.: C: A Reference Manual. Prentice Hall, Englewood Cliffs (1987)
11. https://docs.python.org/2/library/itertools.html
12. Sawada, Joe: A fast algolithm to generate neckleces with fixed content. Theoret. Comput. Sci. **301**, 477–489 (2003)
13. Terasic, DE5-Net FPGA Development Kit. http://www.terasic.com.tw/cgi-bin/page/archive.pl?Language=English&CategoryNo=158&No=526
14. Intel FPGA SDK for OpenCL, Programming Guide. https://www.altera.com/en_US/pdfs/literature/hb/opencl-sdk/aocl_programming_guide.pdf

Performance Tools

TINS: A Task-Based Dynamic Helper Core Strategy for In Situ Analytics

Estelle Dirand[1(✉)], Laurent Colombet[1], and Bruno Raffin[2]

[1] CEA, DAM, DIF, 91297 Arpajon, France
estelle.dirand@cea.fr
[2] Univ. Grenoble Alpes, Inria, CNRS, Grenoble INP, LIG,
38000 Grenoble, France

Abstract. The in situ paradigm proposes to co-locate simulation and analytics on the same compute node to analyze data while still resident in the compute node memory, hence reducing the need for post-processing methods. A standard approach that proved efficient for sharing resources on each node consists in running the analytics processes on a set of dedicated cores, called helper cores, to isolate them from the simulation processes. Simulation and analytics thus run concurrently with limited interference. In this paper we show that the performance can be improved through a *dynamic helper core strategy*. We rely on a work stealing scheduler to implement TINS, a task-based in situ framework with an on-demand analytics isolation. The helper cores are dedicated to analytics only when analytics tasks are available. Otherwise the helper cores join the other cores for processing simulation tasks. TINS relies on the Intel® TBB library. Experiments on up to 14,336 cores run a set of representative analytics parallelized with TBB coupled with the hybrid MPI+TBB ExaStamp molecular dynamics code. TINS shows up to 40% performance improvement over various other approaches including the standard helper core.

1 Introduction

The exascale era will bring more computational capabilities enabling the simulation of more complex phenomena with higher precision. This will generate a growing amount of data. Traditionally, simulation codes output data into the filesystem and these data are later read back for postmortem analytics. However, the growing gap between computational capabilities and IO bandwidth calls for new data processing methods.

The *in situ* paradigm proposes to reduce data movement and to analyze data while still resident in the memory of the compute node by co-locating simulation and analytics on the same compute node [1]. The simplest approach consists in modifying the simulation timeloop to directly call analytics routines. However, several works have shown that an *asynchronous* approach where analytics and simulation run concurrently can lead to a significantly better performance [2–4]. Today, the most efficient approach consists in running the analytics processes on

© The Author(s) 2018
R. Yokota and W. Wu (Eds.): SCFA 2018, LNCS 10776, pp. 159–178, 2018.
https://doi.org/10.1007/978-3-319-69953-0_10

a set of dedicated cores, called helper cores, to isolate them from the simulation processes [3]. Simulation and analytics thus run concurrently on different cores but this static isolation can lead to underused resources if the simulation or the analytics do not fully use all the assigned cores.

In this paper, we introduce TINS, a task-based in situ framework that implements a novel *dynamic helper core* strategy. TINS relies on a work stealing scheduler and on task-based programming. Simulation and analytics tasks are created concurrently and scheduled on a set of worker threads created by a single instance of the work stealing scheduler. Helper cores are assigned dynamically: some worker threads are dedicated to analytics when analytics tasks are available while they join the other threads for processing simulation tasks otherwise, leading to a better resource usage. We leverage the good compositionality properties of task-based programming to seamlessly keep the analytics and simulation codes well separated and a plugin system enables to develop parallel analytics codes outside of the simulation code.

TINS is implemented with the Intel® Threading Building Blocks (TBB) library that provides a task-based programming model and a work stealing scheduler. The experiments are conducted with the hybrid MPI+TBB ExaStamp molecular dynamics code [5] that we associate with a set of analytics representative of computational physics algorithms. We show up to 40% performance improvement over various other approaches, including the standard helper core, on experiments on up to 14,336 Broadwell cores.

The paper is organized as follows. After an overview of related work (Sect. 2), we present the TINS task-based in situ method (Sect. 3) and we compare the dynamic helper core method with state-of-the art approaches (Sect. 4).

2   Related Work

The more direct way to perform in situ processing is called *synchronous* and consists in in-lining analytics code in the simulation code. The total execution time is the addition of simulation and analytics times, plus some possible overheads due to cache trashing. The analytics can directly access the simulation data structures, but more often a copy is performed to build a data structure adapted to the analytics needs [6]. ParaView/Catalyst [7] and VisIt/Libsim [8] are both relying on this approach to enable in situ visualization. They recently worked on a unified in situ API for the simulation codes, called SENSEI [9], to switch between Catalyst, Libsim and the IO framework ADIOS [10] with very limited code modifications.

Parallel simulations are almost never 100% efficient, some cores being idle during communication phases for instance or because some code sections do not provide enough parallelism to feed all the cores. One idea is to harvest these CPU cycles to execute analytics, leading to execution times shorter than with the synchronous execution. This is called *asynchronous in situ*. A simple approach consists in relying on the OS scheduler capabilities to allocate resources. The analytics run its own processes or threads concurrently with the ones of the simulation. The simulation only needs to give a copy of the relevant data to the local in situ analytics processes. The analytics can next proceed concurrently with the simulation. However, works [11,12] show that relying on the OS scheduler does not prove efficient because the presence of analytics processes tends to disturb the simulation.

To circumvent this problem, a common approach consists in dedicating one or more cores, called *helper cores*, to the analytics. The simulation runs on less cores, but, because it is usually not 100% efficient, its performance decreases by less than the ratio of confiscated cores. Damaris [3], FlowVR [2] Functional Partitioning [13], GePSeA [14], Active Buffer [15] or FlexIO [4] support this approach and have demonstrated its benefit in different contexts. Performance gains are usually significant compared to a synchronous approach. However, because the analytics and simulation are both isolated on distinct subsets of cores, this helper core strategy does not allow the analytics to harvest unused cycles of the simulation cores and vice versa.

GoldRush [11] takes a different approach. It implements a custom time-sharing scheduling to interleave simulation and analytics while limiting the interference on the simulation. Goldrush detects sequential sections in the OpenMP code of the simulation to schedule the analytics processes. The simulation sends resume signals to the analytics during these sections while the analytics are suspended otherwise. Experiments show the simulation performance is improved compared to OS controlled scheduling or a synchronous approach. However, Goldrush does not enable overlapping simulation and analytics during short simulation sequential sections and weakly scalable parallel sections.

All previously mentioned approaches applied to MPI or MPI+OpenMP simulations. New programming models are also developed as alternatives to message passing. StarPU [16], PaRSEC [17], Legion [18] and HPX [19] propose task-based runtime systems for distributed heterogeneous architectures. The program defines a directed acyclic graph where vertices are tasks and edges data dependencies between tasks. The runtime is in charge of mapping tasks to resources, and triggering task execution and the necessary data movements when data dependencies are resolved. Early experiments have been reported using Legion for in situ analytics [20,21]. They show that Legion runtime is able to overlap analytics and simulation tasks, but globally the performance is not yet competitive with MPI approaches.

In a more general context the shortcomings of standard OS for scheduling concurrent parallel applications on one multi-core node motivated the development of specific *co-scheduling* strategies. Space-sharing is often favored compared to time-sharing as it usually leads to better performance. But these solutions require a specific OS scheduler or modifications to the parallel runtimes [12,22].

3   The TINS Framework

3.1   Work Stealing and TBB

Task-based programming is becoming a standard for shared memory. The user only needs to delimit the potential parallelism through tasks or loops and the runtime takes care of creating and distributing these tasks to the worker threads it created. In a *work stealing scheduling*, the threads are assigned a set of tasks they have to execute. When a thread has executed all its tasks, it selects another thread and steals part of this victim's tasks if available; otherwise, it tries with another victim. The work stealing scheduler algorithm has a proven performance [23]. Pioneered by Cilk, task-based programming is today also available through Intel® TBB or OpenMP for instance.

In this paper, we use the TBB library that provides a task-based programming model and a work stealing scheduler for shared memory machines. TBB provides mechanisms to guide the task execution, in particular the notions of task_arena (arena in the following) and task_scheduler_observer (observer in the following). An *arena* encapsulates one or several TBB parallel regions where threads share and execute tasks. An arena is defined with a *concurrency level* that fixes the maximum number of tasks that can be executed simultaneously. In other words, the arena concurrency level determines the maximum number of threads that can work inside an arena. An application can contain several arenas. In this situation, when the parallel work encapsulated in an arena has been completed, the worker threads involved in this arena are free to enter another arena if its concurrency level allows it. An *observer* is an object that intercepts when a worker thread enters and leaves a specific arena. We use it to control thread affinity as detailed in Sect. 3.4.

In a TBB application, there will never be more threads running than the number of cores in the processor to avoid core oversubscription. In the case of an application with two concurrent arenas with concurrency levels of n_1 and n_2 on a processor with N cores, two situations can therefore be distinguished:

- if $n_1 + n_2 \leq N$, the concurrent arenas can have as many threads as requested (there will be n_1 threads in the first arena, n_2 in the second);
- if $n_1 + n_2 > N$, the concurrent arenas cannot have as many threads as requested and TBB allocates to each arena a number of threads proportional to the request ($n_1/(n_1 + n_2)N$ and $n_2/(n_1 + n_2)N$ respectively).

3.2   In Situ Processing with Tasks

TINS relies on the TBB work-stealing scheduler to implement a novel task-based in situ processing method. Simulation and analytics tasks are created concurrently and scheduled on a set of worker threads created by a single instance of the TBB scheduler. The use of TBB arenas allows to implement two asynchronous patterns: the standard helper core strategy with a permanent thread isolation and a *dynamic helper core strategy* with a temporary thread isolation.

3.3 Spawning Analytics and Simulation Tasks

Traditionally, a simulation is organized around a timeloop where internal data are updated at each timestep. We consider here a hybrid MPI+TBB simulation where each MPI process runs one instance of the work-stealing scheduler. Following TBB vocabulary, we call *simulation master thread* the simulation main thread started by MPI for each process. When tasks are created, they are distributed among the simulation master thread and the *worker threads* spawned by TBB.

To enable the asynchronous execution of the analytics, we propose the method described in Fig. 1. The simulation master thread spawns an *analytics master thread* at simulation initialization. The simulation and analytics master threads have their own timeloop and arena with different concurrency levels: the simulation master thread creates simulation tasks in the simulation arena while the analytics master thread creates analytics tasks in the analytics arena. Each master thread is responsible for its own arena and cannot enter the other one, while worker threads can change of arena as detailed in Sect. 3.4.

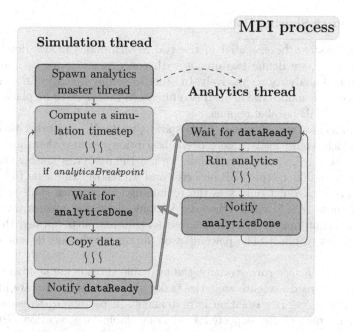

Fig. 1. Timeloops of the simulation (left) and analytics (right) master threads inside one MPI process. The green-framed blocks contain sequential regions (MPI communications for example) and parallel regions where simulation or analytics tasks are scheduled on the worker threads spawned by TBB inside the MPI process. The red arrows depict the synchronization between the master threads. (Color figure online)

The computation of the simulation timestep is left unchanged by TINS, alternating sequential regions with parallel ones where simulation tasks are created.

The user defines an *analytics breakpoint frequency* that sets the frequency of data processing. Every time the simulation reaches such analytics breakpoint, data are copied into a temporary buffer. When data are copied, the simulation master thread notifies the analytics master thread that data are ready to be processed with the `dataReady` signal and resumes the simulation execution.

On the other side, the analytics master thread waits for the simulation master thread `dataReady` signal to launch the analytics on the data written into the temporary buffer. It creates analytics tasks while the simulation master thread creates simulation tasks in its own timeloop, leading to an asynchronous in situ pattern. Once the analytics are executed, the analytics master thread notifies the simulation master thread with the `analyticsDone` signal. This second synchronization is added to avoid having to store more than one temporary buffer. This synchronization can be delayed if enough memory is available to store various buffers. The simulation master thread therefore has to wait for the `analyticsDone` signal before writing data in the temporary buffer. This signal is disabled for the first analytics breakpoint to avoid a deadlock.

3.4   Resource Sharing Policies

Analytics tasks can be executed in the two asynchronous modes described in Fig. 2. To do so, we define two arenas with concurrency levels n_s and n_a for simulation and analytics respectively. In order to simply manage the arenas and the asynchronous modes, we defined two functions that need to be placed before and after the TBB parallel regions.

On a processor with N cores, TBB spawns up to $N-1$ worker threads by default, which would lead to core oversubscription because there are already 2 master threads. To avoid this pitfall, we pin the analytics master thread on the first core thanks to the TBB observer and we restrict the node topology so that the TBB scheduler only sees the remaining $N-1$ cores. This way, there will be at most $N-2$ worker threads. Various pinning strategies were tested on the simulation master thread. Because no solution outperformed the other, we decided not to pin it. The placement of the worker threads depends on the strategy.

In the *static helper core* strategy, the available threads are split in two categories: some threads execute analytics tasks while the other ones are in charge of simulation tasks. The isolation is permanent. In particular, threads remain idle when no task of the expected kind is available for execution. To implement the static helper core strategy, the concurrency levels are chosen such that $n_a + n_s = N$. The TBB observer is used to bind threads that execute analytics tasks on the first n_a cores of the processor while the threads that execute simulation tasks are bound to the remaining cores. The goal is to try as much as possible to gather all threads of the same kind on the same NUMA nodes for a better cache efficiency. Tests showed that it notably improves the performance.

We introduce the *dynamic helper core* policy with a temporary thread isolation. As in the static helper core approach, a set of threads is assigned to analytics

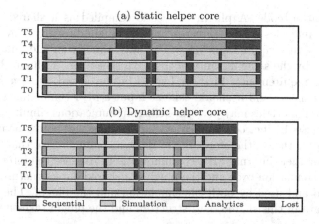

Fig. 2. Gantt diagram of the execution of simulation and analytics tasks on 6 threads (T0 to T5) for a static (a) or dynamic (b) helper core strategy. T0 and T5 are respectively the simulation and analytics master threads, T1, T2 and T3 are worker threads assigned to simulation and T4 is a worker thread assigned to analytics. The diagram represents two iterations of a simulation, both being the alternation of four sequential regions (grey areas) and three parallel regions (blue areas). The analytics is composed of one parallel region (orange areas). The purple areas highlight the periods when the threads are idle. The dynamic helper core strategy enables worker threads to switch to simulation (resp. analytics) tasks when there is no analytics (resp. simulation) work left, while this is not possible with static helper cores. (Color figure online)

tasks execution while the remaining execute simulation tasks. The main difference with the static approach is that the isolation is temporary: when the execution of a simulation (resp. analytics) parallel region is completed, the worker threads involved in the computation can enter the analytics (resp. simulation) arena if its concurrency level permits it. This method aims at reducing the thread idleness periods induced by the static helper core approach. We set $n_s = N - 1$ so that all the worker threads and the simulation master thread can work on simulation tasks if available. Note that the analytics master thread cannot execute simulation tasks because it is not allowed to enter the simulation arena. To restrict the number of threads in the analytics arena, we can choose different values for n_a. $n_a = n_s$ means that half of the threads will execute analytics tasks when both arenas are active while $n_a < n_s$ gives a higher priority to the simulation. We tested various binding strategies for the worker threads, but because they can execute tasks from both arenas, we did not observe that a binding strategy was overcoming the others. We therefore adopted the less constraining one by not binding the worker threads.

3.5 Plugin System

TINS aims at keeping the simulation and analytics codes well separated. We therefore developed a plugin system that allows to develop the analytics outside of the simulation code. A plugin is a code compiled as a shared library. At runtime, the analytics master thread scans the plugin directory provided by the user and loads the required analytics. This way, simulation and analytics tasks are scheduled by the same instance of the TBB scheduler. A plugin should meet the following requirements. First, it has to be developed using a MPI+TBB programming model and it should take as input a MPI communicator. Indeed, simulation and analytics may perform MPI communications simultaneously and they need to use distinct communicators for the messages not to be mixed. The analytics master thread therefore creates its own communicator that the plugins should use for their internal MPI communications. To ease the interoperability between the simulation code and the plugins, a shared data structure also needs to be defined and used by both the simulation and the plugin. The simulation copies the data in this shared data structure and the plugin takes it as input.

4   Experimental Evaluation

We compare the dynamic helper core strategy implemented with TINS with several other approaches on a molecular dynamics simulation using Intel® Xeon processors available in the CCRT French Computing Center.

4.1   ExaStamp Molecular Dynamics Code

ExaStamp [5] is a molecular dynamics code dedicated to material sciences (condensed matter and shock physics). It is written in C++11 and uses MPI and TBB for the different levels of parallelism. ExaStamp is used as a production code and routinely runs on more than 4,000 cores to simulate the displacement of up to 1 billion particles in a 3D system. ExaStamp is well parallelized, leaving limited compute resources under-used: it shows an efficiency of 90% on one node varying the number of cores from 1 to 28, and of 85% when scaling from 1 to 512 nodes. For each particle, the parameters of interest are the index of the particle (idx), its type (type), its position along the three axes (rx, ry, rz) and its velocity along the three axes (vx, vy, vz). To ease the interoperability between ExaStamp and the analytics described below, we defined the ParticleInSitu data structure as a structure of arrays where each array contains $nbPart$ elements, $nbPart$ being the number of particles in the current MPI process. The data structure is shared by the simulation code and the analytics implemented in the plugin system: the simulation produces and fills it and the plugins take it as input.

Implementing the TINS approach in ExaStamp required about 50 extra lines of code. The analytics master thread is implemented as a C++ thread and the synchronization signals between the master threads are implemented with shared booleans. The master threads may perform MPI communications concurrently so we need a thread-safe implementation of MPI with MPI_THREAD_MULTIPLE.

ExaStamp execution is parametrized through an input data file that defines the analytics to be executed, the analytics breakpoint frequency, the execution policy and the size of the arenas. No recompilation is required to change the configuration.

4.2 Analytics

To test TINS, we developed a set of analytics routines representative of the analytics used in computational physics (Table 1). They were chosen to represent different patterns regarding parallelization, MPI communications, cache and memory usage.

Table 1. Analytics implemented to evaluate TINS

Analytics	Description
write_dat	Write the positions of the particles inside each MPI process in a file (one file per MPI process)
statistics_seq	Compute sequentially the mean of the positions for the particles inside each MPI process
statistics_par	Compute in parallel the mean of the positions for the particles inside each MPI process (with 1 TBB parallel reduction)
radial	Compute in parallel a local radial distribution function for the particles inside each MPI process (with 2 nested TBB parallel for)
histogram	Compute in parallel a global histogram of rx positions (locally with 2 TBB parallel reductions, and globally with 2 MPI_REDUCE)

In the write_dat routine, each MPI process writes a file with the positions of each particle at each analytics breakpoint. This analytics mimics a native file writing pattern commonly used in ExaStamp to write particles in an XYZ format suitable for post-processing tools. This analytics plugin neither generates TBB tasks nor MPI communications.

The two statistics routines trigger local computations and do not perform any MPI communication. They both compute the mean of the positions of the particles from the data copied in each MPI process. We implemented a sequential version (statistics_seq) and a parallel version (statistics_par) where the mean is computed through one TBB parallel reduction. Each task consists in a few summations but is very memory intensive. When simulating the behavior of 4,000,000 particles per MPI process, the positions represent approximately 96 MB of data per MPI process, significantly more than the caches available on a Broadwell processor (see below for the processor specifications). Reading these data therefore evicts simulation data from the caches. Moreover, these analytics highlight NUMA effects because data are split between the caches of the different NUMA nodes. To further stress memory accesses for the experiments, the statistics routines can be executed several times at each analytics breakpoint.

The histogram algorithm (histogram) mixes TBB tasks creation and MPI communications. This routine counts how many particles have a position in intervals of the form $[rx_i, rx_i + \Delta x]$. A first collective communication is necessary to determine the bounds of the system: each MPI process computes its own minimum and maximum positions with a TBB parallel reduction and the global bounds are found thanks to a MPI_REDUCE operation. The global domain is then split into smaller intervals of the form $[rx_i, rx_i + \Delta x]$. The number of particles in each interval is computed inside each MPI process thanks to a TBB parallel reduction and the global histogram is then computed with a MPI_REDUCE. The histogram is computed on 1,000 intervals. For experimenting with analytics having different MPI communication loads, we can increase the size of the arrays communicated in the second MPI_REDUCE. This way, we can see the influence of an analytics that spends most of its time in MPI communications.

The local radial distribution function (radial) is a common algorithm in computational physics and consists in a local histogram over the distances between the particles. For each particle, we compute the distance with all the other particles and store them in a local histogram of 1,000 bins. This analytics requires two nested for loops and is parallelized with TBB thanks to the tbb::blocked_range2d feature. This algorithm is used because it demonstrates the effect of a compute intensive analytics.

4.3   I/O Middlewares

We compare the TINS approach with two state-of-the-art in situ frameworks: Damaris [24] and Goldrush [11].

Damaris implements the static helper core strategy. It is a MPI-based approach that starts on each node a certain number of processes for the simulation and the analytics, each one running with their own MPI communicator. Local data transfers from the simulation to the analytics processes are made through a shared memory segment. To limit data copies, Damaris enables the simulation to directly allocate data inside the shared memory segment. The simulation writes data into this shared memory segment and the analytics deallocates data once consumed. We instrumented ExaStamp with the Damaris API and developed Damaris plugins for the five analytics described above, keeping their TBB parallelization when existing. An important difference with TINS is that Damaris starts two distinct instances of TBB scheduler per node: one for running the simulation tasks and the other for the analytics. Damaris does not integrate mechanisms for pinning the processes or threads to the cores. We use TBB observers to bind analytics threads (master and workers) to the helper cores and the simulation threads (master and workers) to the remaining cores. The helper cores are assigned contiguously starting from the first core to keep them running as much as possible on the same sockets. We experienced better performance with this approach.

Goldrush is a C library that implements a custom time-sharing scheduling to trigger analytics during the simulation sequential sections. Each simulation process records the duration of its sequential sections and assumes these sections repeat at each iteration. When a sequential section is long enough, given a user-defined threshold, the simulation process sends a SIGCONT signal to resume the analytics process and a SIGSTOP signal to suspend it at the end of this sequential region. We instrumented ExaStamp with the Goldrush API delimiting the sequential regions where no TBB task is created. We ported the sequential statistics and the parallel one with its TBB parallelization that can run tasks on all cores when resumed by Goldrush.

4.4   Experimental Setups

Experiments run on the Cobalt supercomputer from the CCRT high performance computing center. Each node has two Intel® Broadwell CPUs running at 2.40 GHz and 128 GB of memory. Each CPU has 2 NUMA nodes with 7 cores each and a shared L3 cache of 17,920 KB. Hyperthreading is not activated. The nodes are connected through a EDR InfiniBand network. The codes use Intel® TBB 16.0.3.210, are compiled with icpc compiler (version 17.0.4.196) and are launched with Intel® MPI (version 2017.0.4.196).

Experiments are conducted timing 32 consecutive iterations of ExaStamp, with the analytics performed after each timestep. In production codes, outputs are usually not produced at each timestep to avoid slowing down to much the execution. Here we stress the system by analyzing data at each iteration to make the overheads more visible.

Tests are performed on simulations with 4,000,000 particles per MPI process and one MPI process per node. Simulation codes usually run several MPI processes per node, but we run only one MPI process per node to probe TBB scheduler with a larger pool of cores. We compared the performance of running ExaStamp with 1 process per node and 4 processes per node and measured only a 2% performance drop.

4.5   Results

Comparison with Goldrush

We first compare the TINS approach with the static and dynamic helper core strategies with the Goldrush approach. We ran three analytics on 28 Broadwell cores for a simulation of 4,000,000 particles: the parallel statistics performed 100 and 1,000 times at each analytics breakpoint (stat_par_100 and stat_par_1000) for small and long analytics parallelized with TBB and the sequential statistics computed 1,000 times at each analytics (stat_seq_1000) for a long analytics without parallelization. For each experiment, we tested two static helper core configurations (SHC-a-s) and two dynamic helper core configurations (DHC-a-s) where a and s stand for analytics and simulation arena sizes.

Table 2 shows that the Goldrush approach is efficient on small parallel analytics. For instance, it gives on overhead of only 8% on ExaStamp executed without analytics (ExaStamp-alone) when co-locating the stat_par_100 analytics and it can outperform the TINS approach with 7 static helper cores because too much cores were removed from the simulation in this situation. However, the TINS approach with dynamic helper core strategy can be up to 4.55% faster than the

Table 2. Total execution times in seconds of ExaStamp co-located with three analytics executed with different TINS configurations and with Goldrush for a simulation of 4,000,000 atoms on 28 Broadwell cores (1 MPI process)

	stat_par_100	stat_par_1000	stat_seq_1000
ExaStamp-alone	75.66	75.66	75.66
Goldrush	81.90	92.73	131.53
SHC-1a-27s	77.35	86.05	86.01
SHC-7a-21s	99.00	99.67	101.20
DHC-7a-27s	78.17	81.76	85.84
DHC-27a-27s	79.00	82.29	85.85

Goldrush approach. For longer analytics, like the sequential statistics, the TINS approach with dynamic helper core strategy can be up to 34.74% faster than the Goldrush approach. The long execution time of the stat_seq_1000 analytics reflects that Goldrush only manages to overlap with the simulation a small portion of the analytics because it executes analytics only during long enough sequential periods. The remaining of the analytics computations that Goldrush does not manage to execute during the simulation sequential sections is thus completed after the end of the simulation. The TINS task interleaving strategy prevents this issue by using both the simulation sequential periods and the periods when the simulation is not efficient enough to schedule analytics tasks.

Static versus Dynamic Helper Cores

In order to compare the different in situ strategies, we run a simulation of 256,000,000 particles with 64 MPI processes on 1,792 cores (Figs. 3 and 4). We tested various configurations to stress the memory accesses or the MPI communications for the statistics and the histogram routines. The statistics routines were executed 1 to 1,000 times at each analytics breakpoint. We present here only the results with 100 and 1,000 executions representative of the two main behaviors that emerged from these tests. The histogram was tested with global reductions applied on arrays of 1,000 to 1,000,000,000 integers. We include here the results for the intermediate size of 100,000,000 integers. For large arrays, execution times are similar for all strategies, dominated by the MPI communication. Analytics cost is too short with small array sizes to exhibit significant performance differences.

For each analytics, we tested various numbers of helper cores and arena sizes. damaris-a-s corresponds to Damaris running the analytics on a helper cores and the simulation on the remaining s cores. SHC-a-s (resp. DHC-a-s) corresponds to the TINS approach running the static (resp. dynamic) helper core strategy with an analytics arena of size a and a simulation arena of size s. Each histogram bar gives the total execution time of one strategy. A bar is divided into four areas: left part is the simulation master thread idle (no pattern) and active times (cross pattern); right part is the analytics master thread execution time split into idle (no pattern) and active times (dashed pattern).

For the sake of comparison, we implemented a synchronous version of the algorithm in Fig. 1 where the simulation master thread waits for the analytics-Done signal before computing the next iteration. We also implemented a pure asynchronous case where simulation and analytics tasks are created inside the same arena. Task scheduling is left to the TBB scheduler without any isolation or priority constraint. As a reference we also report the execution time of ExaStamp running on all cores without analytics, giving the best execution time we could expect if perfectly overlapping analytics with the simulation.

First, we notice that the TINS implementation presents a small overhead on the simulation execution time compared to the Damaris implementation. Our first studies tend to show that this overhead comes from the interaction between the two arenas and the observer in the TINS approach. Indeed, we interfere with TBB default data placement when using two arenas while there is only one arena in the Damaris case. This overhead depends on the number of helper cores but never exceeds 8%. On the other side, the execution of memory intensive analytics (statistics_seq and statistics_par) can be up to 75% longer with Damaris than with equivalent static helper core strategies implemented with TINS. Performance measurements with VTune show an important impact of NUMA effects, Damaris having up to 75% of DRAM remote accesses compared to 15% for TINS. Damaris relies on a shared memory segment managed by the Boost library and this shared memory segment is not bound to any specific memory bank. The shared memory segment can therefore be interleaved on different NUMA nodes, leading to performance penalties when data need to be accessed. TINS also relies on a copy but we do not need to create a shared memory segment because analytics and simulation belong to the same process. We tested various binding strategies for the temporary buffer. Compared to a situation where the buffer is not bound, the analytics is 41% quicker when binding the buffer on the NUMA nodes where the analytics worker threads belong and 22% longer when binding it on the NUMA nodes where the simulation worker threads belong. The different binding strategies do not have an impact on the simulation execution time and we decided to simply bind the buffer on the NUMA nodes where the analytics worker threads belong to speed up the analytics.

To compare the static helper core configurations, we can separate the analytics into two groups: the short analytics whose execution time are smaller than the simulation execution time (Fig. 3) and the long analytics whose execution time are equivalent or greater than the simulation execution time (Fig. 4). For short analytics, the best configuration is to dedicate one thread for the analytics. The analytics cannot benefit of any parallelism but the smallest number of threads are confiscated for the simulation and the analytics execution is still faster than the simulation iteration. Increasing the number of helper cores then leads to fewer threads for the simulation, which impacts the simulation execution time. For long analytics, the optimal number of static helper cores is analytics-dependent. Using 4 threads for statistics_par is a good trade off because if we use fewer threads, the analytics cannot benefit from its parallelization and the total execution time is dominated by the analytics execution time. If we use more threads for the analytics, the simulation runs on fewer threads and the total execution time is dominated by the simulation execution time.

The dynamic helper core strategy is in general less sensitive to the configuration. For the small analytics in Fig. 3, there is less than 1% difference for the total execution time from one configuration to another. The different dynamic helper core configurations are therefore equivalent to a static helper core approach where one helper core is used. The analytics can be performed with an overhead of less than 5% with respect to ExaStamp alone and the dynamic helper core strategy can be up to 3% faster than the pure asynchronous approach and 28% faster than the synchronous approach that suffers from NUMA issues.

The results are similar with the sequential statistics performed 1,000 times (Fig. 4), with approximately 1% difference in the total execution time from one configuration to another. In the case of the parallel statistics performed 1,000 times (Fig. 4), setting an analytics arena of size 1 is too restrictive because the analytics cannot benefit from its parallelization. It therefore presents a total execution time 10% longer than the simulation alone while the other dynamic helper core configurations reduce this overhead to 6%. For these analytics, the dynamic helper core strategy is up to 40% better than the Damaris approach set with the appropriate number of static helper cores.

The radial analytics shows a slightly different behavior for the dynamic helper core strategy: increasing the concurrency level of the analytics arena also increases the total execution time. An analytics arena of size 1 induces an overhead of 6% with ExaStamp alone, this overhead growing up to 39% with an analytics arena of size 27. This analytics differs from the others because it executes two nested parallel loops. TBB does not support task switching on nested parallel loops. When a thread enters the analytics arena during simulation sequential periods, it cannot move back to the simulation arena before all the analytics tasks have been executed. In particular, it cannot switch back to support the simulation when the sequential region is over, slowing down the progress of the simulation. This effect is all the more visible as the analytics arena size increases. It is therefore necessary to reduce the size of the analytics arena in the dynamic helper core strategy, sizes of 4 and 7 being good tradeoff in this situation.

Experiments show that TINS implemented with the dynamic helper core strategy gives generally better performance than the static helper core strategy implemented by Damaris. In addition, our system shows greater flexibility for the choice of the number of helper cores, the execution times between the different dynamic configurations being relatively close.

Task versus Analytics Master Thread

TBB constrains master threads to execute only the tasks of the arena they created. Thus the analytics master thread never executes simulation tasks. As we spawn only $N - 2$ worker threads, there is always one core that cannot execute simulation tasks, potentially leading to underusing this core. We tried oversubscription by creating $N - 1$ worker threads, but the performance degrades

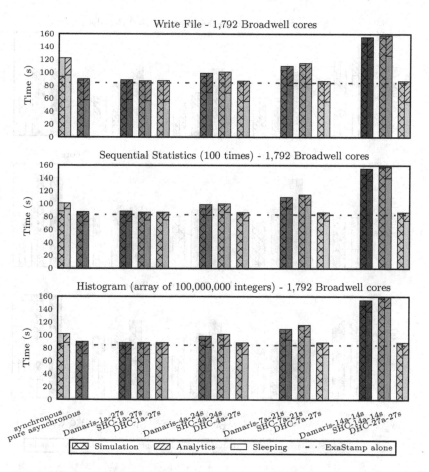

Fig. 3. Comparison of the different strategies on 1,792 Broadwell cores (64 MPI processes) for three analytics quicker than the simulation timestep: file writing (a), sequential statistics performed 100 times (b) and histogram with an array of 100,000,000 integers for the MPI collective communication (c).

significantly. To compare our analytics-master-thread approach with a version without additional master thread, we modified ExaStamp so that the simulation master thread creates an analytics task enqueued in the analytics arena task queue after data are copied. This task creates sub analytics tasks, as in the analytics-master-thread approach. The arena sizes are respectively set to N and n for simulation and analytics. The n threads in the analytics arena are pinned on the first cores, as in the static helper core strategy defined above.

Table 3 compares the execution times of the task approach (task-a-s) and the analytics master thread one (thread-a-s). The results are similar for the histogram computation (less than 2% of difference for the two methods) and the radial analytics (less than 4% of difference). However, the task method completely fails at reproducing the results of the thread method on the

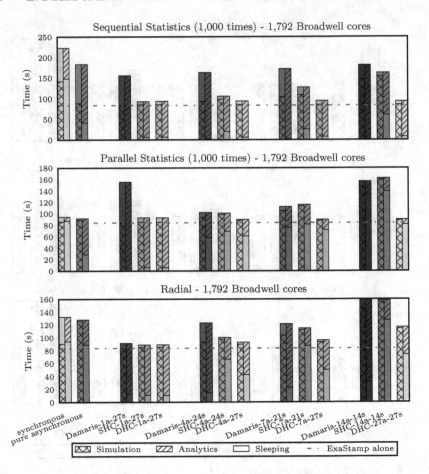

Fig. 4. Comparison of the different strategies on 1,792 Broadwell cores (64 MPI processes) for three analytics equivalent to or larger than the simulation timestep: sequential statistics performed 1,000 times (a), parallel statistics performed 1,000 times and radial.

`statistics_seq` analytics: the total execution time is up to 74% higher with an analytics arena of size 27. Performance measurements with VTune show that the percentage of DRAM remote accesses is of 18.5% with an analytics arena of size 7 and increases to 67.5% with an analytics arena size of 27 while it remains around 15% for TINS. In the thread approach, the sequential analytics will always be executed by the analytics master thread, guaranteeing data locality. In the task approach, we can bind the analytics threads on a set of cores but we cannot guarantee that the task will be executed on a particular thread. The task approach is also more intrusive in the simulation because the simulation needs to enqueue the task while it is left to a separate thread in the TINS approach. The TINS approach shows therefore better performance than a task approach and is less intrusive in the simulation.

Table 3. Execution times in seconds of the task and analytics-master-thread approaches, for three different analytics running the dynamic helper core strategy, with analytics arenas of sizes 7 and 27, on 1,792 Broadwell cores (64 MPI processes).

Time (s)	statistics_seq			radial			histogram		
	Total	Simulation	Analytics	Total	Simulation	Analytics	Total	Simulation	Analytics
task-7-27	110.7	102.6	94.6	93.6	91.6	29.9	90.7	89.0	23.7
thread-7-27	95.1	85.3	87.2	96.0	93.2	45.5	88.8	86.9	18.1
task-27-27	163.1	138.0	146.3	112.9	110.6	39.3	86.5	84.8	22.1
thread-27-27	93.7	85.6	86.3	116.6	114.0	42.6	88.6	86.9	17.6

Iteration Varying Analytics Workload

The analysis of simulation results often requires to execute different types of analytics at different iterations. Typically in production runs, different kinds of analytics are performed as the physics of the system evolves. To encompass this behavior, we execute 3 different statistics: the parallel statistics is computed during 10 iterations, the histogram is computed for the next 10 iterations and the radial distribution function is computed for the last 10 iterations.

Figure 5 compares the results for the different strategies on a simulation of 2 billions atoms using 14,336 Broadwell cores (512 MPI processes). The dynamic helper core approach always gives the best performance, being up to 20% faster than Damaris. As the analytics workload varies, no number of static helper cores is capable of ensuring the best performance for all the iterations. In opposite the dynamic helper core strategy offers more flexibility, leading to a better resource usage. Best results are obtained with an analytics arena of size 4 or 7 because the analytics can run in parallel and the simulation has still exclusive access to enough resources to ensure that its progression is not disturbed by analytics.

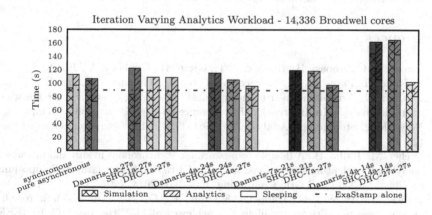

Fig. 5. Comparison of the different strategies on 14,336 Broadwell cores for an analytics scheme where the executed analytics depends on the iteration number.

5   Conclusion

Many previous works investigated how to perform asynchronous in situ processing at a process level for MPI applications. The helper core strategy emerged as the best approach to share the resources. In this paper, we propose the TINS approach that goes one step further by proposing a dynamic helper core strategy with a temporary thread isolation in a task-based programming model. The helper cores are assigned to analytics only when analytics tasks are available while they join the other threads for simulation processing instead. The TINS approach is a minimally intrusive method where it is easy to switch between static and dynamic helper core strategies without code recompilation and that is easy to use by the end-user. It enables use of both the simulation sequential regions and the part of the simulation that are not parallelized well enough. The experiments conducted on up to 14,336 Broadwell cores on representative analytics codes show that the TINS framework implemented with the Intel® TBB library can be up to 40% faster than the Damaris and Goldrush approaches on the ExaStamp molecular dynamics code that shows a good MPI and TBB efficiency. In particular, when the analytics workload varies from an iteration to another, no fixed number of static helper cores is capable of ensuring the best performance while the dynamic helper core strategy proves more flexible. Experiments also show that the obtained performance are close to the raw simulation, demonstrating that our approach enables to perform analytics at a high frequency. Future work will investigate the behavior of TINS on real analytics use cases. We also plan to study how to port TINS on other task-based runtimes, OpenMP in particular.

Acknowledgments. This work was partly funded by the French Programme d'Investissements d'Avenir (PIA) project SMICE. We thank Fang Zheng for having provided the Goldrush code and Matthieu Dorier for his help with Damaris.

References

1. Bennett, J.C., Abbasi, H., Bremer, P.-T., Grout, R., Gyulassy, A., Jin, T., Klasky, S., Kolla, H., Parashar, M., Pascucci, V., Pebay, P., Thompson, D., Yu, H., Zhang, F., Chen, J.: Combining in-situ and in-transit processing to enable extreme-scale scientific analysis. In: International Conference on High Performance Computing, Networking, Storage and Analysis, pp. 49:1–49:9. IEEE Computer Society Press (2012)
2. Dreher, M., Raffin, B.: A flexible framework for asynchronous in situ and in transit analytics for scientific simulations. In: 14th IEEE/ACM International Symposium on Cluster, Cloud and Grid Computing (CCGRID 2014) (2014)
3. Dorier, M., Antoniu, G., Cappello, F., Snir, M., Orf, L.: Damaris: how to efficiently leverage multicore parallelism to achieve scalable, jitter-free I/O. In: IEEE International Conference on Cluster Computing (2012)
4. Zheng, F., Zou, H., Eisnhauer, G., Schwan, K., Wolf, M., Dayal, J., Nguyen, T.A., Cao, J., Abbasi, H., Klasky, S., Podhorszki, N., Yu, H.: FlexIO: I/O middleware for location-flexible scientific data analytics. In: IPDPS 2013 (2013)

5. Cieren, E., Colombet, L., Pitoiset, S., Namyst, R.: ExaStamp: a parallel framework for molecular dynamics on heterogeneous clusters. In: Lopes, L., et al. (eds.) Euro-Par 2014. LNCS, vol. 8806, pp. 121–132. Springer, Cham (2014). https://doi.org/10.1007/978-3-319-14313-2_11
6. Lorendeau, B., Fournier, Y., Ribes, A.: In situ visualization in fluid mechanics using Catalyst: a case study for Code_Saturne. In: IEEE Symposium on Large Data Analysis and Visualization (LDAV) (2013)
7. Fabian, N., Moreland, K., Thompson, D., Bauer, A., Marion, P., Geveci, B., Rasquin, M., Jansen, K.: The ParaView coprocessing library: a scalable, general purpose in situ visualization library. In: Large Data Analysis and Visualization Workshop (LDAV 2011), pp. 89–96 (2011)
8. Whitlock, B., Favre, J.M., Meredith, J.S.: Parallel in situ coupling of simulation with a fully featured visualization system. In: 11th Eurographics Conference on Parallel Graphics and Visualization, pp. 101–109 (2011)
9. Ayachit, U., Whitlock, B., Wolf, M., Loring, B., Geveci, B., Lonie, D., Bethel, E.: The SENSEI generic in situ interface. In: 2nd Workshop on In Situ Infrastructures for Enabling Extreme-Scale Analysis and Visualization (ISAV 2016), pp. 40–44 (2016)
10. Lofstead, J.F., Klasky, S., Schwan, K., Podhorszki, N., Jin, C.: Flexible IO and integration for scientific codes through the adaptable IO system (ADIOS). In: 6th International Workshop on Challenges of Large Applications in Distributed Environments, pp. 15–24 (2008)
11. Zheng, F., Yu, H., Hantas, C., Wolf, M., Eisenhauer, G., Schwan, K., Abbasi, H., Klasky, S.: GoldRush: resource efficient in situ scientific data analytics using fine-grained interference aware execution. In: International Conference on High Performance Computing, Networking, Storage and Analysis (SC 2013), pp. 78:1–78:12 (2013)
12. Harris, T., Maas, M., Marathe, V.J.: Callisto: co-scheduling parallel runtime systems. In: Proceedings of the Ninth European Conference on Computer Systems (EuroSys 2014), pp. 24:1–24:14 (2014)
13. Li, M., Vazhkudai, S.S., Butt, A.R., Meng, F., Ma, X., Kim, Y., Engelmann, C., Shipman, G.: Functional partitioning to optimize end-to-end performance on many-core architectures. In: International Conference for High Performance Computing, Networking, Storage and Analysis, pp. 1–12 (2010)
14. Singh, A., Balaji, P., Feng, W.: GePSeA: a general-purpose software acceleration framework for lightweight task offloading. In: International Conference on Parallel Processing, pp. 261–268 (2009)
15. Ma, X., Lee, J., Winslett, M.: High-level buffering for hiding periodic output cost in scientific simulations. IEEE Trans. Parallel Distrib. Syst. **17**(3), 193–204 (2006)
16. Augonnet, C., Thibault, S., Namyst, R., Wacrenier, P.: StarPU: a unified platform for task scheduling on heterogeneous multicore architectures. Concurr. Comput. Pract. Exper. **23**, 187–198 (2011)
17. Hoque, R., Herault, T., Bosilca, G., Dongarra, J.: Dynamic task discovery in PaR-SEC: a data-flow task-based runtime. In: Proceedings of the 8th Workshop on Latest Advances in Scalable Algorithms for Large-Scale Systems, ScalA 2017, pp. 6:1–6:8. ACM, New York (2017). http://doi.acm.org/10.1145/3148226.3148233
18. Bauer, M., Treichler, S., Slaughter, E., Aiken, A.: Legion: expressing locality and independence with logical regions. In: Proceedings of the International Conference on High Performance Computing, Networking, Storage and Analysis (SC 2012) (2012)

19. Kaiser, H., Heller, T., Adelstein-Lelbach, B., Serio, A., Fey, D.: HPX: a task based programming model in a global address space. In: Proceedings of the 8th International Conference on Partitioned Global Address Space Programming Models (PGAS 2014) (2014)
20. Pébaÿ, P., Bennett, J.C., Hollman, D., Treichler, S., McCormick, P.S., Sweeney, C.M., Kolla, H., Aiken, A.: Towards asynchronous many-task in situ data analysis using legion. In: 2016 IEEE International Parallel and Distributed Processing Symposium Workshops (IPDPSW), pp. 1033–1037, May 2016
21. Heirich, A., Slaughter, E., Papadakis, M., Lee, W., Biedert, T., Aiken, A.: In situ visualization with task-based parallelism. In: Workshop on In Situ Infrastructures on Enabling Extreme-Scale Analysis and Visualization (ISAV 2017) (2017)
22. Cho, Y., Oh, S., Egger, B.: Adaptive space-shared scheduling for shared-memory parallel programs. In: Desai, N., Cirne, W. (eds.) JSSPP 2015-2016. LNCS, vol. 10353, pp. 158–177. Springer, Cham (2017). https://doi.org/10.1007/978-3-319-61756-5_9
23. Blumofe, R.D., Leiserson, C.E.: Scheduling multithreaded computations by work stealing. J. ACM **46**(5), 720–748 (1999)
24. Dorier, M., Sisneros, R., Peterka, T., Antoniu, G., Semeraro, D.: Damaris/Viz: a nonintrusive, adaptable and user-friendly in situ visualization framework. In: IEEE Symposium on Large Data Analysis and Visualization (LDAV) (2013)

Machine Learning Predictions for Underestimation of Job Runtime on HPC System

Jian Guo[1](✉) , Akihiro Nomura[1](✉), Ryan Barton[1](✉), Haoyu Zhang[1](✉),
and Satoshi Matsuoka[1,2,3](✉)

[1] Department of Mathematical and Computing Science,
Tokyo Institute of Technology, Tokyo, Japan
{guo.j.ae,nomura.a.ac,barton.r.aa}@m.titech.ac.jp,
lynkzhang@gmail.com, matsu@is.titech.ac.jp
[2] Global Scientific Information and Computing Center,
Tokyo Institute of Technology, Tokyo, Japan
[3] Real World Big-Data Computing Open Innovation Laboratory,
National Institute of Advanced Industrial Science and Technology, Tokyo, Japan

Abstract. In modern high-performance computing (HPC) systems,
users are usually requested to estimate the job runtime for system
scheduling when they submit a job. In general, an underestimation of job
runtime will cause the HPC system to terminate the job before its completion. If users could be notified that their jobs may not finish before its
allocated time expires, users can take actions, such as killing the job and
resubmitting it after parameter adjustment, to save time and cost. Meanwhile, the productivity of HPC systems could also be vastly improved. In
this paper, we propose a data-driven approach – that is, one that actively
observes, analyzes, and logs jobs – for predicting underestimation of job
runtime on HPC systems. Using data produced by TSUBAME 2.5, a
supercomputer deployed at the Tokyo Institute of Technology, we apply
machine learning algorithms to recognize patterns about whether the
underestimation of job runtime occurs. Our experimental results show
that our approach on runtime-underestimation prediction with 80% precision, 70% recall and 74% F1-score on the entirety of a given dataset.
Finally, we split the entire job data set into subsets categorized by scientific application name. The best precision, recall and F1-score of subsets on runtime-underestimation prediction achieved 90%, 95% and 92%
respectively.

Keywords: HPC · Job log analysis
Underestimation on job runtime · Machine learning

1 Introduction

Modern high-performance computing (HPC) systems are built with an increasing number of CPU/GPU cores, memory, and storage space. Meanwhile, scientific applications have been growing in complexity. However, not all users have

© The Author(s) 2018
R. Yokota and W. Wu (Eds.): SCFA 2018, LNCS 10776, pp. 179–198, 2018.
https://doi.org/10.1007/978-3-319-69953-0_11

enough experience working reasonably with supercomputing resources. Writing and executing programs on an HPC system requires more experience and techniques than on a PC. First, HPC users need to have relevant knowledge about system-specific information, such as parallel programming on multi cores or multi nodes in HPC environments, and how many compute nodes or cores are appropriate for a specific application job. Furthermore, when submitting a job to an HPC system, users are usually requested to estimate the runtime of said job for system scheduling. In general, an underestimated runtime will lead to the HPC system terminating the job before its completion. On the other hand, an overestimated runtime of the job usually results in a longer queuing time. In both cases, the productivity of HPC users is hindered [1]. Especially in the case of underestimation, the system will directly terminate the undergoing job when its estimated runtime expires. Users will lose their processing data, and furthermore, can no longer get the final results they need. Therefore, most users have to resubmit their jobs again and run them again from the beginning, which is a costly situation for users and systems since they waste time and system resources.

Predicting jobs, especially those which may not finish before its allocated time expires, can mitigate wastes of time and system resources by taking early actions for those jobs. For instance, if an ongoing task execution of a job is predicted to be *runtime-underestimated* based on the characteristic patterns, system administrators or an automated agent can explicitly send a notification to the user who submitted the job. The user can fix the problem by killing the job and resubmitting it after parameter adjustment.

In this study, we propose a data-driven approach for predicting job statuses on HPC systems. Here, "data-driven" means that our approach actively observes, analyzes, and logs jobs collected on TSUBAME, a large-scale supercomputer deployed at the Tokyo Institute of Technology. Supervised machine learning algorithms (i.e., XGBoost and Random Forest) are applied to address this binary classification problem (having runtime-underestimation or not).

Our experimental results show that our approach predicts the underestimated job with 80% precision, 70% recall and 74% F1-score on the entirety of a given dataset. Then, we split the entire job data set into subsets categorized by scientific application name. The best precision, recall and F1-score of subsets on job runtime-underestimated prediction achieve 90%, 95% and 92% respectively. This achievement means that, for some scientific applications on HPC systems, our model can be used to accurately predict whether a job can be completed before its estimated runtime expires.

Our specific contributions are:

- We introduced some evaluation metrics (precision, recall, and F1-score on minority classes) which are more fair than metrics used in similar previous studies (overall precision, recall, and F1-score).
- Additionally, we plotted feature importance and revealed surprising hidden patterns between different HPC applications and different features on computing resource usage.

The rest of the paper is organized as follows: Related work about gathering and analyzing job logs in HPC systems are introduced in Sect. 2, followed by an overview description of the dataset and feature engineering used for preprocessing the dataset in Sect. 3. Design and implementation of our machine learning-based prediction methods and the evaluation of our approach are described in Sect. 4. In Sect. 5, we presented detailed analysis based on experiment results and discussion. Finally, we gave our future work and conclude the paper in Sect. 6.

2 Related Work

Gathering and analyzing job logs in HPC systems is a widely studied topic in computer science literature. In recent years, there have been many studies on analyzing job logs focusing on anomaly detection, failure prediction, runtime prediction, and so on.

Klinkenberg et al. [2] proposed and evaluated a method for predicting failures with framed cluster monitoring data and extracted features describing the characteristic of the signals. Authors in [3] presented a machine learning based Random forests (RF) classification model for predicting unsuccessful job executions. In modern supercomputing centers, successful or health jobs occupy a very large part of job databases. However, authors used the overall accuracy as an evaluation metric in those works, which cannot truly reflect unsuccessful execution results. Tuncer et al. [4] presented a method to detect anomalies and performance variations in HPC and Cloud environments. However, they run kernels representing common HPC workloads and infuse synthetic anomalies to mimic anomalies observed in HPC systems, which may deviate from anomaly situations in reality.

There exists research focusing on predicting other job features, such as I/O, CPU, GPU, memory usage and runtime in clusters. McKenna et al. [5] utilized several machine learning methods (kNN, Decision Tree, and RF) for predicting runtime and I/O usage for HPC jobs with training data from job scripts. Rodrigues et al. [6] predicted job execution, wait time, and memory usage with job logs and batch schedulers by an ensemble of machine learning algorithms such as RF and kNN. Fan et al. [7] proposed an online runtime adjustment framework for trade-off between prediction accuracy and underestimation rate in job runtime estimates.

Additionally, others have worked on log file analysis with machine learning, anomaly detection and so on. In this work, we use system log data collected by ganglia to predict whether a job runtime was underestimated. We found that our method has particularly good results at predicting underestimated runtime for some applications after splitting the entire job data set into subset categorized by scientific application name.

To the best of our knowledge, our work is the first to analyze job data and build models according to different HPC scientific applications using machine learning. We discover that different features of computing resource usage, with different weights on the prediction of job runtime-underestimation, ended up affecting HPC applications' runtime.

3   Data Collection and Feature Engineering

Our purpose is to model and predict users' runtime-underestimation on job runtime that wastes time and system resources. To address this, we propose a machine learning-based technique which takes advantage of utilization data of different computing resources as well as users' resource usage requirements at job submission. The technique builds classifiers that can recognize hidden patterns in the collected data, which are necessary to understand what jobs are running in the system and the number of resources allocated at each node.

The overall system architecture from data gathering to result prediction is depicted in Fig. 1.

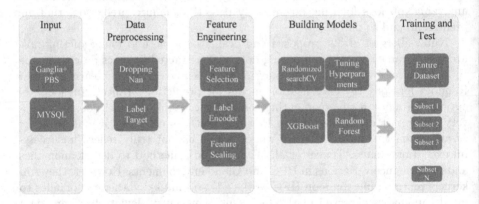

Fig. 1. Overall workflow diagram in this study

3.1   Gathering TSUBAME DATA

TSUBAME 2.5 [8] is GPU supercomputer located at Tokyo Institute of Technology, operated from November 2010 to July 2017, including its ancestor TSUBAME 2.0. TSUBAME 2.5 is well known as "the greenest supercomputer in the world" in the Green500 List [9] on November 2010 and June 2011. The system consists of 1408 compute nodes, each of which has three NVIDIA Tesla K20X GPUs (upgraded from NVIDIA Tesla M2050 on September 2013), two CPUs and SSD as local scratch storage. The nodes are interconnected with dual-rail InfiniBand QDR full fat-tree network. All nodes run SUSE Enterprise Linux 11 and compute jobs are managed by PBS Professional 11. System load (and power) information, including GPU usage, is monitored and recorded using Ganglia [10]. All nodes process information is also recorded via process accounting interface in Linux.

We created MySQL database containing anonymized job history data from PBS's log, associated CPU and GPU usage information as features from Ganglia, and application information from accounting logs of each job. Prediction of online runtime underestimation needs to be based on the progress information, rather than the post-processing of measured information after jobs are finished.

All features regarding computing resource usage were normalized by dividing by used wall clock timings. This provides progress information in the form of a ratio – resource usage related measurements by wall clock units. As they are normalized by time-based value, those normalized performance related measurements serve as appropriate data sources for machine learning based job status prediction. Indeed, this can also be extended to online prediction [3]. In total, 14.3 million jobs were recorded, with a total database size of 8.5 GiB.

Table 1 shows the really world data we collected by Ganglia and PBS from TSUBAME 2.5.

Table 1. List of computing resource usage features based on normalized time series data and job requests information

Features	Description	Features	Description
used_cpupercent	Recorded CPU usage	req_pl	Requested priority
used_mem	Recorded memory usage	req_et	Requested option to extend maximum runtime
used_ncpus	Recorded number of CPU used	nhosts	Calculated number of host involved
used_vmem	Recorded memory address space usage	is_array	1 if the job is a part of array (parameter survey) job
req_mem	Requested memory amount	gpu_utilization	Recorded average GPU utilization per node (0.0–3.0)
req_ncpus	Recorded number of CPU used	num_gpu_used	Number of GPU per node which is actually used
req_walltime	Requested runtime (wallclock time)	app	Recorded application which run inside of the job
req_gpus	Requested number of GPUs per node	grouphash	Anonymized project name
used_walltime	Recorded runtime (wallclock time)	userhash	Anonymized user name
queue_time	Timestamp of job submit	start_time	Timestamp of job submit
end_time	Timestamp of job finish	exit_state	Recorded exit status of job script
year	Fiscal year	month	Month
used_nodesec	Used runtime on per node	used_cputime	Used runtime per CPU
queue	Job class name		

3.2 Feature Engineering

The purpose of a feature, other than being an attribute, would be much easier to understand in the context of a problem. A feature is a characteristic that might help when solving the problem [11]. Features describe the structures inherent in data, and furthermore, they are very important to the predictive models and will influence the result. The quality and quantity of features have direct impact on whether the model is good or not. Therefore, getting enough useful features from the raw data is the first step in building good models for solving our problem.

Feature Selection. From the previous sections, we know that the raw data about compute resources usage was time series data of extreme size. Directly using raw time series data will produce unacceptable compute overhead, which may lead to serious time gaps between data collection and analysis as well as wasted computational resource. Instead of using raw time series data, we selected a set of relevant features from the raw job logs data for use in model construction by normalizing and converting them to MySQL database. In machine learning tasks, this is an essential step to make results easier to interpret by researchers. Additionally one can enjoy shorter training times, avoid the curse of dimensionality and enhanced generalization by reducing overfitting [12].

In this research, our purpose is building a machine learning technique-based model that can predict whether a job is underestimated on its runtime. Therefore we selected features as training set **X** by removing redundant or irrelevant features such as *used_cputime*, *used_nodesec*, *used_walltime*, *queue_time*, *start_time* and *end_time* without incurring much loss of information. This is a preliminary study in which we try to reveal complex patterns hidden in utilization of computing resources, user behaviors, and different applications on an HPC system. Those features are redundant, which have a large impact on the prediction of job runtime.

Additionally, we needed to create the target variable as the test set **y** which is then compared with the results produced with the training set **X**. We label the test set by the following formula:

$$y' = j.used\_walltime - j.req\_walltime$$

where j.used_walltime is actual runtime of a job, and j.req_walltime is user estimated time of a job. If $y' < 0$, we label this job as 0 in the test set y, which means that the actual runtime of this job does not exceed the user's estimated time when its user submitted it. Relatively, if $y' >= 0$, this job will be labeled as 1 in the test set, which indicates runtime-underestimation. In this case, this job will be terminated by the HPC system immediately before its completion. The purpose of our work is to predict whether a job is runtime-underestimated after job submission.

Feature Preprocessing. So far, we have selected enough feature variables as the training set and also have made corresponding labels as the test set. However, there are a few more important things needing to be addressed before we create the training machine learning model.

First is Labelencoding. For most traditional machine learning algorithms, the data fed to them must be in numerical type. Based on Table 1, however, we can see that there are some feature columns that are non-numerical type. For instance,

Table 2. 5 instances with selected 18 features as training set and test set

			Training set (X)				
used_cpupercent	used_mem	used_ncpus	used_vmem	req_mem	req_ncpus	req_walltime	req_gpus
975	974532	3	8.95E+07	1.07E+09	3	3540	3
1733	4.8451e+06	12	5.49226e+06	2.14748e+09	12	10800	0
1196	1.12E+06	192	6.83E+08	2.15E+09	192	86400	48
896	828776	24	3.41E+08	2.15E+09	24	86400	3
1197	2.64E+06	12	9.20E+07	2.15E+09	12	86400	1

			Training set (X)							Test set (y)
req_pl	req_et	nhosts	is_array	gpu_utilization	num_gpu_used	group	queue	user	app	Label: 1 or 0
0	0	1	0	81.0646	3	5	2	5	20	0
0	1	1	0	0	0	11	2	35	8	0
0	1	16	0	48.8958	3	166	5	368	11	0
0	1	1	0	169.295	3	10	5	473	11	0
0	1	1	0	49.8069	3	5	5	185	11	1

the column *queue* is list including [G, H, L128F, S, S96, X] which represents varying queues in TSUBAME 2.5 HPC system. In addition, the column *userhash* and *grouphash* keep hash values from 1 100 users and 421 user groups. Labelencoder can also be used to transform non-numerical variables (as long as they are hashable and comparable) to numerical variables. For example, LabelEncodeing can turn [G, S, G, H, S] into [1, 2, 1, 3, 2], but then the imposed ordinality means that the average of G and H is S. In this work, we used Labelencoder to transform feature variables in columns *userhash*, *grouphash* and *queue* from categorical variables to numerical variables.

Second is feature standardization. Based on Table 1, we can see that the range of values of columns varies widely. For instance, in column *used_mem*, values range from single units to millions of units. Meanwhile, in column *used_cpupercent*, the values range from 0 to hundreds of thousands. In contrast with these two columns, the column *is_array* is bool type (0 or 1). Given this wide variation of training set values in some machine learning algorithms, objective functions will not work properly without normalization. For example, most of classifiers calculate the distance between two points by the Euclidean distance. If one of the features has a broad range of values, the distance will be governed by this particular feature. Therefore, the range of all features should be feature scaled so that each feature contributes approximately proportionately to the final distance.

Feature standardization can make the values of each feature in the data have zero-mean (when subtracting the mean in the numerator) and unit-variance. This method is widely used for normalization in many machine learning algorithms (e.g., SVM, logistic regression, and neural networks). The general method of calculation is to determine the distribution mean and standard deviation for each feature. Next we subtract the mean from each feature. Then we divide the values of each feature by its standard deviation (since mean is already subtracted) [13], which can be presented in the following formula:

$$x' = \frac{x - \bar{x}}{\sigma}$$

Where x is the original feature vector, $\bar{x}$ is the mean of that feature vector, and σ is its standard deviation. We give 5 job instances - with 18 selected features which as Table 2 showed.

One important thing to note, researchers usually split the data into training, validation, and testing sets in the training phase. If we perform feature scaling to take the mean and variance (or standard deviation) over the whole set of predictor variables, future information will be introduced into the training predictor variables; namely, the future information contained in the mean and variance. Therefore, we perform feature scaling over the training data and save the mean and variance. Then we apply feature scaling to the predictor variables of the validation and test data sets, using the training mean and variances. A model can be applied on unseen data which, in general, is not available at the time the model is built. The validation process (including data splitting) simulates this. In order to get a good estimate of the model quality (and generalization power), one needs to restrict the calculation of the normalization parameters (mean and variance) to the training set.

Finally, for data cleaning work, we dropped all log job instances that contain NaN which may be caused by recording error when collecting data. The size of the logs from Jan. 1, 2015 to Dec. 31, 2016 is about one million job instances, which are enough for training and testing our models. Table 3 shows the summary of the entire job data set and subsets categorized by scientific application name. In Table 3, we found that, regardless of the whole dataset or a given subset, both are imbalanced datasets. That is, at least one of the classes accounts for only a small minority of the data. Aside from subset named "*WRF*", the rest are extremely imbalanced subsets. For example, subsets named "Bio: BLAST", "Bio: MEGADOCK" and "MD:Desmond MD", the minority class (labeled 1, having runtime-underestimation) are less than 1%, 1.45% and 2.2% respectively on those subsets. The majority class (labeled 0, not having runtime-underestimation) occupies overall 94.82% over the entire data set.

4   Performance Metrics and Algorithm Coverage for Binary Classification Problem on Imbalanced Dataset

So far, we have realized very clearly that we are dealing with a binary classification problem on an extremely imbalanced dataset. Almost all classifications that will predict every sample as the majority class can still achieve very high performance [14]. We can see that no matter what algorithms it is based on, and no matter what the data subset is, the majority class always has very high scores on all metrics. Therefore, for building models on extremely imbalanced data, the overall classification accuracy is often not an appropriate metric of performance. There are 2 ways that are given by data scientists and researchers to deal with imbalanced

Table 3. Imbalanced subsets categorized by scientific application name

Name of dataset	Number of instance	Number of instance with label 0 (majority class percentage)	Number of instance with label 1 (minority class percentage)
Whole data	987,123	935 926 (94.82%)	51 197 (5.18%)
Ab-Initio: PHASE	454	384 (84.59%)	70 (15.41%)
Bio: BLAST	6 367	6352 (99.76%)	15 (0.23%)
Bio: MEGADOCK	228 728	225 416 (98.54%)	3 312 (1.45%)
CAE: Abaqus	170	143 (84.11%)	27 (15.89%)
CAE: CST MW-Studio	944	861 (91.2%)	83 (8.8%)
CAE: Fluent	467	434 (92.94%)	33 (7.06%)
CAE: LS-DYNA	1 712	1 583 (92.46%)	129 (7.54%)
CAE: MSC Marc	28	28 (100%)	0
CFD: OpenFOAM	4 876	4480 (91.88%)	396 (8.12%)
MATLAB	3 127	2 832 (90.57%)	295 (9.43%)
MD: AMBER	45 554	44 382 (97.43%)	1 172 (2.57%)
MD: CHARMM	103	79 (76.7%)	24 (23.3%)
MD: Desmond MD	4 510	4411 (97.8%)	99 (2.2%)
MD: GROMACS	212 817	205 528 (96.57%)	7 289 (3.43%)
MD: NAMD	3 530	2 871 (81.33%)	659 (18.67%)
MD: Tinker	20 889	20 125 (96.34%)	764 (3.66%)
MD: lammps	1 285	1 147 (89.26%)	138 (10.74%)
MPI	124 828	112 321 (89.98%)	12 507 (10.02%)
Others	4 365	4 044 (92.65%)	321 (7.35%)
Python	208 892	199 368 (95.44%)	9 524 (4.56%)
QM: Gaussian	31 116	29 462 (94.68%)	1 654 (5.32%)
QM: OpenMX	3 786	3 459 (91.36%)	327 (8.64%)
QM: Quantum Espresso	5 276	4482 (84.95%)	794 (15.05%)
QM: VASP	69 445	58 541 (84.3%)	10 904 (15.7%)
RISM	102	102 (100%)	0
Vis: POV-RAY	1 967	1 833 (93.19%)	134 (6.81%)
WRF	1 785	1 258 (70.47%)	527 (29.53%)

data set. First is to collect more minority class data or to re-sample the imbalanced dataset by over-sampling (e.g. adding copies of instances from the minority class) or by under-sampling (e.g. deleting instances from the majority class). We cannot do either of these strategies, because over-sampling will increase the size of the data set thereby greatly extending training time, and under-sampling may lose important information as a consequence of dropped data. Second is to change the performance metrics. There are metrics that have been designed to get fair performance evaluation when working with imbalanced classes.

4.1 Metrics for Evaluating Imbalanced Data

In machine learning tasks with extremely imbalanced datasets, we use a set of alternative metrics such as false positive rate (FPR), true positive rate (TPR), receiver operating characteristic (ROC), Area under the Curve of ROC (AUC), precision, recall, and F1-score to evaluate the performance of our model on imbalanced data:

True Positives (TP): the true positive are the cases when the actual class of the target label was 1 (True) and the predicted is also 1 (True). In this research, the case where a job is actually runtime-underestimated (1) and the model classifies the case as runtime-underestimated (1) falls under True Positives.

True Negatives (TN): the true negative are the cases when the actual class of the target label was 0 (False) and the predicted is also 0 (False). In this research, the case where a job is NOT runtime-underestimated and the model classifies the case as NOT runtime-underestimated falls under True Negatives.

False Positives (FP): the false positive are the cases when the actual class of the target label was 0 (False) and the predicted is 1 (True). In this research, the case where a job is NOT runtime-underestimated and the model classifies the case as runtime-underestimated comes under False Positives.

False Negatives (FN): the false negative are the cases when the actual class of the target label was 1 (True) and the predicted is 0 (False). In this research, the case where there is a runtime-underestimated job and the model classifies the case as NOT runtime-underestimated comes under False Negatives.

$$Accuracy = \frac{TP + TN}{TP + TN + FP + FN} \tag{1}$$

$$Precision = \frac{TP}{TP + FP} \tag{2}$$

$$Recall = \frac{TP}{TP + FN} \tag{3}$$

$$\text{F1-score} = \frac{2 \times Precision \times Recall}{Precision + Recall} \tag{4}$$

$$FPR = \frac{FP}{FP + TN} \tag{5}$$

$$TPR = \frac{TP}{TP + FN} \tag{6}$$

$$SPC = \frac{TN}{TN + FP} \tag{7}$$

The ROC is a kind of curve graph that represents the diagnostic ability for a binary classification problem with all possible threshold values. ROC can be drawn with coordinates ranging between FPR and TPR along the x and y axes. Adjusting the threshold will change the FPR and TPR. In a binary classification problem, the prediction result for each sample is usually made based on a continuous random variable X, which is a "score" computed for this sample. Setting a threshold T, the sample will be classified as "positive" if $X > T$, and "negative" otherwise.

The AUC it indicates the probability that a classifier will rank a randomly chosen positive instance higher than a randomly chosen negative one (assuming 'positive' ranks higher than 'negative') [15]. The AUC is a single metric which can be used for an overall performance summary of a classifier, calculated by following formula:

$$AUC = \int_{\infty}^{-\infty} TPR(T)(-FPR'(T))dT$$

$$= \int_{-\infty}^{\infty} \int_{-\infty}^{\infty} I(T' > T) f_1(T') f_0(T) dT' dT = P(X_1 > X_0) \qquad (8)$$

where X_1 is the score for a positive instance and X_0 is the score for a negative instance, and f_0 is the probability density when the sample actually belongs to class "positive", and f_1 otherwise [16].

Due to space limitations, we will not describe it in detail here. What we need to know about AUC are as follows: The range of the value of AUC is between 0 and 1, the higher the better; When AUC is 1, this means that it is a perfect classifier, and with this prediction classifier, there is at least one threshold that leads to a perfect prediction (no FP and FN). However, there is no perfect classifier in most real world cases. $0.5 < AUC < 1$ means that the performance of this model is better in cases of a random guess. If the AUC is around 0.5, that means the performance of this model is generally the same as the result of a random guess.

The AUC was the first metric used to evaluate the overall accuracy performance of a classifier in the evaluation stage. After the best classifiers were chosen with the AUC, we used ROC to trade off precision vs recall in the minority class, because the majority class always has very high scores on all metrics in extremely imbalanced datasets. F1-score was a useful metric as we desired harmonic average of the precision and recall.

In all classifiers, a trade off will always occur between true negative rate (SPC, specificity) and true positive rate (TPR). The same occurs with precision and recall. In our study, we hope to train a classifier that gives high precision over the minority class (label 1, a job having runtime-underestimation), while maintaining reasonable precision and recall for the majority class. In the case of modeling on extremely imbalanced dataset, quite often the minority class is of great significance. For our imbalanced binary classification problem, we will take advantage of the combination of the above-mentioned evaluation metrics to diagnose our model.

4.2   Machine Learning Algorithms for Imbalanced Data

In this study, we compare two popular supervised machine learning algorithms: Random Forest (RF) [17] and XGBoost [18]. XGBoost is a scalable tree boosting system that implements the gradient boosting decision tree algorithm, which is widely used by data scientists and provides state-of-the-art results on many problems. The reason we chose to compare these two algorithms is that there are tree based models (both based on ensembles of decision trees) that solve tabular data very well, and have certain properties that a deep net does not have (e.g. ease of interpretation and invariant to input scale, and much easier to tune). Both of these methods are widely used as they outperform other distance-based algorithms like logistic regression, support vector machine, kNN in data science [4,14,18–21].

5   Experiment Results and Analysis

Since we split the entire job data set into subsets, there are some subsets in which the absolute number of minority class samples is too small. Therefore, we use the leave-one-out cross-validation (LOOCV) in our work [22]. The LOOCV method keeps a certain percentage of the full data set as a test set, then the rest of the data is used to perform k-fold cross-validation (k-fold CV). Next, it records k scores and calculates the standard deviation (std) of k scores as reference for choosing the best classifier from them. At the same time, it evaluates the robustness of the model. The final performance score of this model can be obtained from using the best-chosen classifier to predict the test set.

Meanwhile, most machine learning algorithms have several hyperparameters that will affect a model's performance. Tuning hyperparameters is an indispensable step to improve a model's performance, which often improve its accuracy or other metrics, like precision and recall, by 3–5%, depending on the algorithm and dataset. In some cases, parameter tuning may improve the accuracy by around 50% [21]. In this study, we train our model and tune hyperparameters via LOOCV with the RandomizedSearchCV function from scikit-learn [23]. The RandomizedSearchCV is an estimator used to optimizing hyperparameters from parameter settings. In contrast to GridSearchCV, not all parameter values are attempted, but rather a fixed number of parameter settings is sampled from the specified distributions. We set 30% of the each dataset as the test set with a random state, n_iter to 50, and we also set AUC as the scoring metric in RandomizedSearchCV. Parameter settings and optimized parameters are presented in Table 4.

5.1   Classification with Entire Dataset

We trained and tuned classifiers with the XGBoost and the RF on the entire dataset. We used the best chosen classifiers based on 5-fold CV on the training set (70% entire dataset) to predict the test set (30% entire dataset). Tables 5 and 6 shows that the XGBoost and the RF have an extremely similar overall performance result. The result consist of similar values of runtime-underestimation prediction

Table 4. Hyperparameters settings of Random Forest, XGBoost and the best parameters after tuning for our study

Algorithm	Hyperparameters	Best parameters after tuning
Random Forest	*n_estimators:* Number of decision trees in the ensemble	n_estimators = 500
	min_weight_fraction_leaf: The minimum number of (weighted) samples for a node to be considered a leaf. Controls the depth and complexity of the decision trees	max_features = 2
	max features: Number of features to consider when computing the best node split	criterion = "entropy"
	criterion: Function used to measure the quality of a split	min_weight_fraction_leaf = 8
XGBoost	*n_estimators:* Number of decision trees in the ensemble	n_estimators = 500
	learningrate: Shrinks the contribution of each successive decision tree in the ensemble	learning rate = 0.8
	maxdepth: Maximum depth of the decision trees. Controls the complexity of the decision trees	max depth = 3
	max_delta_step: Set it to a finite number (say 1) will help convergence	max_delta_step = 2
	max features: Number of features to consider when computing the best node split	max features = "log2"

(in terms of overall precision, recall, and F1-score) in the entire dataset. As we estimated, the precision, recall, and F1-score of the majority class are very high on both algorithms (0.98, and as high as 0.99). In contrast, all metrics on the minority class are lower than those on the majority class (e.g. F1-score: 0.74 vs 0.99). However, the overall average of precision, recall, and F1-score achieved very high scores on both algorithms (all around 0.97), due to combining absolute quantity and relative quantity subsets into an entire imbalanced dataset. There is a slight difference in precision and recall between the two algorithms; XGBoost outperforms the RF in precision by 0.02, while decreases the RF's recall by 0.01. Thus, the precision, recall, and F1-score on the minority class are fairer metrics than those of the majority class when evaluating model performance.

Table 5. Prediction results with entire dataset by XGBoost

Class	Precision	Recall	F1-score	Total
1	0.8	0.7	0.74	15273
0	0.98	0.99	0.99	280864
Avg/Total	0.98	0.97	0.97	296137

	Predicted Positive	Predicted Negative
Actual Positive	10677 (TP)	4596 (FN)
Actual Negative	2749 (FP)	278115 (TN)

Table 6. Prediction results with entire dataset by Random Forest

Class	Precision	Recall	F1-score	Total
1	0.78	0.71	0.74	15304
0	0.98	0.99	0.99	280833
Avg/Total	0.97	0.97	0.97	296137

	Predicted Positive	Predicted Negative
Actual Positive	11178 (TP)	4287 (FN)
Actual Negative	3186 (FP)	277486 (TN)

5.2 Classification with Subset Dataset Categorized by Scientific Application Name

In most HPC systems, there are a huge number of jobs submitted by thousands of users who are potentially grouped into hundreds of user groups. In relevant research about job logs analysis, researchers usually divide logs into subsets with different rules or purposes for seeking hidden patterns from those logs [1–3].

In this research, our main purpose is predicting whether a job may or may not finish before its runtime estimated by its user. The runtime is mainly affected by many factors, such as user behaviors and computing resource usage in the HPC environment. (In this study, we do not consider human intervention from users or administrators, nor random hardware failures). The entire job dataset was split into subsets categorized by scientific application name for mining potential patterns which may affect runtime of HPC applications. According to Table 3, there are almost one million job logs based on 27 pre-installed HPC applications in TSUB-AME 2.5 (except those in the unlabeled "others" class). We used XGBoost and RF to build prediction models with the optimized hyperparameters presented in Table 4 and run them through on each subset by 5-fold LOOCV respectively. The performance evaluation results including AUC, precision and recall on the minority class were plotted in Figs. 2 and 3.

Figure 2 shows the AUC and the standard deviation (std) of the AUC by 5-fold LOOCV for 26 subsets after taking "others" as a subset and removing "RISM", "CAE: MSC", from all training dataset. This was because there is no instance of runtime-underestimation (labeled 1, minority class) in their subsets. The AUC (XGBoost) was chosen as an indicator to sort the results in descending order for observation and analysis purposes. We can see that the XGBoost outperforms or tie

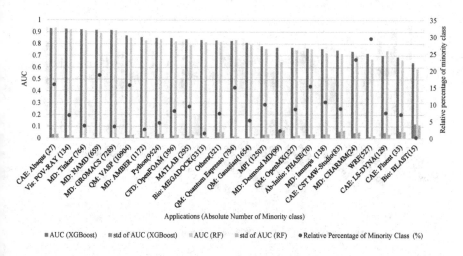

Applications (Absolute Number of Minority class)

■ AUC (XGBoost)   ■ std of AUC (XGBoost)   ■ AUC (RF)   ■ std of AUC (RF)   ● Relative Percentage of Minority Class (%)

Fig. 2. The AUC and its STD after running through subsets with 5-fold LOOCV

with RF slightly in most application subsets with the AUC as the indicator, except application named "CAE: LS-DYNA". The std of AUC show the model stability; the smaller the std is, the more stable the model's performance is. The percentage of minority class of each application was also plotted in Fig. 2. We can see that, for most of cases in this study, the percentage of minority class almost has no impact on the AUC and the std of the AUC. However, we found that, the higher the absolute number of minority class is, the more stable the model is relatively. We believe that the high std of AUC in some subsets is due to the low absolute number of minority class. The AUC shows the overall performance of models. We can see that both algorithms achieved very good AUC on 5 subsets including "CAE: Abaqus", "Vis: POV-RAY", "MD: Tinker", "MD: NAMD" and "MD: GROMACS". Except for "MD: NAMD" by RF, the AUC in the rest of 4 subsets are greater than or equal to 0.9, which means that both algorithms provide very good prediction about runtime-underestimation for those 5 applications in the HPC environment. In contrast to "CAE:Abaqus" and "Vis: POV-RAY", the results of "Bio:BLAST" by both 2 algorithms are the worst in all subsets. Since in "Bio:BLAST" subset, the absolute number (15) and the relative percentage (0.45%) on minority class are much lower than those on other subsets, our models cannot handle with this kind of problem. The "CAE:FLUENT" has similar result with "Bio:BLAST", because of its absolute number (33) on minority class is also very low. But its std of AUC is better than "Bio:BLAST", due to its relative percentage on minority class is higher than "Bio:BLAST".

In Fig. 3, we used best-chosen classifier from 5-fold LOOCV to plot precision and recall in minority class on all subsets, which follows the sorting in Fig. 2. Taking stable, precision, recall and F1-score into consideration together, we think that "Vis: POV-RAY" achieves the best result on minority class by XGBoost (90% precision, 95% recall, 92% F1-score). This figure helps to find out which algorithms

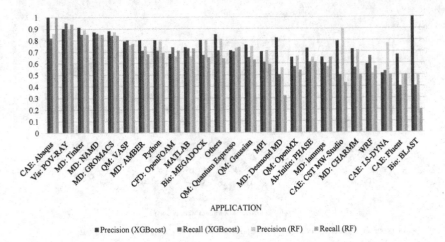

APPLICATION

■ Precision (XGBoost)   ■ Recall (XGBoost)   ■ Precision (RF)   ■ Recall (RF)

Fig. 3. Precision and recall on minority class after running through XGBoost and Random Forest

is good at which metric. For example, if we need the best recall on subset "Vis: POV-RAY", XGBoost will be the best selection to build model.

If we want our model to provide the best precision for "CAE: LS-DYNA", RF should be chosen to build model. In this research, from the user's point of view, the precision is more important than the recall, due to the FP is more important than the FN in the job runtime-underestimated prediction. Since the FP can be much more costly than FN. On the contrary, if looking at the angle of HPC system administrators for saving system resources as much as possible, the recall will be more critical than FP.

Figure 4 represent ROC, AUC and std of AUC after 5-fold CV on "CAE:Abagus" and "Bio: BLAST" by XGBoost. Adjusting the threshold will change the FPR. For instance, increasing the threshold will decrease FP (and increase FN), which corresponds to moving in the left direction on the curve. The curve is more

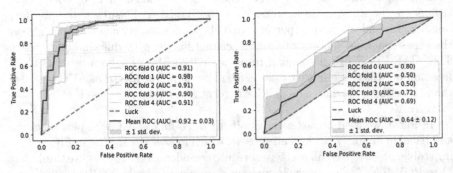

Fig. 4. ROC, AUC and standard deviation after 5-fold CV on subsets "CAE:Abagus" (left) and "Bio: BLAST" (right) by XGBoost

inclined to the upper left corner $(0, 1)$, where the performance of the model is better at distinguishing positive and negative classes. Adjusting the threshold on ROC will be the last step to improve the performance of a model.

5.3   Feature Importance

Feature importance gives a score (F score) for indicating how valuable or useful each feature was when building boosted decision trees based models. With the features

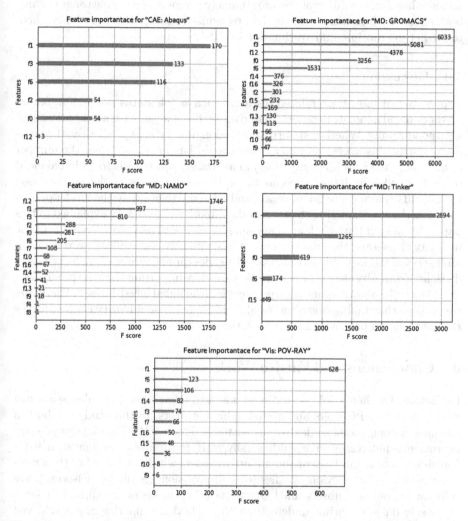

Fig. 5. Important features for different applications; features are automatically named according to their index, f0: *used_cpupercent*, f1: *used_mem*, f2: *used_ncpus*, f3: *used_vmem*, f4: *req_mem*, f5: *req_ncpus*, f6: *req_walltime*, f7: *req_gpus*, f8: *req_pl*, f9: *req_et*, f10:*nhosts*, f11: *is_array*, f12: *gpu_utilization*, f13: *num_gpu_used*, f14: *group*, f15: *queue* and f16: *user*, from f0 to f16 respectively

sorted according to how many times they appear, the more a feature was used to make key decisions within the decision trees, the higher its relative importance was to the model.

In our study, we plotted feature importance in the top 5 AUC indicated subsets with the features ordered according to how many score they have (how important it was) in Fig. 5. We can see that $used\_mem$, $used\_vmem$, $used\_cpupercent$, $req\_walltime$ and $gpu\_utilization$ are the most important features in those applications. However, applications have different weights (namely prediction of runtime-underestimation) on different features (namely computing resource usage), which both affected job runtime. Our method recognized these patterns and used them to predict job runtime-underestimation in HPC systems.

5.4   Discussion

Papers [2–5] demonstrate related research, such as job status prediction, failure prediction and anomaly detection, based on log file analysis with machine learning with good results. Whether abnormal detection or job status prediction, the number of correct instances (majority class) should be much more than the number of incorrect instances (minority class) in a dataset, which leads to an imbalanced dataset just like our dataset presented here. However, in those works, authors used the overall accuracy, precision, recall, and F1-score to evaluate the model performance without considering those of on the minority class. As we explained in this paper, because of the imbalanced absolute number and relative percentage of the majority classes and the minority classes (the minority class will be more than 1 in multi-classification problems), the overall metrics cannot accurately reflect the predictions of minority class. Minority classes are more important than the predictions of majority classes in classification problem with an imbalanced dataset. Therefore, we propose that taking precision, recall, and F1-score on minority classes, rather than overall, is a promising metric for future work.

6   Conclusions and Future Work

Predicting whether a job is runtime-underestimated after job submission can greatly benefit HPC users and system administrators. In this study, we built a machine learning based model to mine patterns hidden in HPC job logs for predicting runtime-underestimation. Additionally, we introduced some evaluation metrics (precision, recall, and F1-score on minority classes) which are more fair than metrics used in similar previous studies (overall precision, recall, and F1-score). We split our dataset into subsets, and found that the best precision, recall, and F1-score of subsets on job runtime-underestimated prediction (minority class) achieved 90%, 95% and 92% respectively. These results outperform some recent related studies to date. Finally, we plotted feature importance and revealed surprising hidden patterns between different HPC applications and different features on computing resource usage.

As future work, we would like to improve prediction by extracting more features such as the network traffic I/O, the standard deviation of computing resource usage etc. which may affect the prediction performance. Also, we would like to do more test with data collected from different time periods to prove and improve the robustness of our model.

Acknowledgment. This work was supported by JST CREST Grant Number JPMJCR1303 and JPMJCR1687, Japan. This work was partially conducted as research activities of AIST - Tokyo Tech Real World Big-Data Computation Open Innovation Laboratory (RWBC-OIL).

References

1. Zhang, H., You, H., Hadri, B., Fahey, M.: HPC usage behavior analysis and performance estimation with machine learning techniques. In: Proceedings of the International Conference on Parallel and Distributed Processing Techniques and Applications (PDPTA), the Steering Committee of The World Congress in Computer Science, Computer Engineering and Applied Computing (WorldComp), p. 1 (2012)
2. Klinkenberg, J., Terboven, C., Lankes, S., Müller, M.S.: Data mining-based analysis of HPC center operations. In: 2017 IEEE International Conference on Cluster Computing (CLUSTER), pp. 766–773. IEEE (2017)
3. Yoo, W., Sim, A., Wu, K.: Machine learning based job status prediction in scientific clusters. In: SAI Computing Conference (SAI), pp. 44–53. IEEE (2016)
4. Tuncer, O., Ates, E., Zhang, Y., Turk, A., Brandt, J., Leung, V.J., Egele, M., Coskun, A.K.: Diagnosing performance variations in HPC applications using machine learning. In: Kunkel, J.M., Yokota, R., Balaji, P., Keyes, D. (eds.) ISC 2017. LNCS, vol. 10266, pp. 355–373. Springer, Cham (2017). https://doi.org/10.1007/978-3-319-58667-0_19
5. McKenna, R., Herbein, S., Moody, A., Gamblin, T., Taufer, M.: Machine learning predictions of runtime and IO traffic on high-end clusters. In: 2016 IEEE International Conference on Cluster Computing (CLUSTER), pp. 255–258. IEEE (2016)
6. Rodrigues, E.R., Cunha, R.L., Netto, M.A., Spriggs, M.: Helping HPC users specify job memory requirements via machine learning. In: Proceedings of the Third International Workshop on HPC User Support Tools, pp. 6–13. IEEE Press (2016)
7. Fan, Y., Rich, P., Allcock, W.E., Papka, M.E., Lan, Z.: Trade-off between prediction accuracy and underestimation rate in job runtime estimates. In: 2017 IEEE International Conference on Cluster Computing (CLUSTER), pp. 530–540. IEEE (2017)
8. Matsuoka, S.: The TSUBAME 2.5 evolution. TSUBAME e-Sci. J. **10**, 2–8 (2013)
9. Feng, W., Cameron, K.: The Green500 list: encouraging sustainable supercomputing. Computer **40**(12), 50–55 (2007)
10. Massie, M.L., Chun, B.N., Culler, D.E.: The ganglia distributed monitoring system: design, implementation, and experience. Parallel Comput. **30**(7), 817–840 (2004)
11. Brownlee, J.: Discover feature engineering, how to engineer features and how to get good at it. Machine Learning Process (2014)
12. Bermingham, M.L., Pong-Wong, R., Spiliopoulou, A., Hayward, C., Rudan, I., Campbell, H., Wright, A.F., Wilson, J.F., Agakov, F., Navarro, P., et al.: Application of high-dimensional feature selection: evaluation for genomic prediction in man. Sci. Rep. **5**, 1–12 (2015)

13. Grus, J.: Data Science from Scratch: First Principles with Python. O'Reilly Media, Inc., Sebastopol (2015)
14. Chen, C., Liaw, A., Breiman, L.: Using random forest to learn imbalanced data, vol. 110. University of California, Berkeley (2004)
15. Fawcett, T.: An introduction to ROC analysis. Pattern Recogn. Lett. **27**(8), 861–874 (2006)
16. Powers, D.M.: Evaluation: from precision, recall and F-measure to ROC, informedness, markedness and correlation (2011)
17. Liaw, A., Wiener, M., et al.: Classification and regression by randomforest. R News **2**(3), 18–22 (2002)
18. Chen, T., Guestrin, C.: XGBoost: a scalable tree boosting system. In: Proceedings of the 22nd ACM SIGKDD International Conference on Knowledge Discovery and Data Mining, pp. 785–794. ACM (2016)
19. Song, R., Chen, S., Deng, B., Li, L.: eXtreme gradient boosting for identifying individual users across different digital devices. In: Cui, B., Zhang, N., Xu, J., Lian, X., Liu, D. (eds.) WAIM 2016. LNCS, vol. 9658, pp. 43–54. Springer, Cham (2016). https://doi.org/10.1007/978-3-319-39937-9_4
20. Nielsen, D.: Tree boosting with XGBoost-why does XGBoost win "every" machine learning competition? Master's thesis, NTNU (2016)
21. Olson, R.S., La Cava, W., Mustahsan, Z., Varik, A., Moore, J.H.: Data-driven advice for applying machine learning to bioinformatics problems. arXiv preprint arXiv:1708.05070 (2017)
22. Cawley, G.C., Talbot, N.L.: Efficient leave-one-out cross-validation of kernel fisher discriminant classifiers. Pattern Recogn. **36**(11), 2585–2592 (2003)
23. Pedregosa, F., Varoquaux, G., Gramfort, A., Michel, V., Thirion, B., Grisel, O., Blondel, M., Prettenhofer, P., Weiss, R., Dubourg, V., Vanderplas, J., Passos, A., Journapeau, D., Brucher, M., Perrot, M., Duchesnay, E.: Scikit-learn: machine learning in Python. J. Mach. Learn. Res. **12**, 2825–2830 (2011)

A Power Management Framework with Simple DSL for Automatic Power-Performance Optimization on Power-Constrained HPC Systems

Yasutaka Wada[1](✉), Yuan He[2], Thang Cao[3], and Masaaki Kondo[3]

[1] Meisei University, Tokyo, Japan
yasutaka.wada@meisei-u.ac.jp
[2] Shenyang University of Technology, Shenyang, Liaoning, China
heyuan@sut.edu.cn
[3] The University of Tokyo, Tokyo, Japan
{cao,kondo}@hal.ipc.i.u-tokyo.ac.jp

Abstract. To design exascale HPC systems, power limitation is one of the most crucial and unavoidable issues; and it is also necessary to optimize the power-performance of user applications while keeping the power consumption of the HPC system below a given power budget. For this kind of power-performance optimization for HPC applications, it is indispensable to have enough information and good understanding about both the system specifications (what kind of hardware resources are included in the system, which component can be used as a "power-knob", how to control the power-knob, etc.) and user applications (which part of the application is CPU-intensive, memory-intensive, and so on). Because this situation forces both the users and administrators of power-constrained HPC systems pay much effort and cost, it has been highly demanded to realize a simple framework to automate a power-performance optimization process, and to provide a simple user interface to the framework. To tackle these concerns, we propose and implement a versatile framework to help carry out power management and performance optimization on power-constrained HPC systems. In this framework, we also propose a simple DSL as an interface to utilize the framework. We believe this is a key to effectively utilize HPC systems under the limited power budget.

Keywords: HPC · Performance · Power · Optimization

1 Introduction

The need for high performance computing (HPC) in modern society never recedes as more and more HPC applications are highly involved in every aspect of our daily life. To achieve exascale performance, there are many technical challenges waiting to be addressed, ranging from the underlying device technology to exploiting parallelism in application codes. Numerous reports including Exascale

© The Author(s) 2018
R. Yokota and W. Wu (Eds.): SCFA 2018, LNCS 10776, pp. 199–218, 2018.
https://doi.org/10.1007/978-3-319-69953-0_12

Study from DARPA [2] and Top Ten Exascale Research Challenges from DOE [12] have identified power consumption as one of the major constraints in scaling the performance of HPC systems. In order to bridge the gap between required and current power/energy efficiency, one of the most important research issues is developing a power management framework which allows power to be more efficiently consumed and distributed.

Power management is a complicated process involving the collection and analysis of statistics from both hardware and software, power allocation and control by available power-knobs, code instrumentation/optimization, and so on. For large scale HPC systems, it would be more complex since handling these tasks at scale is not easy. So far, these tasks are mostly carried out in a discrete and hand-tuned way for a specific hardware or software component. This fact causes several problems and limitations.

First, the lack of cooperation/automation makes power management very difficult and time-consuming. It is desirable that power management process is able to be carried out under a common convention with little effort from users and system administrators. Second, though there are many existing tools to be potentially used for power optimization, each of them is usually designed for different purpose. For example, PDT and TAU are used for application analysis, RAPL is dedicated to power monitoring and capping while cpufreq targets mainly for performance/power tuning [10,18,23]. It is necessary to have a holistic way to use them together. Third, different HPC systems have different capabilities for power management, resulting in system or hardware-specific ad-hoc solutions. Of course, these are not portable. Therefore, it is crucial to provide a generalized interface for portability and extensibility. Fourth, power management sometimes needs a collaborative effort from both users and administrators. Many existing solutions fail to draw a clear border between them.

To address these problems, some of power management related tools and APIs such as GeoPM [5] and PowerAPI [8] have been developed. These tools/APIs are user-centric and need hand-tuning efforts for efficient power management. Hence, we design and implement a versatile power management framework targeting at power constrained large scale HPC systems. We try to provide a standard utility to people of different roles when managing/using such systems. Through this framework, we provide an extensible hardware/software interface between existing/future power-knobs and related tools/APIs so that system administrators can help supercomputer users make full use of valuable power budget. Since the framework defines clear roles for people participating and software components, power management and control can be carried out securely. The framework contains a very simple domain-specific language (DSL) which serves as a front-end to many other utilities and tools. This enables users to create, automate, port and re-use power management solutions.

This paper makes the following contributions:

- We design and implement a versatile framework to meet the necessity of performance optimization and power management for power-constrained large scale HPC systems.

- By showing three case studies, we demonstrate how this framework works and how it is used to carry out certain power management tasks under different power control strategies.
- We also prove the effectiveness of this framework through these three case studies.

The rest of this paper is organized as follows. Section 2 covers the background and related work, while Sect. 3 presents details of the power management framework and its components. Section 4 is about the DSL. In Sect. 5, we demonstrate this framework through a few case studies and make discussions on the results. Finally, Sect. 6 concludes this paper.

2 Related Work

To make full use of a given power budget on power-constrained HPC systems, many aspects such as system configurations and application characteristics are required to be considered when applying power-performance optimization for applications. This section covers related research efforts for some of these aspects.

2.1 Power-Performance Optimization

Power-performance optimization methodologies typically aim at maximizing application performance while satisfying given constraints (power budget, energy consumption, application execution deadline, etc.). Most of them are mainly based on "power-shifting" among hardware components [9,13,19] or among applications/jobs [3,17,20,24,26]. Usually we have a large number of jobs running on a HPC system, and hence optimizing power-performance in both intra- and inter-application cases is important.

Intra-application Optimization. Some power-performance optimization methods focus on the optimization of an application by accommodating power budgets from one hardware component to another.

For example, Miwa et al. proposed power-shifting method to shift the power budget from network resources among nodes to CPUs in order to utilize unused power created when network equipment with the Energy Efficient Ethernet Standard [7] are deployed for the interconnections among nodes [13]. Gholkar et al. proposed a technique to optimize the number of processors to be used in a job under given power budgets [6]. Inadomi et al. proposed power-performance optimization method which considers manufacturing variations in a large system [9,19].

Though these power-performance optimization methods succeeded to improve the execution performance of applications, each method employs its own optimization process and it is required to develop a unified way or framework to apply the optimizations.

Inter-application Optimization. In most HPC systems, users submit a large number of jobs, and the system scheduler allocates some of the jobs considering the number of nodes needed by each job, estimated execution time, and so on. In addition to the intra-application power-performance optimization, it is important to optimally allocate power budgets among running jobs.

Cao et al. developed a demand-aware power management approach [24]. With this approach, job scheduler allocates power budget and hardware resources to run jobs considering their demands and the total system power consumption. They also developed an approach for cooling-aware job scheduling and node allocations [3]. The aim of this approach is to shift power from cooling facilities to compute nodes as much as possible by keeping low inlet temperature. Sakamoto et al. developed extensible power-aware resource management based on slurm resource manager [20]. By using this resource management framework, job scheduler can correct and utilize the power consumption data of each application and node. Patki et al. proposed a resource management system which makes it possible to apply back-fill job scheduling considering system power utilization [17]. Chasapis et al. proposed a runtime optimization method which changes concurrency levels and socket assignment considering manufacturing variability of chips and the relationships among chips in NUMA nodes [4]. Wallace et al. proposed "data-driven" job scheduling strategy [26] which observes the power profile of each job and use it at runtime to decide power budget distribution among jobs running on the system which has limited power budget.

2.2   Interfaces to Control Power-Knobs

To realize power-performance optimization, user applications need to access and control power-knobs and obtain power consumption values for various hardware. These power-knobs may come from different vendors so we need a unified interface to access them.

Recent Intel processors are equipped with RAPL interface to apply power-capping to CPU and DRAM [10]. RAPL allows us to monitor and restrict the power consumption of both CPU and DRAM. Also, NVML [15] provides the API to manage both power consumption and operating frequency of NVIDIA's GPUs. PAPI (Performance API) is now developed with functionalities to access NVML and RAPL interfaces [27]. With these functionalities, user applications are allowed to have access to these interfaces in the same way as to other hardware performance counters if the system administrator gives the permission to them. Though PAPI supports various processor architectures, it mainly provides us interfaces to monitor hardware counter information and is not for controlling the hardware. Power API has also been developed to provide standardized interfaces to measure/control power on HPC systems [8]. It provides us unified interfaces and abstraction layers to users, system administrators, applications, and so on.

However, users are still required to insert API calls into the application source code to realize power-performance optimized applications. In addition, each system has its own power-performance characteristics, and this makes the optimization process much harder and requires users to spend large cost and effort. To alleviate the difficulties, it is desirable to develop a simple and easy-to-use interface to control and monitor power-knobs. This simple interface should play an important function for the unified framework.

2.3 Performance Profiling and Analysis Tools

Not only optimizing applications, but also gathering performance data of applications is essential. Detailed analysis information of a user application is required to apply power-performance optimization more effectively.

Until now, many performance analysis tools have been developed. TAU [21] is one of such performance analysis tools, with which one can collect application profiling information and visualize the data with it. Most of these tools are basically developed to give us a simple and easy way to collect application profiling data, and recently they can help collect power consumption data together with performance data by using PAPI and similar libraries. SPECpower [11] consists of a set of benchmark programs and provides instructions to measure the performance and power consumption of computer systems. SPECpower can be used to collect detailed data for comparing different systems.

However, it is difficult to utilize such information for power-performance optimization as in practice, many kinds of user applications run on many different systems. In addition, most of the performance analysis tools and methodologies assume that the user optimizes their applications manually according to the information obtained through such tools.

2.4 Domain Specific Language to Describe System Performance and Configuration

To make it easy to develop power-performance optimized applications, using a DSL is already considered. ASPEN [22] is a DSL to describe both system architecture and application characteristics in order to model the performance of an application on a system. ASPEN is good at estimating performance of the system described with it, but the power consumption is just an estimation based on given parameters. To realize power-performance optimization on real systems, it is required to know the actual power profile on target systems.

2.5 Towards a Versatile Power Management Framework

Most of the works above, related to power-performance optimization/management on power-constrained HPC systems, could help us carry out good power management. However, we still need to pay much cost and effort to apply them to many kinds of user applications, and it is difficult to make all users know well about the system they want to use, in addition to their application characteristics. Furthermore, if the system is replaced, they are forced to optimize their applications again while getting knowledge about the new system.

In this paper, we aim to provide a simple and easy way to realize power-performance managed/optimized application by using a versatile power management framework which has access to all kinds of information from the systems, users, and applications. This framework applies power-performance optimization to the application automatically, and can reduce users' burden drastically.

3   The Proposed Power Management Framework

The main objective of the framework proposed in this paper is to make the power management and power-performance optimizations processes more facilitating and flexible for both users and system administrators. In this framework, we assume a standard HPC system with its hierarchical structure as shown in Fig. 1. The target system consists of multiple compute nodes, interconnection network, and the storage subsystem. Each node consists of multiple processors, DRAM modules, and accelerators like GPUs. Each processor has multiple cores. We assume some of the hardware components have power-knobs to control power consumption of the executing programs, but their availability to the users depends on the control permission or the operational policy specified by the system administrator.

3.1   Overview and Power Management Workflow Control

To optimize power-performance efficiency and to manage power consumption of HPC applications to be executed, we have to take care of many things including: (1) what kinds of hardware components the system has and how much power is consumed in them, (2) what kinds of power-knobs are available and how to control them, (3) how the applications behave at runtime, and (4) what is the relationship between performance and power consumption of the application.

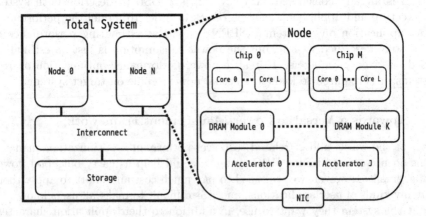

Fig. 1. The outline of a target HPC system

Based on these information, (5) we have to design a power-performance optimization algorithm. One of the most burdensome tasks is (6) to assemble and utilize existing tool-sets for collecting the necessary information and actually controlling power-knobs.

It requires the user to pay much cost and time to consider these tasks. Our framework is designed to provide or to support the following functionalities which help users and administrators carry out power management/control effectively without taking care of the above mentioned issues:

- Analyzing source code and applying automatic instrumentation
- Measuring and controlling application power consumption and performance
- Optimizing an application under given power budget
- Specifying and defining the target machine specification
- Calibrating hardware power consumption of the system

The outline of the framework is presented in Fig. 2. One of the benefit of the framework is the fact that workflow of power-performance optimization and control can be specified in higher abstraction level. Details of how to use libraries for controlling power-knobs, how to profile and analyze the application code, and how to instrument power management pragmas in the code or the job submission script are hidden from users. Moreover, the framework provides high modularity and flexibility so that libraries or tool-set used in the framework and also power optimization algorithms are customizable.

In order to provide customizability and flexibility, we developed a simple DSL as the front-end for these supported tools and for selecting the power optimization algorithm. Note that in current version of the framework, we support RAPL/cpufreq utils for accessing power-knobs [9,19] and TAU/PDT for code

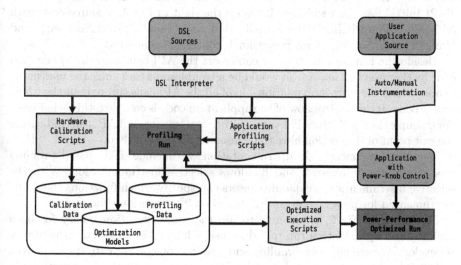

Fig. 2. The overview of the power-performance optimization framework

instrumentation and profiling. However, these are extensible and other tool-sets are easily supported.

This framework requires only two sets of inputs, the DSL code and the user application source code. Based on them, our framework offers a semi-automatic way of power-performance optimizations. Meanwhile, the administrators and users can be free from the effort to understand the inside of the optimization workflow. Once the DSL source code is prepared, the proposed framework provides an easy way to realize optimized execution of user applications.

Note that our framework supports two types of users. One is simply supercomputer "user" and the other is "administrator". An administrator is able to specify machine configurations, enable/disable power-knobs and calibrate the hardware while a user is not allowed to do so. Switching between them is carried out with the DSL.

3.2   Application Instrumentation for Profiling and Optimization

To realize power-performance profiling and optimized execution of a user application, the application is required to be instrumented with API calls to get profiling data and to control power-knobs. In current version of our workflow, it is assumed that PDT based instrumentation tool [9,19,25] is used for automatic instrumentation. For example, the user should instruct the instrumentation tool to insert API calls before/after each function call, parallel loop, and so on to control the power-knobs. This process can also be carried out with the DSL.

Figure 3 shows an example of the automatic instrumentation by the framework. As shown on the left in Fig. 3, our automatic instrumentation tool assumes that its input is a source code written with MPI. The instrumentation tool detects the entry/exit points of each function in the source code and inserts API calls. The tool also inserts an initialization API call just after "MPI_Init()". As the result, as shown on the right in Fig. 3, a source code with API calls ("PomPP_Init()" for initialization, and "PomPP_Start_Section()" and "PomPP_Stop_Section()" for power-knob control) is generated.

Beside the framework, the user can insert the API calls into the application code by themselves. However, it would be a troublesome task since the user needs a sanity check for start-stop relationship of all the API calls throughout the whole source code. If the control flow of the application code is complex, this is not easy. For example, in Fig. 3, "func1" has two return statements, and API calls indicating the exit point of the section have to be inserted for both of them.

For the automatic code instrumentation, we include TAU based profiling tool [21] in the framework and it allows selective instrumentation. With the selective instrumentation capability, users can specify which functions should be instrumented for power-knob control based on its execution time and so on.

As shown in Fig. 2, we assume to use the same execution binary for both profiling and optimization run to reduce users' labor. To realize this, the library is developed to enable both profiling and power-knob control with the same API call [9,19]. The library can change its behavior based on the user setting via environment variables.

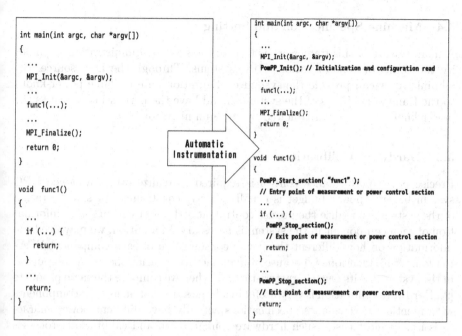

Fig. 3. An example of the automatic instrumentation for both profiling and power-knob control

3.3 Power Control and Application Optimization

In the current implementation of the framework, we assume to decide power-capping and power distribution in advance statically. For the optimization, the user is asked to run at least two scripts generated by the DSL described in Sect. 4.

The first one is the script to generate power-performance profiling data for the application. This script runs the instrumented application several times and generates power consumption profiling data of the available power-knobs with several settings of them.

The second one is the script for optimized application run. In this script, power-knob settings are decided in advance based on the information given by the hardware calibration data, the profiling data of the target application, and other given constraints (power budget, allowed slowdown in the execution time, and so on). This decision is written to a file, and is referred to find out when and how the power-knobs should be controlled while running the application.

In our current implementation, it is assumed that the script or program, which is used to make a decision for the optimized power capping values, is prepared by the system administrator in advance, because the administrator is responsible to decide which power-knobs to be opened for user applications and what kind of power-performance models are desirable.

3.4 Machine Specification and Setting

A main feature of this framework is to help the system administrators set/modify the configurations of various HPC systems. Through the DSL source, the administrator can provide the system configuration and available power-knobs to the framework. Users of the system should have the permission to access the power-knobs as if they are allowed by the administrator.

3.5 Hardware Calibration

Precise power-performance control is required to realize overprovisioned HPC system because power budget is usually strictly constrained for safe operation of the system. To realize the precise control, actual power consumption information of each component in the system is necessary. In addition, we may need the information on how different the power consumption of each component is. As Inadomi et al. mentioned, because of manufacturing variations, each component in the system has its own characteristic even when we compare the same products [9]. Hardware calibration is very useful in a large scale system as even components with identical performance specifications actually have different power characteristics. In most cases, such hardware configuration and calibration processes are only required once per system right after the system is installed.

Therefore, the proposed framework provides the scripts for the hardware calibration based on the information given by the administrators. The scripts run some microbenchmarks and collect the power-performance relationship information for each component. With this information and the profiling data of user applications, our framework decides how much power budgets should be allocated for each power-knob.

4 DSL to Control Power Management Workflow

As a front-end to our framework, we have developed a simple DSL to provide a uniform gateway to tools and utilities in the framework. It helps to create power management algorithms and processes. The DSL interpreter is developed based on ANTLR v4 [1, 16] with very simple semantics.

Using this DSL leads to several advantages. First, this simple DSL provides a unified way to access to various functionalities supported by this framework. Second, system configurations, optimization processes and algorithms are composed in this DSL such that they can be easily reused and extended. Third, given the code written in this DSL, automation is possible which dramatically improves productivity.

4.1 Semantics of the DSL

Source code written in our DSL is composed of a basic element which is called the "statement". Each statement has a command, which is used to specify an action.

For example, Listing 1, 2 and 3 illustrate statements manipulating objects defined in this DSL. Listing 1 shows how system configuration is set and Listing 2 shows how to use an application as the microbenchmark to calibrate the hardware. Listing 3 is about how a job is submitted with a socket power cap of 70 W.

Listing 1. DSL Code Snippets for System Configuration

```
 1  CREATE MACHINE M
 2  ADD M POMPP_NPKGS_PER_NODE 2
 3  ADD M POMPP_NCORES_PER_PKG 12
 4  ADD M POMPP_TOTAL_NODES 965
 5  ADD M POMPP_MAX_FREQ 16
 6  ADD M POMPP_MIN_FREQ 12
 7  ADD M POMPP_PKG_TDP 130.0
 8  ADD M POMPP_DRAM_TDP 62.0
 9  ADD M POMPP_PKG_MIN 64.0
10  ADD M POMPP_DRAM_MIN 30.0
11  ADD M POMPP_MODULE_MIN 46.0
12  SWITCH M
```

Listing 2. DSL Code Snippets for Hardware Calibration

```
 1  CREATE JOB EP_C
 2  ADD EP_C EXEC_PATH <absolute path to the executable>
 3  ADD EP_C JOB_TYPE CALIBRATION
 4  ADD EP_C PVT_PATH <absolute path to the power variation table>
 5  SUBMIT EP_C
```

Listing 3. DSL Code Snippets to Submit a Job with a Specified Power Cap

```
 1  CREATE JOB EP_G
 2  ADD EP_G EXEC_PATH <absolute path to the executable>
 3  ADD EP_G JOB_TYPE GENERAL
 4  ADD EP_G MODULE_POWER 70
 5  ADD EP_G CONTROL_MODE RAPL
 6  SUBMIT EP_G
```

So far, commands supported by this DSL are "CREATE", "DELETE", "ADD", "REMOVE", "GET", "SET", "LIST", "INSERT", "SWITCH" and "SUBMIT". When initializing objects, "CREATE" is used so it is followed by a type and an object name while "ADD" is used to add attribute and it is followed by an attribute and its value. "GET" and "SET" are used to retrieve and modify attributes of an object while "REMOVE" is used to remove an attribute of an object and "DELETE" is used to delete an object. In addition, "LIST" is used to list objects created; "INSERT" is used for manual instrumentation; and "SUBMIT" means to submit a job to the HPC system. Finally, "SWITCH" is used to switch between "user" and "administrator" or used to switch to different sets of machine configurations. In the scope of this DSL, an administrator is also a user, but with more commands/capabilities available. For example, an administrator can submit a job just like a user but a user is not allowed to calibrate the hardware. Therefore, when switching to the "administrator" role, a password is required to prevent an administrator from misuses of privileged commands. All commands are summarized in Table 1.

Supported types in this "DSL" include "MACHINE", "JOB" and "MODEL". "MACHINE" is used to represent set of system configurations, while "JOB"

Table 1. Commands in the DSL

CREATE/DELETE	Creating or deleting an object
ADD/REMOVE	Adding or removing an attribute for an object
GET/SET	Setting or getting the value of an attribute
LIST	Listing objects
INSERT	Manual instrumentation to application source
SWITCH	Switching between user/admin or switching to a different machine
SUBMIT	Submitting jobs to the system

is used to represent a job to run on the system and "MODEL" is defined as the relationship between performance and power consumption, which can be used to optimize the execution process of an application to satisfy power or performance requirements according to a mathematical model. Such models are used to generate power caps from the profiling and hardware calibration data.

In addition to commands and types above, arrays and loops are also supported in this DSL. Arrays are used to create objects as a batch and loops simply help improve the productivity of this DSL. Through all these supported features, this DSL stands between the user/system administrator and our framework and allows the framework to be accessed in a more unified manner and also realizes more complex power management tasks.

4.2 Implementation of the DSL Interpreter

The DSL interpreter is designed and implemented with ANTLR v4. During interpretation, various DSL statements are translated into shell scripts and application instrumentation for different purposes such as hardware calibration, application profiling, job submission, specifying power control in the application, interfaces to other tools and so on. This interpretation process is uniform for different systems but different hardware configurations may lead to variations in the results.

Along with any created instances of a defined type in this DSL, there is also an XML file created to store their attributes. For example, an instance of the type "job" will have an accompanying XML file which stores its attributes such as its name, path, executable, power caps and so on.

5 Case Studies and Evaluation

In this section, we provide three case studies to demonstrate some of the functionalities of our framework. All these case studies are firstly programmed with the DSL and then interpreted on a gateway node of an HPC system with its specifications shown in Table 2.

Table 2. Evaluation environment and parameters

Number of nodes	16
Processor	Intel Xeon E5-2680
Number of sockets per node	2
Number of cores per socket	8
Memory size per node	128 GB
Interconnect	Infiniband FDR
OS	Red Hat Linux Enterprise with kernel 2.6.32
Compiler	FUJITSU Software Technical Computing Suite
MPI	Open MPI 1.6.3
Applications	EP and IS (Class D) from the NPB Suite

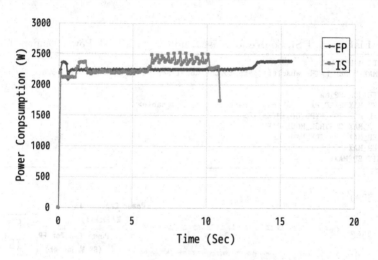

Fig. 4. Power profiles of EP and IS

Listing 4. DSL Source for Profiling

```
1  CREATE JOB EP_P
2  ADD EP_P EXEC_PATH <absolute path to the executable>
3  ADD EP_P JOB_TYPE PROFILING
4  ADD EP_P PVT_PATH <absolute path to the power variation table>
5  ADD EP_P ITERATIONS 5
6  ADD EP_P PROFILE_NAME EP
7  SUBMIT EP_P
```

In these case studies, we employed RAPL interface [10] as the available power-knob, and considered only CPU power to be controlled through the RAPL under the assumption that DRAM power consumption has strong correlations with CPU performance and power. We used two applications (EP and IS) from the NPB benchmark suite [14] to carry out these case studies. To understand their performance and power characteristics, profiling is necessary and the results are shown in Fig. 4 with an interval of 100 ms. The profiling processes are also specified with our DSL as in Listing 4. How power capping should be applied during the profiling process depends on the system and the power-performance model to be used, and our framework can be easily extended to follow them.

5.1   Case Study 1: Peak Power Demand as the Power Cap for Applications

The first case study shows how a maximum power demand of an application is used as the power cap for the application. This case study requires our framework to insert power-knob control API calls to the user application. Such API calls are inserted into the application source file, and help both the profiling process and capping tasks.

Listing 5. DSL Source for Case Study 1 (with Peak Power Demand)

```
 1  CREATE MODEL MAX
 2  ADD MAX MODEL_PATH <absolute path to the model script to find out max power>
 3
 4  CREATE JOB EP_MAX
 5  ADD EP_MAX EXEC_PATH <absolute path to the executable>
 6  ADD EP_MAX JOB_TYPE OPTIMIZATION
 7  ADD EP_MAX CONTROL_MODE RAPL
 8  ADD EP_MAX PROFILE_NAME EP
 9  ADD EP_MAX MODEL_TO_USE MAX
10  SUBMIT EP_MAX
```

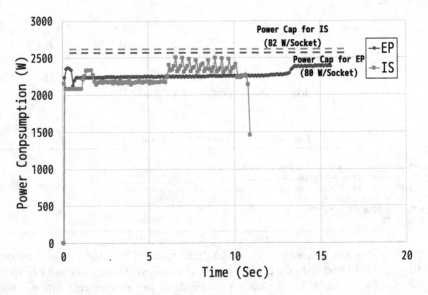

Fig. 5. Power performance optimization results under case study 1 (with peak power demand)

For this case study, first we profile a target application without any power cap to get its general power profile, and then search for its peak power consumption in the profile. After finding the peak power consumption, we then launch a production run with it as the power cap so that the application does not suffer from any performance loss under the guarantee that the power consumption will not exceed given power budget. The DSL source (for EP) for this case study is shown in Listing 5.

Figure 5 presents the power profiles of two applications under the peak power demand. As expected, there is no performance loss observed in this case study.

5.2 Case Study 2: Average Power Demand as the Power Cap for Applications

The second case study is used to prove how the average power demand of an application is obtained through profiling and used as the power cap for the application. Such power caps can help save the power and may lead to more energy-efficient runs. Saved power can be distributed to other jobs simultaneously running on the same system by the system software like a job scheduler. The DSL source (for EP) for this case study is shown in Listing 6.

In this case study, first we run the target application without any power capping to get its general power profile like Case Study 1, and then obtained average power consumption through a simple calculation. We set the power caps with this average value for a power optimized run.

Figure 6 presents the power profiles of two applications under the average power demand. For each application, there is a performance loss compared to Case Study 1, but the power consumption is much less.

Listing 6. DSL Source for Case Study 2 (with Average Power Demand)

```
 1  CREATE MODEL AVERAGE
 2  ADD AVERAGE MODEL_PATH <absolute path to the model script to find out the average power>
 3
 4  CREATE JOB EP_AVE
 5  ADD EP_AVE EXEC_PATH <absolute path to the executable>
 6  ADD EP_AVE JOB_TYPE OPTIMIZATION
 7  ADD EP_AVE CONTROL_MODE RAPL
 8  ADD EP_AVE PROFILE_NAME EP
 9  ADD EP_AVE MODEL_TO_USE AVERAGE
10  SUBMIT EP_AVE
```

5.3 Case Study 3: Power Cap to Satisfy a User-Defined Deadline While Minimizing Power Consumption

The third case study is used to show how a linear performance/power model of the application is constructed through profiling and how we use this model to derive the power cap according to user's performance demand for the application.

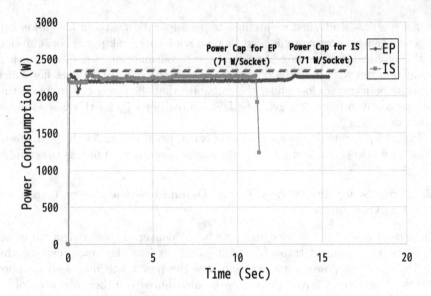

Fig. 6. Power performance optimization results under case study 2 (with average power demand)

Listing 7. DSL Source for Case Study 3 (within a Slowdown of 2)

```
1  CREATE MODEL LINEAR
2  ADD LINEAR MODEL_PATH <absolute path to the script of a linear model between performance
     and power>
3
4  CREATE JOB EP_LINEAR
5  ADD EP_LINEAR EXEC_PATH <absolute path to the executable>
6  ADD EP_LINEAR JOB_TYPE OPTIMIZATION
7  ADD EP_LINEAR CONTROL_MODE RAPL
8  ADD EP_LINEAR PROFILE_NAME EP
9  ADD EP_LINEAR MODEL_TO_USE LINEAR
10 ADD EP_LINEAR PERFORMANCE_TARGET 0.5
11 SUBMIT EP_LINEAR
```

In addition to the power profiles shown in Fig. 4, four extra rounds of profiling are required for this case study. The first two extra rounds are launched with the peak power demand to find the shortest runtime. Then through the third extra round of profiling where we set the power caps to a very small value (10 W/Socket), we found that the minimum amount of power needed to run both applications properly is around 30 W. We then set the power cap to 30 W per socket and profile the forth extra round to find the runtime of the applications. Using these profiled data, we can construct a linear performance/power model for each application as shown in Fig. 7.

Using the models shown in Fig. 7, performance demand can be set from the users when they submit their jobs through the DSL code. For example, if the user allows the runtime to be doubled, the corresponding power caps can be found from these two models as 59 W and 34 W for EP and IS, respectively. The DSL source (for EP) for this case study is shown in Listing 7.

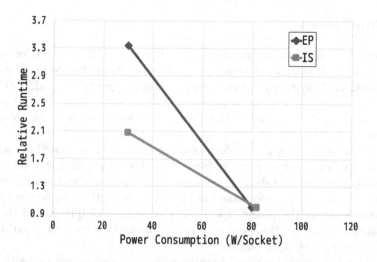

Fig. 7. The linear performance/power models for EP and IS

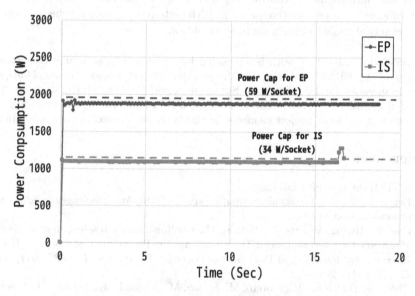

Fig. 8. Power performance optimization results under case study 3 (within a slowdown of 2)

Figure 8 presents the power profiles of the two applications under power caps obtained from the models to allow the elapsed time to be shorter than twice the runtime under the peak power demand. Obviously, these two models are not accurate enough so that both applications are slowed down for less than two times (1.20x and 1.53x, respectively). Regardless of the accuracy of such models, at least user's performance demand is satisfied while the allocated power is dramatically cut.

6   Conclusions

We have demonstrated a versatile power management framework for power-constrained HPC systems to tackle the problem of power limitation. With this framework, HPC system administrators can easily specify and calibrate their system hardware. Meanwhile, it is also helpful for tasks such as how the user applications should be tuned to maximize the performance or to cut the power demand.

To verify the validity and usefulness of our framework, we tested it with several case studies. In these case studies, we applied power management to two selected applications and showed how a simple power model with linear relationship between the CPU performance and power consumption can be constructed and used to derive the power cap. These case studies simply proved that our framework can provide the users an easy way to apply power optimization and management to their applications.

In our future work, we plan to evaluate the proposed framework with other power and performance optimization policies/algorithms, and to improve it with more functionalities such as cooperation with system software, job schedulers and other external tools to enrich its functionalities.

Acknowledgment. This work is supported by the Japan Science and Technology Agency (JST) CREST program for the research project named "Power Management Framework for Post-Petascale Supercomputers". We are also grateful to the Research Institute for Information Technology of Kyushu University for providing us the resources and to all project members for their valuable comments and cooperation.

References

1. ANTLR. http://www.antlr.org/
2. Bergman, K., et al.: Exascale computing study: Technology challenges in achieving exascale systems (2008)
3. Cao, T., Huang, W., He, Y., Kondo, M.: Cooling-aware job scheduling and node allocation for overprovisioned HPC systems. In: Proceedings of the 31st IEEE International Parallel and Distributed Processing Symposium (IPDPS 2017), pp. 728–737, May 2017
4. Chasapis, D., Casas, M., Moretó, M., Schulz, M., Ayguadé, E., Labarta, J., Valero, M.: Runtime-guided mitigation of manufacturing variability in power-constrained multi-socket NUMA nodes. In: Proceedings of the 2016 International Conference on Supercomputing (ICS 2016), pp. 5:1–5:12, June 2016
5. GeoPM. https://github.com/geopm
6. Gholkar, N., Mueller, F., Rountree, B.: Power tuning HPC jobs on power-constrained systems. In: Proceedings of the 2016 International Conference on Parallel Architectures and Compilation (PACT 2016), pp. 179–191, September 2016
7. IEEE Std 802.3az-2010 (2010). https://standards.ieee.org/findstds/standard/802.3az-2010.html
8. Laros III, J.H., DeBonis, D., Grant, R., Kelly, S.M., Levenhagen, M., Olivier, S., Pedretti, K.: High performance computing - power application programming interface specification version 1.3, May 2016

9. Inadomi, Y., Patki, T., Inoue, K., Aoyagi, M., Rountree, B., Schulz, M., Lowenthal, D., Wada, Y., Fukazawa, K., Ueda, M., Kondo, M., Miyoshi, I.: Analyzing and mitigating the impact of manufacturing variability in power-constrained supercomputing. In: Proceedings of the International Conference for High Performance Computing, Networking, Storage and Analysis (SC15), pp. 78:1–78:12, November 2015

10. Intel Corporation: Intel® 64 and IA-32 architectures software developer's manual, September 2016

11. Lange, K.D.: Identifying shades of green: the SPECpower benchmarks. Computer 42(3), 95–97 March, 2009

12. Lucas, R., et al.: Top ten exascale research challenges (2014)

13. Miwa, S., Nakamura, H.: Profile-based power shifting in interconnection networks with on/off links. In: Proceedings of the International Conference for High Performance Computing, Networking, Storage and Analysis (SC15), pp. 37:1–37:11, November 2015

14. NAS parallel benchmarks 3.3. http://www.nas.nasa.gov/

15. NVIDIA Corporation: NVML reference manual (2015)

16. Parr, T.: The Definitive ANTLR 4 Reference, 2nd edn. Pragmatic Bookshelf, Dallas (2013)

17. Patki, T., Lowenthal, D.K., Sasidharan, A., Maiterth, M., Rountree, B.L., Schulz, M., de Supinski, B.R.: Practical resource management in power-constrained, high performance computing. In: Proceedings of the 24th International Symposium on High-Performance Parallel and Distributed Computing, pp. 121–132, June 2015

18. PDT. https://www.cs.uoregon.edu/research/pdt/home.php

19. PomPP Library and Tools. https://github.com/pompp/pompp_tools

20. Sakamoto, R., Cao, T., Kondo, M., Inoue, K., Ueda, M., Patki, T., Ellsworth, D.A., Rountree, B., Schulz, M.: Production hardware overprovisioning: real-world performance optimization using an extensible power-aware resource management framework. In: Proceedings of the 31st IEEE International Parallel and Distributed Processing Symposium (IPDPS 2017), pp. 957–966, May 2017

21. Shende, S.S., Malony, A.D.: The TAU parallel performance system. Int. J. High Perform. Comput. Appl. 20(2), 287–331 (2006)

22. Spafford, K.L., Vetter, J.S.: Automated design space exploration with aspen. Sci. Program. 7:1–7:10 (2015)

23. TAU. https://www.cs.uoregon.edu/research/tau/home.php

24. Cao, T., Thang, C., He, Y., Kondo, M.: Demand-aware power management for power-constrained HPC systems. In: Proceedings of 16th IEEE/ACM International Symposium on Cluster, Cloud and Grid Computing (CCGrid 2016), pp. 21–31, May 2016

25. Wada, Y., He, Y., Thang, C., Kondo, M.: The PomPP framework: from simple DSL to sophisticated power management for HPC systems. In: HPC Asia 2018 Poster Session, January 2018

26. Wallace, S., Yang, X., Vishwanath, V., Allcock, W.E., Coghlan, S., Papka, M.E., Lan, Z.: A data driven scheduling approach for power management on HPC systems. In: Proceedings of the International Conference for High Performance Computing, Networking, Storage and Analysis (SC16), pp. 56:1–56:11, November 2016

27. Weaver, V.M., Johnson, M., Kasichayanula, K., Ralph, J., Luszczek, P., Terpstra, D., Moore, S.: Measuring energy and power with PAPI. In: Proceedings of the 41st International Conference on Parallel Processing Workshops (ICPPW-2012), pp. 262–268, September 2012

Scalable Data Management of the Uintah Simulation Framework for Next-Generation Engineering Problems with Radiation

Sidharth Kumar[1](✉), Alan Humphrey[1], Will Usher[1], Steve Petruzza[1],
Brad Peterson[1], John A. Schmidt[1], Derek Harris[2], Ben Isaac[2],
Jeremy Thornock[2], Todd Harman[2], Valerio Pascucci[1], and Martin Berzins[1]

[1] SCI Institute, University of Utah, Salt Lake City, UT, USA
{sidharth,ahumphrey}@sci.utah.edu
[2] Institute for Clean and Secure Energy, Salt Lake City, UT, USA

Abstract. The need to scale next-generation industrial engineering problems to the largest computational platforms presents unique challenges. This paper focuses on data management related problems faced by the Uintah simulation framework at a production scale of 260K processes. Uintah provides a highly scalable asynchronous many-task runtime system, which in this work is used for the modeling of a 1000 megawatt electric (MWe) ultra-supercritical (USC) coal boiler. At 260K processes, we faced both parallel I/O and visualization related challenges, e.g., the default file-per-process I/O approach of Uintah did not scale on Mira. In this paper we present a simple to implement, restructuring based parallel I/O technique. We impose a restructuring step that alters the distribution of data among processes. The goal is to distribute the dataset such that each process holds a larger chunk of data, which is then written to a file independently. This approach finds a middle ground between two of the most common parallel I/O schemes–file per process I/O and shared file I/O–in terms of both the total number of generated files, and the extent of communication involved during the data aggregation phase. To address scalability issues when visualizing the simulation data, we developed a lightweight renderer using OSPRay, which allows scientists to visualize the data interactively at high quality and make production movies. Finally, this work presents a highly efficient and scalable radiation model based on the sweeping method, which significantly outperforms previous approaches in Uintah, like discrete ordinates. The integrated approach allowed the USC boiler problem to run on 260K CPU cores on Mira.

1 Introduction

The exponential growth in High performance computing (HPC) over the past 20 years has fueled a wave of scientific insights and discoveries, many of which

---

S. Kumar and A. Humphrey—Authors contributed equally.

© The Author(s) 2018
R. Yokota and W. Wu (Eds.): SCFA 2018, LNCS 10776, pp. 219–240, 2018.
https://doi.org/10.1007/978-3-319-69953-0_13

would not be possible without the integration of HPC capabilities. This trend is continuing, for example, the DOE Exascale Computing Project [18] lists 25 major application focus areas [20] in energy, science, and national security. The primary challenge in moving codes to new architectures at exascale is that, although present codes may have good scaling characteristics on some current architectures, those codes may likely have components that are not suited to the high level of parallelism on these new computer architectures, or to the complexity of real-world applications at exascale. One of the major challenges faced by modern scalable scientific codes is with regard to data management. As the gap between computing power and available disk bandwidth continues to grow, the cost of parallel I/O becomes an important concern, especially for simulations at the largest scales. Large-scale simulation I/O can be roughly split into two use cases: checkpoint restarts in which the entire state of a simulation must be preserved exactly, and analysis dumps in which a subset of information is saved. Both checkpointing and analysis dumps are important, yet due to poor I/O scaling and little available disk bandwidth, the trend of large-scale simulation runs is to save fewer and fewer results. This not only increases the cost of faults, since checkpoints are saved less frequently, but ultimately may affect the scientific integrity of the analysis, due to the reduced temporal sampling of the simulation. This paper presents a simple to implement method to enable parallel I/O, which we demonstrate to efficiently scale up to 260K processes.

For most applications, the layout of data distributed across compute cores does not translate to efficient network and storage access pattern for I/O. Consequently, performing naive I/O leads to significant underutilization of the system. For instance, the patch or block size of simulations is typically on the order of 12^3 to 20^3 voxels (cells), mainly because a scientist typically works under a restricted compute budget, and smaller patch sizes lead to faster execution of individual computational timesteps (see Fig. 1), which is critical in completion of the entire simulation. Small patch sizes do not bode well for parallel I/O, with either file-per-process I/O or shared file I/O.

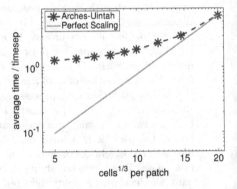

Fig. 1. Time taken for execution of a timestep for different patch sizes. Execution time starts to increase rapidly after a patch size of 12^3.

We find a middle ground by introducing a restructuring-based parallel I/O technique. We virtually regrid the data by imposing a restructuring phase that alters the distribution of data among processes in a way such that only a few processes end up holding larger patches/blocks, which are then written to a file independently. The efficacy and scalability of this approach is shown in Sect. 3.

In order to gain scientific insight from such large-scale simulations, the visualization software used must also scale well to large core counts and datasets, introducing additional challenges in performing scientific simulations at scale for domain scientists. To address I/O challenges on the read side of the scientific pipeline, we also use our scalable parallel I/O library in combination with the ray tracing library OSPRay [24] to create a lightweight remote viewer and movie rendering tool for visualization of such large-scale data (Sect. 4).

Finally, we introduce a new, efficient radiation solve method into Uintah based on spatial transport sweeps [2,4]. The radiation calculation is central to the commercial 1000 megawatt electric (MWe) ultra-supercritical (USC) coal boiler being simulated in this work, as radiation is the dominant mode of heat transfer within the boiler itself. To improve parallelism within these spatial sweeps, the computation is split into multiple stages, which then expose spatial dependencies to the Uintah task scheduler. Using the provided information about the stage's dependencies, the scheduler can efficiently distribute the computation, increasing utilization. For the target boiler problem discussed in this paper, we find this method up to 10× faster than previous reverse Monte Carlo ray tracing methods (Sect. 5) due to this increased utilization.

This work demonstrates the efficacy of our approach by adapting the Uintah computational framework [8], a highly scalable asynchronous many-task (AMT) [7] runtime system, to use our I/O system and spatial transport sweeps within a large-eddy simulation (LES). This work is aimed at predicting the performance of a commercial 1000 MWe USC coal boiler, and has been considered as an ideal exascale candidate given that the spatial and temporal resolution requirements on physical grounds give rise to problems between 50 to 1000 times larger than those we can solve today.

The principal contributions of this paper are:

1. A restructuring-based parallel I/O scheme.
2. A data parallel visualization system using OSPRay.
3. A faster approach to radiation using a spatial transport sweeps method.

2   Background

2.1   Uintah Simulation Framework

Uintah [22] is a software framework consisting of a set of parallel software components and libraries that facilitate the solution of partial differential equations on structured adaptive mesh refinement (AMR) grids. Uintah currently contains four main simulation components: (1) the multi-material ICE code for both low- and high-speed compressible flows; (2) the multi-material, particle-based code MPM for structural mechanics; (3) the combined fluid-structure interaction (FSI) algorithm MPM-ICE; and (4) the Arches turbulent reacting CFD component that was designed for simulating turbulent reacting flows with participating media radiation. Separate from these components is an AMT runtime, considered as a possible leading alternative to mitigate exascale challenges at the runtime system-level, which shelters the application developer from the complexities introduced by future architectures [7]. Uintah's clear separation between the application layer and the underlying runtime system both keeps the application developer insulated from complexities of the underlying parallelism Uintah provides, and makes it possible to achieve great increases in scalability through changes to the runtime system that executes the taskgraph, without requiring changes to the applications themselves [17].

Uintah decomposes the computational domain into a structured grid of rectangular cuboid cells. The basic unit of a Uintah simulation's Cartesian mesh (composed of cells) is termed a *patch*, and simulation variables that reside in Uintah's patches are termed *grid* or *particle* variables. The Uintah runtime system manages the complexity of inter-nodal data dependencies, node-level parallelism, data movement between the CPU and GPU, and ultimately task scheduling and execution that make up a computational algorithm [19], including I/O tasks. The core idea is to use a directed acyclic graph (DAG) representation of the computation to schedule work, as opposed to, say, a bulk synchronous approach in which blocks of communication follow blocks of computation. This graph-based approach allows tasks to execute in a manner that efficiently overlaps communication and computation, and includes out-of-order execution of tasks (with respect to a topological sort) where possible. Using this task-based approach also allows for improved load balancing, as only nodes need to be considered, not individual cores [8].

2.2 Related Work

Many high-level I/O libraries have been developed to help structure the large volumes of data produced by scientific simulations, such as HDF5 and PnetCDF. The hierarchical data format (HDF5) [10] allows developers to express data models organized hierarchically. PnetCDF [14] is a parallel implementation of the network common data form (netCDF), which includes a format optimized for dense, regular datasets. Both HDF5 and PnetCDF are implemented using MPI and both leverage MPI-IO collective I/O operations for data aggregation. In practice, shared file I/O often does not scale well because of the global communication necessary to write to a single file. ADIOS [15] is another popular library used to manage parallel I/O for scientific applications.

On the visualization front, VisIt [9] and ParaView [3] are popular distributed visualization and analysis applications. They are typically executed in parallel, coordinating visualization and analysis tasks for massive simulation data. The data are typically loaded at full resolution, requiring large amounts of system memory. Moreover, both can be used for remote visualization, where a remote server (or servers) is responsible for rendering and operating on the data and the user interacts remotely through a lightweight client. Our renderer works similarly, allowing for remote visualization and offline movie rendering. Furthermore, our viewer supports running on any CPU architecture, via OSPRay [24], which is now integrated in ParaView and being integrated into VisIt. However, in contrast to these larger visualization packages, our viewer is tuned specifically for interactive visualization and movie rendering, allowing for better rendering performance and enabling us to take better advantage of parallel I/O for fast data loading.

The 1000 MWe USC coal boiler being modeled by Uintah in this work has thermal radiation as a dominant heat transfer mode, and involves solving the conservation of energy equation and radiative heat transfer equation (RTE) simultaneously. This radiation calculation, in which the radiative-flux divergence at each cell of the discretized domain is calculated, can take up to 50% of the overall CPU time per timestep [11] using the discrete ordinates method (DOM) [6], one of the standard approaches to computing radiative heat transfer. Using a reverse Monte Carlo ray tracing approach combined with a novel use of Uintah's adaptive mesh refinement infrastructure, this calculation has been made to scale to 262K cores [11], and further adapted to run on up to 16K GPUs [12]. The spatial transport sweeps method discussed in Sect. 5 shows great promise for future large-scale simulations.

2.3 System Configuration

The Mira supercomputer [1] at Argonne National Laboratory is an IBM Blue Gene/Q system that enables high-performance computing with low power consumption. The Mira system has 16 cores per node, 1024 nodes per rack, and 48 racks, providing a total of 768K cores. Each node has 16 GB of RAM and the network topology is a 5D torus. There are two I/O nodes for every 128 compute nodes, with one 2 GB/s bandwidth link per I/O node. Mira uses the GPFS file system. Ranks are assigned with locality guarantees on the machine, which our I/O system can also take advantage of. Initial results of weak and strong scaling studies of the target problem on Mira are shown in Fig. 2.

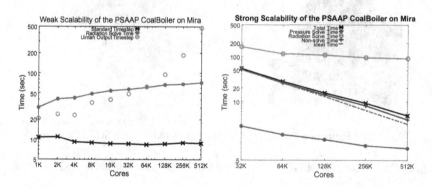

Fig. 2. Strong and weak scalability of the coal boiler simulation on Mira using the discrete ordinates solver. In these initial studies, we found scaling issues with the I/O and radiation solve components of Uintah that needed to be addressed for the production runs. Note the radiation solve is not executed each timestep, and not included in the total time for a timestep.

2.4 Target Boiler Problem

GE Power is currently building new coal-fired power plants throughout the world and evaluating new designs for these boilers. Many of these units will potentially be 1000 MWe, twin-fireball USC units (Fig. 3a). Historically, twin-fireball (or 8-corner) units became part of the GE Power product offering because of the design uncertainty in scaling 4-corner units from a lower MWe rating to a much higher MWe rating. In order to decrease risk, both from GE Power's perspective and the customer's, two smaller units were joined together to form a larger unit capable of producing up to 1090 MWe.

Simulation plays a key role in designing new boilers, allowing engineers to build, test, and optimize new designs at very low cost. When viewed as a large-scale computational problem, there are considerable challenges to simulating the boiler at acceptable accuracy and resolution to gain scientific insight about the design. The geometric complexity of the boiler is considerable, and presented a significant challenge for the combustion modelers. The boiler measures 65 m × 35 m × 15 m and contains 430 separated over-fired air (SOFA) inlets (Fig. 3b), which inject pulverized coal and oxygen into the combustion chamber. Moreover, the boiler has division panels, plates, super-heaters and re-heater tubing with about 210 miles of piping walls, and tubing made of 11 metals with varying thickness. Both the 8-corner units and 4-corner units have different mixing and wall absorption characteristics that must be fully understood in order to have confidence in their respective designs. One key piece of the design that must be understood is how the SOFA inlets should be positioned and oriented, and what effect this has on the heat flux distribution throughout the boiler.

   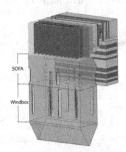

(a) Entire unit.   (b) Primary wind-box and SOFA locations.

Fig. 3. CAD rendering of GE Power's 1000 MWe USC two-cell pulverized coal boiler.

3 Restructured Parallel I/O

File-per process I/O and single shared file I/O are two of the most commonly used parallel I/O techniques. However, both methods fail to scale at high core counts. An I/O-centric view of the typical simulation pipeline is as follows: the simulation domain is first divided into cells/elements (usually pixels or voxels), and then the elements are grouped into patches. Each patch is assigned a rank or processor number. Rank assignment is done by the simulation software using a deterministic indexing scheme (for example, row-order or Z-order). When performing file-per-process I/O, each process creates a separate file and independently writes its patch data to the file. This approach works well for relatively small numbers of cores; however, at high core counts this approach performs poorly, as the large number of files overwhelms the parallel file system. When using single shared file I/O, performance also decreases as the core count increases, as the time spent during data exchange involved in the aggregation step becomes significant, impeding scalability [5]. In this work we tackle both the communication bottleneck of the aggregation phase in single shared file I/O and the bottleneck of creating a hierarchy of files in file-per-process I/O by proposing a middleground approach through a restructuring-based parallel I/O technique. The main idea is to regrid the simulation domain in a restructuring phase.

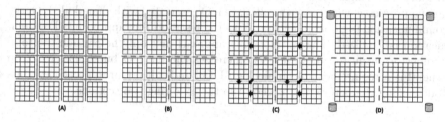

Fig. 4. Schematic diagram of restructuring-based parallel I/O. (A) The initial simulation patch size is 4 × 4. (B) A new grid of patch size 8 × 8 is imposed. (C) The restructuring phase is executed using MPI point-to-point communication. (D) Finally, using the restructured grid, every patch is written to a separate file.

Starting from the original simulation grid (Fig. 4(A)), we begin restructuring by imposing a new grid on the simulation domain (Fig. 4(B)). The patch size of the imposed grid is larger than the initial patch size assigned by the simulation. As mentioned in Fig. 1, the patch size assigned by the simulation is on the order of 12^3 to 20^3, while the patch size of the new restructured grid is typically twice that in each dimension. The simulation data is then restructured-based on the new grid/patch configuration (Fig. 4(C)). During the restructuring, MPI point-to-point communication is used to move data between processes [13]. Note that the communication is distributed in nature and confined to small subsets of processes, which is crucial for the scalability of the restructuring phase. At the end of the restructuring phase, we end up with large-sized patches on a subset of processes (Fig. 4(D)). Given that the new restructured patch size is always bigger than the patch size assigned by the simulation (or equal in size at worst), we end up with fewer patches held on a subset of the simulation processes. Throughout the restructuring phase the data remains in the application layout. Once the restructuring phases concludes, each processes holding the restructured patches create a file and writes its data to the file. This scheme of parallel I/O finds a middle-ground between file-per-process-based parallel I/O and shared file I/O, both in terms of the total number of files generated and the extent of communication required during the data aggregation phase. With our approach, the total number of files generated is given by the following formula:

$$\texttt{number\_of\_files} = \left\lceil \frac{\texttt{bounds\_x}}{\texttt{nrst\_x}} \right\rceil \times \left\lceil \frac{\texttt{bounds\_y}}{\texttt{nrst\_y}} \right\rceil \times \left\lceil \frac{\texttt{bounds\_z}}{\texttt{nrst\_z}} \right\rceil$$

Based on the restructuring box size ($\texttt{nrst\_x} \times \texttt{nrst\_y} \times \texttt{nrst\_z}$), we can have a range of total number of outputted files. The number of files will be equal to the number of processes (i.e., file-per-process I/O) when the restructuring patch size is equal to the simulation patch size. The number of files will be one (i.e., shared-file I/O) when the restructuring patch size is equal to the entire simulation domain ($\texttt{bounds\_x} \times \texttt{bounds\_y} \times \texttt{bounds\_z}$). For most practical scenarios, the latter situation is not feasible due to limitations on the available memory on a single core. With file-per-process I/O, there is no communication among processes, whereas with collective I/O associated with shared file I/O, the communication is global in nature. With the restructuring approach, all communication is localized. The restructuring approach not only helps tune the total number of outputted files, but also increases the file I/O burst size, which in general is a requirement to obtain high I/O bandwidth. Our approach exhibits good scaling characteristics, as shown in the following two sections.

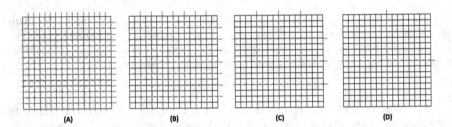

Fig. 5. Three variations of restructuring-based parallel I/O. (A) No restructuring, each patch is held by a process and is written out separately to a file. (B) Restructuring phase with new patches containing 2^2 simulation patches, creating 4× fewer files. (C) New patch size of 4^2 simulation patches, creating 16× fewer files (D) New patch size of 8^2 simulation patches, creating 64× fewer files. Communication is limited to groups of (B) 4, (C) 16, and (D) 64 processes.

3.1   Parameter Study

The tunable parameter in our proposed I/O framework that has the greatest impact on performance is the patch size used for restructuring. The patch size affects both the degree of network traffic and the total number of outputted files. To understand the impact of the parameter, we wrote a micro-benchmark to write out a 3D volume. In our evaluations on the Mira supercomputer, we kept the number of processes fixed at 32768. Each process wrote a 16^3 subvolume of double precision floating point data to generate a total volume of 1 gigabyte (512^3). We used four restructuring box sizes – 32^3, 64^3, 128^3 and 256^3; the number of files generated, respectively, varied as 4096 ($512^3/32^3$), 512 ($512^3/64^3$), 64 ($512^3/128^3$), 8 ($512^3/256^3$). The number of processes involved in communication during the restructuring phase increases with the box size. For example, with a restructuring box of size 32^3, communication is limited to groups of 8 processes ($32^3/16^3$), whereas with a restructuring box of size 256^3, communication takes place with a group of 4096 processes. See Fig. 5 for an example. In order to provide a baseline for the results obtained, we also ran IOR benchmarks. IOR is a general-purpose parallel I/O benchmark [23] that we configured to perform both file-per-process as well as shared file I/O. For shared file I/O, all the processes wrote to a single file using MPI collective I/O. The results can be seen in Fig. 6. The file-per-process I/O performs the worst and this is because the underlying GPFS [21] parallel file system of Mira is not adept at handling large numbers of files. Although we did not run any benchmarks of the Lustre PFS [16], it is more suited to handling large numbers of files, especially at low core counts. This is mainly because GPFS is a block-based distributed filesystems where the metadata server controls all the block allocation, whereas the Lustre filesystem has a separate metadata server for pathname and permission checks. Furthermore, the Lustre metadata server is not involved in any file I/O operations, which avoids I/O scalability bottlenecks on the metadata server. The constraint on the number of files makes our approach highly suitable for GPFS file systems. Note that both file systems start to get saturated with file per-process I/O at high core counts.

The performance of restructuring-based parallel I/O improves with larger box sizes, reaching peak performance with a box size of 128^3. At that patch size, the restructuring approach achieves a 3.7× improvement over the IOR benchmark's shared file I/O approach (using MPI collective I/O) because our approach's *aggregation* phase is localized in nature, involving only small groups of processes, as opposed to MPI collective I/O's underlying global communication. However, we observe performance degradation at a restructuring box size of 256^3. The reason for this degradation can be understood by looking at a time breakdown between the restructuring (communication) phase and the file I/O phase (Fig. 6). As can be seen, communication time (red) increases with larger restructuring boxes. Although the file I/O time continues to decrease with increasing box size, the restructuring time begins to dominate at 256^3, and as a result overall performance suffers. We believe our design is flexible enough to be tuned to generate small numbers of large shared files or a large number of files, depending on which is optimal for the target system.

3.2   Production Run Weak Scaling Results

With Uintah's default I/O subsystem, every node writes data for all its cores into a separate file. Therefore, on Mira there is one file for every 16 cores (16 cores

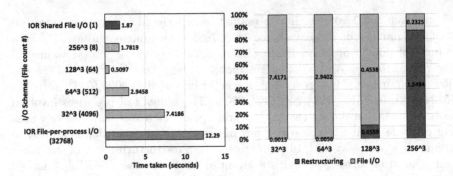

Fig. 6. (Left) Performance of restructuring-based parallel I/O with varying box sizes. (Right) Time breakdown between restructuring (communication) and file I/O for different box sizes. (Color figure online)

per node). This form of I/O is an extension to the file-per process style of I/O commonly adopted by many simulations. An XML-based meta-data file is also associated with every data file that stores type, extents, bounds, and other relevant information for each of the different fields. For relatively small core counts this I/O approach works well. However, I/O performance degrades significantly for simulations with several hundreds of thousands of patches/processors. The cost of both reads and writes for large numbers of small files becomes untenable.

We extended the Uintah simulation framework to use the restructuring-based I/O scheme, and evaluated the weak scaling performance of the I/O system when writing data for a representative Uintah simulation on Mira. In each run, Uintah wrote out 20 timesteps consisting of 72 fields (grid variables). The patch size for the simulation was 12^3. The number of cores was varied from 7,920 to 262,890. Looking at the performance results in Fig. 7, our I/O system scales well for all core counts and performs better than the original Uintah UDA I/O system. The restructuring-based I/O system demonstrates almost linear scaling up to 262,890 cores whereas the performance of file-per-node I/O starts to decline after

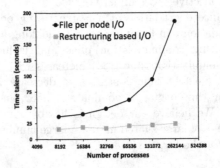

Fig. 7. Weak scaling results of restructuring-based parallel I/O compared to Uintah's file per node I/O approach. Our I/O system outperforms Uintah's default I/O at all core counts, attaining 10× performance improvement at 260K cores.

16,200 cores. At 262,890 cores, our I/O system achieves an approximate speed-up of 10× over Uintah's default file-per-node I/O.

The restructuring-based I/O system was then used in production boiler simulations, carried out at 260K cores on Mira. Due to the improved performance of the I/O system, scientists were able to save data at a much higher temporal frequency. In terms of outputs, close to 200 terabytes of data was written which, using our new restructuring I/O strategy, required only 2% of the entire simulation time. If the simulation were run using the Uintah's default file-per-process node output format, nearly 50% of the time of the computation would be spent on I/O, reducing the number of timesteps that could be saved, or increasing the total computation time significantly.

4   Scalable Visualization with OSPRay

When trying to visualize the data produced on Mira using the Cooley visualization cluster at ANL, VisIt rendered at interactive framerates for smaller datasets; however, when trying to visualize the recent large simulations using all the cores on each node would consume too much memory, resulting in crashes or significantly reduced performance due to swapping. To address these issues and allow for quick, interactive visualization and high-quality offline movie rendering, we wrote a lightweight renderer using OSPRay [24] which uses the restructuring-based parallel I/O to read the data. OSPRay is a CPU-based open-source ray tracing library for scientific visualization, and includes high-quality and high-performance volume rendering, along with support for rendering distributed data with MPI.

OSPRay includes support for two modes of MPI-parallel rendering: an offload mode, where data is replicated across nodes, and subregions of the image are distributed; and a distributed mode, where different ranks make OSPRay API calls independently to setup their local data, and then work collectively to render

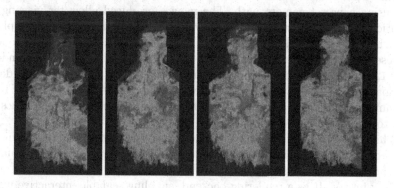

Fig. 8. Frames from the movie showing the O^2 field over time. Using restructuring-based parallel I/O backend and OSPRay we were able to render an animation of the full 1030 timesteps in two hours using 128 KNL nodes on Theta.

the distributed data using sort-last compositing [24]. To leverage the benefits of the restructuring-based parallel I/O in the viewer, we implemented our renderer using the distributed mode of OSPRay, with each rank responsible for loading and rendering a subregion of the dataset. To properly composite the distributed data OSPRay requires the application to specify a set of regions on each rank, which bound the data owned by that rank. In our case this is trivially the bounds of the single subregion owned by the rank. The renderer supports two usage modes, allowing for interactive remote visualization and offline movie rendering for creating production animations of the evolution of the boiler state.

The interactive viewer runs a set of render worker processes on the compute nodes, with one per node as OSPRay uses threads for on-node parallelism. The user then connects over the network with a remote client and receives back rendered JPG images, while sending back over the network camera and transfer function changes to interact with the dataset. To decouple the interface from network latency effects and the rendering framerate, we send and receive to the render workers asynchronously, and always take the latest frame and send the latest application state. With this application, users can explore the different timesteps of the simulation and different fields of data interactively on their laptop, with the rendering itself performed on Theta or Cooley. When rendering on 16 nodes of Theta with a 1080 × 1920 framebuffer (oriented to match the vertical layout of the boiler), the viewer was able to render at 11 FPS, allowing for interactive exploration.

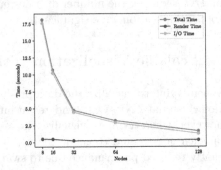

Fig. 9. Strong scaling of movie rendering on Theta.

The offline movie renderer is run as a batch application and will render the data using a preset camera path. The movies produced allow for viewing the evolution of the boiler state smoothly over time, as the timesteps can be played through at a constant rate, instead of waiting for new timesteps or fields to load. A subset of frames from this animation is shown in Fig. 8, which was rendered using 128 nodes on Theta. The majority of the time spent in the movie rendering is in loading the data, which scales well with the presented I/O scheme (Fig. 9). The animation is rendered at 1080 × 1920 with a high number of samples per pixel to improve image quality.

While our lightweight viewer is valuable for visual exploration, it is missing the large range of additional analysis tools provided by production visualization and analysis packages like VisIt. To this end, we are working on integrating OSPRay into VisIt as a rendering backend, enabling scalable interactive visualization for end users.

5 Radiation Modeling: Spatial Transport Sweeps

The heat transfer problem arising from the clean coal boilers being modeled by the Uintah framework has thermal radiation as a dominant heat transfer mode and involves solving the conservation of energy equation and radiative heat transfer equation (RTE) simultaneously [11]. Scalable modeling of radiation is currently one of the most challenging problems in large-scale simulations, due to the global, all-to-all nature of radiation [17], potentially affecting all regions of the domain simultaneously at a single instance in time. To simulate thermal transport, two fundamental approaches exist: random walk simulations and finite element/finite volume simulations, e.g., discrete ordinates method (DOM) [6], which involves solving many large systems of equations. Additionally, the algorithms used for radiation can be used recursively with different spatial orientations and different spectral properties, requiring hundreds to thousands of global, sparse linear solves. Consequently, the speed, accuracy, and limitations of the method must be appropriate for a given application.

Uintah currently supports two fundamentally different approaches to solving the radiation transport equation (RTE) to predict heat flux and its divergence (operator) in these domains. We provide an overview of these supported approaches within Uintah and introduce a third approach, illustrating its performance and scaling with results up to 128K CPU cores on Mira for a radiation benchmark problem.

5.1 Solving the Radiation Transport Equation

The heat flux divergence can be computed using:

$$\nabla Q = 4 * \pi * S - \int_{4\pi} I_\Omega d\Omega, \tag{1}$$

where S is the local source term for radiative intensity, and I_Ω is computed using the RTE for grey non-scattering media requiring a global solve via:

$$\frac{dI_\Omega}{ds} = k * (S - I_\Omega) \tag{2}$$

Here, s is the 1-D spatial coordinate oriented in the direction in which intensity I_Ω is being followed, and k is the absorption or attenuation coefficient. The lack of time in the RTE implies instantaneous transport of the intensity, appropriate for most applications. The methods for solving the RTE discussed here aim to solve for I_Ω using Eq. 2, which can then be integrated to compute the radiative flux and divergence.

5.2 Discrete Ordinates

The discrete ordinates method [6], used in our Mira simulations, solves the RTE by discretizing the left-hand side of Eq. 2, which results in a 4 or a 7-point stencil, depending on the order of the first derivative. Instabilities arise when using the higher order method, so often the 7-point stencil is avoided, or a combination of the two stencils is used. The 4-point stencil results in numerical diffusion that impacts the fidelity of the solve, but for low ordinate counts can improve solution accuracy. As shown by Fig. 2, this method has been demonstrated to scale, but it is computationally expensive, due to the numerous global sparse linear solves. In the case shown, as many as 30–40 backsolves were required per radiation step, with up to an order of magnitude more solves required in other cases. It should be noted that, due to their computational cost, the radiation solves are computed roughly once every 10 timesteps, as the radiation solution does not change quickly enough to warrant a more frequent radiation calculation.

5.3 Reverse Monte Carlo Ray Tracing

Reverse Monte Carlo Ray Tracing (RMCRT) [11] has been implemented on both CPUs and GPUs [11,12], and is a method for solving Eq. 2 by tracing radiation rays from one cell to the next, as described in detail in [11,12]. Reverse Monte Carlo (as opposed to forward) is desirable because rays are then independent of all other ray tracing processes, and are trivially parallel. RMCRT exhibits high accuracy with sufficient ray sampling and is can easily simulate various scattering effects. However, RMCRT can have a very large memory footprint when geometry is replicated on each node to facilitate local ray tracing. To reduce this memory footprint and the required communication, RMCRT leverages the AMR support within Uintah to use a fine mesh locally and a coarse mesh distally. RMCRT uses Monte Carlo processes to model scattering physics and is a direct method, outperforming discrete-ordinates with significant scattering. Numerical diffusion is non-existent for RMCRT. When computation resources are abundant and the solid-angle [11] can be well resolved, RMCRT is preferred to discrete-ordinates, where numerical diffusion hurts accuracy. This method has been made to scale up to 256K CPU cores and up to 16K GPUs within the Uintah framework [11,12,19], and is used for the large-scale, GPU-based boiler simulations, as detailed in [19].

5.4 Spatial Transport Sweeps Method

The Uintah infrastructure allows for solving for the intensities with a 4-point stencil known as *spatial transport sweeps*, a *sweeping method* [2,4], or simply *sweeps*. It is this method that we cover in detail in this work.

Sweeps is a lightweight spatially serial algorithm in which spatial dependencies dictate the speed of the algorithm. These dependencies impose serialized inter-nodal communication requirements, and account for the bulk of the algorithm's cost. While the sweeping method is inherently serial, it can be parallelized over many ordinate directions and spectral frequencies. The radiation sweeping mechanism uses the older A-matrix construction from the linear solve, and performs recursive back substitution on the A-matrix to solve for the intensities. This process is done in stages for each intensity and phase, both of which are defined below. Although this staging process is serialized by the reliance of corner-to-corner dependencies, it can show good performance when sweeping a large quantity of independent solves. For a non-scattering medium, the angular and spectral intensities are all independent of each other, allowing for parallelization of the solve.

On large, distributed memory systems, the intensities are stored on multiple compute nodes, making communication between them expensive and inefficient. To address this problem, one processor (or node) needs to operate only on intensities that have satisfied their spatial dependency. The method shown here is based on the algorithm for a simple rectangular domain; however, it further supports identification of these dependencies for complex domains with non-rectangular shapes. To most easily convey the methodology used, we start by describing the algorithm on a rectangular domain.

Consider a domain with 3×3 sub-units. Within Uintah, these sub-units are referred to as *patches*. A diagram showing how these patches are divided is shown in Fig. 10. The number labeling each patch (Fig. 10a) designates the phase in which a sweep is relevant for a single intensity, from the $x + y + z + octant$, with a single wave number. Note that these phases are defined as:

$$P = x_i + y_i + z_i \qquad (3)$$

where x_i, y_i, and z_i are the patch indices in the x, y, and z directions. The patch indices are defined as the number of patches away from the origin patch. Hence, the total number of phases required to complete a single complete full-domain sweep is:

$$P_{max} = x_{max} + y_{max} + z_{max} \qquad (4)$$

where $x_{max}, y_{max}, z_{max}$ are the maximum. Numbers designate the designated phase indices of the patches within the domain. We determine the patch indices using the sub-domain with the patch ID provided by Uintah.

Uintah numbers its patches in the order of z, y, x (Fig. 10b). From this we can determine the point in space in which the sweep is currently located using modulo operators, the patch dimensions, and the patch ID. The patch index is then converted to the patch indices x_i, y_i, z_i for each patch. Using the Uintah

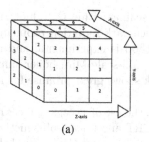
(a)

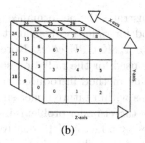
(b)

Fig. 10. A rectangular domain divided into 27 sub-domains, labeled by the designated phase (a) and Uintah patch ID (b).

task scheduler, we can indicate to a task what this phase is. This process is more complicated when conducting sweeps with multiple intensity directions. First, consider additional intensities that are in the x^+, y^+, z^+ directions. To keep as many processors busy as possible in the computation, we create stages.

A stage S is defined as $S = I + P$, where I is the intensity index relevant to a single octant. We know the maximum number of stages via the equation $S_{max} = I_{max} + P_{max}$. Now we have an algorithm that describes the sweeping in a single direction, for intensities of the same octant: next, we will discuss how to extend this to all octants. The phase equation for the x^-, y^-, z^- octant results in:

$$P = x_{max} - x_i + y_{max} - y_i + z_{max} - z_i \tag{5}$$

Hence, a total of eight phase equations are possible, depending on the combination of directions. We discuss two equations in detail in this paper. The task designates the stage and intensity, and then computes a function mapping its patch ID to its spatial patch index using a series of modulos. If the patch and intensity are relevant to the local processor, then it executes, otherwise it exits the task.

Spatial Scheduling-Supporting Sweeps Within Uintah. In order to spatially schedule the sweeping tasks, a Uintah patch subset must be identified during the Uintah task-scheduling phase. It is convenient to use Eq. 5 to accomplish this. Iterating over the phase P and two patch indices y_i and z_i allows us to collect the relevant patches to a sweeping phase P, which results in P_{max} patch subsets per octant. These patch subsets can be reused for each intensity solve. The patch subsets are used in the Uintah task-requires call to the infrastructure that manages ghost cells, which greatly reduces communication costs. The sweep is propagated across the domain by having one independent task per stage. To propagate information from patch to patch within Uintah, a requires modifies dependency chain is created, where the requires is conditioned on a patch subset only relevant to the patches on which the sweep is occurring. The patch subset is defined as all patches with the same phase number P, as shown in Fig. 10a.

5.5   Sweeps: Scaling and Performance Results

Table 1 illustrates the performance and weak scaling within Uintah of the sweeping method for radiation transport on a benchmark radiation problem, run on Mira up to 128K CPU cores. Note this method is experimental and although DOM was used for the radiation solve in the full-scale Mira boiler simulations, the sweeping method introduced in this work shows great promise for radiation calculations within future boiler simulations.

For the target boiler problems in question, the use of sweeps reduces radiation solve times by a factor of 10 relative to RMCRT and linear solve methods. The differences in the solution times between the linear solve (DOM) in Table 1 and Fig. 2 are attributed to differences between the benchmark calculation and the target boiler simulation. Within the target boiler (CFD) simulation, the previous

Table 1. Weak scaling results on the model radiation problem.

Cores	16	256	4056	65536	131072	262144
Time DO	91	189	399	959	1200	1462
DO iter.	90	180	400	900	1300	1500
Sweeps time	1.9	3.4	4.4	9.09	13.9	

solve can also be used as an initial guess, thus accelerating convergence and making it possible for DOM to use as few as 30–40 iterations as compared to the much larger number of backsolves shown in Table 1. In contrast to a static problem, no initial guess is available, and significantly more iterations are used with DOM than is the case in a full boiler simulation (as shown in Table 1), in which as many as 1500 iterations are used. However, we note that for this problem each DOM iteration takes about a second. Hence, the best that DOM could achieve would be about 40 s, even if a good initial guess is available. In this way sweeps outperforms both the actual observed cost and the optimistic estimated cost of DOM with its linear solve using 40 iterations by a factor of between 4 and 10. However, the sweeping algorithm has not currently scaled beyond 128K cores due to its large memory footprint and, additionally, it can be slower than the linear solver for systems with very high attenuation. This is because the sparse linear solvers are iterative, but they converge quickly for systems with large attenuation, as the impact of radiation can be isolated to a subset of the domain for these systems.

For systems with scattering, DOM typically lags the scattering term and then resolves until the intensities converge to within a certain tolerance. The convergence can be costly for systems where the scattering coefficients are significantly larger than the absorption coefficients. Given these very encouraging results, applying sweeps to the full problem and improving its memory use are clearly the next steps.

6   Mira Production Cases – Results

In making use of the improvements to scalability of the entire code, two production cases were considered using the geometry, inlet parameters and operating parameters of a GE Power 8 Corner Unit. The first case represented the operation of the commercial unit that is currently in production, whereas the second case represented alterations to the inlet parameters to investigate a more uniform energy distribution. Each case was run for approximately 20 s of physical time, which is considered sufficient for the boiler to achieve a steady state distribution.

Table 2 shows the computational aspects of the 2 cases that were run on Mira, simulating the 8-corner unit. Each production case was run at 260K cores with 455 M grid cells at a resolution of 4.25 cm with 16 MPI ranks per node using a timestep of $8e^{-5}$ and about 400 MB of memory per rank. Table 2 shows that between the first and second cases additional speed-ups were achieved in the

Table 2. Computational aspects of 8-corner boiler simulations

Item	Original inlets	Modified inlets
Number of cells	455 M	455 M
Cell resolution	4.25 cm	4.25 cm
MPI ranks	260,712	260,712
MPI ranks/node	16	16
Memory/rank	412 MB	372 MB
dt	8e−5	8e−5
Time/timestep	4.5 s	3.0 s
Pressure solve	1.9 s	1.0 s
Radiation solve	101 s	79.3 s
Data to disk	5.5 min	33.2 s
Data dumps	77	1030
Data size	9.9 TB	180 TB
# Timesteps	236,500	220,979
Simulated time	19.38 s	17.92 s
CPU hours	97 M	110 M

pressure solve due to work being done in Uintah/Arches. The most significant performance improvement was the switch of the I/O library, with the presented restructuring-based I/O, which resulted in 33 s write times, compared to the 5.5 min required on the Original Inlets case which used the legacy Uintah I/O system. Ultimately, the Modified Inlets case wrote 1030 datasets allowing for the creation of 3D rendered movies of the simulation.

Though validation of the simulation data against experimental data was performed, the proprietary nature of both the simulation and experimental data makes publication of these comparisons problematic. However, working closely with the GE Power engineers made it possible to validate the results of these simulations against their previous results. Figure 11 depicts the heat absorption profile (x-axis) as a function of the elevation in the boiler (y-axis), and shows the average absorption profile predicted in the unmodfied inlet configuration (Original Inlets) is different from the tentative estimates due to the higher fidelity modeling performed with Arches, but it is in relatively good agreement with the actual absorption profile based on discussions with GE Power engineers and the existing proprietary data provided. The second case was run with changes to the inlet geometry parameters to optimize gas-side energy imbalance (GSEI) by changing the flow pattern in the wind-box as well as the SOFA inlets.

The key result from this work is the confidence that has been established with GE Power to demonstrate that high resolution LES simulations are a useful tool for exploring a range of operating conditions, with the potential to be used for future designs. This is the first time that computational design at this scale has

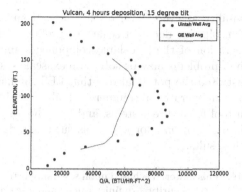

Fig. 11. Heat absorption profile as a function of the elevation. The solid green line shows GE Power's wall-averaged absorption profile tentative estimates for the expected operating conditions in the unit. The blue dots show the average absorption profile computed from unmodified inlet case. (Color figure online)

been used for such a complex combustion problem with petascale simulations. Future studies of the unit will investigate design and operation adjustments to achieve incremental improvements in gas-side energy imbalance. GE will consider testing the new conditions in the existing unit when significant improvements are discovered.

7 Conclusions

This work has introduced an excellent exascale candidate problem through the successful simulation of a commercial, 1000 megawatt electric (MWe) ultra-supercritical (USC) boiler, the largest currently in production worldwide, using Large-Eddy Simulation (LES) predictions, requiring 280 Million CPU hours on Mira. The overall objective of this work was in understanding how we can solve such a problem through the use of an AMT runtime to efficiently schedule and execute computational tasks, including I/O, and to leverage scalability improvements in the runtime itself, linear solvers, I/O, and computational algorithms. To achieve the results shown in this work for production-level petascale computations significant code and algorithmic innovations were required, including novel adaptations of I/O system that achieved a nearly order of magnitude improvement in I/O performance.

Through this work, we have exposed areas even within an advanced, scalable runtime system that need careful design consideration for post-petascale and eventually exascale platforms, particularly when globally coupled problems such as radiation are considered. For example, while existing radiation methods used in Uintah scale, it is clear from the results presented that the use of the sweeps method for problems of this scale and size needs to be investigated further, to see if it is possible to reduce the overall simulation time significantly. A key lesson this work conveys is that the success of large, production-scale simulations depends upon scalability at every level of the code. If any single component within the simulation pipeline does not scale, the problem cannot be solved. It is through the integration of these scalable components and subsystems that the next generation of problems may be solved on exascale systems. Finally, our results have demonstrated the potential role that LES simulations can have on analysis and design of an operational commercial boiler and that simulations can be used as a design tool for future systems, and that choosing fast scalable and hardware appropriate algorithms, for key areas such as radiation is important in achieving scalable results.

Acknowledgements. This material is based upon work supported by the Department of Energy, National Nuclear Security Administration, under Award Number(s) DE-NA0002375. An award of computer time was provided by the Innovative and Novel Computational Impact on Theory and Experiment (INCITE) program. This research used resources of the Argonne Leadership Computing Facility, which is a DOE Office of Science User Facility supported under contract DE-AC02-06CH11357. The authors would like to thank the Intel Parallel Computing Centers program. We would like to thank all those involved with Uintah past and present.

References

1. Mira home page. https://www.alcf.anl.gov/mira
2. Adams, M.P., Adams, M.L., Hawkins, W.D., Smith, T., Rauchwerger, L., Amato, N.M., Bailey, T.S., Falgout, R.D.: Provably optimal parallel transport sweeps on regular grids. Technical report, Lawrence Livermore National Laboratory (LLNL), Livermore, CA (2013)
3. Ayachit, U.: The ParaView Guide: A Parallel Visualization Application. Kitware Inc., New York (2015)
4. Bailey, T., Hawkins, W.D., Adams, M.L., Brown, P.N., Kunen, A.J., Adams, M.P., Smith, T., Amato, N., Rauchwerger, L.: Validation of full-domain massively parallel transport sweep algorithms. Technical report, Lawrence Livermore National Laboratory (LLNL), Livermore, CA (2014)
5. Balaji, P., Chan, A., Thakur, R., Gropp, W., Lusk, E.: Toward message passing for a million processes: characterizing MPI on a massive scale blue gene/P. Comput. Sci. Res. Dev. **24**(1), 11–19 (2009)
6. Balsara, D.: Fast and accurate discrete ordinates methods for multidimensional radiative transfer. Part I, basic methods. J. Quant. Spectrosc. Radiat. Transf. **69**(6), 671–707 (2001)
7. Bennett, J., Clay, R., Baker, G., Gamell, M., Hollman, D., Knight, S., Kolla, H., Sjaardema, G., Slattengren, N., Teranishi, K., Wilke, J., Bettencourt, M., Bova, S., Franko, K., Lin, P., Grant, R., Hammond, S., Olivier, S., Kale, L., Jain, N., Mikida, E., Aiken, A., Bauer, M., Lee, W., Slaughter, E., Treichler, S., Berzins, M., Harman, T., Humphrey, A., Schmidt, J., Sunderland, D., McCormick, P., Gutierrez, S., Schulz, M., Bhatele, A., Boehme, D., Bremer, P., Gamblin, T.: ASC ATDM level 2 milestone #5325: asynchronous many-task runtime system analysis and assessment for next generation platforms. Technical report, Sandia National Laboratories (2015)

8. Berzins, M., Beckvermit, J., Harman, T., Bezdjian, A., Humphrey, A., Meng, Q., Schmidt, J., Wight, C.: Extending the uintah framework through the petascale modeling of detonation in arrays of high explosive devices. SIAM J. Sci. Comput. **38**(5), 101–122 (2016)
9. Childs, H., Brugger, E., Whitlock, B., Meredith, J., Ahern, S., Pugmire, D., Biagas, K., Miller, M., Harrison, C., Weber, G.H., Krishnan, H., Fogal, T., Sanderson, A., Garth, C., Bethel, E.W., Camp, D., Rübel, O., Durant, M., Favre, J.M., Navrátil, P.: VisIt: an end-user tool for visualizing and analyzing very large data. In: High Performance Visualization-Enabling Extreme-Scale Scientific Insight, pp. 357–372 (2012)
10. HDF5 home page. http://www.hdfgroup.org/HDF5/
11. Humphrey, A., Harman, T., Berzins, M., Smith, P.: A scalable algorithm for radiative heat transfer using reverse Monte Carlo ray tracing. In: Kunkel, J.M., Ludwig, T. (eds.) ISC High Performance 2015. LNCS, vol. 9137, pp. 212–230. Springer, Cham (2015). https://doi.org/10.1007/978-3-319-20119-1_16
12. Humphrey, A., Sunderland, D., Harman, T., Berzins, M.: Radiative heat transfer calculation on 16384 GPUs using a reverse Monte Carlo ray tracing approach with adaptive mesh refinement. In: 2016 IEEE International Parallel and Distributed Processing Symposium Workshops (IPDPSW), pp. 1222–1231, May 2016
13. Kumar, S., Vishwanath, V., Carns, P., Levine, J., Latham, R., Scorzelli, G., Kolla, H., Grout, R., Ross, R., Papka, M., Chen, J., Pascucci, V.: Efficient data restructuring and aggregation for I/O acceleration in PIDX. In: 2012 International Conference for High Performance Computing, Networking, Storage and Analysis (SC), pp. 1–11, November 2012
14. Li, J., Liao, W.-K., Choudhary, A., Ross, R., Thakur, R., Gropp, W., Latham, R., Siegel, A., Gallagher, B., Zingale, M.: Parallel netCDF: a high-performance scientific I/O interface. In: Proceedings of SC 2003: High Performance Networking and Computing, Phoenix, AZ. IEEE Computer Society Press, November 2003
15. Lofstead, J., Klasky, S., Schwan, K., Podhorszki, N., Jin, C.: Flexible IO and integration for scientific codes through the adaptable IO system (ADIOS). In: Proceedings of the 6th International Workshop on Challenges of Large Applications in Distributed Environments, CLADE 2008, pp. 15–24. ACM, New York, June 2008
16. Lustre home page. http://lustre.org
17. Meng, Q., Humphrey, A., Schmidt, J., Berzins, M.: Investigating applications portability with the Uintah DAG-based runtime system on petascale supercomputers. In: Proceedings of the International Conference on High Performance Computing, Networking, Storage and Analysis, SC 2013, pp. 96:1–96:12. ACM, New York (2013)
18. U. D. of Energy: Exascale computing project (2017). https://exascaleproject.org/
19. Peterson, B., Humphrey, A., Schmidt, J., Berzins, M.: Addressing global data dependencies in heterogeneous asynchronous runtime systems on GPUs. In: Third International Workshop on Extreme Scale Programming Models and Middleware, ESPM2. IEEE Press (2017, submitted)
20. Russell, J.: Doug Kothe on the race to build exascale applications (2017). https://www.hpcwire.com/2017/05/29/doug-kothe-race-build-exascale-applications/
21. Schmuck, F., Haskin, R.: GPFS: a shared-disk file system for large computing clusters. In: Proceedings of the 2002 Conference on File and Storage Technologies (FAST), pp. 231–244 (2002)
22. Scientific Computing and Imaging Institute: Uintah web page (2015). http://www.uintah.utah.edu/

23. Shan, H., Antypas, K., Shalf, J.: Characterizing and predicting the I/O performance of HPC applications using a parameterized synthetic benchmark. In: Proceedings of Supercomputing, November 2008
24. Wald, I., Johnson, G., Amstutz, J., Brownlee, C., Knoll, A., Jeffers, J., Günther, J., Navratil, P.: OSPRay - a CPU ray tracing framework for scientific visualization. IEEE Trans. Visual. Comput. Graph. **23**(1), 931–940 (2017)

Linear Algebra

High Performance LOBPCG Method for Solving Multiple Eigenvalues of Hubbard Model: Efficiency of Communication Avoiding Neumann Expansion Preconditioner

Susumu Yamada[1](✉), Toshiyuki Imamura[2], and Masahiko Machida[1]

[1] Japan Atomic Energy Agency, Kashiwa, Chiba, Japan
yamada.susumu@jaea.go.jp
[2] RIKEN, Kobe, Hyogo, Japan

Abstract. The exact diagonalization method is a high accuracy numerical approach for solving the Hubbard model of a system of electrons with strong correlation. The method solves for the eigenvalues and eigenvectors of the Hamiltonian matrix derived from the Hubbard model. Since the Hamiltonian is a huge sparse symmetric matrix, it was expected that the LOBPCG method with an appropriate preconditioner could be used to solve the problem in a short time. This turned out to be the case as the LOBPCG method with a suitable preconditioner succeeded in solving the ground state (the smallest eigenvalue and its corresponding eigenvector) of the Hamiltonian. In order to solve for multiple eigenvalues of the Hamiltonian in a short time, we use a preconditioner based on the Neumann expansion which uses approximate eigenvalues and eigenvectors given by LOBPCG iteration. We apply a communication avoiding strategy, which was developed considering the physical properties of the Hubbard model, to the preconditioner. Our numerical experiments on two parallel computers show that the LOBPCG method coupled with the Neumann preconditioner and the communication avoiding strategy improves convergence and achieves excellent scalability when solving for multiple eigenvalues.

1 Introduction

Since the High-T_c superconductor was discovered many physicists have tried to understand the mechanism behind the superconductivity. It is believed that strong electron correlations underlie the phenomenon, however the exact mechanism is not yet fully understood. One of the numerical approaches to the problem is the exact diagonalization method. In this method the eigenvalue problem is solved for the Hamiltonian derived exactly from the Hubbard model [1,2], which is a model of a strongly-correlated electron system. When we solve the ground state (the smallest eigenvalue and its corresponding eigenvector) of the

© The Author(s) 2018
R. Yokota and W. Wu (Eds.): SCFA 2018, LNCS 10776, pp. 243–256, 2018.
https://doi.org/10.1007/978-3-319-69953-0_14

$x_0 :=$ an initial guess, $p_0 := 0$
$x_0 := x_0/|x_0|$, $X_0 := Ax_0$, $P_0 := 0$, $\mu_{-1} := (x_0, X_0)$,
$w_0 := X_0 - \mu_{-1}x_0$
do $k=0, \dots$ until convergence
$\quad W_k := Aw_k$
$\quad S_A := \{w_k, x_k, p_k\}^T \{W_k, X_k, P_k\}$
$\quad S_B := \{w_k, x_k, p_k\}^T \{w_k, x_k, p_k\}$
$\quad$ Solve the generalized eigenvalue problem $S_A v = \mu S_B v$ to obtain the smallest
eigenvalue μ_k and the corresponding eigenvector $v = (\alpha, \beta, \gamma)^T$,
$\quad x_{k+1} := \alpha w_k + \beta x_k + \gamma p_k$, $x_{k+1} := x_{k+1}/|x_{k+1}|$,
$\quad p_{k+1} := \alpha w_k + \gamma p_k$, $p_{k+1} := p_{k+1}/|p_{k+1}|$
$\quad X_{k+1} := \alpha W_k + \beta X_k + \gamma P_k$, $X_{k+1} := X_{k+1}/|x_{k+1}|$,
$\quad P_{k+1} := \alpha W_k + \gamma P_k$, $P_{k+1} := P_{k+1}/|p_{k+1}|$
$\quad w_{k+1} := T^{-1}(X_{k+1} - \mu_k x_{k+1})$, $w_{k+1} := w_{k+1}/|w_{k+1}|$
enddo

Fig. 1. Algorithm of LOBPCG method for matrix A. Here the matrix T is a preconditioner.

Hamiltonian, we can understand its properties at absolute zero ($-273.15\,^\circ$C). Many computational methods for the problem have been proposed. Since the Hamiltonian from the Hubbard model is a huge sparse symmetric matrix, an iteration method, such as the Lanczos method [3] or the LOBPCG method (see Fig. 1) [4,5], is usually utilized for solving the eigenvalue problem.

The convergence of the LOBPCG method depends strongly on the use of a preconditioner. We previously confirmed that the zero-shift point Jacobi preconditioner, which is a shift-and-invert preconditioner [6] using an approximate eigenvalue, gives excellent convergence properties for the Hubbard model with the trapping potential [7]. However, we also reported that the benefit of the preconditioner strongly depends on the characteristics of the non-zero elements of the Hamiltonian and that the preconditioner does not always improve the convergence [8]. Therefore we proposed a novel preconditioner using the Neumann expansion for solving the ground state of the Hamiltonian and demonstrated that this preconditioner improves convergence for a Hamiltonian that is difficult to solve with the zero-shift point Jacobi preconditioner [8]. Moreover we applied a communication avoiding strategy, which was developed considering the properties of the Hubbard model, to the preconditioner.

In order to understand more details of strongly correlated electron systems in particular properties at temperatures near absolute zero, we must solve for the several smallest eigenvalues and corresponding eigenvectors of the Hamiltonian. The LOBPCG method can solve multiple eigenvalues by using a block of vectors.

In this paper, we extend the Neumann expansion preconditioner to the LOBPCG method for solving multiple eigenvalues and corresponding eigenvectors. Moreover, we demonstrate that the preconditioner improves the convergence properties and can achieve excellent parallel performance.

The paper is structured as follows. In Sect. 2 we briefly introduce related work for solving the ground state of the Hubbard model using the LOBPCG method. Section 3 describes the use of the Neumann expansion preconditioner with the communication avoiding strategy for solving for multiple eigenvalues and their corresponding eigenvectors. Section 4 demonstrates the parallel performance of the algorithm on the SGI ICE X and K supercomputers. A summary and conclusions are given in Sect. 5.

2 Related Work

2.1 Hamiltonian-Vector Multiplication

When solving the ground state of a symmetric matrix using the LOBPCG method, the most time-consuming operation is the matrix-vector multiplication. The Hamiltonian derived from the Hubbard model (see Fig. 2) is

$$H = -t \sum_{i,j,\sigma} c_{j\sigma}^{\dagger} c_{i\sigma} + \sum_{i} U_i n_{i\uparrow} n_{i\downarrow}, \qquad (1)$$

where t is the hopping parameter from one site to another, and U_i is the repulsive energy for double occupation of the i-th site by two electrons [1,2,7]. Quantities $c_{i,\sigma}$, $c_{i,\sigma}^{\dagger}$ and $n_{i,\sigma}$ are the annihilation, creation, and number operator of an electron with pseudo-spin σ on the i-th site, respectively. The indices in formula (1) for the Hamiltonian denote the possible states for electrons in the model. The dimension of the Hamiltonian for the n_s-site Hubbard model is

$$\binom{n_s}{n_\uparrow} \times \binom{n_s}{n_\downarrow},$$

where $n_\uparrow$ and $n_\downarrow$ are the number of the up-spin and down-spin electrons, respectively.

The diagonal element in formula (1) is derived from the repulsive energy U_i in the corresponding state. The hopping parameter t affects non-zero elements with

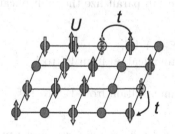

Fig. 2. A schematic figure of the 2-dimensional Hubbard model, where t is the hopping parameter and U is the repulsive energy for double occupation of a site. Up arrows and down arrows correspond to up-spin and down-spin electrons, respectively.

column-index corresponding to the original state and row-index corresponding to the state after hopping. Since the ratio U/t greatly affects the properties of the model, we have to execute many simulations varying this ratio to reveal the properties of the model.

When considering the physical properties of the model, we can split the Hamiltonian-vector multiplication as

$$Hv = Dv + (I_\downarrow \otimes A_\uparrow)v + (A_\downarrow \otimes I_\uparrow)v, \tag{2}$$

where $I_{\uparrow(\downarrow)}$, $A_{\uparrow(\downarrow)}$ and D are the identity matrix, a sparse symmetric matrix derived from the hopping of an up-spin electron (a down-spin electron), and a diagonal matrix from the repulsive energy, respectively [7]. Since there is no regularity in the state change by electron hopping, the distribution of non-zero elements in matrix $A_{\uparrow(\downarrow)}$ is irregular.

Next, a matrix V is constructed by the following procedures from a vector v. First, decompose the vector v into n blocks, and order in the two-dimensional manner as follows,

$$v = (\underbrace{v_{1,1}, v_{2,1}, \ldots, v_{m_\uparrow,1}}_{\text{the first block}}, \underbrace{v_{1,2}, v_{2,2}, \ldots, v_{m_\uparrow,2}}_{\text{the second block}}, \cdots, \underbrace{v_{1,m_\downarrow}, v_{2,m_\downarrow}, \ldots, v_{m_\uparrow,m_\downarrow}}_{\text{the } m_\downarrow\text{-th block}})^T,$$

where $m_\uparrow$ and $m_\downarrow$ are the dimensions of the Hamiltonian for up-spin and down-spin electrons, i.e.

$$m_\uparrow = \binom{n_s}{n_\uparrow}, m_\downarrow = \binom{n_s}{n_\downarrow}.$$

The subscripts on each element of v formally indicate the row and column within the matrix V. Therefore V is a dense matrix. The k-th elements of the matrix D, d_k, are used in the same manner to define a new matrix $\bar{D}$. The multiplication in Eq. (2) can then be written as

$$V_{i,j}^{new} = \bar{D}_{i,j}V_{i,j} + \sum_k A_{\uparrow i,k}V_{k,j} + \sum_k V_{i,k}A_{\downarrow j,k} \tag{3}$$

where the subscript i, j of the matrix is represented as the (i, j)-th element and V and $\bar{D}$. Accordingly we can parallelize the multiplication $Y = HV (\equiv Hv)$ as follows:

CAL 1: $Y^c = \bar{D}^c \odot V^c + A_\uparrow V^c$,
COM 1: all-to-all communication from V^c to V^r,
CAL 2: $W^r = V^r A_\downarrow^T$,
COM 2: all-to-all communication from W^r to W^c,
CAL 3: $Y^c = Y^c + W^c$.

where superscripts c and r denote column wise and row wise partitioning of the matrix data for the parallel calculation. The operator $\odot$ means an element wise multiplication. The parallelization strategy requires two all-to-all communication operations per multiplication.

2.2 Preconditioner of LOBPCG Method for Solving the Ground State of Hubbard Model

Zero-Shift Point Jacobi Preconditioner. A suitable preconditioner improves the convergence properties of the LOBPCG method. As a consequence many preconditioners have been proposed. Preconditioners for the Hamiltonian derived from the Hubbard model also have been proposed. For the Hubbard model, the zero-shift point Jacobi (ZSPJ) preconditioner, which is a shift-and-invert preconditioner using an approximate eigenvalue obtained during LOBPCG iteration, has excellent convergence properties for Hamiltonians where the diagonal elements predominate over the off-diagonal elements, i.e. cases where the repulsive energy U is large [7,8].

Neumann Expansion Preconditioner. For the Hubbard model with a small repulsive energy, a preconditioner using the Neumann expansion was previously proposed [8]. The expansion is

$$(I - M)^{-1} = I + M + M^2 + M^3 + \cdots . \tag{4}$$

The expansion converges when the operator norm of the matrix M is less than 1 ($\|M\|_{op} < 1$) [9]. Here the matrix M is

$$M = I - \frac{2}{\lambda_{\max} - \lambda_{\min}}(H - \lambda_{\min}I),$$

where $\lambda_{\min}$ and $\lambda_{\max}$ are the smallest and largest eigenvalues, respectively. When the exact eigenvalues are utilized for $\lambda_{\min}$ and $\lambda_{\max}$, $\|M\|_{op}$ is equal to 1. Since the LOBPCG method calculates an approximation of the smallest eigenvalue, we consider the residual error of this approximation and make a low estimate of $\lambda_{\min}$. The Gershgorin circle theorem is used to assign a $\lambda_{\max}$ that is an overestimate of the true value. The inequality $\|M\|_{op} < 1$ is hence obeyed and the expansion (4) can converge, i.e. the inverse matrix of $\frac{2}{\lambda_{\max} - \lambda_{\min}}(H - \lambda_{\min}I)$. The expansion is an effective preconditioner for the smallest eigenvalue $\lambda_{\min}$. In practice the Gershgorin circle theorem may give estimates for $\lambda_{\max}$ that are much too large. Multiplying by a damping factor α can help alleviate this inefficiency. We found 0.9 to be an appropriate α in numerical tests.

2.3 Communication Avoiding Neumann Expansion Preconditioner for Hubbard Model

When we execute the LOBPCG method with the s-th order Neumann expansion preconditioner, we calculate $s + 1$ matrix-vector multiplications, Hv, H^2v, $\ldots$, and $H^{s+1}v$, per iteration. As the multiplications $(I_\downarrow \otimes A_\uparrow)$ and $(A_\downarrow \otimes I_\uparrow)$ are commutative Yamada et al. proposed a communication avoiding strategy for the Hamiltonian-vector multiplication [8]. Then, H^2 is given as

$$
\begin{aligned}
H^2 &= (I_\downarrow \otimes A_\uparrow)(D + (I_\downarrow \otimes A_\uparrow)) + (A_\downarrow \otimes I_\uparrow)(D + (A_\downarrow \otimes I_\uparrow)) \\
&\quad + D(D + (I_\downarrow \otimes A_\uparrow) + (A_\downarrow \otimes I_\uparrow)) + (I_\downarrow \otimes A_\uparrow)(A_\downarrow \otimes I_\uparrow) + (A_\downarrow \otimes I_\uparrow)(I_\downarrow \otimes A_\uparrow) \\
&= (I_\downarrow \otimes A_\uparrow)(D + (I_\downarrow \otimes A_\uparrow) + 2(A_\downarrow \otimes I_\uparrow)) \\
&\quad + (A_\downarrow \otimes I_\uparrow)(D + (A_\downarrow \otimes I_\uparrow)) + D(D + (I_\downarrow \otimes A_\uparrow) + (A_\downarrow \otimes I_\uparrow)).
\end{aligned}
$$

As a result, $Y_1 = Hv$ and $Y_2 = H^2v$ can be calculated by the following algorithm:

CAL 1: $Y^c = \bar{D}^c \odot V^c + A_\uparrow V^c$,
COM 1:   all-to-all communication from V^c to V^r,
CAL 2: $W^r = V^r A_\downarrow^T$,
COM 2:   all-to-all communication from W^r to W^c,
CAL 3: $Y_1^c = Y^c + W^c$,
CAL 4: $Y^c = Y_1^c + W^c$,
CAL 5: $Y^c = \bar{D}^c \odot Y_1^c + A_\uparrow Y^c$,
CAL 6: $W^r = \bar{D}^r \odot V^r + W^r$,
CAL 7: $W^r = W^r A_\downarrow^T$,
COM 3:   all-to-all communication from W^r to W^c,
CAL 8: $Y_2^c = Y^c + W^c$.

The algorithm requires three all-to-all communication operations. On the other hand, when using the original algorithm described in Sect. 2.1, four all-to-all communication operations are required to calculate the same multiplication. However, the new algorithm has extra calculations, CAL 4 and CAL 6, as compared to the original one. Therefore when the cost of one all-to-all communication operation is larger than that of the extra calculations, we expect to achieve speedup with the communication avoiding strategy. The algorithm can not be directly applied to the multiplication H^{s+1} for $s \geq 2$. In this case, the multiplication H^{s+1} is calculated by appropriately combining Hv and H^2v operations.

3 Neumann Expansion Preconditioner for Multiple Eigenvalues of Hubbard Model

3.1 How to Calculate Multiple Eigenvalues Using LOBPCG Method

The LOBPCG method for solving the m smallest eigenvalues and corresponding eigenvectors carries out recurrence with m vectors simultaneously (see Fig. 3). In this algorithm, the generalized eigenvalue problem has to be solved. We can solve the problem using the LAPACK function dsyev, if the matrix S_B is a positive definite matrix. Although theoretically S_B is always a positive definite matrix, numerically this is not always the case. The reason is that the norms of the vectors $w_k^{(i)}$ and $p_k^{(i)}$ ($i = 1, 2, \ldots, m$) become small as the LOBPCG iteration converges, and it is possible that trailing digits are lost in the calculation of S_B. Therefore we set the matrix S_B to the identity matrix by orthogonalizing the vectors per iteration. In the following numerical tests, we utilize the TSQR method for the orthgonalization [10, 11].

$x_0^{(i)} :=$ an initial guess, $p_0^{(i)} := 0,\ i = 1, \ldots, m$
$x_0^{(i)} = x_0^{(i)}/\|x_0^{(i)}\|,\ i = 1, \ldots, m$
$X_0^{(i)} := A x_0^{(i)},\ P_0^{(i)} := 0,\ i = 1, \ldots, m$
$\mu_{-1}^{(i)} := (x_0^{(i)}), X_0^{(i)},\ w_0^{(i)} := X_0^{(i)} - \mu_{-1}^{(i)} x_0^{(i)},\ i = 1, \ldots, m$
do $k=0, \ldots$ until convergence
$\quad W_k^{(i)} := A w_k^{(i)},\ i = 1, \ldots, m$
$\quad S_A := \{w_k^{(1)}, \ldots, w_k^{(m)}, x_k^{(1)}, \ldots, x_k^{(m)}, p_k^{(1)}, \ldots, p_k^{(m)}\}^T$
$\qquad \{W_k^{(1)}, \ldots, W_k^{(m)}, X_k^{(1)}, \ldots, X_k^{(m)}, P_k^{(1)}, \ldots, P_k^{(m)}\}$
$\quad S_B := \{w_k^{(1)}, \ldots, w_k^{(m)}, x_k^{(1)}, \ldots, x_k^{(m)}, p_k^{(1)}, \ldots, p_k^{(m)}\}^T$
$\qquad \{w_k^{(1)}, \ldots, w_k^{(m)}, x_k^{(1)}, \ldots, x_k^{(m)}, p_k^{(1)}, \ldots, p_k^{(m)}\}$
$\quad$ Solve the generalized eigenvalue problem $S_A v = \mu S_B v$ to obtain the m smallest eigenvalues $\mu^{(i)}$ and the corresponding eigenvectors $v^{(i)} = (\alpha^{(i)}, \beta^{(i)}, \gamma^{(i)})^T$ ($i = 1, \ldots, m$),
$\quad x_{k+1}^{(i)} := \sum_{j=1}^{m} \{\alpha^{(j)} w_k^{(j)} + \beta^{(j)} x_k^{(j)} + \gamma^{(j)} p_k^{(j)}\},\ i = 1, \ldots, m$
$\quad p_{k+1}^{(i)} := \sum_{j=1}^{m} \{\alpha^{(j)} w_k^{(j)} + \gamma^{(j)} p_k^{(j)}\},\ i = 1, \ldots, m$
$\quad X_{k+1}^{(i)} := \sum_{j=1}^{m} \{\alpha^{(j)} W_k^{(j)} + \beta^{(j)} X_k^{(j)} + \gamma^{(j)} P_k^{(j)}\},\ i = 1, \ldots, m$
$\quad P_{k+1}^{(i)} := \sum_{j=1}^{m} \{\alpha^{(j)} W_k^{(j)} + \gamma^{(j)} P_k^{(j)}\},\ i = 1, \ldots, m$
$\quad \mu_k^{(i)} := (x_{k+1}^{(i)}, X_{k+1}^{(i)})/(x_{k+1}^{(i)}, x_{k+1}^{(i)}),\ i = 1, \ldots, m$
$\quad w_{k+1}^{(i)} := T^{(i)-1}(X_{k+1}^{(i)} - \mu_k^{(i)} x_{k+1}^{(i)}),\ i = 1, \ldots, m$
enddo

Fig. 3. LOBPCG method for solving the m smallest eigenvalues and corresponding eigenvectors. $T^{(i)}$ is a preconditioner for the i-th smallest eigenvalues. This algorithm requires m matrix-vector multiplication operations and m preconditioned ones per iteration.

3.2 Neumann Expansion Preconditioner of LOBPCG Method for Solving Multiple Eigenvalues

When we calculate multiple eigenvalues (and corresponding eigenvectors) using the LOBPCG method, we can individually apply a preconditioning operation to each vector corresponding to the eigenvectors. We set the matrix M_i using the Neumann expansion preconditioner for the i-th smallest eigenvalue λ_i of the Hamiltonian as

$$M_i = I - \frac{2}{\lambda_{\max} - \lambda_i}(H - \lambda_i I).$$

Since we obtain approximate eigenvalues after each iteration of the LOBPCG method, we consider the residual errors of these approximations to define an appropriate λ_i. The matrix M_i has $(i-1)$ eigenvalues whose absolute values are greater than or equal to 1. In this case, the Neumann expansion using M_i can not converge. The eigenvectors corresponding to the eigenvalues agree with those corresponding to the eigenvalues $\lambda_1, \lambda_2, \ldots, \lambda_{i-1}$ of the Hamiltonian, and then, they are calculated during the LOBPCG iteration simultaneously. Accordingly, we orthogonalize the vectors $x_k^{(i)}$, $w_k^{(i)}$, and $p_k^{(i)}$ ($i = 1, 2, \ldots, m$) in the order that takes away the components of the vectors $x_k^{(1)}, x_k^{(2)}, \ldots, x_k^{(i-1)}$ from $w_k^{(i)}$ given by the Neumann expansion preconditioner using M_i. That is, we orthogonal the vectors utilizing the algorithm including the following operation

$$w_k^{(j)} := w_k^{(j)} - \sum_{i=1}^{j-1} (w_k^{(j)}, x_k^{(i)}) x_k^{(i)}. \tag{5}$$

The formula (5) can approximately remove the components of the eigenvectors corresponding to the eigenvalues, whose absolute values are greater than or equal to 1, from the preconditioned vectors. Therefore we expect that the Neumann expansion using M_i becomes an appropriate preconditioner for solving for multiple eigenvalues.

4   Performance Result

4.1   Computational Performance and Convergence Property

We examined the computational performance and convergence properties of the LOBPCG method. We solved the 2-D 4×5-site Hubbard model with 5 up-spin electrons and 5 down-spin ones. The dimension of the Hamiltonian derived from the model is about 240 million. The number of non-zero off-diagonal elements is about 1.6 billion. We solved for one, five and 10 eigenvalues (and corresponding eigenvectors) of the Hamiltonian on 768 cores (64 MPI processes × 12 OpenMP threads) of the SGI ICE X supercomputer (see Table 1) in Japan Atomic Energy Agency (JAEA). Table 2 shows the results for a weak interaction case ($U/t = 1$) and a strong one ($U/t = 10$). Table 3 shows the elapsed times of some representative operations.

The results for $U/t = 1$ indicate that point Jacobi (PJ) and zero-shift point Jacobi (ZSPJ) preconditioners hardly improve the convergence compared to without using a preconditioner at all. When we solve for many eigenvalues, the PJ and ZSPJ preconditioners have little effect on the speed of the calculation. On the other hand, the Neumann expansion preconditioner can decrease the number of iterations required for convergence. Moreover, the larger the Neumann expansion series s, the fewer iterations required. When we solve for only

Table 1. Details of SGI ICE X

Processor	Intel Xeon E5-2680v3 (2.5 GHz, 30 MB L2 cache)
FLOPS per processor	480 GFLOPS
Number of cores per CPU	12
Number of processors per node	2
Memory of node	64 GB
Memory bandwidth	68 GB/s
Network	Infini Band 6.8 GB/s
Compiler	Intel compiler

Table 2. Elapsed time and number of iterations for convergence of LOBPCG method using zero-shift point Jacobi (ZSPJ), Neumann expansion (NE), or communication avoiding Neumann expansion (CANE) preconditioner. Here, s is the number of the Neumann expansion series.

(a) One eigenvalue (The ground state)

	Number of iterations (top) & Elapsed time (sec) (bottom)								
	No precon.	PJ	ZSPJ	NE			CANE		
				$s = 1$	$s = 2$	$s = 3$	$s = 1$	$s = 2$	$s = 3$
$U/t = 1$	133	133	132	69	59	46	69	59	46
	9.16	9.19	9.13	8.79	11.06	10.78	7.40	9.18	8.94
$U/t = 10$	184	132	124	95	81	65	94	81	64
	13.03	9.08	8.61	12.07	14.65	15.62	10.05	12.62	12.79

(b) 5 eigenvalues

	Number of iterations (top) & Elapsed time (sec) (bottom)								
	No precon.	PJ	ZSPJ	NE			CANE		
				$s = 1$	$s = 2$	$s = 3$	$s = 1$	$s = 2$	$s = 3$
$U/t = 1$	199	190	168	81	77	59	86	72	54
	171.75	164.57	145.28	89.44	103.31	93.69	87.89	91.21	77.16
$U/t = 10$	293	217	240	159	156	108	155	142	105
	250.77	186.35	204.97	172.90	208.80	171.37	156.41	179.12	149.59

(c) 10 eigenvalues

	Number of iterations (top) & Elapsed time (sec) (bottom)								
	No precon.	PJ	ZSPJ	NE			CANE		
				$s = 1$	$s = 2$	$s = 3$	$s = 1$	$s = 2$	$s = 3$
$U/t = 1$	551	777	624	319	257	184	340	302	198
	1221.55	1672.69	1369.91	911.56	897.79	759.40	863.57	936.35	680.48
$U/t = 10$	398	298	313	232	184	161	201	177	137
	996.19	740.98	763.42	720.22	704.14	705.03	579.98	607.46	515.60

the smallest eigenvalue, the total elapsed time increases as s increases. The reason is that the elapsed time of the Hamiltonian-vector multiplication operation is dominant over the whole calculation for solving the only smallest eigenvalue (see Table 3). When we solve multiple eigenvalues, the TSQR operation becomes dominant. Therefore when the series number s becomes large, it is possible to achieve speedup of the computation.

Next, we discuss the results for $U/t = 10$. The results indicate that the PJ preconditioner improves the convergence properties. On the other hand, ZSPJ for small m improves convergence, however, its convergence properties when solving for multiple eigenvalues are almost the same as those for the PJ preconditioner. When we solve for multiple eigenvalues using the Neumann expansion preconditioner, the solution is obtained faster than using the PJ or ZSPJ preconditioners. Moreover, as the Neumann expansion series s increases, the Neumann expansion

Table 3. Elapsed time for operations per iteration. This table shows the results using the zero-shift point Jacobi (ZSPJ), Neumann expansion (NE), and communication avoiding Neumann expansion (CANE). Here, the Neumann expansion series s is equal to 1. For $m = 1$, instead of executing TSQR, we calculate S_B ,moreover, ZSPJ preconditioner is calculated together with x, p, X, P.

	Elapse time per iteration (sec)								
	$m = 1$			$m = 5$			$m = 10$		
	ZSPJ	NE	CANE	ZSPJ	NE	CANE	ZSPJ	NE	CANE
Hw (& H^2w)	0.061	0.117	0.100	0.276	0.545	0.448	0.568	1.088	0.909
TSQR	—	—	—	0.407	0.408	0.407	1.498	1.503	1.502
S_A (& S_B)	0.007	0.007	0.007	0.073	0.073	0.073	0.255	0.257	0.254
x, p, X, P	0.008	0.007	0.007	0.107	0.122	0.121	0.301	0.331	0.332
Preconditioner	—	0.003	0.003	0.018	0.015	0.014	0.035	0.030	0.028

Table 4. Speedup ratio for the elapsed time per iteration using the Neumann expansion preconditioner and communication avoiding strategy.

	Speedup ratio								
	$m = 1$			$m = 5$			$m = 10$		
	$s = 1$	$s = 2$	$s = 3$	$s = 1$	$s = 2$	$s = 3$	$s = 1$	$s = 2$	$s = 3$
$U/t = 1$	1.19	1.20	1.21	1.08	1.06	1.11	1.13	1.13	1.20
$U/t = 10$	1.19	1.16	1.20	1.08	1.06	1.11	1.08	1.12	1.16

preconditioner improves the convergence properties and the total elapsed time decreases, especially when m is large.

Finally, we talk about the effect of the communication avoiding strategy. Table 4 shows the speedup ratio for the elapsed time using the Neumann expansion preconditioner per iteration and the communication avoiding strategy. In all cases the communication avoiding strategy realizes speedup. When we solve for only the smallest eigenvalue (and its corresponding eigenvector), the speedup ratio is almost the same as that for the matrix-vector multiplication, because the multiplication cost is dominant. On the other hand, when we solve for multiple eigenvalues, the calculation cost except the multiplication becomes dominant. Therefore the speedup ratio is a little smaller than that for only the multiplication. Furthermore, when the Neumann expansion series s is equal to 3, we confirm that the ratio improves. In this case, since four multiplications (Hw, H^2w, H^3w and H^4w) are executed per iteration, the ratio of the multiplication cost increases. Moreover, we can execute four multiplication operations by two communication avoiding multiplications. Therefore, the ratio for $s = 3$ is better than that for $s = 1$.

4.2   Parallel Performance

In order to examine the parallel performance of the LOBPCG method using the Neumann expansion preconditioner, we solved for the 10 smallest eigenvalues and corresponding eigenvectors of the Hamiltonian derived from the 4×5-site Hubbard model for $U/t = 1$ with 6 up-spin and 6 down-spin electrons. We used the LOBPCG method with ZSPJ, NE, and CANE preconditioners using hybrid parallelization on SGI ICEX in JAEA and the K computer in RIKEN (see Table 5). The results are shown in Table 6. The results indicate that all preconditioners achieve excellent parallel efficiency. The communication avoiding strategy on SGI ICEX decreases the elapsed time per iteration by about 15%. On the other hand, the communication avoiding strategy on the K computer did not realize speedup when using a small number of cores. The ratio of the network bandwidth to FLOPS per node of the K computer is larger than that of SGI ICEX, so it is possible that the cost of the extra calculations (CAL 4 & CAL 6) is larger than that of the all-to-all communication operation. However since the cost of the all-to-all communication operation increases as the number of the cores increases, the strategy realizes speedup on 4096 cores. Therefore, the strategy has a potential of speedup for parallel computing using a sufficiently large number of cores, even if the ratio of the network bandwidth to FLOPS is large.

Although the LOBPCG method using NE has four times more Hamiltonian-vector multiplications per iteration than the method with ZSPJ, the former takes about twice the elapsed time of the latter. The reason is that the calculation operations except the multiplication is dominant in this case. Therefore, we conclude that in order to solve for multiple eigenvalues of the Hamiltonian derived from the Hubbard model using the LOBPCG method in a short computation time, it is crucial to reduce the number of the iterations for the convergence even if the calculation cost of the preconditioner is large.

Table 5. Details of K computer

Processor	SPARCTM 64 VIIIfx (2 GHz, 6 MB L2 cache)
FLOPS per processor	128 GFLOPS
Number of cores per CPU	8
Number of processors per node	1
Memory of node	16 GB
Memory bandwidth	64 GB/s
Network	Torus network (Tofu) 5 GB/s
Compiler	Fujitsu compiler

Table 6. Parallel performance of LOBPCG method on SGI ICEX and K computer. This table shows the number of iterations, the total elapsed time, and the elapsed time per iteration of LOBPCG method using zero-shift point Jacobi (ZSPJ), Neumann expansion (NE), or communication avoiding Neumann expansion (CANE) preconditioner. Here, the Neumann expansion series s is 3.

(a) SGI ICEX

	Number of iterations (top)		
	Elapsed time (sec) (middle)		
	Elapsed time per iteration (sec) (bottom)		
	ZSPJ	NE	CANE
64 MPI × 12 OpenMP	591	226	225
	9501.694	5886.533	4921.302
	16.077	26.047	21.872
128 MPI × 12 OpenMP	605	246	229
	4611.478	3662.846	2909.048
	7.622	14.890	12.703
256 MPI × 12 OpenMP	601	244	226
	2259.070	2043.231	1603.456
	3.759	8.374	7.095

(b) K computer

	Number of iterations (top)		
	Elapsed time (sec) (middle)		
	Elapsed time per iteration (sec) (bottom)		
	ZSPJ	NE	CANE
128 MPI × 8 OpenMP	503	209	230
	5775.971	3752.884	4596.063
	11.483	17.956	19.983
256 MPI × 8 OpenMP	551	224	303
	3231.566	2085.268	2974.883
	5.865	9.309	9.818
512 MPI × 8 OpenMP	862	243	250
	2548.534	1327.093	1130.652
	2.957	5.461	4.523

5   Conclusions

In this paper we applied the Neumann expansion preconditioner to the LOBPCG method to solve for multiple eigenvalues and corresponding eigenvectors of the Hamiltonian derived from the Hubbard model. We examined the convergence properties and parallel performance of the algorithms. Since the norm of the matrix used in the Neumann expansion should be less than 1, we transform it using approximate eigenvalues calculated by the LOBPCG iteration and the upper bounds of the eigenvalues by the Gershgorin circle theorem. Moreover, we orthogonalize the iteration vectors in the order that removes the components of the eigenvectors corresponding to the eigenvalues, whose absolute values are greater than or equal to 1, from the preconditioned vectors.

The Neumann expansion preconditioner with the communication avoiding strategy can achieve speedup even for problems which are hardly improved by the conventional preconditioners. Furthermore, a numerical experiment indicated that the LOBPCG method using this preconditioner has excellent parallel efficiency on thousands cores, and the communication avoiding strategy based on the property of the Hubbard model realizes speedup for parallel computers if a sufficiently large number of cores are used. Therefore, we confirm that the preconditioner based on the Neumann expansion is suitable for solving the eigenvalue problem derived from the Hubbard model using the LOBPCG method.

Acknowledgments. Computations in this study were performed on the SGI ICE X at the JAEA and the K computer at RIKEN Advanced Institute for Computational Science (project ID:ra000005). This research was partially supported by JSPS KAKENHI Grant Number 15K00178.

References

1. Rasetti, M. (ed.): The Hubbard Model: Recent Results. World Scientific, Singapore (1991)
2. Montorsi, A. (ed.): The Hubbard Model. World Scientific, Singapore (1992)
3. Cullum, J.K., Willoughby, R.A.: Lanczos Algorithms for Large Symmetric Eigenvalue Computations, vol. 1: Theory. SIAM, Philadelphia (2002)
4. Knyazev, A.V.: Preconditioned eigensolvers - an oxymoron? Electron. Trans. Numer. Anal. **7**, 104–123 (1998)
5. Knyazev, A.V.: Toward the optimal eigensolver: locally optimal block preconditioned conjugate gradient method. SIAM J. Sci. Comput. **23**, 517–541 (2001)
6. Saad, Y.: Numerical Methods for Large Eigenvalue Problems: Revised Edition. SIAM (2011)
7. Yamada, S., Imamura, T., Machida, M.: 16.447 TFlops and 159-Billion-dimensional exact-diagonalization for trapped Fermion-Hubbard Model on the Earth Simulator. In: Proceedings of SC 2005 (2005)
8. Yamada, S., Imamura, T., Machida, M.: Communication avoiding Neumann expansion preconditioner for LOBPCG method: convergence property of exact diagonalization method for Hubbard model. In: Proceedings of ParCo 2017 (2017, accepted)
9. Barrett, R., et al.: Templates for the Solution of Linear Systems: Building Blocks for Iterative Methods. SIAM, Philadelphia (1994)
10. Langou, J.: AllReduce algorithms: application to Householder QR factorization. In: Proceedings of the 2007 International Conference on Preconditioning Techniques for Large Sparse Matrix Problems in Scientific and Industrial Applications, pp. 103–106 (2007)
11. Demmel, J., Grigori, L., Hoemmen, M., Langou, J.: Communication-avoiding paralleland sequential QR factorizations, Technical report, Electrical Engineering and Computer Sciences, University of California Berkeley (2008)

Application of a Preconditioned Chebyshev Basis Communication-Avoiding Conjugate Gradient Method to a Multiphase Thermal-Hydraulic CFD Code

Yasuhiro Idomura[1(✉)], Takuya Ina[1], Akie Mayumi[1], Susumu Yamada[1], and Toshiyuki Imamura[2]

[1] Japan Atomic Energy Agency, Kashiwa, Chiba 227-0871, Japan
idomura.yasuhiro@jaea.go.jp
[2] RIKEN, Kobe, Hyogo 650-0047, Japan

Abstract. A preconditioned Chebyshev basis communication-avoiding conjugate gradient method (P-CBCG) is applied to the pressure Poisson equation in a multiphase thermal-hydraulic CFD code JUPITER, and its computational performance and convergence properties are compared against a preconditioned conjugate gradient (P-CG) method and a preconditioned communication-avoiding conjugate gradient (P-CACG) method on the Oakforest-PACS, which consists of 8,208 KNLs. The P-CBCG method reduces the number of collective communications with keeping the robustness of convergence properties. Compared with the P-CACG method, an order of magnitude larger communication-avoiding steps are enabled by the improved robustness. It is shown that the P-CBCG method is 1.38× and 1.17× faster than the P-CG and P-CACG methods at 2,000 processors, respectively.

1 Introduction

Krylov subspace methods are widely used for solving linear systems given by extreme scale sparse matrices, and thus, their scalability is one of critical issues towards exascale computing. In nuclear engineering, exascale computing is needed for Computational Fluid Dynamics (CFD) simulations of turbulent flows such as multiphase thermal-hydraulic simulations of nuclear reactors and fusion plasma simulations. In these CFD simulations, implicit solvers based on Krylov subspace methods occupy dominant computational costs, and the scalability of such CFD simulations largely depends on the performance of Krylov solvers.

The current Peta-scale machines are characterized by extreme concurrency reaching at ~100 k computing nodes. In addition to this feature, on future exascale machines, which may be based on many-core processors or accelerators, significant acceleration of computation is expected. In Ref. [1], we optimized stencil computation kernels from CFD simulations on the latest many-core

© The Author(s) 2018
R. Yokota and W. Wu (Eds.): SCFA 2018, LNCS 10776, pp. 257–273, 2018.
https://doi.org/10.1007/978-3-319-69953-0_15

processors and GPUs, and significant performance gains were achieved. However, the accelerated computation revealed severe bottlenecks of communication.

Krylov solvers involve local halo data communications for stencil computations or sparse matrix vector operations SpMVs, and global data reduction communications for inner product operations in orthogonalization procedures for basis vectors. Although communication overlap techniques [2] may reduce the former latency, it can not be applied to the latter. In order to resolve this issue at mathematics or algorithm levels, in Refs. [3,4], we have introduced communication-avoiding (CA) Krylov methods to a fusion plasma turbulence code GT5D [5] and a multiphase thermal-hydraulic CFD code JUPITER [6].

The implicit solver in the GT5D is well-conditioned, and the communication-avoiding general minimum residual (CA-GMRES) method [7] was stable for large CA-steps $s > 10$. On the other hand, the Poisson solver in the JUPITER is ill-conditioned, and the convergence of the left-preconditioned communication-avoiding conjugate gradient (P-CACG) method [7] was limited for $s \leq 3$. Even with $s = 3$, the strong scaling of the JUPITER on the K-computer [8] was dramatically improved by reducing the number of global data reduction communications to $1/s$. However, for practical use, it is difficult to operate CA Krylov solvers at the upper limit of CA-steps, because the Poisson operator is time dependent and its condition number may increase in time. Therefore, we need to use more robust CA Krylov methods at CA-steps well below the upper limit, beyond which they become numerically unstable. In order to resolve this issue, in this work, we introduce the preconditioned Chebyshev basis communication-avoiding conjugate gradient (P-CBCG) method to the JUPITER, and examine its robustness and computational performance on the Oakforest-PACS, which consists of 8,208 KNLs.

The reminder of this paper is organized as follows. Related works are reviewed in Sect. 2. In Sect. 3, we explain CA Krylov subspace methods used in this work. In Sect. 4, we discuss numerical properties and kernel performances of CA Krylov solvers. In Sect. 5, we present the convergence property of CA Krylov methods and the computational performances of CA Krylov solvers on the JAEA ICEX and the Oakforest-PACS. Finally, a summary is given in Sect. 6.

2   Related Works

The CACG method is based on the so-called s-step CG method, in which the data dependency between SpMV and inner product operations in the standard CG method is removed. Van Rosendale [9] first developed a s-step version of the CG method. Chronopoulos and Gear [10] called their own variant of the CG method as the s-step CG method. However, the above works did not change SpMV operations for generating the s-step basis. Toledo optimized the computation of the s-step basis in the s-step CG method [11], in which the number of words transferred between levels of the memory hierarchy is reduced. The CACG method by Hoemmen [7] reduced communications between levels of the memory hierarchy and between processors by a matrix power kernel (MPK) [12].

Carson [13] showed the performance of the CACG method on the Hopper super-computer using a simple Poisson model problem.

CA-preconditioning is based on sparse approximate inverses with the same sparsity pattern as the matrix A, or block Jacobi (BJ) and polynomial precon-ditioners [9,11,14]. For instance, in BJ preconditioning, each processor indepen-dently solves its local problem. However, when the local preconditioner has data dependency over the whole local problem as in ILU factorization, it is difficult to construct a MPK without additional communications, because each local SpMV requires preconditioned input vector elements from neighboring processors. To avoid the additional communications, Yamazaki et al. [15] proposed an under-lap approach, in which each subdomain is divided into an inner part and the remaining surface part, and preconditioning for the latter is approximated by point Jacobi preconditioning. However, in our previous work [3], it was shown that for ill-conditioned problems given by the JUPITER, the underlap approach leads to significant convergence degradation, and a hybrid CA approach, in which SpMVs and BJ preconditioning are unchanged and CA is applied only to inner product operations, was proposed.

In most of performance studies [4,13,15], CA Krylov methods were applied to well-conditioned problems, where CA-steps are extended for $s > 10$. How-ever, in Ref. [3], it was shown that for ill-conditioned problems given by the JUPITER, the P-CACG method is numerically stable only within a few CA-steps even with the original BJ preconditioning. This issue is attributed to the monomial basis vectors, which are aligned to the eigenvector with the maximum eigenvalue as s increases, and the other eigen-components become relatively smaller and are hidden by the round-off errors. This violates the linear inde-pendency of the monomial basis vectors, and makes them ill-conditioned, when each basis vectors are not orthogonalized after creating it. To resolve this issue, Hoemmen [7] proposed to use the Newton basis vectors and the Chebyshev basis vectors. Suda et al. [16] proposed the P-CBCG method, which was tested with point Jacobi preconditioning on the K-computer [17]. In this work, we apply the P-CBCG method with BJ preconditioning to the JUPITER, compare its convergence property and numerical stability against the P-CACG method, and demonstrate its computational performance on the Oakforest-PACS.

3   Krylov Solvers in JUPITER Code

3.1   Code Overview

In the JUPITER code [6], thermal-hydraulics of the molten material in nuclear reactors is described by the equations of continuity, Navier-Stokes, and energy, assuming Newtonian and incompressible viscous fluids. The dynamics of gas, liquid, and solid phases of multiple components consisting of fuel pellets, fuel cladding, the channel box, the absorber, reactor internal components, and the atmosphere are described by an advection equation of the volume of fluid (VOF) function. The main computational cost ($\sim$90%) comes from computation of the pressure Poisson equation, because the Poisson operator given by the density has extreme contrast $\sim 10^7$ between gas and solid phases, and is ill-conditioned. The Poisson equation is discretized by the second order accurate centered finite difference scheme (7 stencils) in the Cartesian grid system (x, y, z). The linear system of the pressure Poisson equation, which is a symmetric block diagonal sparse matrix, is solved using Krylov subspace methods explained in the following subsections. These Krylov solvers use the compressed diagonal storage (CDS) format, which enables highly efficient direct memory access for the block diagonal sparse matrix than the compressed sparse row (CSR) format, which is commonly used in many matrix libraries, and are parallelized using a MPI+OpenMP hybrid parallelization model, in which MPI is used for coarse 3D domain decomposition in (x, y, z) and fine 1D domain decomposition in z is applied to each domain via OpenMP. BJ preconditioning is applied to each fine subdomain so that it is computed in thread parallel.

3.2   Preconditioned Conjugate Gradient (P-CG) Method

In the original version of the JUPITER, the pressure Poisson equation was computed using the P-CG method [18] with BJ preconditioning, in which ILU factorization [18] is applied to each block. In the P-CG method in Algorithm 1, a single iteration consists of SpMV, BJ preconditioning, two inner product operations, and three vector operations (AXPYs). Here, the SpMV requires a local halo data communication per iteration, and the inner product operations need two global data reduction communications (All_reduce) per iteration. One All_reduce at line 4 transfers two elements including the norm of residual vector, while the other All_reduce at line 8 sends one element.

Algorithm 1. Preconditioned Conjugate Gradient (P-CG) method

Input: $Ax = b$, Initial guess x_1
Output: Approximate solution x_i
1: $r_1 := b - Ax_1, z_1 = M^{-1}r_1, p_1 := z_1$
2: **for** $j = 1, 2, \dots$ until convergence **do**
3:      Compute $w := Ap_j$
4:      $\alpha_j := \langle r_j, z_j \rangle / \langle w, p_j \rangle$
5:      $x_{j+1} := x_j + \alpha_j p_j$
6:      $r_{j+1} := r_j - \alpha_j w$
7:      $z_{j+1} := M^{-1}r_{j+1}$
8:      $\beta_j := \langle r_{j+1}, z_{j+1} \rangle / \langle r_j, z_j \rangle$
9:      $p_{j+1} := z_{j+1} + \beta_j p_j$
10: **end for**

3.3   Preconditioned Communication-Avoiding Conjugate Gradient (P-CACG) Method

The P-CACG method in Algorithm 2 [7] is based on a three term recurrence variant of CG (CG3) method [18]. The CG3 method is decomposed into the outer loop and the inner s-step loop, and the algorithm is modified so that the latter is processed without any communication. At the k-th outer loop, firstly, the

---

Algorithm 2. Preconditioned Communication Avoiding CG (P-CACG) method

---

Input: $Ax = b$, Initial guess x_1
Output: Approximate solution x_i

1: $z_0 := 0, z_1 := b - Ax_1$
2: $q_0 := 0, q_1 := M^{-1}z_1$
3: **for** $k = 0, 1, 2, ...$ until convergence **do**
4:     $v_{sk+1} := z_{sk+1}$
5:     Compute $\underline{V}_k$ $(v_{sk+1}, M^{-1}Av_{sk+1}, ..., (M^{-1}A)^s v_{sk+1})$
6:     Compute $\underline{W}_k$ $(M^{-1}\underline{W}_k = \underline{V}_k)$
7:     $G_{k,k-1} := \underline{V}_k^* Z_{k-1}, G_{kk} := \underline{V}_k^* \underline{W}_k$
8:     $G_k = \begin{pmatrix} D_{k-1} & G_{k,k-1}^* \\ G_{k,k-1} & G_{kk} \end{pmatrix}$
9:     **for** $j = 1$ to s **do**
10:        Compute d_{sk+j} that satisfies $Aq_{sk+j} = [Z_{k-1}, \underline{W}_k]d_{sk+j}$ and $M^{-1}Aq_{sk+j} = [Q_{k-1}, \underline{V}_k]d_{sk+j}$
11:        Compute g_{sk+j} that satisfies $z_{sk+j} = [Z_{k-1}, \underline{W}_k]g_{sk+j}$ and $q_{sk+j} = [Q_{k-1}, \underline{V}_k]g_{sk+j}$
12:        $\mu_{sk+j} := g_{sk+j}^* G_k g_{sk+j}$
13:        $\nu_{sk+j} := g_{sk+j}^* G_k d_{sk+j}$
14:        $\gamma_{sk+j} := \mu_{sk+j}/\nu_{sk+j}$
15:        **if** $sk + j = 1$ **then**
16:            $\rho_{sk+j} := 1$
17:        **else**
18:            $\rho_{sk+j} := \left(1 - \frac{\gamma_{sk+j}}{\gamma_{sk+j-1}} \cdot \frac{\mu_{sk+j}}{\mu_{sk+j-1}} \cdot \frac{1}{\rho_{sk+j-1}}\right)^{-1}$
19:        **end if**
20:        $u_{sk+j} := [Q_{k-1}, \underline{V}_k]d_{sk+j}$
21:        $y_{sk+j} := [Z_{k-1}, \underline{W}_k]d_{sk+j}$
22:        $x_{sk+j+1} := \rho_{sk+j}(x_{sk+j} + \gamma_{sk+j}q_{sk+j}) + (1 - \rho_{sk+j})x_{sk+j-1}$
23:        $q_{sk+j+1} := \rho_{sk+j}(q_{sk+j} + \gamma_{sk+j}u_{sk+j}) + (1 - \rho_{sk+j})q_{sk+j-1}$
24:        $z_{sk+j+1} := \rho_{sk+j}(z_{sk+j} + \gamma_{sk+j}y_{sk+j}) + (1 - \rho_{sk+j})z_{sk+j-1}$
25:    **end for**
26: **end for**

---

s-step monomial basis vectors $\underline{V}_k$ (line 5) and the corresponding preconditioned basis vectors $\underline{W}_k$ (line 6) are generated at once. Secondly, the Gram matrix G_k (line 8) is computed for the inner product operations, which are replaced as $\mu = \langle z, q \rangle = g_{sk+j}^* G_k g_{sk+j}$ (line 12) and $\nu = \langle Aq, q \rangle = g_{sk+j}^* G_k d_{sk+j}$ (line 13). Here, d_{sk+j} (line 10) and g_{sk+j} (line 11) are defined so that they satisfy $Aq_{sk+j} = [Z_{k-1}, \underline{W}_k]d_{sk+j}$ and $z_{sk+j} = [Z_{k-1}, \underline{W}_k]g_{sk+j}$, respectively. Here, x^* denotes its transpose. At the j-th inner loop, these coefficients are computed to obtain the inner products, and then, the solution vector x_{sk+j} (line 22) and two sets of the residual vectors, the unpreconditioned residual vector z_{sk+j} (line 24) and the preconditioned residual vector q_{sk+j} (line 23), are updated by the three term recurrence formulae. In exact arithmetic, s iterations of the P-CG3 method and one outer loop iteration of the P-CACG method are equivalent.

In Ref. [3], we compared convergence properties of the pressure Poisson solver between the original BJ preconditioning and CA preconditioning based on the underlap approach [15], and significant convergence degradation was observed with the latter preconditioning. In addition, if one uses a MPK with CA preconditioning, s-step halo data is transferred at once. The number of halo data communication directions are significantly increased from 6 (bidirectional in x, y, z) to 26 (including three dimensional diagonal directions), and redundant computations are needed for the halo data. In order to avoid these issues, in this work, we use the BJ preconditioning with a hybrid CA approach [3]. In the P-CACG method, dominant computational costs come from the s-step SpMVs (line 5) and the following BJ preconditioning (line 6) in the outer loop, GEMM operations for constructing the Gram matrix (line 7) in the outer loop, and three vector operations for the three term recurrence formulae (lines 22–24) in the inner loop. Here, the size of GEMM operations depends on s, and thus, their arithmetic intensity is increased with s. If one applies cache blocking optimization, coefficients of the three term recurrence formulae can be reused for s-steps, and the arithmetic intensity of three vector operations is also improved by extending s. The SpMV requires one local halo data communication per inner iteration as in the P-CG method, while the Gram matrix computation needs only one All_reduce for $s(s + 1)$ elements of $G_{k,k-1}$ and $(s + 2)(s + 1)/2$ upper-triangular elements of $G_{k,k}$ per outer iteration. In addition, we compute the norm of residual vector $r_{sk} = b - Ax_{sk+1}$ for the convergence check, which require one All_reduce per outer iteration. Therefore, the P-CACG method requires two All_reduces per outer iteration.

3.4 Preconditioned Chebyshev Basis Communication-Avoiding Conjugate Gradient (P-CBCG) Method

The P-CBCG method [16] is shown in Algorithm 3. Unlike the P-CACG method which is based on the CG3 method, the P-CBCG method computes two term recurrences as in the P-CG method. The inner product operations are performed using the so-called look-unrolling technique [9] instead of a Gram matrix approach in the P-CACG method. A multi-step CG method constructed using the above approach is computed using s-step Chebyshev basis vectors. Here, the preconditioned Chebyshev basis vectors (line 10) are computed using Algorithm 4. In this algorithm, the basis vectors are generated using $T_j(AM^{-1})$, which is the j-th Chebyshev polynomials scaled and shifted within $[\lambda_{min}, \lambda_{max}]$ and thus, satisfies $|T_j(AM^{-1})| < 1$, where λ_{min} and λ_{max} are the minimum and maximum eigenvalues of AM^{-1}. In the monomial basis vectors, the generated vectors are aligned to the eigenvector with λ_{max} as s increases, and the other eigencomponents become relatively smaller and are hidden by the round-off errors. This violates the linear independency of the monomial basis vectors, and makes them ill-conditioned, when each basis vector is not orthogonalized after creating it. On the other hand, the minimax property of Chebyshev polynomials helps to keep the basis vectors well-conditioned without orthogonalizing each basis vector. By using this method, one can construct a Krylov subspace, which is mathematically equivalent to that given by the monomial basis vectors, with much less impact of the round-off errors, and s can be extended compared with

Algorithm 3. Preconditioned Chebyshev Basis communication avoiding CG (P-CBCG) method

---
Input: $Ax = b$, Initial guess x_0
Output: Approximate solution x_i
1: $r_0 := b - Ax_0$
2: Compute S_0 $(T_0(AM^{-1})r_0, T_1(AM^{-1})r_0, ..., T_{s-1}(AM^{-1})r_0)$
3: $Q_0 = S_0$
4: **for** $k = 0, 1, 2, ...$ until convergence **do**
5:      Compute $Q_k^* A Q_k$
6:      Compute $Q_k^* r_{sk}$
7:      $a_k := (Q_k^* A Q_k)^{-1} Q_k^* r_{sk}$
8:      $x_{s(k+1)} := x_{sk} + Q_k a_k$
9:      $r_{s(k+1)} := r_{sk} - A Q_k a_k$
10:     Compute S_{k+1} $(T_0(AM^{-1})r_{s(k+1)}, T_1(AM^{-1})r_{s(k+1)}, ..., T_{s-1}(AM^{-1})r_{s(k+1)})$
11:     Compute $Q_k^* A S_{k+1}$
12:     $B_k := (Q_k^* A Q_k)^{-1} Q_k^* A S_{k+1}$
13:     $Q_{k+1} := S_{k+1} - Q_k B_k$
14:     $A Q_{k+1} := A S_{k+1} + A Q_k B_k$
15: **end for**

CA Krylov methods based on the monomial basis vectors. In this work, $\lambda_{\max}$ is computed by a power method, while $\lambda_{\min}$ is approximated as zero.

In the P-CBCG method, dominant computational costs come from the preconditioned Chebyshev basis vector generation involving the SpMVs and the BJ preconditioning (line 10) and the remaining matrix computations. The SpMVs at line 10 require s local halo data communications, while the matrix computations at lines 5, 11 need global data reduction communications. Therefore, the P-CBCG method requires two All_reduces per s-steps. One All_reduce at lines 5, 6 transfers $s(s+1)/2$ upper-triangular elements of $Q_k^* A Q_k$, s elements of $Q_k^* r_{sk}$, and one element for the norm of residual vector, while the other All_reduce sends s^2 elements of $Q_k^* A S_{k+1}$.

Algorithm 4. Preconditioned Chebyshev basis

Input: r_{sk}, Approximate minimum/maximum eigenvalues of AM^{-1}, $\lambda_{\min}, \lambda_{\max}$
Output: S_k $(\tilde{z}_0, \tilde{z}_1, ..., \tilde{z}_{s-1})$, AS_k $(A\tilde{z}_0, A\tilde{z}_1, ..., A\tilde{z}_{s-1})$
1: $\eta := 2/(\lambda_{\max} - \lambda_{\min})$
2: $\zeta := (\lambda_{\max} + \lambda_{\min})/(\lambda_{\max} - \lambda_{\min})$
3: $z_0 := r_{sk}$
4: $\tilde{z}_0 := M^{-1} z_0$
5: $z_1 := \eta A \tilde{z}_0 - \zeta z_0$
6: $\tilde{z}_1 := M^{-1} z_1$
7: **for** $j = 2, 3, ..., s$ **do**
8:      $z_j := 2\eta A \tilde{z}_{j-1} - 2\zeta z_{j-1} - z_{j-2}$
9:      $\tilde{z}_j := M^{-1} z_j$
10: **end for**

---

4   Kernel Performance Analysis

4.1   Computing Platforms

In this work, we estimate computing performances of the P-CG, P-CACG, and P-CBCG solvers on computing platforms in Table 1. The JAEA ICEX is based on the Xeon E5-2680v3 processor (Haswell) and the dual plane $4 \times$ FDR Infiniband with a hyper cube topology, and the Oakforest-PACS (KNL) consists of the Xeon Phi 7250 processor (Knights Landing) and the Omni Path with a fat tree topology. The compilers used are the Intel Fortran compiler 16.0.1 with the Intel MPI library 5.0 (-O3 -mcmodel= large -qopenmp -fpp -align array64byte -no-prec-div -fma -xHost) and the Intel Fortran compiler 17.0.4 with the Intel MPI library 2017 (-O3 -mcmodel= large -qopenmp -fpp -align array64byte -no-prec-div -fma -axMIC-AVX512) on ICEX and KNL, respectively. In this work, cross-platform comparisons are performed using the same number of processors. Since ICEX is based on a NUMA architecture with two processors per node, we assign two MPI processes per node. As for OpenMP parallelization, we use 12 and 68 threads on ICEX and KNL, respectively. On KNL, we choose 68 threads without hyper threading to avoid performance degradation in MPI communications [4]. Although KNL has hierarchical memory architecture consisting of MCDRAM (16 GByte, B~480 GByte/s) and DDR4 (96 GByte), we suppress the problem size below 16 GB per node and use only MCDRAM in a flat mode.

In this section, we analyze a single processor performance for the three solvers using a small problem size of $N = 104 \times 104 \times 265$, which corresponds to a typical problem size on a single processor. The achieved performance is compared against the modified roofline model [19], in which a theoretical processing time of each kernel is estimated by the sum of costs for floating point operations and memory access, $t_{RL} = f/F + b/B$. Here, f and b are the numbers of floating point operations and memory access of the kernel. F and B are the

Table 1. Specifications of the JAEA ICEX and the Oakforest-PACS (KNL).

	ICEX	KNL
Number of nodes	2,510	8,208
Total performance [PFlops]	2.41	25.00
Number of cores per node	12×2	68
Peak performance F [GFlops/processor]	480	3046
STREAM bandwidth B [GByte/s/processor]	58	480(MCDRAM)
B/F	0.12	0.16
Cache [MB/cores]	30/12	1/2
Memory per node [GByte]	64	16
Interconnect bandwidth [GByte/s]	13.6	12.5

peak performance and the STREAM memory bandwidth of the processor. The performance ratios of F and B between ICEX and KNL are 6.3× and 8.6×, respectively.

Table 2. Kernel performance analysis (Floating point operation f [Flop/grid], Memory access b [Byte/grid], Arithmetic intensity f/b, Roofline time $t_{RL} = f/F + b/B$ [ns/grid], Peak performance F [Flops], STREAM bandwidth B [Byte/s], Elapse time t [ns/grid], Sustained performance P [GFlops], Roofline ratio $R_{RL} = t_{RL}/t$, and ICEX/KNL ratio R_{ICEX}) in the kernel benchmarks using a single processor of ICEX and KNL.

Algorithm	Kernel	f	b	f/b	ICEX				KNL				
					t_{RL}	t	P	R_{RL}	t_{RL}	t	P	R_{RL}	R_{ICEX}
P-CG	SpMV	15.00	80.00	0.19	1.40	1.94	7.75	0.72	0.17	0.28	52.78	0.60	6.81
	BJ	20.00	128.00	0.16	2.24	2.53	7.90	0.88	0.27	0.46	43.26	0.59	5.48
	Vector	4.00	40.00	0.10	0.69	0.72	5.55	0.96	0.08	0.10	39.74	0.84	7.16
	Total	39.00	248.00	0.16	4.33	5.19	7.52	0.84	0.53	0.85	46.03	0.62	6.12
P-CACG ($s = 3$)	SpMV	13.00	80.00	0.16	1.40	1.83	7.11	0.76	0.17	0.24	54.59	0.72	7.68
	BJ	14.00	120.00	0.12	2.09	2.02	6.94	1.03	0.25	0.44	31.87	0.58	4.59
	Gram	18.67	29.33	0.64	0.54	0.54	34.70	1.01	0.07	0.13	142.86	0.51	4.12
	3-term	41.67	80.00	0.52	1.46	1.42	29.26	1.02	0.18	0.49	84.20	0.36	2.88
	Total	87.33	309.33	0.28	5.49	5.81	15.04	0.94	0.67	1.30	67.03	0.52	4.46
P-CBCG ($s = 12$)	CB	30.58	228.67	0.13	3.98	4.91	6.22	0.81	0.49	0.89	34.46	0.55	5.54
	Matrix	93.17	83.33	1.12	1.62	1.79	51.98	0.91	0.20	0.63	147.14	0.32	2.83
	Total	123.75	312.00	0.40	5.61	6.71	18.45	0.84	0.69	1.52	81.38	0.45	4.41

4.2   P-CG Solver

Computational kernels of the P-CG method consist mainly of SpMV (lines 3, 4), BJ (lines 7, 8), and Vector (AXPYs, lines 5, 6, 9). Here, SpMV and BJ involve the following inner product operations in the same loop. The numbers of floating point operations f and memory access b and the resulting arithmetic intensity f/b of each kernel are summarized in Table 2. Since the pressure Poisson equation is solved using the second order accurate centered finite difference scheme, SpMV and BJ have relatively low arithmetic intensity $f/b < 0.2$. In addition, the remaining AXPYs are memory-intensive kernels with $f/b = 0.1$. Therefore, the high memory bandwidth on KNL has a great impact on the acceleration of the P-CG solver, and the performance ratio between ICEX and KNL exceeds $R_{ICEX} > 6$. Although AXPYs in Vector achieve ideal sustained performances with the performance ratio against the roofline model $R_{RL} \sim 0.9$ both on ICEX and KNL, stencil computations in SpMV and BJ show performance degradation from $R_{RL} \sim 0.8$ on ICEX to $R_{RL} \sim 0.6$ on KNL.

4.3   P-CACG Solver

Computational kernels of the P-CACG method consist mainly of SpMV (lines 5, 6), BJ (lines 5, 6), Gram (lines 7, 8), and 3-term (lines 20–24). The arithmetic intensity of the P-CACG method changes depending on s, because the arithmetic intensity of Gram and 3-term are proportional to s. Gram scales as $f = 2(s+1)(2s+1)/s$ and $b = 8(3s+2)/s$. 3-term scales as $f = (8s^2+12s+2)/s$ and $b = 48(s+2)/s$, where the s-dependency comes from cache blocking optimization [3]. In Table 2, the kernel performance is summarized at $s = 3$, which is the upper limit of CA-steps in the benchmark problem in Sect. 5. SpMV and BJ in the P-CACG method have lower f and b than the P-CG method, because they do not involve inner product operations. Compared with SpMV and BJ, Gram and 3-term have higher arithmetic intensity $f/b > 0.5$, and thus, an impact of additional computation in the P-CACG method on the total computational cost ($\sim$1.12× on ICEX) is much lower than the increase of f ($\sim$2.24×) from the P-CG method. These compute-intensive kernels achieve ideal performances with $R_{RL} \sim 1$ on ICEX. However, they show significant performance degradation with $R_{RL} \sim 0.4$ on KNL, and thus, the performance ratio is limited to $R_{ICEX} \sim 4.46$.

4.4 P-CBCG Solver

Computational kernels of the P-CACG method consist mainly of the Chebyshev basis computation CB (line 10), and the remaining matrix computations Matrix. The arithmetic intensity of the P-CBCG method depends on s as in the P-CACG method. CB scales as $f = 2(9s+4)/s$ and $b = 8(4s+35)/s$, and Matrix scales as $f = (7s+2)(s+1)/s$ and $b = 40(2s+1)/s$. In Table 2, the kernel performance is summarized for $s = 12$, which is used in the benchmark problem in Sect. 5. Although f of the P-CBCG method becomes 3.17× larger than the P-CG method, the increase of computational cost is suppressed to 1.3× on ICEX, because of the improved arithmetic intensity. However, on KNL, the performance ratio between the P-CG and P-CBCG methods is expanded to 1.79×, because the compute-intensive Matrix kernel shows performance degradation from $R_{RL} \sim 0.9$ on ICEX to $R_{RL} \sim 0.3$ on KNL. As a result, the performance ratio between ICEX and KNL is limited to $R_{ICEX} \sim 4.41$.

5 Numerical Experiment

5.1 Convergence Property

In the present numerical experiment, we compute nonlinear evolutions of molten debris in a single fuel assembly component of nuclear reactor (see Fig. 1). The problem size is chosen as $N = 800 \times 500 \times 3,540 \sim 1.4 \times 10^9$, which was used also in the former works [3,6]. The problem treats multi-phase flows consisting of gas and multi-component liquid and solid of fuel pellets, fuel cladding, the channel box, the absorber, and the other reactor internal components. The convergence property and the computational performance are investigated for fully developed multi-phase flows, which give the largest iteration number. Because of the large problem size and the extreme density contrast of multi-phase flows, the pressure Poisson equation is ill-conditioned, and the P-CG solver is converged

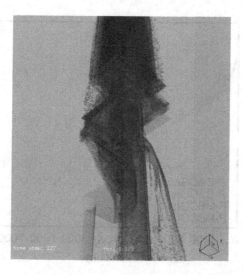

Fig. 1. Visualization of nonlinearly evolved multiphase flows of molten debris in reactor internal components computed by the JUPITER with $N = 800 \times 500 \times 3,540$.

with $\sim 6,000$ iterations (see Fig. 2). Here, the convergence condition is given by the relative residual error of $|b - Ax|/|b| < 10^{-8}$.

The convergence properties of the P-CG, P-CACG, P-CBCG, and P-MBCG solvers are summarized in Fig. 2. Here, the P-MBCG method is a variant of the P-CBCG method, in which the Chebyshev basis vectors at lines 2, 10 are replaced by the monomial basis vectors $S_k(r_{sk}, (AM^{-1})r_{sk}, (AM^{-1})^2 r_{sk}, ..., (AM^{-1})^{s-1} r_{sk})$. Although the P-MBCG method is mathematically similar to the P-CACG method, the former uses the two term recurrence formulae, while the latter is based on the CG3 method or the three term recurrence formulae. In Ref. [20], it was shown that Krylov subspace methods based on three term recurrences give significantly less accurate residuals than those with two term recurrences. In this work, we examine this point for CA Krylov subspace methods. As shown in Ref. [3], the convergence of the P-CACG solver is limited to $s = 3$, while in the P-MBCG solver, the convergence is somewhat extended to $s = 5$. On the other hand, in the P-CBCG method, the convergence property is dramatically extended to $s = 40$. These observations show that the main cause of the convergence degradation is not the three term recurrence formulae, but the ill-conditioned monomial basis vectors. Another important property is in the P-CBCG solver, the convergence property becomes worse gradually above the upper limit of CA-steps, while the P-CACG and P-MBCG solvers breaks down immediately above the upper limit. This property is important for practical use in extreme-scale CFD simulations.

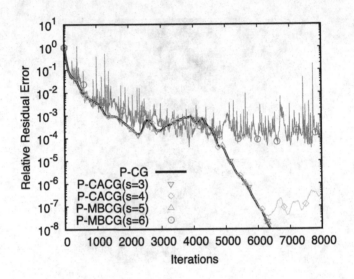

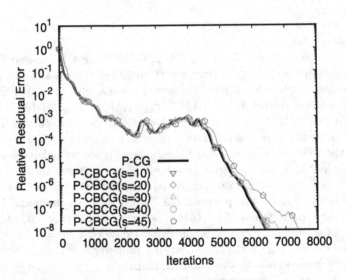

Fig. 2. Comparisons of convergence properties among the P-CG, P-CACG, P-CBCG, and P-MBCG (a variant of the P-CBCG method using the monomial basis vectors) solvers. The relative residual error $|b - Ax|/|b|$ is plotted for the JUPITER with $N = 800 \times 500 \times 3,540$. The computation is performed using 800 processors on ICEX.

5.2   Strong Scaling Test

In the P-CACG solver, we use $s = 3$, which is the upper limit of CA-steps from the viewpoint of numerical stability. On the other hand, the choice of s in the

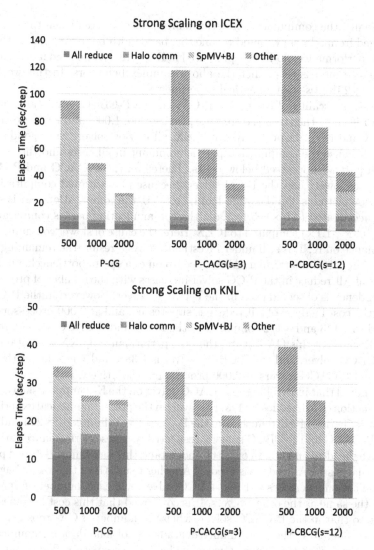

Fig. 3. Strong scaling of the P-CG, P-CACG($s = 3$), and P-CBCG($s = 12$) solvers using 500, 1,000, and 2,000 processors (MPI processes) on ICEX and KNL. The cost distribution in a single time step is shown.

P-CBCG solver is rather flexible, and the optimum s depends on the following factors. Firstly, the number of All_reduce is reduced to $1/s$ compared to the P-CG method. Here, the communication data size scales as $\sim s^2$. Secondly, the numbers of floating point operations and memory access per iteration in Matrix kernel scale as $f \sim s$ and $b \sim const.$, respectively, and the arithmetic intensity of Matrix scales as $f/b \sim s$. Thirdly, cache efficiency of CB is affected by the number of basis vectors. Therefore, the computational performance of each kernel varies depending on s. Finally, the communication performance is also affected when the data size is changed from a latency bound regime to a bandwidth bound regime. Although a simple performance model was presented in Refs. [13,17], we need more detailed performance models to predict the above complex behaviors. In this work, we chose $s = 12$ from s-scan numerical experiments.

The strong scaling of the P-CG, P-CACG, and P-CBCG solvers are summarized in Fig. 3. In the strong scaling test, we use 500, 1,000, and 2,000 processors on ICEX and KNL, respectively. On ICEX, all Krylov solvers show good strong scaling, because the computation part is dominant in all cases and the communication part is suppressed below ~10 s. Therefore, the P-CACG and P-CBCG solvers are slower than the P-CG solver, because of additional computation in CA Krylov methods. On the other hand, on KNL, the computation part is significantly accelerated ($3.5 \times \sim 5.1\times$) and the communication part is comparable or slower ($0.3\times \sim 1.1\times$) compared to ICEX. Here, the cause of slower communication performance on KNL is still under investigation. As a result, the remaining communication part, in particular, All_reduce becomes a severe bottleneck. On KNL, the cost of All_reduce in the P-CG solver increases with the number of processors. This tendency is observed even in the P-CACG solver. However, in the P-CBCG solver, the cost increase of All_reduce is suppressed, and at 2,000 processors, it is reduced to ~1/3 and ~1/2 compared to the P-CG and P-CACG solvers, respectively. Because of this CA feature, the best performance on KNL is obtained by the P-CBCG solver, and the P-CBCG solver is $1.38\times$ and $1.17\times$ faster than the P-CG and P-CACG solvers at 2,000 processors, respectively.

It is noted that in Ref. [3], the P-CACG solver on the K-computer showed ideal cost reduction of All_reduce by $1/s$. However, in the present numerical experiment, the cost reduction of All_reduce from the P-CG solver is limited to ~2/3 and ~1/3 in the P-CACG and P-CBCG solvers, respectively. These performance ratios are far above the ideal one $1/s$. In order to understand this issue, more detailed performance analysis for All_reduce is needed. Another issue is that the cost of halo data communications increases in the P-CBCG solver, while the number of SpMVs is almost the same as the other solvers. It is confirmed that this cost becomes comparable to that in the P-CACG solver, when the number of CA-steps is reduced to $s = 3$. Therefore, the performance degradation of halo data communications seems to depend on the memory usage, which increases with s. These issues will be addressed in the future work.

6 Summary

In this work, we applied the P-CBCG method to the pressure Poisson equation in the JUPITER. We analyzed numerical properties of the P-CACG and P-CBCG methods in detail, and compared it against the P-CG method, which was used in the original code. The P-CACG and P-CBCG methods reduce data reduction communications to $1/s$, but additional computation is needed for CA procedures. The P-CACG ($s = 3$) and P-CBCG ($s = 12$) methods have ~2× and ~3× larger f, while the increase in b is only ~1.25×. Because of the improved arithmetic intensity f/b, the resulting computational costs of the P-CACG and P-CBCG solvers on a single processor were respectively suppressed to $\sim$1.1$\times$ and $\sim$1.3$\times$ on ICEX, while they were expanded to $\sim$1.5$\times$ and $\sim$1.8$\times$ on KNL.

We tested convergence properties of CA Krylov subspace methods based on the monomial basis vectors (P-CACG, P-MBCG) and the Chebyshev basis vectors (P-CBCG). In the comparison between the P-CACG and P-MBCG methods, which are based on three term recurrences and two term recurrences, the latter showed slightly improved convergence. However, the convergence of both solvers were limited for $s \ll 10$. On the other hand, the convergence of the P-CBCG method was extended to $s \sim 40$, and the robustness of CA Krylov solvers was dramatically improved.

Strong scaling tests of the P-CG, P-CACG ($s = 3$), and P-CBCG ($s = 12$) solvers were performed using 500, 1,000, and 2,000 processors on ICEX and KNL. On ICEX, the computational costs were dominated by the computation part, and all three solvers showed good strong scaling. As the communication part is minor, the P-CG solver was fastest on ICEX. On the other hand, on KNL, the computation part was significantly accelerated, and the remaining communication part, in particular, All_reduce became a severe bottleneck. By reducing the cost of All_reduce, the best performance was achieved by the P-CBCG solver, and the P-CBCG solver is 1.38$\times$ and 1.17$\times$ faster than the P-CG and P-CACG solvers at 2,000 processors, respectively. As the P-CBCG method satisfies both high computational performance and excellent robustness, it is promising algorithm for extreme scale simulations on future exascale machines with limited network and memory bandwidths.

Acknowledgement. The authors would like to thank Dr. S. Yamashita for providing the JUPITER for the present benchmark, and Dr. T. Kawamura for the visualization image. This work is supported by the MEXT (Grant for Post-K priority issue No.6: Development of Innovative Clean Energy). Computations were performed on the Oakforest-PACS (Univ. Tokyo/Univ. Tsukuba) and the ICEX (JAEA).

References

1. Asahi, Y., et al.: Optimization of fusion Kernels on accelerators with indirect or strided memory access patterns. IEEE Trans. Parallel Distrib. Syst. **28**(7), 1974–1988 (2017)
2. Idomura, Y., et al.: Communication-overlap techniques for improved strong scaling of Gyrokinetic Eulerian code beyond 100k cores on the K-computer. Int. J. High Perform. Comput. Appl. **28**(1), 73–86 (2014)
3. Mayumi, A., et al.: Left-preconditioned communication-avoiding conjugate gradient methods for multiphase CFD simulations on the K computer. In: Proceedings of the 7th Workshop on Latest Advances in Scalable Algorithms for Large-Scale Systems, ScalA 2016, Piscataway, NJ, USA, pp. 17–24. IEEE Press (2016)
4. Idomura, Y., Ina, T., Mayumi, A., Yamada, S., Matsumoto, K., Asahi, Y., Imamura, T.: Application of a communication-avoiding generalized minimal residual method to a gyrokinetic five dimensional Eulerian code on many core platforms. In: Proceedings of the 8th Workshop on Latest Advances in Scalable Algorithms for Large-Scale Systems, ScalA 2017, New York, NY, USA, pp. 7:1–7:8. ACM (2017)

5. Idomura, Y., et al.: Study of ion turbulent transport and profile formations using global gyrokinetic full-f Vlasov simulation. Nucl. Fusion **49**, 065029 (2009)

6. Yamashita, S., Ina, T., Idomura, Y., Yoshida, H.: A numerical simulation method for molten material behavior in nuclear reactors. Nucl. Eng. Des. **322**(Suppl. C), 301–312 (2017)

7. Hoemmen, M.: Communication-avoiding Krylov subspace methods. Ph.D. thesis, University of California, Berkeley (2010)

8. Fujitsu Global: K computer. http://www.fujitsu.com/global/about/businesspolicy/tech/k/

9. Van Rosendale, J.: Minimizing inner product data dependencies in conjugate gradient iteration. NASA contractor report (1983)

10. Chronopoulos, A., Gear, C.: s-step iterative methods for symmetric linear systems. J. Comput. Appl. Math. **25**(2), 153–168 (1989)

11. Toledo, S.A.: Quantitative performance modeling of scientific computations and creating locality in numerical algorithms. Ph.D. thesis, Massachusetts Institute of Technology (1995)

12. Demmel, J., Hoemmen, M., Mohiyuddin, M., Yelick, K.: Avoiding communication in sparse matrix computations. In: 2008 IEEE International Symposium on Parallel and Distributed Processing, pp. 1–12, April 2008

13. Carson, E.C.: Communication-avoiding Krylov subspace methods in theory and practice. Ph.D. thesis, University of California, Berkeley (2015)

14. Chronopoulos, A., Gear, C.W.: Implementation of preconditioned s-step conjugate gradient methods on a multiprocessor system with memory hierarchy. Technical report, Department of Computer Science, Illinois University, Urbana, USA (1987)

15. Yamazaki, I., Anzt, H., Tomov, S., Hoemmen, M., Dongarra, J.: Improving the performance of CA-GMRES on multicores with multiple GPUs. In: 2014 IEEE 28th International Parallel and Distributed Processing Symposium, pp. 382–391, May 2014

16. Suda, R., Cong, L., Watanabe, D., Kumagai, Y., Fujii, A., Tanaka, T.: Communication-avoiding CG method: new direction of Krylov subspace methods towards exa-scale computing. RIMS Kôkyûroku **1995**, 102–111 (2016)

17. Kumagai, Y., Fujii, A., Tanaka, T., Hirota, Y., Fukaya, T., Imamura, T., Suda, R.: Performance analysis of the Chebyshev basis conjugate gradient method on the K computer. In: Wyrzykowski, R., Deelman, E., Dongarra, J., Karczewski, K., Kitowski, J., Wiatr, K. (eds.) PPAM 2015. LNCS, vol. 9573, pp. 74–85. Springer, Cham (2016). https://doi.org/10.1007/978-3-319-32149-3_8

18. Saad, Y.: Iterative Methods for Sparse Linear Systems, 2nd edn. Society for Industrial and Applied Mathematics, Philadelphia (2003)

19. Shimokawabe, T., et al.: An 80-fold speedup, 15.0 TFlops full GPU acceleration of non-hydrostatic weather model ASUCA production code. In: 2010 ACM/IEEE International Conference for High Performance Computing, Networking, Storage and Analysis, pp. 1–11, November 2010

20. Gutknecht, M.H., Strakos, Z.: Accuracy of two three-term and three two-term recurrences for Krylov space solvers. SIAM J. Matrix Anal. Appl. **22**(1), 213–229 (2000)

Optimization of Hierarchical Matrix Computation on GPU

Satoshi Ohshima[1]([✉]), Ichitaro Yamazaki[2], Akihiro Ida[3], and Rio Yokota[4]

[1] Kyushu University, Fukuoka, Japan
ohshima@cc.kyushu-u.ac.jp
[2] University of Tennessee, Knoxville, USA
iyamazak@icl.utk.edu
[3] The University of Tokyo, Tokyo, Japan
ida@cc.u-tokyo.ac.jp
[4] Tokyo Institute of Technology, Tokyo, Japan
rioyokota@gsic.titech.ac.jp

Abstract. The demand for dense matrix computation in large scale and complex simulations is increasing; however, the memory capacity of current computer system is insufficient for such simulations. Hierarchical matrix method ($\mathcal{H}$-matrices) is attracting attention as a computational method that can reduce the memory requirements of dense matrix computations. However, the computation of $\mathcal{H}$-matrices is more complex than that of dense and sparse matrices; thus, accelerating the $\mathcal{H}$-matrices is required. We focus on $\mathcal{H}$-matrix - vector multiplication (HMVM) on a single NVIDIA Tesla P100 GPU. We implement five GPU kernels and compare execution times among various processors (the Broadwell-EP, Skylake-SP, and Knights Landing) by OpenMP. The results show that, although an HMVM kernel can compute many small GEMV kernels, merging such kernels to a single GPU kernel was the most effective implementation. Moreover, the performance of BATCHED BLAS in the MAGMA library was comparable to that of the manually tuned GPU kernel.

1 Introduction

The scale of computer simulations continues to increase as hardware capability advances from post-Peta to Exascale. At such scales, the asymptotic complexity of both computation and memory is a serious bottleneck if they are not (near) linear. In addition, the deep memory hierarchy and heterogeneity of such systems are a challenge for existing algorithms. A fundamental change in the underlying algorithms for scientific computing is required to facilitate exascale simulations, i.e., (near) linear scaling algorithms with high data locality and asynchronicity are required.

In scientific computing, the most common algorithmic components are linear algebra routines, *e.g.*, matrix - vector multiplication, matrix-matrix multiplication, factorization, and eigenvalue problems. The performance of these components has been used as a proxy to measure the performance of large scale systems.

© The Author(s) 2018
R. Yokota and W. Wu (Eds.): SCFA 2018, LNCS 10776, pp. 274–292, 2018.
https://doi.org/10.1007/978-3-319-69953-0_16

Note that the general usefulness of the high performance LINPACK benchmark for supercomputers has long been disputed, and recent advancements of dense linear algebra methods with near linear complexity could be the final nail in the coffin.

Dense matrices requires $\mathcal{O}(N^2)$ storage and have a multiplication/factorization cost of $\mathcal{O}(N^3)$. Hierarchical low-rank approximation methods, such as $\mathcal{H}$-matrices [1], hierarchical semi-separable matrices [2], hierarchical off-diagonal low-rank matrices [3], and hierarchical interpolative factorization methods [4], reduce this storage requirement to $\mathcal{O}(N \log N)$ and the multiplication/factorization cost to $\mathcal{O}(N \log^q N)$, where, q denotes a positive number. With such methods, there is no point performing large scale dense linear algebra operations directly. Note that, we refer to all hierarchical low-rank approximation methods as $\mathcal{H}$-matrices in this paper for simplicity.

$\mathcal{H}$-matrices subdivide a dense matrix recursively, i.e., off-diagonal block division terminates at a coarse level, whereas diagonal blocks are divided until a constant block size obtained regardless of the problem size. Here, off-diagonal blocks are compressed using low-rank approximation, which is critical to achieving $\mathcal{O}(N \log N)$ storage and $\mathcal{O}(N \log^q N)$ arithmetic complexity. Recently, $\mathcal{H}$-matrices have attracted increasing attention; however, such efforts have a mathematical and algebraic focus. As a result, few parallel implementations of the $\mathcal{H}$-matrix code have been proposed.

In this paper, we focus on a parallel implementation. Specifically, we target matrix - vector multiplications on GPUs. Of the many scientific applications that involve solving large dense matrices, we selected electric field analysis based on boundary integral formulation. Our results demonstrate that orders of magnitude speedup can be obtained by merging many matrix - vector computations into a single GPU kernel and proper implementation of batched BLAS operations in the MAGMA library [5–7].

The remainder of this paper is organized as follows. An overview of the $\mathcal{H}$-matrices and its basic computation are presented in Sect. 2. In Sect. 3, we focus on $\mathcal{H}$-matrix - vector multiplication (HMVM) and propose various single GPU implementations. Performance evaluation results are presented and discussed in Sect. 4, and conclusions and suggestions for future work are given in Sect. 5.

2   Hierarchical Matrix Method ($\mathcal{H}$-matrices)

$\mathcal{H}$-matrices are an approximation technique that can be applied to the dense matrices in boundary integral equations and kernel summation. The $\mathcal{O}(N^2)$ storage requirement $\mathcal{O}(N^3)$ factorization cost of $\mathcal{H}$-matrices can be reduced to $\mathcal{O}(N \log^q N)$. Therefore, $\mathcal{H}$-matrices allow calculations at scales that are otherwise impossible. In the following, we describe the formulation of $\mathcal{H}$-matrices using boundary integral problems as an example.

2.1   Formulation of $\mathcal{H}$-matrices for Boundary Integral Problems

Let H be a Hilbert space of functions in a $(d-1)$-dimensional domain $\Omega \subset \mathbb{R}^d$ and H' be the dual space of H. For $u \in H$, $f \in H'$, and a kernel function of a convolution operator g: $\mathbb{R}^d \times \Omega \to \mathbb{R}$, we consider following the integral equation:

$$\int_\Omega g(x,y)u(y)\mathrm{d}y = f. \tag{1}$$

To calculate (1) numerically, we divide domain Ω into elements $\Omega^h = \{\omega_j : j \in J\}$, where J is an index set. When we use weighted residual methods, the function u is approximated from a d-dimensional subspace $H^h \subset H$. Given a basis $(\varphi_i)_{i \in \mathcal{I}}$ of H^h for an index set $\mathcal{I} := \{1, ..., N\}$, the approximant $u^h \in H^h$ to u can be expressed using a coefficient vector $\phi = (\phi_i)_{i \in \mathcal{I}}$ that satisfies $u^h = \sum_{i \in \mathcal{I}} \phi_i \varphi_i$. Note that the supports of the basis $\Omega^h_{\varphi_i} := \mathrm{supp}\,\varphi_i$ are assembled from the sets ω_j. Equation (1) is reduced to the following system of linear equations.

$$A\phi = B. \tag{2}$$

Here, assume that we have two subsets (i.e., clusters) $s, t \in \mathcal{I}$, where the corresponding domains are defined as follows:

$$\Omega^h_s := \bigcup_{i \in s} \mathrm{supp}\,\varphi_i, \quad \Omega^h_t := \bigcup_{i \in t} \mathrm{supp}\,\varphi_i. \tag{3}$$

A cluster pair (s,t) is 'admissible', if the Euclidian distance between Ω^h_s and Ω^h_t is sufficiently large compared to their diameters:

$$\min\{\mathrm{diam}(\Omega^h_s), \mathrm{diam}(\Omega^h_t)\} \le \eta \, \mathrm{dist}(\Omega^h_s, \Omega^h_t), \tag{4}$$

where η is a positive constant number depending on the kernel function g and the division Ω^h. For the domain corresponding to the admissible cluster pairs $x \in \Omega^h_s$, $y \in \Omega^h_t$, we assume that the kernel function can be approximated at certain accuracy using a degenerate kernel such as

$$g(x,y) \cong \sum_{\nu=1}^k g_1^\nu(x) g_2^\nu(y), \tag{5}$$

where k is a positive number. Such kernel functions are employed in various scientific applications, e.g., electric field analysis, mechanical analysis, and earthquake cycle simulations. The kernel functions in such applications can be written as follows:

$$g(x,y) \in \mathrm{span}(\{|x-y|^{-p}, p > 0\}). \tag{6}$$

When we consider static electric field analysis as a practical example, the kernel function is given by

$$g(x,y) = \frac{1}{4\pi\epsilon}|x-y|^{-1}. \tag{7}$$

Here, ϵ denotes the electric permittivity. Figure 1 shows the calculation result when a surface charge method is used to calculate the electrical charge on the surface of the conductors. We divided the surface of the conductor into triangular elements and used step functions as the base function φ_i of the BEM.

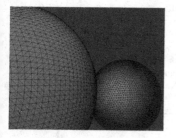

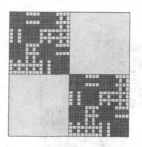

Fig. 1. Calculated surface charge density and triangular elements dividing the conductor surface.

Fig. 2. Partition structure of $\mathcal{H}$-matrix $\tilde{A}_{\mathcal{H}}^K$ for the two-sphere model in Fig. 1. Dark and light red blocks represent dense sub-matrices and low-rank sub-matrices, respectively. (Color figure online)

An $\mathcal{H}$-matrix $\tilde{A}_{\mathcal{H}}^K$, the approximation of A in (2), is characterized by a partition $\mathcal{H}$ of $N \times N$ with blocks $h = s_h \times t_h \in \mathcal{H}$ and block-wise rank K (Fig. 2). Note that most off-diagonal blocks in $\tilde{A}_{\mathcal{H}}^K$ have a low-rank, and the diagonal blocks remain dense. A low-rank matrix $\tilde{A}_{\mathcal{H}}^K|^h$, which approximates a sub-matrix $A_{\mathcal{H}}|^h$ of the original matrix corresponding to block h, is expressed as

$$\tilde{A}_{\mathcal{H}}^K|^h := \sum_{\nu=1}^{k_h} v^\nu (w^\nu)^T, \tag{8}$$

where $v^\nu \in \mathbb{R}^{s_h}$, $w^\nu \in \mathbb{R}^{t_h}$, and $k_h \leq K$. Typically, the upper limit K of the ranks of sub-matrices is set such that $\|A - \tilde{A}_{\mathcal{H}}^K\|_{\mathcal{F}} \leq \epsilon$ for a given tolerance ϵ.

For $x, b \in \mathbb{R}^{\mathcal{I}}$, we consider the following equation:

$$\tilde{A}_{\mathcal{H}}^K x = b. \tag{9}$$

To solve (9), we use a Krylov subspace method, such as the BiCGSTAB method. The HACApK library [8] and ppOpen-APPL/BEM [9,10] implement these computations in parallel and distributed computer environments using the MPI and OpenMP.

2.2   BiCGSTAB Method for the Hierarchical Matrix

We select BiCGSTAB method to solve (2) because the coefficient matrices are not positive definite. Similar to the BiCGSTAB method for a dense matrix, most of the execution time of the BiCGSTAB method for an $\mathcal{H}$-matrix is spent in HMVM. Low-rank sub-matrix - vector multiplication involves two dense matrix - vector multiplications; therefore, HMVM results in many dense matrix - vector multiplications (Fig. 3). Figure 4 shows the pseudo code of the HMVM kernel in ppOpen-APPL/BEM which is optimized for multi-core CPUs. The original code was implemented in Fortran; however, to develop a GPU version of HMVM, we have developed a C version that is nearly the same as the algorithm in the original code. Hereafter, we refer to this kernel as the *OMP kernel*.

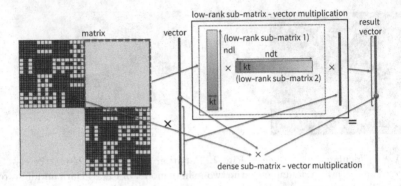

Fig. 3. HMVM calculation

```
#pragma omp for
for(ip=0; ip<number_of_leaves; ip++){
    if(leaf[ip]==low-rank_sub-matrix){
        tmpvec2 <= sub-matrix_2 * vector;        low-rank sub-matrix
        tmpvec  <= sub-matrix_1 * tmpvec2;        - vector multiplication
    }
    if(leaf[ip]==small_dense_sub-matrix)
        tmpvec <= sub-matrix * vector;            small dense sub-matrix
    }                                              - vector multiplication
    for(...;...;...){
#pragma omp atomic
        result <= result + tmpvec;
    }
}
```

Fig. 4. Pseudo code of the HMVM kernel (*OMP kernel*); the range of the loops in each sub-matrix - vector multiplication depends on the target leaves.

HMVM comprises many low-rank sub-matrix - vector multiplications for off-diagonal blocks and dense sub-matrix - vector multiplications for diagonal blocks. These matrix - vector calculations correspond to the leaves of a tree structure; thus, we refer to both low-rank sub-matrix - vector multiplication and dense sub-matrix - vector multiplication as leaves. This parallel implementation requires atomic addition because multiple leaves may have partial values of the same index of the result vector. Although it can be eliminated using atomic operations in each matrix - vector multiplications, the *OMP kernel* merges partial results after sub-matrix - vector multiplication because atomic operations in sub-matrix - vector multiplication incur additional computation cost and cannot obtain better performance than previous implementations. Note that the length of the parallel loop is sufficient for current parallel processors because our target matrices have greater than thousands of leaves.

3 $\mathcal{H}$-matrix Computation on GPU

The BiCGSTAB method employs basic matrix and vector operations. Here, HMVM is a dominant component in terms of the time to solution. Therefore, we

```
● Host (CPU) side code
for(ip=0; ip<number_of_leaves; ip++){
  if(leaf[ip]==low-rank_sub-matrix){
    cublasDgemv( tmpvec2 <= sub-matrix_2 * vector );    low-rank sub-matrix
    cublasDgemv( tmpvec  <= sub-matrix_1 * tmpvec2 );   - vector multiplication
  }                                                     on GPU
  if(leaf[ip]==small_dense_sub-matrix)                  small dense sub-matrix
    cublasDgemv( tmpvec <= sub-matrix * vector );       - vector multiplication
  }                                                     on GPU
}
cuda_vadd<<<>>>(); // merging temporary vectors (tmpvec) to result on GPU
```

Fig. 5. Pseudo code of the HMVM kernel with CUBLAS (*CUBLAS kernel*); red text indicates functions executed on the GPU. (Color figure online)

```
#pragma omp for
for(ip=0; ip<number_of_leaves; ip++){
  if(leaf[ip]==low-rank_sub-matrix){
    dgemv_( tmpvec2 <= sub-matrix_2 * vector );    low-rank sub-matrix
    dgemv_( tmpvec  <= sub-matrix_1 * tmpvec2 );   - vector multiplication
  }
  if(leaf[ip]==small_dense_sub-matrix)             small dense sub-matrix
    dgemv_( tmpvec <= sub-matrix * vector );       - vector multiplication
  }
  for(...;...;...){
#pragma omp atomic
    result <= result + tmpvec;
  }
}
```

Fig. 6. Pseudo code of the HMVM kernel with MKL (*MKL kernel*); red text indicates MKL functions. (Color figure online)

consider a GPU implementation of HMVM on an NVIDIA Tesla P100 (Pascal architecture) GPU [11].

3.1 BLAS GEMV

As discussed in Sect. 2, HMVM consists of many dense sub-matrix - vector multiplications. A dense matrix - vector multiplication can be replaced by the well-known general matrix vector product calculation (GEMV) in BLAS, and this calculation is provided by some BLAS libraries for NVIDIA GPUs, e.g., the CUBLAS [12] and MAGMA libraries. Therefore, using these BLAS libraries, we can implement HMVM relatively easily. Here, we use CUBLAS for GPUs. In addition, to compare performance, we also implement HMVM using the Math Kernel Library (MKL) for CPUs. Hereafter, we refer to these kernels as the *CUBLAS* and *MKL kernels*. Figures 5 and 6 show the pseudo code of an HMVM kernel using the *CUBLAS* and *MKL kernels*, respectively.

3.2 Simple GEMV Kernels

BLAS libraries are useful; however, they cannot always achieve optimal performance. Generally, such libraries perform optimally for large matrix calculations.

- Host (CPU) side code

```
for(ip=0; ip<number_of_leaves; ip++){
  if(leaf[ip]==low-rank_sub-matrix){
    myDgemv1<<<g,b>>>(...); // tmpvec2 <= sub-matrix_2 * vector    ] low-rank sub-matrix
    myDgemv2<<<g,b>>>(...); // tmpvec  <= sub-matrix_1 * tmpvec2   |  - vector multiplication
  }                                                                   on GPU
  if(leaf[ip]==small_dense_sub-matrix)                             ] small dense sub-matrix
    myDgemv2<<<g,b>>>(...); // tmpvec  <= sub-matrix * vector       |  - vector multiplication
  }                                                                   on GPU
}
cuda_vadd<<<>>>(); // merging temporary vectors (tmpvec) to result on GPU
```

- Device (GPU) side code

```
__global__ void myDgemv1(...){          __global__ void myDgemv2(...){
  int gid = blockIdx.x,  glen = gridDim.x;   int gid = blockIdx.x,  glen = gridDim.x;
  int tid = threadIdx.x, tlen = blockDim.x;  int tid = threadIdx.x, tlen = blockDim.x;
  double tmp;                                double tmp;
  for(il=gid; il<rows; il+=glen){            for(il=gid; il<rows; il+=glen){
    for(it=tid; it<cols; it+=tlen){            for(it=tid; it<cols; it+=tlen){
      tmp += matrix[m+it] * vector[v+it];        tmp += matrix[m+it] * vector[v+it];
    }                                          }
    reduction_and_write_tmp_                   reduction_and_atomicAdd_tmp_
    to_vector_on_globalmemory                  to_vector_on_globalmemory
  }                                          }
}                                        }
```

Fig. 7. Pseudo code of the HMVM kernel with CUDA (*SIMPLE kernel*); the entire GPU kernel calculates a single GEMV, and each thread block calculates one GEMV row.

In contrast, HMVM involves many small GEMV calculations. With GPUs, if the CUBLAS GEMV function is used in HMVM, performance will be low because of the lack of parallelism. Moreover, launching GPU kernels requires significant time. In addition, the *CUBLAS kernel* launches a GEMV kernel for each leaf; thus, the incurred overhead will increase execution time.

To evaluate and reduce this overhead, we implemented two HMVM kernels using CUDA.

The first is a GEMV kernel that performs a single GEMV calculation using the entire GPU, and each thread block calculates one GEMV row. Threads in the thread block multiply the matrix and vector elements and calculate the total value using a reduction operation. The reduction algorithm is based on an optimized example code in the CUDA toolkit, which we refer to as the *SIMPLE kernel*. Figure 7 shows the pseudo code of an HMVM kernel using the *SIMPLE kernel*. The execution form (i.e., the number of thread block and threads per block) is an optimization parameter.

Note that many of the GEMV calculations in the HMVM are small; thus, it is difficult for the *SIMPLE kernel* to obtain sufficient performance. To improve performance, some parts of the GPU should calculate a single GEMV in parallel. Thus, we developed an advanced kernel in which a single GEMV kernel is calculated by one thread block, and each line in a single GEMV is calculated by a single warp. Moreover, to eliminate data transfer between the CPU and GPU, two GEMV calculations in low-rank sub-matrix - vector multiplication are merged to a single GPU kernel, and shared memory is used rather

- Host (CPU) side code

```
for(ip=0; ip<number_of_leaves; ip++){
  if(leaf[ip]==low-rank_sub-matrix){
    myDgemvA<<<1,b,,s[ip]>>>(...); // tmpvec2 <= sub-matrix_2 * vector ⎤  low-rank sub-matrix
  }                                 // tmpvec  <= sub-matrix_1 * tmpvec2 ⎦  - vector multiplication
  if(leaf[ip]==small_dense_sub-matrix)                                      on GPU
    myDgemvB<<<1,b,,s[ip]>>>(...); // tmpvec  <= sub-matrix * vector  ⎤  small dense sub-matrix
  }                                                                    ⎦  - vector multiplication
}                                                                        on GPU
cudaThreadSynchronize();
cuda_vadd<<<>>>(); // merging temporary vectors (tmpvec) to result on GPU
```

- Device (GPU) side code

```
__global__ void myDgemvA(...){            __global__ void myDgemvB(...){
  int wid  = threadIdx.x/32; // WARP ID      int wid  = threadIdx.x/32; // WARP ID
  int wlen = blockDim.x/32;                  int wlen = blockDim.x/32;
  int xid  = threadIdx.x%32, xlen = 32;      int xid  = threadIdx.x%32, xlen = 32;
  double tmp;                                double tmp;
  __shared__ double tmpvec[];                for(il=wid; il<ndl; il+=wlen){
  for(il=wid; il<kt; il+=wlen){                for(it=xid; it<ndt; it+=xlen){
    for(it=xid; it<ndt; it+=xlen){               tmp += matrix[m+it] * vector[v+it];
      tmp += matrix2[m+it] * vector[v+it];     }
    }                                          reduction_and_atomicAdd_tmp_
    reduction_and_write_tmp_                   to_vector_on_globalmemory
    to_tmpvec_on_sharedmemory                }
  }                                        }
  __syncthreads();
  for(it=wid; it<ndl; it+=wlen){
    for(il=xid; il<kt; il+=xlen){
      tmp += matrix1[m+il] * tmpvec[v+il];
    }
    reduction_and_atomicAdd_tmp_
    to_vector_on_globalmemory
  }
}
```

Fig. 8. Pseudo code of the HMVM kernel with CUDA (*ASYNC kernel*); one thread block calculates one GEMV, each warp in the thread blocks calculates a single line, two GEMV calculations of low-rank sub-matrix - vector multiplication are merged into a single GPU kernel, and multiple GPU kernels are launched asynchronously.

than global memory. Note that we refer to this kernel as the *ASYNC kernel*. Figure 8 shows the pseudo code of an HMVM kernel with the *ASYNC kernel*. Here, the execution form is also an optimization parameter, similar to the *SIMPLE kernel*; however, the number of thread blocks is always one and multiple GPU kernels are launched concurrently using CUDA stream. Moreover, atomic function is used to merge the partial results because the atomic addition operation of the P100 is fast enough and this implementation can make memory management easy.

3.3 All-in-One Kernel

It is well known that launching a GPU kernel requires much more time than launching a function executed on a CPU. In previous HMVM kernels, the number of launched GPU kernels has depended on the number of leaves; therefore, GPU kernels are launched many times, which may degrade performance. To address

- Host (CPU) side code

```
myHMVM<<<g,b>>>(...);
```

- Device (GPU) side code

```
__global__ void myHMVM(...){
  int gid  = blockIdx.x,      glen = gridDim.x;
  int wid  = threadIdx.x/32,  wlen = blockDim.x/32; // wid = WARP ID
  int xid  = threadIdx.x%32,  xlen = 32;
  double tmp;
  __shared__ double tmpvec[];
  for(ip=gid; ip<number_of_leaves; ip+=glen){
    if(leaf[ip]==low-rank_sub-matrix){
      for(il=wid; il<kt; il+=wlen){
        for(it=xid; it<ndt; it+=xlen){
          tmp += matrix2[m+it] * vector[v+it];
        }
        reduction_and_write_tmp_to_tmpvec_on_sharedmemory
      }
      __syncthreads();
      for(it=wid; it<ndl; it+=wlen){
        for(il=xid; it<kt; il+=xlen){
          tmp += matrix1[m+it] * tmpvec[v+it];
        }
        reduction_and_atomicAdd_tmp_to_vector_on_globalmemory
      }
    }
    if(leaf[ip]==small_dense_sub-matrix){
      for(il=wid; il<ndl; il<wlen){
        for(it=xid; it<ndt; it+=xlen){
          tmp += matrix[m+it] * vector[v+it];
        }
        reduction_and_write_tmp_to_vector_on_globalmemory
      }
    }
    __syncthreads();
  }
}
```

low-rank sub-matrix – vector multiplication on GPU

small dense sub-matrix – vector multiplication on GPU

Fig. 9. Pseudo code of the HMVM kernel with CUDA (*A1 kernel*); the entire HMVM calculation is executed by a single GPU kernel.

this issue, we have created a new GPU kernel that calculates all sub-matrix - vector multiplications using a single GPU kernel, which we refer to as the *A1 kernel*.

Figure 9 shows the pseudo code of an HMVM kernel with the *A1 kernel*. In this kernel, each leaf is calculated by a single warp, and the basic algorithm of each leaf is similar to that of the *ASYNC kernel*. Although the loop for the number of leaves is executed on the CPU in the *ASYNC kernel*, this loop is executed on the GPU in the *A1 kernel*. Similar to the *ASYNC kernel*, here, the execution form is an optimization parameter.

3.4   BATCHED BLAS

Similar to HMVM, many small BLAS calculations are required in various applications, such as machine learning, graph analysis, and multi-physics. To

```
void magmablas_dgemv_vbatched (
    magma_trans_t trans, magma_int_t* m, magma_int_t* n, double alpha,
    magmaDouble_ptr dA_array[], magma_int_t* ldda,
    magmaDouble_ptr dx_array[], magma_int_t* incx,
    magmaDouble_ptr dy_array[], magma_int_t* incy,
    magma_int_t batchCount, magma_queue_t queue);
```

Fig. 10. Example interface of BATCHED MAGMA BLAS (magmablas_dgemv_vbatched).

```
● Host (CPU) side code
for(ip=0; ip<number_of_leaves; ip++){
  if(leaf[ip]==low-rank_sub-matrix){
    dA_array[m++] = sub-matrix_2[ip];      dx_array[v++] = tmpvector;   }  prepare information about
    dA_array[m++] = sub-matrix_1[ip];      dx_array[v++] = tmpvector;   }  low-rank sub-matrix
  }                                                                         - vector multiplication

  if(leaf[ip]==small_dense_sub-matrix)                                      prepare information about
    dA_array[m++] = sub-matrix[ip];        dx_array[v++] = tmpvector;   }  small dense sub-matrix
  }                                                                         - vector multiplication
}
magmablas_dgemv_vbatched_atomic(..., dA_array, ..., dx_array, ..., dy_array, ...); // calc on GPU
```

Fig. 11. Pseudo code of the HMVM kernel with BATCHED MAGMA BLAS (*BATCHED kernel*).

accelerate many small BLAS calculations, batched BLAS has been proposed by several BLAS library developers. For example, MKL, MAGMA, and CUBLAS provide batched BLAS functions. Although gemm is the main target function of batched BLAS, MAGMA provides batched gemv functions for a GPU [13]. Figure 10 shows one of the interfaces of the batched gemv function in MAGMA.

Note that we implemented an HMVM kernel using the batched gemv function of MAGMA [14]. Figure 11 shows the pseudo code of our HMVM kernel with BATCHED MAGMA BLAS, which we refer to as the *BATCHED kernel*. In this kernel, the calculation information is constructed in the loop of leaves on the CPU, and the GPU calculates the entire HMVM calculation using the magmablas_dgemv_vbatched_atomic function. Note that the magmablas_dgemv_vbatched_atomic function is not the original BATCHED MAGMA function, i.e., it is a function that we modified to use atomic addition to produce the results.

4   Performance Evaluation

4.1   Execution Environment

In this section, we discuss the performance obtained on the Reedbush-H super-computer system at the Information Technology Center, The University of Tokyo [15]. Here, we used the Intel compiler 16.0.4.258 and CUDA 8.0.44. We used the following main compiler options: -qopenmp -O3 -xCORE-AVX2 -mkl=sequential for the Intel compiler (icc and ifort) and -O3 -gencode

Table 1. Execution environment.

Processor	Xeon E5-2695 v4	Tesla P100
Architecture	Broadwell-EP (BDW)	Pascal
# cores	18	3584 (64 cores × 56 SMs)
Clock speed	2.1 GHz (upto 3.3 GHz)	1328 MHz (upto 1480 MHz)
Peak performance (DP)	604.8 GFLOPS	5.3 TFLOPS
Memory type & bandwidth (STREAM Triad)	DDR4 65 GB/s	HBM2 550 GB/s
Processor	Xeon Gold 6140	Xeon Phi 7150
Architecture	Skylake-SP (SKX)	Knights Landing (KNL)
# cores	18	68
Clock speed	2.3 GHz (upto 3.7 GHz)	1.4 GHz (upto 1.6 GHz)
Peak performance (DP)	1324.8 GFLOPS	3046.4 GFLOPS
Memory type (STREAM Triad) & bandwidth	DDR4 95 GB/s	MCDRAM 495 GB/s DDR4 85 GB/s

`arch=compute_60`, `code="sm_60,compute_60"` for CUDA (nvcc). The *MKL kernel* is called at the multi-threaded region; thus, sequential MKL is linked. Note that threaded MKL obtained near by the same performance in all cases. Here, we used MAGMA BLAS 2.2.

Moreover, to compare performance with other current processors, we measured the performance on a Skylake-SP CPU and a Knights Landing processor. The Skylake-SP processor is installed in the ITO supercomputer system (test operation) at Kyushu University [16], and Intel compiler 17.0.4 with `-qopenmp -O3 -xCORE-AVX512 -mkl=sequential` compiler options was used. The Knights Landing processor is installed in the Oakforest-PACS at JCAHPC [17] and Intel compiler 17.0.4 with `-qopenmp -O3 -xMIC-AVX512 -mkl=sequential` compiler options was used.

Table 1 shows the hardware specifications of all target hardware. Note that we focus on the performance of a single socket in this paper. The execution times of the Broadwell-EP (BDW) and Skylake-SP (SKX) were measured using all 18 CPU cores. The cluster mode of Knights Landing (KNL) was the quadrant mode, and the memory mode was flat (i.e., only MCDRAM was used). Note that the KNL execution times were measured using 64 threads with scatter affinity and hyper-threading degrades performance.

4.2 Target Data

The four matrices in Table 2 are the target matrices of this evaluation. These matrices were generated from electric field analysis problems. Here, the 10ts and 100ts matrices were generated from a problem with a single spherical object,

Table 2. Target matrices.

Matrix name	10ts	216h	human_1x1	100ts
Number of lines	10,400	21,600	19,664	101,250
Number of leaves	23,290	50,098	46,618	222,274
Number of approximate matrices pairs	8,430	17,002	16,202	89,534
Number of small dense matrices	14,860	33,096	30,416	132,740
Amount of $\mathcal{H}$-matrix (MByte)	136	295	298	2,050

and the 216h matrix was generated from a problem with two spherical objects. In addition, a human_1x1 matrix was generated from a problem with a single human-shaped object.

The sizes of the low-rank sub-matrices and small dense sub-matrix of each target matrix are shown in Fig. 12, where the two left graphs of each matrix show the size of the low-rank sub-matrices and the right shows the size of the small dense sub-matrix.

With the 10ts and 100ts matrices, the size of the approximate matrices ndt and ndl was less than approximately 200 (some were close to 700). Note that all ranks kt were very small (the largest was 23). With the small dense matrices, all matrix lengths were less than 100, and many were less than 30.

With the 216h and human_1x1 matrices, the aspect ratio of the small dense matrices was similar to that of the 10ts and 100ts matrices. With the approximate matrices, although kt was greater than that of the 10ts and 100ts matrices, the aspect ratio was similar. However, although nearly all ndt and ndl lengths were less than 1000, a few matrices had ndt and ndl lengths that were greater than 5000.

Note that the sizes of these matrices depend on the target matrix. Moreover, the size is controlled by the matrix assembling algorithm and HACApK parameters. The above sizes were generated using current usual HACApK parameter settings. It is expected that optimizing the matrix size will affect HMVM performance, and this will be the focus of future work.

4.3 Performance Evaluation

In this subsection, we discuss execution time and performance. Note that the dominant part of the BiCGSTAB method is HMVM; therefore we focus on the execution time of the HMVM. Moreover, the BiCGSTAB method does not modify the matrix data in its own kernel; thus, the each execution time does not include the time required to perform data transfer between the main memory and the GPU in the main iteration of the BiCGSTAB method. Figures 13 and 14 show the execution times for the target matrices. All times are the average execution time of 100 HMVM calculations in 50 BiCGSTAB iterations. As mentioned in the previous section, although the execution form (i.e., grid layout) of the *SIMPLE, ASYNC,* and *A1 kernels* are the optimization parameters, only

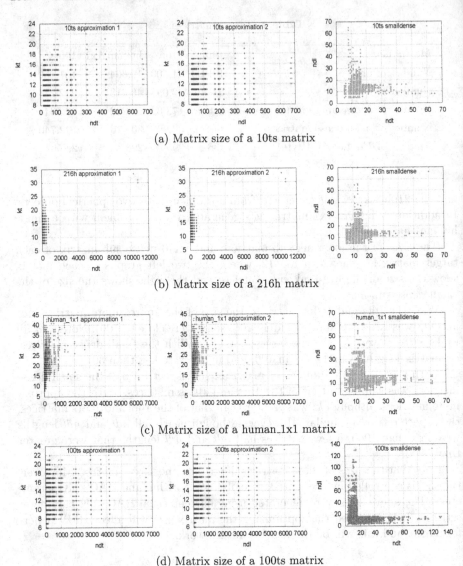

(a) Matrix size of a 10ts matrix

(b) Matrix size of a 216h matrix

(c) Matrix size of a human_1x1 matrix

(d) Matrix size of a 100ts matrix

Fig. 12. Matrix sizes.

the fastest cases are shown and the chosen forms are shown at Table 3. Note that the *ASYNC kernel* launches many GEMV kernels asynchronously with a single thread block. The "#leaves" grids of the *A1 kernel* indicate that the number of thread blocks is equal to the number of leaves, and the outermost GPU kernel loop is eliminated.

Figure 13(a) shows the execution times of all measurements on the Reedbush-H. As can be seen, the *CUBLAS*, *SIMPLE*, and *ASYNC kernels* were too slow for a performance comparison with the fast kernels. Figure 13(b) shows graphs with a limited Y-axis from Fig. 13(a). Relative to the CPU execution time, the *OMP* and *MKL kernels* obtained nearly the same performance with all target matrices. Focusing on the GPU execution time, it is clear that the execution times of the *CUBLAS*, *SIMPLE*, and *ASYNC kernels* were much greater than that of the *A1* and *BATCHED kernels*. The major difference between these two groups is the number of launched GPU kernels. As mentioned in the previous section, launching GPU kernels requires more time than executing functions on the CPU and causes long execution times with the three slower kernels. Therefore, although the *ASYNC kernel* improves the performance compared to the *CUBLAS* and *SIMPLE kernels*, its performance is much slower than that of the *A1* and *BATCHED kernels*. On the other hand, the *A1* and *BATCHED kernels* obtained much higher performance than the other kernels. Note that the *A1 kernel* showed better performance than the *BATCHED kernel* because the batched functions in MAGMA BLAS include computations that are unnecessary for HMVM calculation or the execution form is unoptimized.

The execution time ratio of the *OMP kernel* (BDW) to the *A1 kernel* was 17.37% with the 10ts matrix, 24.22% with the 216h matrix, 18.18% with the human_1x1 matrix, and 14.45% with the 100ts matrix, and the execution time ratio of the *OMP kernel* (BDW) to the *BATCHED kernel* was 34.39% with the 10ts matrix, 32.07% with the 216h matrix, 31.43% with the human_1x1 matrix, and 21.67% with the 100ts matrix. Considering that the calculation performance ratio of the GPU to CPU was 11.4% and the memory performance was 10.5%, there might be room to improve the GPU implementation.

Figure 14 shows the execution times of the *A1 kernel*, *BATCHED kernel*, and CPU (i.e., the *OMP* and *MKL kernels*) on the Broadwell-EP (BDW), Skylake-SP (SKX), and Knights Landing (KNL). All times of the KNL are the average execution time of 100 HMVM calculations in 50 BiCGSTAB iterations, but that of the SKX are average execution time of greater than 10 iterations because of the resource limitation of the test operation.

Relative to the performance of SKX, both the *OMP* and *MKL kernels* required nearly 30% less execution time than the *OMP kernel* of the BDW. By considering the performance gap between the BDW and SKX in terms of specification, i.e., the SKX has 45% greater memory bandwidth and more than 200% greater calculation performance than the BDW, it was expected that the SKX would obtain higher performance than 30%. However, HMVM calculation involves various loop length, and it is not a suitable calculation for AVX512; therefore, the obtained performance is not unexpected. On the other hand, there are large differences between the *OMP kernel* and *MKL kernel* of the KNL. However, it is difficult to describe the reason why the performance of the *MKL kernel* was unstable because the MKL implementation is undisclosed. There might be room to improve the KNL implementation. By considering the performance gap between the BDW and KNL in terms of specification, i.e., the KNL has 7.6 times greater memory bandwidth and 5.0 times greater calculation performance than the BDW. The *OMP kernel* of the KNL obtained 34% to 57% better perfor-

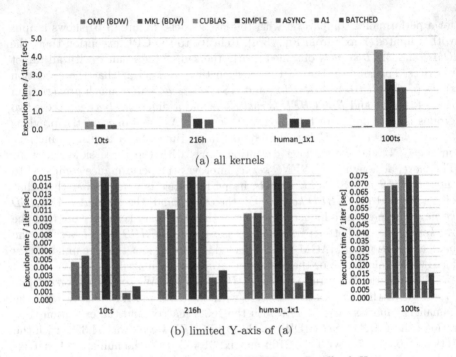

(a) all kernels

(b) limited Y-axis of (a)

Fig. 13. Execution times of HMVM on Reedbush-H

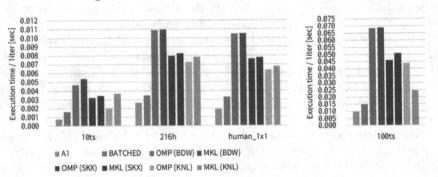

Fig. 14. HMVM execution times.

mance than the *OMP kernel* of the BDW. Similar to the SKX, the KNL has much higher peak performance than the BDW; thus the performance improvement of the KNL is insufficient relative to the performance gap between the BDW and KNL.

Figure 15 shows the entire execution time of the BiCGSTAB method in all target environments. Here, although the iteration count was not exactly the same, only the total computation times are compared. Nearly all vector and matrix calculations of the BiCGSTAB method were executed on the GPU with the *A1 kernel*. Similarly, nearly all vector and matrix calculations of the

Table 3. Best execution form of each GPU kernel: number of thread block and threads per thread block

	10ts	216h	human_1x1	100ts
SIMPLE	168, 64	112, 64	168, 64	168, 64
ASYNC	1, 256	1, 256	1, 256	1, 224
A1	#leaves, 96	#leaves, 256	#leaves, 256	#leaves, 192

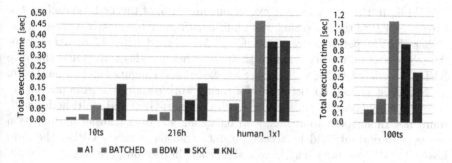

Fig. 15. BiCGSTAB execution times: BDW, SKX, and KNL were the fastest with *OMP* and *MKL kernels*

BiCGSTAB method were executed on the GPU using MAGMA BLAS with the *BATCHED kernel.* To simplify the evaluation, only the shortest times of the *OMP* and *MKL kernels* for each hardware configuration are shown. The execution times of the *A1* and *BATCHED kernels* were less than that of the other processors, and the *A1 kernel* demonstrated the fastest performance with all target matrices. Note that the SKX was faster than the BDW for all matrices and was faster than the KNL with the 10ts, 216h, and human_1x1 matrices. However, the KNL showed a shorter execution time than the BDW and SKX with the 100ts matrix. The reason for this may be that the 100ts matrix has a greater number of large sub-matrices than the other matrices. Note that the larger target matrix, the greater performance KNL obtained relatively.

5   Conclusion

Using $\mathcal{H}$-matrices is an essential technique to solve large and complex computer simulations using a small amount of memory. In this paper, we focus on the BiCGSTAB method with $\mathcal{H}$-matrices for electric analysis problems on GPUs. Since matrix - vector multiplication is a dominant part of the execution time of the BiCGSTAB method, we primarily focused on the performance and implementation of HMVM. We implemented five GPU kernel variations and compared the execution times of several CPUs and a manycore processor. The results indicate that, because HMVM requires many small GEMV computations and launching GPU kernels requires a long time, merging the computation of GEMV kernels into a single kernel (i.e., the *A1 kernel*) was the most effective implementation. This implementation obtained much better performance among the compared processors. Moreover, the BATCHED BLAS function of MAGMA, which executes many BLAS computations using a single GPU kernel (*BATCHED kernel*), obtained good performance. Although the performance of the *BATCHED kernel* was less than that of the *A1 kernel* with all matrices, developing the *A1 kernel* requires much more time and labor than the *BATCHED kernel*. Therefore, it would be beneficial to implement an *A1 kernel*-based HMVM library in HACApK. In the best case, the execution time ratio of the *OMP kernel* on the Broadwell-EP to the *A1 kernel* was 14.45% with the 100ts matrix. Owing to the higher HMVM performance, the BiCGSTAB method with *A1 kernel* demonstrated overall better performance than the other kernels on the GPU (i.e., the NVIDIA Tesla P100), as well as the Skylake-SP and Knights Landing hardware.

Note that various opportunities for future work remain. For example, we are currently implementing and evaluating in the multi-GPU and multi-nodes environments. In such environments, load balancing and data transfer optimization are very important, and to accelerate data transfer between GPUs, the data layout in GPU memory may have a significant impact on performance. Simplification of partition structure of H-matrices used in lattice H-matrices would be required to improve load balancing and communication pattern [18]. Currently, it is uncertain whether the *A1* and *BATCHED kernels* have good data layouts. The data layouts of approximate and small dense matrices can be modified by configuring the parameters of the matrix assembly process in the HACApK library. The relationship between the data layout of matrices and performance is an interesting topic. Moreover, optimization of the execution forms of GPU kernel in *A1 kernel* to various target matrices is an important issue; thus, evaluating the performance of various matrices is required. In addition, we are considering providing an implementation of our HMVM kernel in HACApK.

Acknowledgements. This work was partially supported by JSPS KAKENHI Grant Number 17H01749, JST/CREST, German Priority Programme 1648 Software for Exascale Computing (SPPEXA-II), and "Joint Usage/Research Center for Interdisciplinary Large-scale Information Infrastructures" and "High Performance Computing Infrastructure" in Japan (Project ID: jh160041). Computations were primarily performed using the computer facilities at the Information Technology Center, The University of Tokyo (Reedbush), the Research Institute for Information Technology, Kyushu University (ITO), and JCAHPC (Oakforest-PACS).

References

1. Hackbusch, W.: A sparse matrix arithmetic based on H-Matrices, Part I: introduction to h-matrices. Computing **62**, 89–108 (1999)
2. Chandrasekaran, S., Dewilde, P., Gu, M., Lyons, W., Pals, T.: A fast solver for HSS representations via sparse matrices. SIAM J. Matrix Anal. Appl. **29**(1), 67–81 (2006)
3. Ambikasaran, S.: Fast Algorithms for Dense Numerical Linear Algebra and Applications. Ph.D thesis, Stanford University (2013)

4. Ho, K.L., Ying, L.: Hierarchical interpolative factorization for elliptic operators: differential equations. Commun. Pure Appl. Math. **69**(8), 1415–1451 (2016)
5. MAGMA: MAGMA (2017). http://icl.cs.utk.edu/magma/. Accessed 11 Aug 2017
6. Dongarra, J., Duff, I., Gates, M., Haidar, A., Hammarling, S., Higham, N.J., Hogg, J., Lara, P.V., Zounon, M., Relton, S.D., Tomov, S.: A Proposed API for Batched Basic Linear Algebra Subprograms. Draft Report, May 2016 (2016)
7. Batched BLAS: Batched BLAS (2017). http://icl.utk.edu/bblas/. Accessed 23 Dec 2017
8. Ida, A., Iwashita, T., Mifune, T., Takahashi, Y.: Parallel hierarchical matrices with adaptive cross approximation on symmetric multiprocessing clusters. J. Inf. Process. **22**(4), 642–650 (2014)
9. Iwashita, T., Ida, A., Mifune, T., Takahashi, Y.: Software framework for parallel BEM analyses with H-matrices using MPI and OpenMP. Procedia Comput. Sci. **108**, 2200–2209 (2017). International Conference on Computational Science, ICCS 2017, Zurich, Switzerland, 12–14 June 2017
10. ppOpen-HPC: Open Source Infrastructure for Development and Execution of Large-Scale Scientific Applications on Post-Peta-Scale Supercomputers with Automatic Tuning (AT) (2017). http://ppopenhpc.cc.u-tokyo.ac.jp/ppopenhpc/. Accessed 11 Aug 2017
11. NVIDIA: Tesla P100 Most Advanced Data Center Accelerator (2017). http://www.nvidia.com/object/tesla-p100.html. Accessed 11 Aug 2017
12. NVIDIA: cuBLAS: CUDA Toolkit Documentation (2017). http://docs.nvidia.com/cuda/cublas/. Accessed 11 Aug 2017
13. Dong, T., Haidar, A., Tomov, S., Dongarra, J.: Optimizing the SVD bidiagonalization process for a batch of small matrices. Procedia Comput. Sci. **108**, 1008–1018 (2017). International Conference on Computational Science, ICCS 2017, Zurich, Switzerland, 12–14 June 2017
14. Yamazaki, I., Abdelfattah, A., Ida, A., Ohshima, S., Tomov, S., Yokota, R., Dongarra, J.: Analyzing Performance of BiCGStab with Hierarchical Matrix on GPU cluster. In: 2018 IEEE International Parallel and Distributed Processing Symposium (IPDPS) (2018, in press)
15. Information Technology Center, The University of Tokyo: Reedbush Supercomputer System (2017). http://www.cc.u-tokyo.ac.jp/system/reedbush/index-e.html. Accessed 08 Aug 2017
16. Research Institute for Information Technology, Kyushu University: Supercomputer system ITO (2018). https://www.cc.kyushu-u.ac.jp/scp/system/ITO/. Accessed 09 Feb 2018 (in Japanese)
17. JCAHPC (Joint Center for Advanced HPC): Oakforest-PACS (2018). http://jcahpc.jp/eng/ofp_intro.html. Accessed 09 Feb 2018
18. Ida, A.: Lattice H-matrices on distributed-memory systems. In: 2018 IEEE International Parallel and Distributed Processing Symposium (IPDPS) (2018, in press)

Author Index

Printed in the United States
By Bookmasters